CARLING

10,000
Football
Facts & Questions

CARLING 10,000 Football

Facts & Questions

Frank Nicklin & Henry Russell

Cartoons by
Peter Coupe

STOPWATCH

Published by Stopwatch Publishing Limited

For Bookmark Limited
Desford Road
Enderby
Leicester
LE9 5AD

This edition published 1999

Printed and bound in Finland

The views and opinons of the writer are not necessarily
those of Bass Brewers Limited

Cartoons by Peter Coupe
Compiled by Frank Nicklin & Henry Russell

© Stopwatch Publishing Limited
1st Floor
1–7 Shand Street
London
SE1 2ES

info@stopwatch.co.uk

ISBN 1 900032 04 X

Contents

Foreword

Mark Hunter

Marketing Director, Bass Brewers

On behalf of Carling – official sponsors of the Carling Premiership –
I welcome you to the 1999/2000 edition of Carling 10,000 Football Facts and
Questions. Once again, we are delighted to be associated with a publication that
is so widely used by fans as their companion to the beautiful game.

In no other country is the passion for the game so alive or intense. This book
reflects this passion and our insatiable appetite for the game, and a quick look
through its 676 pages reveals why it's such an essential read.

From Ajax to York City, this book contains everything you would wish to
know about your team, its rivals, the records and the heroes. 10,000 Football Facts
and Questions provides a hugely diverse source of information and statistics,
coupled with fascinating facts, and a fun and interactive quiz element.
It is the perfect combination for the football fan.

This season takes us into a new Millennium where, yet again, we are sure
to see more dazzling individual performances and collective team performances
that have graced the Carling Premiership since 1993 and
other international football competitions.

Equally impressive as the action on the pitch is your increasing dedication
to the game. And, just to prove this point, here's one statistic that kicks off
this superb book: in the Carling Premiership, match attendances have increased
by 45% since 1993 and for the first time in the competition's history,
the average match attendance exceeded 30,000.

Carling wishes you all a great Millennium season.

Happy reading!

Mark Hunter

Marketing Director – Bass Brewers

CARLING 10,000 FOOTBALL FACTS & QUESTIONS

Football Quizzes

Quiz Contents

FA CUP
AND
CHARITY
SHIELD

Quiz 1

FA Cup

1   Who won the first FA Cup in 1871-72?

2   **Where was that game played?**

3   Who beat Derby County 6-0 to record the biggest FA Cup Final win?

4   **Which player has scored the most FA Cup goals this century?**

5   Who has made the most FA Cup appearances?

6   **Who is the youngest player to play in an FA Cup Final at Wembley?**

7   Name the youngest scorer in an FA Cup Final

8   **Who is the oldest scorer in an FA Cup Final?**

9   Who is the youngest FA Cup Final captain?

10 **Who became the oldest player in the FA Cup, almost 20 years after scoring the winning goal for Manchester City in the Final?**

11 Who is the oldest player to play in an FA Cup Final?

12 **Who holds the record for most FA Cup wins?**

13 Who were the last team outside the top division to play in the FA Cup Final?

14 **Which was the only club to be relegated from the top flight after appearing in an FA Cup Final during the 1980s?**

15 Which team appeared in three successive finals in the 1990s?

1 The Wanderers 2 The Kennington Oval 3 Bury 4 Ian Rush (Chester, Liverpool) 5 Ian Callaghan (Liverpool, Swansea, Crewe), 88 matches 6 Paul Allen (West Ham United, 1980), 17 yrs 256 days 7 Norman Whiteside (Manchester United, 1983), 18 yrs 19 days 8 Bert Turner (Charlton Athletic, 1946), 36 yrs 312 days 9 David Nish (Leicester City, 1969), 21 yrs 7mths 10 Billy Meredith, 49yrs 8mths 11 Walter Hampson (Newcastle, 1924), 41 yrs 8mths 12 Manchester United, nine 13 Sunderland (1992) 14 Brighton (1983) 15 Manchester United (1994, 1995, 1996)

 # Quiz 2

FA Cup

1 **Which club lost successive Finals in the 1980s?**

2 Which two players have made the most Finals appearances at Wembley (including replays)?

3 **Which Sunderland player tied the record for most loser's medals in 1992?**

4 Who was a winner with different clubs in successive 1970s Finals?

5 **Who played for QPR in the 1982 Final against Tottenham and then for Tottenham in the 1987 Final?**

6 Who scored for different teams in two of the first three Finals of the 1990s?

7 **Who became the only on-loan player to play in the Final, winning with Manchester United in 1990?**

8 Which father and son have both appeared in Finals with Tottenham?

9 **Which Chile international played for Newcastle in the 1951 Final and scored the winning goal for them in the 1952 Final?**

10 Which Belgian-born player made four Final appearances in six years?

11 **Who was the first American to play in a Final?**

12 Name the last three managers to have won the Cup as player and manager of the same club?

13 **Who is the youngest manager of a Cup Final winning team?**

14 Who is the only foreigner to captain his club to a Final win?

15 **Who has scored the most goals in FA Cup Finals?**

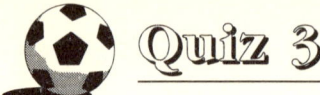

Quiz 3

FA Cup

1 Who scored the second fastest FA Cup Final goal at Wembley in 1955?

2 Which Manchester United player made two substitute appearances in Finals while still a teenager?

3 Who is the youngest goalkeeper to play in an FA Cup Final?

4 Who are the only non-English club to win the FA Cup?

5 Who was the last player to score in every round of the FA Cup in the same season?

6 Since the Football League was formed, only one non-league club have won the Cup. Who are they?

7 Who were the last non-league team to beat a side from the top flight?

8 Which six teams have won the FA Cup and League Championship double?

9 Who was the last team to be runner-up in the FA Cup and League Championship in the same year?

10 Which Scottish club reached two FA Cup Finals?

11 Which club entered the 1992-93 FA Cup but went into liquidation before playing a match?

12 When was the last all-London FA Cup Final?

13 When was the first all-Merseyside FA Cup Final?

14 Which two teams played in the first semi-final to be staged at Wembley?

15 Who became the first player to miss a penalty in the Final?

(Liverpool v Everton) **14 Arsenal v Tottenham, 1991** 15 Charlie Wallace (Aston Villa, 1913)
10 Queen's Park (1884,1885) 11 Maidstone United **12** 1982 **(Tottenham v QPR)** 13 1986
Arsenal (1971), **Liverpool** (1986), **Manchester United** (1994,1996) 9 Everton (1986)
Coventry, 1989) **8 Preston North End** (1889), **Aston Villa** (1897), **Tottenham** (1961),
(Chelsea, 1970) **6 Tottenham Hotspur of the Southern League** (1901) 7 Sutton United (v
1976,1977) 3 Peter Shilton (Leicester City, 1969) **4 Cardiff City** (1927) 5 Peter Osgood
1 Jackie Milburn (Newcastle United, 45 seconds) **2 David McCreery (Manchester United,**

Quiz 4

FA Cup

1 Which two international strikers have had their penalty kicks saved in Wembley Cup Finals?

2 And which two goalkeepers saved the kicks?

3 Which goalkeeper broke his neck in the 1956 Cup Final, but carried on playing to get a winners medal?

4 Which club has made the most semi-final appearances?

5 Who was the first player to be sent off in the Final?

6 Who was the referee?

7 Who was the last man to be sent-off in an FA Cup semi-final?

8 Which four Nationwide League sides have reached three FA Cup semi-finals, and lost all of them?

9 Which two teams contested the lowest attended semi-final in 1988?

10 Which ground has staged the most FA Cup semi-finals?

11 Which Chelsea player was refused a winners' medal in 1970 because he was wearing a Leeds shirt he had exchanged after the whistle and an official believed he played for Leeds?

12 Which striker scored a hat-trick against West Bromwich for non-league Woking in 1991?

13 Which Cup winners are the only club to have beaten top-flight teams in every round?

14 Which Cup Final song reached number three in the charts in 1988?

15 Who were Hereford's scorers when the Southern League side beat Newcastle United 2-1 in a third round replay in 1972?

---

1 Liverpool's John Aldridge (1988), Tottenham's Gary Lineker (1991) 2 Dave Beasant (Wimbledon, 1988), Mark Crossley (Nott'm. Forest, 1991) 3 Bert Trautmann (Manchester City) 4 Everton 5 Kevin Moran (Manchester United, 1985) 6 Peter Willis 7 Lee Dixon (Arsenal, 1993) 8 Millwall, Norwich City, Stoke City, Oldham Athletic 9 Luton v Wimbledon 10 Villa Park (45) 11 David Webb 12 Tim Buzaglo 13 Manchester United (1948) 14 Liverpool's 'Anfield Rap' 15 Ronnie Radford, Ricky George

CARLING 10,000 FOOTBALL FACTS & QUESTIONS

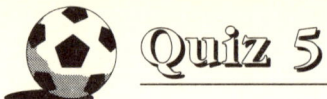 ## Quiz 5

FA Cup

1 Who was the scorer when Sunderland beat Leeds in the 1973 Cup Final?

2 **Which Wimbledon goalkeeper saved Peter Lorimer's penalty in the fourth round draw with Leeds in 1975?**

3 Who played for Manchester United in the Cup Final of 1979 against Arsenal, and then scored against the Londoners for Wrexham in 1992?

4 **Which was the first club to win the Cup on three occasions?**

5 Who was the first player to score a hat-trick in a Wembley FA Cup Final in 1953?

6 **Who became the first player to score in successive FA Cup Finals at Wembley?**

7 Who was the first substitute to appear in a Cup Final?

8 **Who was the first substitute to score in the Final?**

9 Which two substitutes scored twice when they came on in the 1989 Final?

10 **Who were the last team to win the Cup with eleven English players?**

11 When was the first FA Cup Final played at Wembley?

12 **Who was the first person to win the Cup as player and manager of the same club?**

13 Which two teams played in the first Wembley FA Cup Final that went to a replay?

14 **What was the first Cup Final replay to be played at Wembley?**

15 Which was the first Cup Final to produce gate receipts of £1million?

---

1 Ian Porterfield 2 **Dickie Guy** 3 Mickey Thomas 4 **The Wanderers** (1872,1873,1876)
5 Stan Mortensen (Blackpool) 6 **Bobby Johnstone (Manchester City, 1955,1956)**
7 Derek Clarke (West Bromwich Albion, 1968) 8 **Eddie Kelly (Arsenal, 1971)** 9 Stuart McCall
(Everton), Ian Rush (Liverpool) 10 **West Ham (1975)** 11 1923 12 **Stan Seymour
(Newcastle, 1924 (player), 1961,1952 (manager)** 13 Chelsea and Leeds, 1970 14 1981,
Tottenham v **Manchester City** 15 1985, Manchester United v Everton

Quiz 6

FA Cup

1 **Which two teams contested the first FA Cup tie to be decided on penalties in 1991?**

2 Which two teams became the first Cup Final sides to have the players' names on the back of their shirts?

3 **Who was the first black player to captain a Cup Final side?**

4 And which other black player captained the same side in the replay?

5 **Who was the first Premiership side to win the Cup?**

6 Who scored in Liverpool's 1992 FA Cup Final success and came on as a substitute in the 1996 Final?

7 **Who scored in the Manchester United v Brighton Final in 1983 and then played in the 1987 Final for Tottenham?**

8 Which Wigan player was carried off on a stretcher after 20 minutes of a 1965 first round replay against Doncaster Rovers but returned to the field to score a hat-trick?

9 **Who was the last non-league team to reach the Final?**

10 How many Final appearances have Bristol City made?

11 **Which team won the FA Cup in 1911, only eight years after forming?**

12 When was the last FA Cup Final played outside London?

13 **When was the last time both semi-finals were played at Wembley?**

14 Who were the first winners of the Littlewoods-sponsored FA Cup?

15 **What was the name of the white horse that pushed the crowds back in Wembley's first Cup Final?**

---

1 **Birmingham City v Stoke City, third place play-off, 1972** 2 Arsenal, Sheffield Wednesday, 1993 3 **Viv Anderson, Sheffield Wednesday, 1993** 4 Carlton Palmer 5 **Arsenal** 6 Michael Thomas 7 **Gary Stevens** 8 H.Lyons, 1965 9 **Southampton** 10 One (1909) 11 **Bradford City** 12 1915 13 1994 14 Everton, 1995 15 Billy

 # Quiz 7

FA Cup

1 Which Nationwide League club are the only founder member of the Football League not to have won the FA Cup?

2 Who were the first Football League club to win the FA Cup in 1889?

3 William Townley was the first player to score a hat-trick in the Cup Final in 1890. But who did he play for?

4 Who became the first non-league team to reach the Final?

5 Who scored the first FA Cup Final goal at Wembley?

6 Which club had to apply for re-election to the Football League, just seven years after winning the Cup?

7 When was the first all-Lancashire FA Cup Final?

8 What year did the Cup Final teams first wear numbers on their shirts?

9 Which two Manchester City players won FA Cup medals in 1934, but were later in the Munich air crash of 1958?

10 Name the referee of the 1934 Final who later became president of FIFA?

11 Which former Liverpool manager played in Preston's 1938 FA Cup winning team?

12 Which team has reached four FA Cup Finals, and has lost all of them?

13 Portsmouth kept the Cup for seven years, but only reached the Final once. How come?

14 Which London club played in successive Finals in the 1940s?

15 Which team came from 3-1 down to beat Bolton 4-3 in the 1953 Final?

1 Stoke City 2 **Preston North End** 3 Blackburn Rovers 4 **Southampton, 1900** 5 David Jack (Bolton, 1923) 6 **Cardiff City** 7 1926 (Bolton v Manchester City) 8 1933 9 Frank Swift and Sir Matt Busby 10 **Sir Stanley Rous** 11 Bill Shankly 12 **Leicester City** 13 They won in 1939, but the competition was suspended beacues of the Second World War 14 **Charlton Athletic** 15 Blackpool

Quiz 8

FA Cup

1 How many loser's medals did Sir Stanley Matthews collect?

2 Which team scored 37 goals on their way to winning the Cup?

3 **Which team won the Cup in the 1940s without playing a home tie?**

4 Which non-league side failed to get into the first round just once between 1949 and 1972?

5 **Who won the Cup three times in five years in the 1950s?**

6 How many FA Cup Final appearances did George Best make?

7 **How long did West Ham have to wait to make their second appearance in the Cup Final?**

8 Which teams contested a third round tie that went to four replays in 1955?

9 **Which goalkeeper broke his jaw after only six minutes in the 1957 Cup Final, but returned later as an outfield player?**

10 When was the last of Bolton's FA Cup wins?

11 **Who played in goal for Leicester City in the 1961 Cup Final against Tottenham?**

12 Who were the last team to win successive FA Cup Finals?

13 **Who scored the 100th Cup Final goal at Wembley?**

14 Which two sides faced each other in three successive FA Cup ties each year between 1961 and 1963?

15 **How many days did it take to play all the third round matches in 1963?**

Quiz 9

FA Cup

1　Wembley stadium was refurbished for the 1966 World Cup finals. But which two teams played the first FA Cup Final in the re-built stadium?

2　**Which FA Cup Final scorer's father played with Sir Matt Busby in the Finals of 1933 and 1934?**

3　Which two Manchester United players won the FA Cup in 1963, having been in the losing United sides of 1957 and 1958?

4　**How many Midlands teams won the Cup betwen 1961 and 1997?**

5　Who were the last team to come back from two goals down to win a Cup Final?

6　**Which player, who did not have his name in the official programme, scored twice in the 1966 Final?**

7　Which two former England goalkeepers played in losing Cup Finals for the same club in the 1960s?

8　**Which teams played in the Centenary Final?**

9　Who scored a last-minute penalty to give Arsenal a draw in the 1971 semi-final against Stoke?

10　**Who played in goal for Tottenham in the 1981 Cup Final?**

11　Which player was on the losing side in successive Finals before winning with Leeds in 1972?

12　**Who were the first holders of the Cup to lose a Final at Wembley?**

13　Which Cup Final was played on April 11th to help the England players prepare for the World Cup finals?

14　**Who scored twice when Colchester United beat Leeds in the fifth round in 1971?**

15　Which team had their names on the back of their tracksuits before the 1961 Cup Final?

 Quiz 10 FA Cup

1 **Which two-time FA Cup loser with Leicester City won the Cup with Arsenal in 1971?**

2 Who is the highest-capped England player never to have won an FA Cup Final winners medal?

3 **Which team appeared in three Finals in four years during the 1970's?**

4 How many internationals were in Sunderland's Cup-winning side of 1973?

5 **Who were the last team outside the top flight to win the Cup?**

6 How many FA Cup matches did Fulham play in the 1974-75 season?

7 **Which two former FA Cup winners were in the Fulham side in the 1975 Final?**

8 Which FA Cup Final manager scored the winning goal for non-league Yeovil when they beat Sunderland in 1948?

9 **Who was the first player to captain English and Scottish FA Cup winning teams?**

10 Who lost an FA Cup Final as player in 1954, and as manager in 1967 and 1976 before winning the trophy with Manchester United?

11 **Which Final-winning manager was an unused sub for West Ham in the 1975 Final?**

12 Who scored Arsenal's late winner in the 1979 Final against Manchester United?

13 **Who captained his side to three FA Cup triumphs at Wembley?**

14 Who had to taken off suffering with 'sunstroke and emotion' after scoring an FA Cup Final winner?

15 **Who scored Southampton's winning goal in the 1976 Final?**

 **Quiz 11**   **FA Cup**

1   How many games did it take Arsenal to beat Liverpool in the FA Cup semi-final of 1980?

2   Who is the only player to play in five post-war FA Cup Finals for the same team?

3   Who was the Manchester City captain in their 1969 Cup success who later went on to become their manager?

4   Who scored both goals in the 1981 FA Cup Final?

5   Which club played in five FA Cup Finals from 1971 to 1980?

6   When Brighton reached the Cup Final in 1983 they beat Liverpool in the fifth round with a goal from a former Liverpool Cup Final goalscorer. Who was it?

7   Roy Dwight played for Nottingham Forest in the 1959 Final. His nephew was at Wembley for the 1984 Final. Who is he?

8   Who scored two Cup Final goals in three years in the 1980s?

9   Because of the Hillsborough disaster in 1989 the semi-final between Liverpool and Nottingham Forest was replayed at another ground. Where?

10   Which teams contested the 100th Cup Final?

11   Who is the only goalkeeper to captain his team in the Cup Final?

12   What was wrong with Tottenham's shirts in the 1987 Final?

13   Who played in six Cup Finals in Scotland before playing, and scoring, in the 1983 FA Cup Final?

14   Who scored for Coventry in the 1987 Final against the same club he had faced in another Final?

15   Who played for only the first two minutes of the 1982 Final for QPR before limping off injured?

Quiz 12

FA Cup

1 **Who made his last appearance for Tottenham in the 1987 Final?**

2 Who captained Brighton in the 1983 Cup Final instead of suspended Steve Foster?

3 **Which former Cup winner managed Crystal Palace to the Final in 1990?**

4 Who scored an own goal in the 1991 Final?

5 **Who became the first side to win a semi-final on penalties?**

6 Who beat Cup holders Liverpool in a third round replay at Anfield in 1993?

7 **Who scored Arsenal's winner in the semi-final against Tottenham in 1993?**

8 Who invented the FA Cup?

9 **Who was the first man to captain a winning side in successive Finals?**

10 Who is the last Scotsman to captain an FA Cup winning side?

11 **Which Russian goalkeeper played in a Cup Final?**

12 Which Danish international played in the 1986, 1988 and 1992 FA Cup Finals?

13 **Which striker played in the 1983 Final and later went on to become a football commentator for Spanish television?**

14 Which two brothers played in the 1977 Final?

15 **Who scored with a 20-yard volley in the 1981 Final replay?**

Quiz 13

FA Cup

1. Which former Real Madrid and Marseille star played for Wimbledon in the 1988 Cup Final?

2. **Who was the first Dutchman to play in an FA Cup Final?**

3. Who scored Manchester United's winner in the 1990 FA Cup Final replay?

4. **Who was the last club to lose in the Final, but succeed the following year?**

5. Who is the last player-manager to play in the Final?

6. **Who scored Arsenal's last minute winner in the 1993 Final replay?**

7. Apart from Ian Wright, who scored Crystal Palace's other goal in the 1990 Final?

8. **Who scored for both clubs in the 1987 Final?**

9. Who captained West Ham to FA Cup wins in 1975 and 1980?

10. **Which two players played in the 1968 Cup Final and then went on to win the FA Cup as managers of the same team?**

11. When did Luton Town last play in the FA Cup Final?

12. **Which two teams played out a 4-6 third round match in 1948?**

13. Who scored Crystal Palace's winning goal in their 4-3 semi-final win over Liverpool in 1990?

14. **Which two Everton strikers scored twice in a 4-4 fifth round replay against Liverpool in 1991?**

15. Which Cup Final featured two pairs of brothers on the field?

---

1 Laurie Cunningham **2 Arnold Muhren (Manchester United, 1983)** 3 Lee Martin **4 Manchester United (1995, 1996)** 5 Glenn Hoddle (Chelsea, 1994) **6 Andy Linighan** 7 Gary O'Reilly **8 Gary Mabbutt** 9 Billy Bonds **10 Howard Kendall and Joe Royle** 11 1959 **12 Aston Villa and Manchester United** 13 Alan Pardew **14 Graeme Sharp, Tony Cottee** 15 1876

 ## Quiz 14

FA Cup

1   **Has there ever been an FA Cup semi-final played outside England?**

2   Which club's 4-0 victory at Brighton in 1973 was the biggest away win for a non-league side?

3   **Who scored after just 45 seconds on his senior debut in an FA Cup tie in January 1953?**

4   Which club played successive away ties in different rounds in the same · season but on the same ground?

5   **Which club reached a Cup Final after losing a game in the competition in the same season?**

6   Who became the first player to play in the FA Cup for two different clubs in the same season?

7   **Which Premiership team reached their first FA Cup semi-final in 1997?**

8   Who were the last third division team, before Chesterfield in 1997, to reach the semi-finals?

9   **Which team beat six Division One sides to FA Cup victory?**

10 Who was refused a Cup winners medal from the royal box, and had it presented on the pitch after the official ceremony?

11 **Which team collected a £30 clothing voucher as a bonus for winning the Cup?**

12 Which Cup Final was dubbed the 'Friendly Final'?

13 **What was significant about J.F. Mitchell, who played in the 1922 Final for Preston?**

14 When was the first FA Cup Final televised?

15 **Which famous cricketer has a brother who played in the 1983 Final?**

---

1 **Yes. In Edinburgh in 1885** 2 Watton and Hersham 3 **Albert Taylor (Luton Town)**
4 Preston North End They played Manchester City and Manchester United at Maine Road
5 **Charlton Athletic They lost to Fulham in 1946 but the ties that season was played
over two legs** 6 Jimmy Scoular in 1946 (Gosport and Portsmouth) 7 **Middlesbrough**
8 Plymouth Argyle 9 **Manchester United (1948)** 10 Kevin Moran (Manchester United, 1985)
11 **Everton (1933)** 12 Liverpool v Everton (1986) 13 **He wore glasses on the pitch**
14 1938 15 Mike Gatting. His brother, Steve, played for Brighton and Hove Albion

Quiz 15

FA Cup

1 Which team took the FA Cup on their tour of South Africa in 1952?

2 **Who asked for a transfer just an hour before the 1960 Final?**

3 Which wine-bar waiter played in the 1987 semi-final?

4 **Who scored for Oldham in the 1994 semi-final against Manchester United?**

5 How many players did Mansfield Town have booked in their third round tie against Crystal Palace in 1963?

6 **Which English club have played FA Cup ties in all three other home countries, against Linfield, Queen's Park and Cardiff City?**

7 Who went 16 matches without a win in the competition, from February 1952 to March 1963?

8 **The official record attendance for an FA Cup tie is 126,047. What year?**

9 Which team reached two successive Finals without being drawn at home?

10 **Which three England World Cup winners have never played in an FA Cup Final?**

11 Which England player played his last game for his club in an FA Cup Final, and was stretchered off after only 16 minutes?

12 **Who scored for Sutton United in their 2-1 third round victory over Coventry in 1989?**

13 Who beat Sutton 8-0 in the following round?

14 **Who was sent-off in Manchester United's semi-final replay against Crystal Palace in 1995?**

15 Who was sent-off for West Ham in the 1991 semi-final against Nottingham Forest?

Quiz 16

FA Cup

1. **Who scored Arsenal's consolation goal in their 3-1 semi-final defeat against Tottenham in 1991?**

2. Which Footballer of the Year captained his side to victory in the 1964 Final?

3. **Which goalkeeper replaced Gary Sprake for Leeds' 1970 Final replay?**

4. Who scored both of West Ham's goals in the 1975 Final?

5. **Who scored the winning goal for York City against Arsenal in 1985, and scored in the Cup Final two years later?**

6. Which non-league team celebrated scoring goals by waddling along the ground like ducks?

7. **Who did Arsenal beat 3-0 in the semi-final of 1978?**

8. Which London club won in their first FA Cup Final in the 1980s?

9. **Who became the first player this century to play in three FA Cup Finals against the same club?**

10. How many goal-less FA Cup Finals have there been at Wembley?

11. **Name the last two players to be voted Footballer of the Year and captain an FA Cup winning side?**

12. What have Sir Stanley Matthews, Harry Johnston, Nat Lofthouse, Tom Finney, Don Revie, Syd Owen, Jimmy Adamson, Bobby Collins, Billy Bremner, Alan Mullery, Emlyn Hughes, Neville Southall, Gary Lineker, Clive Allen, John Barnes and Chris Waddle all got in common?

13. **Which man made more than 500 appearances for Coventry and was the club's managing director when they won the Cup in 1987?**

14. Which player lost two front teeth after colliding with a team-mate in the 1981 Final?

15. **Who beat Hyde FC 26-0 in 1887 for the biggest win in FA Cup history?**

Quiz 17

FA Cup

1 Who scored Chelsea's goal in the 1996 semi-final at Villa Park?

2 **Which of the Neville brothers came on as a sub in the 1996 FA Cup Final?**

3 Who scored Everton's winner in the 1995 Final?

4 **Which two England goalkeepers played in the 1993 Final?**

5 Who finished a 20-year association with Arsenal by winning his second FA Cup winners medal?

6 **Who scored Manchester United's second goal in a 3-0 fourth round win at Reading in 1996?**

7 Liverpool conceded only one goal on their way to the 1996 Final. Who scored against them?

8 **Up to the 1997 Final, which Premiership club hasn't beaten Manchester United in the FA Cup for 76 years?**

9 Who scored Wimbledon's winner in their 1988 semi-final against Luton?

10 **Which two teams met twice in four years in FA Cup semi-finals in the 1990s?**

11 Who held Brighton to a 2-2 draw in the first round in 1995?

12 **Who did Fulham beat 7-0 in the first round in 1995?**

13 By what scoreline did Oxford United beat Dorchester in the first round of 1995?

14 **How many goals were scored in the 1995-96 first round tie between Shrewsbury and Marine?**

15 Who has made three appearances in the Final for Tottenham and one for Chelsea in the space of 13 years?

Quiz 18

FA Cup

1   Name the last Fourth Division club to reach the quarter-finals.

1   What year was it?

3   Tony Philliskirk scored five goals in a first round tie against Kingstonian in 1992, but does not have it officially recognised because the game was abandoned. Who was he playing for?

4   Which former president of the FA appeared in nine of the first 12 FA Cup Finals?

5   Which three former Liverpool players have all won three Cup winners' medals with the club?

6   What was the amazing feat of all 12 Manchester United players who played in the 1985 Final?

7   Only once in the competition's history have all the quarter-finals been won by the away teams. In which season?

8   Has there ever been an FA Cup Final where the top division was not represented?

9   Which club, in 1994-95, was originally banned from the competition but re-admitted on appeal?

10 Who scored Chesterfield's only goal in their 1996-97 quarter-final win over Wrexham?

11 Which Premiership club beat Blackburn in the fourth round of the 1996-97 season?

12 Who scored a last-minute own goal to send the fifth round tie between Leicester and Chelsea to a replay in 1996-97?

13 Who defeated Leeds at Elland Road to win a place in the 1996-97 quarter-finals?

14 Chelsea came back from 2-0 down at half-time to beat Liverpool in the 1996-97 fourth round. Who scored twice for the Londoners?

15 Which Hull City striker scored six goals in a first round replay against Whitby Town in the 1996-97 season?

1 Cambridge United 2 1990 3 Peterborough United 4 James Forrest 5 Ian Rush, Bruce Grobbelaar and Steve Nicol 6 They were all internationals 7 1986-87 8 No 9 Tottenham 10 Chris Beaumont 11 Coventry 12 Chelsea's Eddie Newton 13 Portsmouth 14 Gianluca Vialli 15 Duane Darby

Quiz 19

FA Cup

1   Which club has won the English FA Cup most often?

2   **Which team has appeared in four FA Cup Finals and never won the trophy?**

3   With which club did Don Revie win an FA Cup winners' medal in 1956?

4   **To the end of the 20th century, how many different clubs have won the FA Cup?**

5   Which club has appeared most often in English FA Cup Finals?

6   **Which Manchester United player began the 1957 FA Cup Final in goal, but was injured and had to leave the field, later returning to the wing?**

7   Up to the end of the 20th century, which club had recorded eight FA Cup victories?

8   **Which was the last team to win the FA Cup for the first time?**

9   Who was the FA Cup-winning captain of Manchester United in 1957?

10 **Which club has appeared most often in the semi-finals of the English FA Cup?**

11 Which four survivors of the Munich air crash played for Manchester United in the 1958 FA Cup Final?

12 **Who won the first FA Cup after the end of the First World War?**

13 How many of the 50 eligible teams entered the first FA Cup in 1871-72?

14 **Which team has appeared in five FA Cup Finals but won the trophy only once, in 1922?**

15 Who won the FA Cup in 1898 and 1959?

1 Manchester United 2 **Leicester City** 3 Manchester City 4 **Forty-two** 5 Manchester United 6 **Ray Wood** 7 Tottenham Hotspur 8 **Wimbledon in 1988** 9 Roger Byrne 10 **Everton** 11 Bobby Charlton, Harry Gregg, Bill Foulkes, Dennis Viollet 12 **Aston Villa** 13 Fifteen 14 **Huddersfield Town** 15 Nottingham Forest

Quiz 20

FA Charity Shield

1 **What are the usual qualifications for the two teams that contest the FA Charity Shield?**

2 In which year was the FA Charity Shield first played?

3 **In the 74 fixtures up to 1997, how many different teams had appeared in it?**

4 Which team has appeared in it most often?

5 **In which year was the Charity Shield first played at Wembley?**

6 How many times has the match not been decided in 90 minutes?

7 **Until 1974, what happened to the Shield when the matches were drawn?**

8 How did that change in 1974?

9 **Which team was the first to win the Charity Shield on penalties?**

10 Who did they beat?

11 **Of the teams in questions 9 and 10, which one won the Championship and which the FA Cup?**

12 To date, which is the only other team to have won the Charity Shield on penalties?

13 **Who were their opponents on that day?**

14 What do the following teams have in common? Blackpool; Bolton Wanderers; Brighton and Hove Albion; The 1950 Canadian Touring Team; Cardiff City; The Corinthians; Coventry City; Derby County; An FA XI; Huddersfield Town; Leicester City; Northampton Town; Portsmouth; Preston North End; Southampton; Swindon Town; Wimbledon; The England 1950 World Cup Team

15 **Despite never having won either the League Championship or the FA Cup, Leicester City won the 1971 Charity Shield. How come?**

---

1 **League Champions versus FA Cup winners** 2 1908 3 40 4 Liverpool (18 times) 5 1974
6 11 times 7 **The trophy was shared for six months each** 8 Shield decided on penalties
9 **Liverpool** 10 Leeds United 11 **Leeds were champions; Liverpool were the Cup winners**
12 Manchester United in 1993 13 **Arsenal** 14 They have all appeared in only one Shield
15 **Arsenal won the double that year, so the Shield was contested between Liverpool,**
the Cup runners-up and Leicester City, Division Two champions

Quiz 21

FA Charity Shield

1　**What was the highest score in a Charity Shield?**

2　Which team appeared in four consecutive Shields in the years 1933-36, winning twice and losing twice?

3　**Which two teams played each other in four consecutive Charity Shields in the years 1923-26, each winning it twice?**

4　Which team won the Charity Shield four times running between 1984 and 1987?

5　**Which two internationals were sent off in the 1974 match?**

6　Name the three teams that have shared the trophy but never won it outright.

7　**For various reasons, the Charity Shield has not always been between the Champions and the Cup winners. Of the times that these two teams have played each other, how many times have the Champions won the trophy outright?**

8　How many times have the Cup winners won it outright?

9　**What was unique about the first Charity Shield match, a 1-1 draw between Manchester United and Queen's Park Rangers?**

10　When Tottenham Hotspur became the first modern team to win the double in 1961, who did they push and overrun in the Charity Shield?

11　**There have to date there have been only two 0-0 draws, in 1977 and 1991. Which teams were involved?**

12　In 1996, Manchester United won the double. Why were Newcastle United chosen to play them in the Charity Shield?

13　**Who won the Charity Shield in 1938 and then again in 1948, the next time it was played, thus becoming the longest-ever holders of the trophy?**

14　What is the common link between Blackpool, Bolton Wanderers, Brighton and Hove Albion, Cardiff, Coventry City, Derby County, Huddersfield Town, Leicester City, Northampton Town, Portsmouth, Preston North End, Southampton, Swindon Town and Wimbledon?

15　**Who were the first Cup winners to win the Charity Shield?**

---

1 **Manchester United 8 Swindon Town 4** (1911) 2 Arsenal 3 **The Professionals and the Amateurs** 4 Everton 5 **Billy Bremner (Leeds United) and Kevin Keegan (Liverpool)** 6 Aston Villa (1981), Portsmouth (1949), West Ham United (1964) 7 42 times 8 12 times 9 **It was the only one to be replayed (Man U won it 4-0)** 10 An FA XI 11 **Liverpool v Manchester United and Arsenal v Tottenham Hotspur** 12 Because they had been runners-up in that year's Premiership 13 **Arsenal** 14 They have all played one, lost one 15 **Tottenham Hotspur in 1921**

LEAGUE CUP

 # Quiz 1

League Cup

1   In which year did the first Final of the League Cup take place?

2   **In which year did the first Wembley Final take place?**

3   Who were the winners of the first League Cup?

4   **Who were the Second Division underdogs who reached the 1961 Final, and led 2-0 after the first leg?**

5   Who scored the winning goal in the first-ever League Cup Final?

6   **Who was the Spurs manager who refused to let his side take part in the first League Cup?**

7   Which Fourth Division side reached the 1962 Final?

8   **Who put the holders out of the competition in 1962?**

9   The 196 Final was completed in which month?

10   **Which Villa player was the top scorer in the 1961 competition?**

11   Who were the first winners of the League Cup who did not play their football in the top flight?

12   **Who holds the all-time scoring record in the League Cup?**

13   Which Welsh international scored a brace for Birmingham in the 1963 Final?

14   **Which club reached the Final in 1964 and 1965?**

15   Which club, now no longer in the League, reached the fifth round in 1964 only to be beaten 6-0 by West Ham?

 ## Quiz 2

League Cup

1   **Which future England manager scored a penalty in the 1965 Final?**

2   Who was the legendary English goalkeeper who played in both the 1964 and 1965 Finals?

3   **Which club reached the Final three times in five years between 1966 and 1970?**

4   Which Stoke player scored ten goals in the 1963-64 season?

5   **Which Premiership striker's father was the top scorer in the 1964-65 season while playing for Aston Villa?**

6   Whose brainchild was the League Cup, leading it to be labelled his 'folly'?

7   **In which year was the introduction of a European place for the winners?**

8   Which two clubs were the only teams not to enter the 1967 competition?

9   **Which club won the 1967 competition, but could not qualify for Europe because they were not a First Division club?**

10 Which Leeds full-back scored the only goal of a dour 1968 Final?

11 **Which team lost in the Final in 1968 and 1969?**

12 Which television commentator played in goals for Arsenal in the 1969 Final?

13 **Which Swindon player scored a brace in the 1969 final to shock Arsenal?**

14 Who were the first club to win a place in Europe through the competition?

15 **Which Manchester City stalwart scored a penalty in the 1970 semi-final derby clash?**

 **Quiz 3**   **League Cup**

1   Who was the Villa manager who led them to victory in 1975 after two previous Final defeats?

2   Which two England internationals scored Manchester City's goals in the 1976 Final victory over Newcastle?

3   Which Villa player and future manager was the top scorer in the 1976-77 campaign?

4   Which Welsh international scored a last-minute goal to give Villa a second replay in the 1977 Final against Everton?

5   For how many minutes did Aston Villa and Everton play to decide the 1977 competition?

6   Which 18-year old keeper was drafted in to keep goal for Forest against Liverpool in the 1978 Final?

7   Who did Phil Thompson bring down in a profesional foul to give Forest and penalty and eventually victory in the 1978 Final?

8   Which team upset Liverpool in the 1979 championship when they beat the favourites in the second round?

9   Which bargain basement striker, bought from a local non-League club, scored a brace for Forest in the final against Southampton in 1979?

10   Which club reached three consecutive Finals at the end of the Seventies?

11   Which fellow First Division side did Arsenal beat 7-0 in the second round of the 1979-80 competition?

12   Who was the Liverpool keeper who brought down Garry Birtles in the semi-final of the 1979-80 competition?

13   Which former winners reached the semi-finals in 1980 while still a Third Divison side?

14   Which Wolves player took advantage of confusion between Peter Shilton and David Needham to score the only goal of the 1980 Final?

15   Who won their first League Cup in 1981?

 Quiz 4   League Cup

1   Who scored West Ham's only goal in the replay for the 1981 Final?

2   Which Liverpool player was the top scorer for the 1980-81 competition?

3   How many consecutive League Cups did Liverpool claim?

4   By what name was the League Cup known between 1982 and 1986?

5   Which Liverpool player scored a brace in the 1982 Final, when the Reds beat Tottenham in extra-time?

6   Which former Liverpool keeper was beaten three times by his old club in the 1982 final?

7   Which Liverpool manager led them to victory in 1983 and then retired?

8   When Burnley beat Bury 8-4 in the 1982-83 competition, how many different players scored for Burnley?

9   Who was the Burnley manager sacked by his club on the day of their fifth round victory over Tottenham Hotspur?

10 What was the Wembley crowd when Liverpool met Manchester United in the 1983 Final?

11 Which Manchester United player was the competition's top scorer in 1982-83?

12 Who scored the opening goal in the 1983 Final, giving Manchester United an early lead?

13 At which ground was the 1984 replay held?

14 Which Third Division side held Liverpool to a draw at Anfield in the 1984 semi-finals?

15 In which year did Liverpool meet Everton at Wembley for the first time in history?

1 Paul Goddard 2 Kenny Dalglish 3 Four 4 Milk Cup 5 Ronnie Whelan 6 Ray Clemence
7 Bob Paisley 8 Eight – one of which was a Bury player 9 Brian Miller 10 100,000
11 Steve Coppell 12 Norman Whiteside 13 Maine Road 14 Walsall 15 1984

Quiz 5

League Cup

1 Which two teams met in a 'derby' game in the 1985 semi-finals?

2 **Which team won the 1985 competition in the same year that they were relegated from the First Division?**

3 Whose own goal gave Norwich victory in 1985?

4 **Who ended Liverpool's amazing run in the competition when they beat them 1-0 in the third round of the 1984-85 competition?**

5 Who played in goal for Norwich in their victory over Sunderland in the 1985 Final, winning his second winner's medal?

6 **Who won their first major trophy when they triumphed in the 1986 Final?**

7 Which First Division team did Fourth Division Swindon beat in the third round of the 1985-86 competition?

8 **Whose goal for QPR at Loftus Road eventually gave them a place in the 1986Final?**

9 What was the final score when Oxford beat QPR in the 1986 Final?

10 **Who began their sponsorship of the League Cup in 1987?**

11 Which First Division team was beaten by Fourth Division Cambridge in the second round of the 1986-87 tournament?

12 **Who were Chelsea beaten by in the third round of the 1986-87 tournament?**

13 Who scored all three goals for Tottenham when they met Arsenal in the 1987 semi-finals?

14 **Who scored a brace for Arsenal in the 1987 Final, giving them the cup on their third Wembley visit?**

15 After which Final was the League Cup trophy broken?

1 Norwich and Ipswich 2 **Norwich** 3 Gordon Chisholm 4 **Tottenham** 5 Chris Woods 6 **Oxford Utd** 7 Sheffield Wednesday 8 **Terry Fenwick** 9 3-0 10 **Littlewoods** 11 Wimbledon 12 **Cardiff City** 13 Clive Allen 14 **Charlie Nicholas** 15 1987

 **Quiz 6**

League Cup

1 Which club lifted their ban on away fans in order to compete in the 1987-88 competition, and went on to win the tournament?

2 Who were Luton playing in the 1987-88 quarter-finals when crowd trouble broke out?

3 Who was the replacement keeper who saved a penalty for Luton in the 1988 Final?

4 Who scored a brace for Luton as they won the 1988 cup against Arsenal?

5 Who took the penalty for Arsenal in the 1988 Final that would have given them a two-goal lead?

6 Which Forest player finished the 1988-89 competition as top scorer?

7 Which Fourth Division side put First Division Middlesbrough out of the 1988-89 competition?

8 Which Third Division side reached the 1989 semi-finals only to be beaten by Nottingham Forest in extra-time?

9 Whose extra-time goal gave Nottingham Forest a place in the 1989 Final?

10 Who did Luton beat in the semi-finals of the 1988-89 competition?

11 Who scored the goals for Forest in their 3-1 victory over Luton in the 1989 Final?

12 Which scorer in the 1989 Final later became a member of the Crazy Gang?

13 Nottingham Forest's fifth visit to the League Cup Final came in which year?

14 Which Fourth Division side drew 1-1 at Stamford Bridge before winning the second leg in 1989-90?

15 Who put six goals past West Ham in their semi-final first leg in 1990?

 Quiz 7   League Cup

1 Who scored the only goal of the 1990 Final?

2 **Who sponsored the League Cup in 1991 and 1992?**

3 Who hit a hat-trick for Manchester United when they beat Arsenal in the fourth round of the 1990-91 competition?

4 **Which Coventry hat-trick man from the 1990-91 quarter-finals later played for Blackburn?**

5 Whose hat-trick for Manchester United in the 1990-91 quarter-finals put out Southampton?

6 **Who did Sheffield Wednesday beat in the semi-finals of the 1990-91 tournament?**

7 Who scored the only goal of the 1991 Final?

8 **What was the aggregate score when Sheffield Wednesday beat Chelsea in the 1991 semi-finals?**

9 How many of Manchester United's League Cup Final team of 1991 were still at the club in 1997?

10 **Peterborough United put out which two top-flight teams in the 1991-92 competition?**

11 Which Tranmere player was top scorer in the 1991-92 competition?

12 **Who scored his 100th goal for Manchester United in the 1992 Final?**

13 Which Second Division team reached the 1992 semi-finals, only to lose to Manchester United in extra-time?

14 **Which teams contested the 1993 FA and League Cup Finals?**

15 Scarborough beat which Premiership team 3-0 in the second leg of the second round of the 1992-93 tournament?

 Quiz 8   League Cup

1   Who were the only non-Premiership side in the 1992-93 quarter-finals?

2   Who scored Arsenal's only goal when they scraped through against Scarborough in the fourth round of the 1992-93 competition?

3   **Who scored a brace for Sheffield Wednesday when they beat Blackburn in the 1992-93 semi-finals?**

4   Who scored Wednesday's goal in the 1993 Final, which they eventually lost 2-1?

5   **Who scored Arsenal's equaliser when they beat Sheffield Wednesday in the 1993 Final?**

6   Who scored the winner for Arsenal in the 1993 Final, but then had his arm broken when Tony Adams dropped him while celebrating?

7   **Who began their sponsorship of the League Cup in the 1992-93 season?**

8   Aston Villa won the trophy in 1994. How many times had they won it before?

9   **Who scored all five goals when Liverpool beat Fulham in the second round (second leg) in 1993-94?**

10 Who scored the Manchester United winner against Portsmouth to give them a semi-final place?

11 **Who were the only non-Premiership side to reach the 1994 semi-finals?**

12 Who did Manchester United beat in the semi-finals of the 1993-94 competition?

13 **What score was the 1994 semi-final first leg between Tranmere and Aston Villa?**

14 Who scored the Villa goal against Tranmere in the second leg of the 1994 semi-final, which took the game to penalties?

15 **Who was the Villa goalkeeper who saved a penalty against Tranmere to give them a 1994 Final berth?**

 **Quiz 9**   **League Cup**

1   Who scored two goals for Villa in the 1994 final against Manchester United?

2   Which player was shown the red card in the 1994 Final?

3   Who put Leeds out of the competition at the second round stage in 1994-95?

4   Which two players scored twice when Crystal Palace beat Aston Villa in the fourth round of the 1994-95 competition?

5   Who scored the Bolton goal which gave them their first semi-final place, in the 1995 tournament?

6   Who was the leading scorer in the 1994-95 tournament?

7   Who scored the goal which gave Bolton victory over Swindon in 1994-95, booking their place in the final?

8   Who scored Liverpool's two goals as they progressed from the 1994-95 semi-finals?

9   Who did Liverpool beat in the 1994-95 semi-finals?

10 Which Liverpool star played against the Reds in the 1995 Final?

11   Who scored the goals for Liverpool in the 1995 Final?

12 Whose screamer gave Bolton some consolation in the 1995 Final?

13   What was the final score in the 1995 final between Liverpool and Bolton?

14 How many appearances have Aston Villa made in the Final?

15   Who were Villa's opponents in the 1996 Final?

---

1 Dean Saunders 2 Andrei Kanchelskis 3 Mansfield 4 Chris Armstrong and Gareth Southgate 5 David Lee 6 Jan – Aage Fjortoft 7 John McGinlay 8 Robbie Fowler 9 Crystal Palace 10 Jason McAteer 11 Steve McManaman 12 Alan Thompson 13 2-1 14 Seven 15 Leeds

 ## Quiz 10

League Cup

1 What was the final aggregate score when Charlton beat Wimbledon in the second round of the 1995-96 competition?

2 Which minnows put Manchester United out of the 1995-96 Cup?

3 Which Yorkshire side put Nottingham Forest out of the 1995-96 tournament?

4 A goal from which veteran gave Reading victory over Southampton in the fourth round in 1995-96?

5 Who was sent off in the 1995-96 quarter-final between Arsenal and Newcastle?

6 Who scored a brace in the 1995-96 quarter-final between Arsenal and Newcastle?

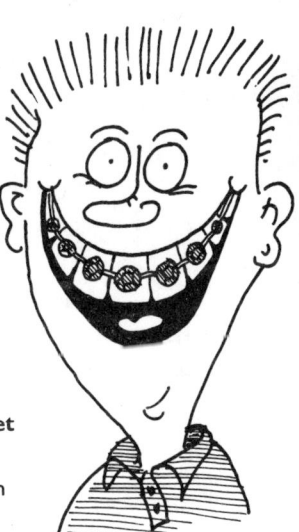

7 Who scored the only goal in the Midlands derby quarter-final between Villa and Wolves in 1995-96?

8 What was the aggregate score in the 1995-96 semi-final between Birmingham and Leeds?

9 Which two Africans were on the scoresheet when Leeds beat Birmingham in the 1995-96 semi-finals?

10 Who scored a brace for Arsenal in their semi-final clash with Aston Villa in 1995-96?

11 Who netted two for Aston Villa when they met Arsenal in the 1995-96 semi-finals?

12 Who played in goal for Leeds in the 1996 Final when they lost 3-0 to Aston Villa?

13 Who scored Villa's opening goal in the 1996 Final?

14 Who was the top scorer in the 1995-96 tournament, his side reaching the semi-finals?

15 Who scored the third and final goal in the 1996 Final to top off a tremendous season?

Quiz 11

League Cup

1 Which Second Division side reached the semi-finals of the 1996-97 tournament?

2 Which player, who had been at both clubs, was sent off in the 1996-97 clash between Birmingham and Coventry?

3 How many goals did Middlesbrough put past Hereford in the second round in 1996-97?

4 Which Premiership side did York City put out of the 1996-97 tournament?

5 Which side gave Chelsea a scare in 1996-97 when they won 3-1 at Stamford Bridge?

6 Who did Charlton hold to a draw at the Valley in the 1996-97 season?

7 Who put holders Villa out of the 1996-97 tournament?

8 Who did Middlesbrough beat in the quarter-finals of the 1996-97 competition?

9 Who scored Leicester's only goal when they overcame Ipswich in the 1996-97 quarter-finals?

10 Who scored the winner when Stockport beat Southampton to reach the 1996-97 semi-finals?

11 What was the aggregate score when Middlesbrough beat Stockport in the 1996-97 semi-finals?

12 Whose goal gave Leicester a win over Wimbledon in the semi-finals in 1996-97 on the away goals rule?

13 Who was the Stockport manager who led them into the Coca-Cola Cup semi-finals?

14 Who scored the opening goal of the Wimbledon v Leicester semi-final in 1997?

15 In what month was the Final of the 1996-97 competition held?

EUROPEAN FOOTBALL

 **Quiz 1**   **European Championships**

1 In which year was the first Final held?

2 **The USSR were awarded a walkover into the semi-finals in the 1960 championships. Why?**

3 Which stadium hosted the first Final, attracting only 17,966 spectators?

4 **How many teams entered the first championships?**

5 Which Dane was the top scorer in the 1964 Championship with 11 goals?

6 **Which was the first tournament entered by England?**

7 Why did Greece refuse to play Albania in 1964, giving the Albanians a walkover into the second round?

8 **In which city did England play their first European game v France?**

9 The home leg v France in 1962 was which English manager's last game in charge?

10 **Which manager took over the reins for the second leg, which England lost 5-2?**

11 Which team did Northern Ireland upset to go into the second round of the 1964 competition?

12 **Which future N. Ireland manager scored in that game?**

13 Which legendary Soviet goalkeeper and European Footballer of the Year saved a penalty to help them beat Italy in the 1964 championships?

14 **Which footballing minnow put Holland out of the 1964 competition, despite electing to play both legs in Holland?**

15 Which Swede played his 80th international in the second round tie they eventually lost to the Soviets?

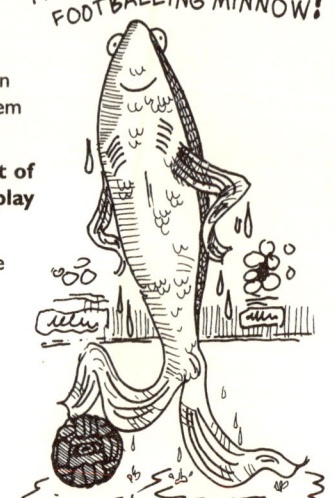

THE AMAZING... FOOTBALLING MINNOW!

 ## Quiz 2 European Championships

1 **A crowd of over 100,000 saw Spain beat which country in the 1964 Final?**

2 Which legendary Italian topped the scoring charts for the 1968 championships?

3 **Which player scored the winning goal for Republic of Ireland v Czechoslovakia in the 1968 qualifying competition, only days after breaking through to the Fulham first team?**

4 Which future Wimbledon manager played in that campaign for the Republic of Ireland?

5 **Which team did West Germany meet in the game billed as the 'Match of the Year' in the 1968 qualifying competition?**

6 Which country held West Germany to a 0-0 draw in 1968 to ensure that the World Cup finalists did not qualify for the European quarter-finals?

7 **Which Celtic veteran made his international debut at the age of 36 at Wembley v England in Scotland's qualifying game for the 1968 championship?**

8 Which Northern Ireland player put paid to Scotland's hopes of qualifying for the 1968 tournament?

9 **The biggest-ever European Championship crowd of 134,000 were attracted to which venue?**

10 Which English player limped off with a broken toe v Scotland, but came back on to score in the qualifying for the 1968 tournament?

11 **By which unusual method did Italy progress to the 1968 Final?**

12 Who became the first English player to be sent off in an international when he was red-carded in the 1968 semi-final?

13 **Who were England's two scorers when they beat the Soviet Union in the 1968 third-place play-off?**

14 Which team won the 1968 championships in front of a home crowd?

15 **Which German topped the 1972 scoring charts with 11, and was the undoubted star of the tournament?**

1 Soviet Union 2 Luigi Riva 3 Turlock O'Connor 4 Joe Kinnear 5 Czechoslovakia 6 Albania 7 Ronnie Simpson 8 George Best 9 Hampden Park (Scotland v England in 1968) 10 Jackie Charlton 11 They beat the Soviet Union on the toss of a coin 12 Alan Mullery 13 Bobby Charlton and Geoff Hurst 14 Italy 15 Gerd Muller

 **Quiz 3** Sonorous **European Championships**

1 Which country's World Cup squad was hit by a series of bans for alleged 'commercial activities', leaving them with a decimated 1972 European Championship team?

2 Who scored England's equaliser at Wembley v Switzerland to help them into the 1972 Finals?

3 Which British team lost all their away games and won all their home games while trying to qualify for the 1972 Finals?

4 Who was the goalkeeper who helped West Germany scrape into the 1972 quarter-finals after only drawing in Turkey?

5 Who scored the only English goal in their 1972 quarter-final defeat by West Germany?

6 Which country hosted the final stages of the 1972 tournament?

7 Who reached their third Final in four attempts in 1972, losing to West Germany?

8 Which Irish player topped the scoring charts for the 1976 European Championships, although his country failed to qualify for the quarter-finals?

9 Which manager was in charge of England's campaign to qualify for the 1976 Finals?

10 Who scored all five goals when England beat Cyprus at Wembley while trying to qualify for the 1976 European Championships?

11 Which England player scored against Czechoslovakia in a game which ended 2-1 and effectively ended their chances of qualifying for the 1976 competition?

12 Who were the only team to beat Wales in their qualification for the 1976 quarter-finals?

13 Who was the Welsh manager who led them to their first European quarter-final?

14 Which 34-year-old Wrexham player was the Welsh hero when he scored the winner against Austria to ensure their qualification for the 1976 quarter-finals?

15 Who was the Scottish keeper for the 1976 campaign, which ended at the group stages?

Quiz 4 — European Championships

1 **Who was Ireland's player-manager for their 1976 campaign, which also ended at the group stages?**

2 When the Republic of Ireland travelled to Russia in 1975 which club side was playing as the Soviet national team?

3 **Which team embarrassed East Germany with a 2-1 win, winning their first game in the history of the competition in the group stages of the 1976 competition?**

4 The quarter-final between Wales and Yugoslavia in 1976 was almost abandoned. Why?

5 **The 1976 Final was the first to be decided by penalties. Who were the two teams involved?**

6 Who was the only player to miss in the 1976 penalty shoot-out?

7 **Which English player top-scored in the 1980 campaign with seven goals?**

8 Which country was chosen to host the 1980 Finals?

9 **What was the final result in the first-ever meeting between the Republic and Northern Ireland in the qualifying for the 1980 championships?**

10 Who were the only team to take a point from England in the 1980 qualifying stage?

11 **Which England player was substituted in their game v Bulgaria in 1979 after scoring and then clashing with Grancharov?**

12 Who scored from the penalty spot to give Scotland a win over Norway in the 1980 qualifying tournament?

13 **Who scored Scotland's only goal when they were trounced 3-1 by Belgium in the 1980 group stages?**

14 Which country was the surprise package of the 1980 qualifying tournament, reaching the Finals despite failing to win away from home?

15 **Which Welsh player was sent off against Turkey in 1979 after breaking the cheekbone of Mustapha I, who was duly taken off to be replaced by Mustapha II?**

---

1 Johnny Giles 2 Dynamo Kiev 3 Iceland 4 The Yugoslav keeper Maric was hit by a beer can thrown by a Welsh fan 5 Czechoslovakia and West Germany 6 Uli Hoeness 7 Kevin Keegan 8 Italy 9 0-0 10 Republic of Ireland 11 Peter Barnes 12 Archie Gemmill 13 John Robertson 14 Greece 15 Byron Stevenson

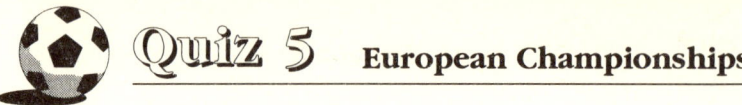

Quiz 5 — European Championships

1   Who was the unlikely hat-trick hero when West Germany beat Holland in the 1980 Finals?

2   **Who were England's opponents in the 1980 Finals when the Italian police used tear gas to disperse rioting fans?**

3   Who had a 'goal' disallowed in that 1-1 draw?

4   **Who scored the only goal for Italy in their victory over England in the 1980 tournament?**

5   Whose ineffective tackle allowed Graziani to cross for the goal?

6   **Who scored a brace in the 1980 Final to give West Germany victory?**

7   Who were their opponents?

8   **Which French genius was the star of the 1984 tournament and finished as top scorer?**

9   Which country hosted the 1984 finals?

10 **Which West Ham player scored for Belgium in their 1983 qualifying game against East Germany?**

11 Who scored Scotland's two goals when they beat East Germany for their only victory of the group stages for the 1984 tournament?

12 **Who scored England's two goals in the opening game of their 1984 qualifying campaign against Denmark?**

13 Who scored the last-minute equaliser for Denmark to make the score 2-2?

14 **Which team did England beat 3-0 for Bobby Robson's first victory as manager?**

15 Who scored a hat-trick in his first appearance on the England starting line-up when they beat Luxembourg 9-0 at Wembley in 1983?

1 Klaus Allofs 2 **Belgium** 3 Tony Woodcock 4 **Marco Tardelli** 5 Phil Neal 6 **Horst Hrubesch** 7 Belgium 8 **Michel Platini** 9 France 10 **Francois Van Der Elst** 11 John Wark and Paul Sturrock 12 **Trevor Francis** 13 Jesper Olsen 14 **Greece** 15 Luther Blissett

 # Quiz 6 European Championships

1 Who handled the ball in England's crunch tie with Denmark at Wembley in Dec 1983, giving away a penalty?

2 Who stepped up to score the penalty and put an end to England's hopes of qualifying?

3 **Wales could have qualified for the 1984 finals had they beaten Yugoslavia in Cardiff. Who scored the Welsh goal in the 1-1 draw?**

4 Which Northern Ireland player scored the only goal in their historic home victory over West Germany in 1982?

5 **Which Northern Ireland player won his 100th cap against Austria in a European Championship game in 1983?**

6 Which Manchester United player scored his first international goal in the same game?

7 **Which team qualified for the 1984 Finals with a 12-1 win over Malta, prompting claims of match-fixing as they had to win by 11 clear goals?**

8 Which team failed to qualify for the finals because of that freak result?

9 **Which future Charlton Athletic player broke his leg in the opening game of the 1984 Finals?**

10 Which French defender headbutted Jesper Olsen, getting himself sent off and suspended for the next three games?

11 **Which 18-year-old Belgian orchestrated their victory over Yugoslavia in the 1984 Finals?**

12 Platini scored two hat-tricks in the 1984 Finals. Which teams were on the receiving end of his stunning displays?

13 **Which veteran Portuguese striker scored on his record 65th international appearance v Romania, taking them through to the 1984 semi-finals?**

14 Whose 119th-minute cross set up Platini for the semi-final winner over Portugal in 1984?

15 **Who was the Spanish goalkeeper and captain who dropped the ball over the line from a Platini free-kick in the Final?**

1 **Phil Neal** 2 Allan Simonsen 3 **Robbie James** 4 Ian Stewart 5 **Pat Jennings** 6 Norman Whiteside 7 **Spain** 8 Holland 9 **Allan Simonsen** 10 Manuel Amoros 11 **Enzo Scifo** 12 Belgium and Yugoslavia 13 **Nene** 14 Jean Tigana 15 Luis Arconada

 # Quiz 7   European Championships

1   Which country was selected as the venue for the 1988 Finals?

2   Who were the only team to take a point from England in their qualification for the 1988 Finals?

3   How many goals did Gary Lineker score in England's six qualifying games?

4   How many goals did England put past Turkey at Wembley in 1987?

5   Which two players scored the only goals of Northern Ireland's unsuccessful qualifying campaign for the 1988 Finals?

6   The 8-0 victory by Holland over Cyprus in the 1988 qualifying competition was declared void. Why?

7   Which Welsh player was refused permission to play against Denmark in the 1988 qualifying by his Italian bosses?

8   Who scored the winning goal for Wales in that game in Cardiff?

9   Which veteran Republic of Ireland defender was controversially picked for their 1988 qualifying game v Scotland and silenced the critics with a winning goal?

10   Which Scottish player ensured the Republic of Ireland's qualification for the 1988 Finals when his late goal took both points against Bulgaria?

11   Which English referee took control of the opening match of the 1988 Finals when Italy drew with West Germany?

12   Which Italian scored his first international goal in that game?

13   Who was the Italian goalkeeper whose extra steps were penalised, leading to the West German equaliser?

14   Which Spaniard's clearly offside goal helped them to victory over Denmark in their first match of the 1988 Finals?

15   Which future Premiership stars scored for West Germany and Italy respectively in that 1988 tournament?

1 West Germany 2 Turkey 3 Five 4 Eight 5 Colin Clarke and Jimmy Quinn
6 The Cypriot keeper was injured by a smokebomb thrown by Dutch fans. The game was replayed behind closed doors and Holland won 4-0 7 Ian Rush 8 Mark Hughes
9 Mark Lawrenson **10 Gary Mackay** 11 Keith Hackett **12 Robert Mancini** 13 Walter Zenga
14 Emilio Butragueno 15 Jurgen Klinsmann and Gianluca Vialli

Quiz 8 — European Championships

1 Which German scored his first and second international goals in their win over Spain in the 1988 Finals?

2 Who was the Danish goalkeeper who had a nightmare game against Italy in 1988, gifting them a 2-0 victory when they only required a draw to qualify for the semi-finals?

3 Who was the manager of West Germany in 1988?

4 Whose goal gave the Republic of Ireland victory over England in their clash in the 1988 Finals?

5 Who was the England keeper beaten by that goal?

6 That game almost turned around because of a timely England substitution. Who replaced Neil Webb?

7 When Holland and England met in the 1988 Finals, which Dutch striker scored a hat-trick to end England's semi-final hopes?

8 Which player scored the only England goal in that game?

9 Who was Ireland's manager who almost took them into the 1988 semi-finals?

10 Whose superb volley gave the Republic the lead in their game v the Soviet Union in 1988?

11 What was the result in the game between the Soviet Union and England which sealed England's nightmare 1988 tournament?

12 Ireland needed only a draw against Holland to reach the semi-finals. Which Dutch player came on as a substitute to score a late goal and spoil the party?

13 Who presented Peter Shilton with a bouquet of flowers for his 100th cap in the 1988 Finals?

14 Holland met West Germany in the 1988 semi-finals. When was the last time that Holland had beaten the Germans?

15 Which German player suffered stomach pains in the warm-up to that Holland semi-final and so had to be replaced for that game?

1 **Rudi Voller** 2 Peter Schmeichel 3 **Franz Beckenbauer** 4 Ray Houghton 5 **Peter Shilton** 6 Glenn Hoddle 7 **Marco Van Basten** 8 Bryan Robson 9 **Jackie Charlton** 10 Ronnie Whelan 11 3-1 12 Wim Kieft 13 **Ruud Gullit** 14 1956 15 Pierre Littbarski

 ## Quiz 9   European Championships

1   Who tripped Klinsmann to give West Germany a penalty in their semi-final?

2   Who stepped up to score the semi-final penalty for West Germany in the 1988 Finals?

3   Which German player tripped Marco Van Basten to give Holland a penalty?

4   Who was the German keeper, later to play in the Premiership, who was beaten by Ronald Koeman's penalty?

5   Whose pass set up Van Basten for his winner against West Germany in the 1988 semi-finals?

6   How many Soviet players had been booked going into their semi-final clash with Italy in 1988?

7   Who scored the Soviet Union's second goal to send them into the 1988 Final?

8   Who scored the first Dutch goal in the 1988 Finals between Holland and the Soviet Union?

9   Whose cross set up Van Basten for the 1988 Final's second goal?

10   In which city was the 1988 Final held?

11   Who was the manager of the winning Dutch team?

12   Which Danish player featured in the 1988 tournament at the age of 38?

13   Which French striker finished the 1992 tournament as the top scorer in the campaign with 11 goals?

14   Which country was selected as hosts for the 1992 Finals?

15   Which team were delayed en route to their qualifying game in Reykjavik in 1990, held at Heathrow for alleged shoplifting offences?

 **Quiz 10** European Championships

1 **Which ex-Nottingham Forest player helped Iceland to a historic qualifying win over Spain?**

2 Which Scottish player scored the winner against Romania at Hampden Park to begin their successful qualifying campaign for the 1992 tournament?

3 **What was the score when Scotland met Bulgaria in Sofia while trying to qualify for the 1992 championships?**

4 Which player was penalised for handling the ball in his own area when the Scots travelled to Romania for their qualifier?

5 **How many goals did Scotland score in their two ties with San Marino in the 1992 qualification campaign?**

6 Which team qualified for the 1992 tournament ahead of Italy?

7 **Which country did the Faroe Islands beat in their first ever European Championship game?**

8 Brian Laudrup pulled out of the Danish international team after disagreements with their manager. Who was he?

9 **The Danes finished second in their qualifying group but made it to the Finals. Why?**

10 What score was Northern Ireland's home fixture against the Faroe Islands?

11 **Who scored his first international goal for two years when Wales met Belgium at Cardiff Arms Park for their qualifier in 1990?**

12 Which Welsh player was sent off against Luxembourg in the same qualifying series?

13 **Who was the scorer when Wales pulled off a magnificent victory over Germany in 1991?**

14 Who were the only team to take a point from Holland in their qualification for the 1992 championships?

15 **Who was the England manager when they began their campaign to qualify for the 1992 tournament?**

1 Toddy Orlygsson 2 Ally McCoist 3 1-1 4 Gordon Durie 5 Six 6 Soviet Union
7 Austria 8 Richard Moller-Nielsen 9 Yugoslavia disqualified because of civil war 10 1-1
11 Ian Rush 12 Clayton Blackmore 13 Ian Rush 14 Finland 15 Graham Taylor

 ## Quiz 11 European Championships

1 Who scored an Irish hat-trick when they demolished Turkey in 1990?

2 **Which controversial figure was dropped for England's visit to the Republic of Ireland in their qualifying game?**

3 Who scored the two goals when England met the Republic at Wembley?

4 **Whose scrambled goal gave England the points in Turkey to leave them favourites to qualify for 1992?**

5 Who scored the goal 13 minutes from the final whistle to earn England a draw against Poland and seal their qualification for the 1992 Finals?

6 **Who was the French goalkeeper who kept them in the opening game of the 1992 Finals against Sweden?**

7 Which English player was drafted in at right-back against Denmark because of injuries?

8 **Who replaced him late in the game and twice came close to scoring?**

9 Which Danish player, later to play in England, beat Chris Woods but hit the post in that game?

10 **Which French player headbutted Stuart Pearce in their 1992 Championship game?**

11 Which English player cleared off the line from an Angloma header in the France v England clash in 1992?

12 **Which Swedish player scored their only goal as they beat Denmark in the group stages of the 1992 championships?**

13 Who scored England's only goal of the 1992 Finals?

14 **Who chipped the deciding penalty in the shoot-out to win the 1976 Finals for Czechoslovakia?**

15 Who replaced Gary Lineker when Graham Taylor substituted him in their final 1992 game against Sweden?

 Quiz 12 European Championships

1 In which minute did Brolin score the winner in that game?

2 Who scored the winner for Denmark against France, sealing their move into the 1992 semi-finals?

3 **Which future Premiership star scored the only goal when Holland met Scotland in the group stages of the 1992 Finals?**

4 Which German played on until half-time against the CIS despite suffering a broken arm after 20 minutes in 1992?

5 **Whose last-minute 'fall' earned Germany a free-kick and the equaliser against the CIS in the 1992 Finals?**

6 Who scored the free-kick for Germany to draw their game with the CIS in 1992?

7 **Who was the Scotland manager who guided them in the 1992 Finals?**

8 Who scored Germany's first goal in their 2-0 win over Scotland in 1992?

9 **Which Scottish defender deflected Stefan Effenberg's cross into his own net for the second German goal in 1992?**

10 Which German player came on as a substitute against Scotland in 1992 but went off five minutes later after clashing heads with Stuart McCall?

11 **Which future Premiership keeper played in the 1992 Finals for the CIS?**

12 What was the score in the 1992 clash between Holland and Germany?

13 **Who scored his first international goal in Scotland's 3-0 win over the CIS in 1992?**

14 Who was brought down for a penalty in Scotland's 3-0 victory over the CIS in 1992?

15 **Who was Germany's keeper in their semi-final tie with Sweden in**

Quiz 13 European Championships

1   Which lofty striker scored Sweden's final goal of the 1992 championships?

2   **Who scored a brace for Germany in their semi-final clash with Sweden in 1992?**

3   Who scored a brace for Denmark in their semi-final game against Holland in 1992?

4   **Which Danish player suffered an horrific knee injury in their clash with Holland in the 1992 semi-finals?**

5   Who scored Holland's 85th-minute equaliser in their semi-final with Denmark in 1992?

6   **In the penalty shoot-out to decide the semi-final between Holland and Denmark in 1992, who was the only man to miss?**

7   In which city was the final of the 1992 championships held?

8   **Which future Premiership player scored in the 1992 Final between Denmark and Germany?**

9   Which was the only team not to play a qualifying game for the 1996 Championship?

10 **Which two Premiership players scored in Romania's win over Azerbaijan in the qualifying tournament for Euro '96?**

11 Which three countries reached the Finals for the first time in 1996?

12 **Which player topped the scoring charts for the European qualifying rounds with 12 goals?**

13 Who were the only nation to beat Italy in their qualification for the 1996 Championship?

14 **In which English city did Holland play the Republic of Ireland for the final place in Euro '96?**

15 Who scored the winner when Northern Ireland beat Austria in Vienna in the qualification stages of Euro '96?

 **Quiz 14** European Championships

1 **Who scored for the Welsh in Dusseldorf when they pulled off a draw against Germany in their unsuccessful qualifying campaign for Euro '96?**

2 Which two players topped the Scottish scoring charts in their qualifying campaign for Euro '96?

3 **Who scored the opening goal of Euro '96?**

4 Which Swiss player equalised with a penalty against England in 1996?

5 **Who provided the pass for England's opening goal of Euro '96?**

6 Who captained the England team for their first game of Euro '96?

7 **Which three Glasgow Rangers' players scored goals in the 1996 championships?**

8 At which ground did Scotland eke out a draw with Holland in the 1996 tournament?

9 **Holland appealed for a penalty in their Euro '96 tie with Scotland, claiming handball. Which player was accused?**

10 Which player was judged to have fouled Gordon Durie to earn Scotland their penalty against England in 1996?

11 **Whose penalty did David Seaman save in the 1996 clash between England and Scotland?**

12 Which Scottish defender did Paul Gascoigne beat for the second goal of their 2-0 victory in 1996?

13 **Which player came on at half-time as a substitute for Stuart Pearce against Scotland in 1996 but was later replaced by Sol Campbell when he picked up an injury?**

14 Who came on to score the only Dutch goal against England in 1996, sealing their move through to the quarter-Finals and knocking out Scotland?

15 **Alan Shearer scored two goals against Holland in Euro '96. Who scored the other two in their 4-1 victory?**

 **Quiz 15** **European Championships**

1   Who scored Scotland's only goal of the 1996 championships?

2   **Which two players were sent off in the 1996 game between Spain and Bulgaria?**

3   At which ground did France beat Romania 1-0 in Euro '96?

4   **Who was the only man to score for Bulgaria in the 1996 championships?**

5   What was the final score between France and Spain when they met in Euro '96?

6   **Who scored Spain's winner against Romania to take them through to the 1996 quarter-Finals?**

7   Who was Germany's impressive full-back who scored against the Czech Republic in the group stages of Euro '96?

8   **Who netted a brace for Italy against Russia in Euro '96, but was dropped from the starting line-up for the next game?**

9   Who was the Italian manager whose tactical mistakes saw his team fail to qualify for the 1996 quarter-Finals?

10 **Which two teams did not win a single point in the 1996 championships?**

11 What was the score in the 1996 tie between Croatia and Portugal?

12 **Which England player was booked in their quarter-final clash with Spain in 1996, ruling him out of the semi-finals?**

13 Which Spaniard's penalty hit the bar in their quarter-final clash with England in 1996?

14 **Whose penalty did David Seaman save in England's quarter-final clash in 1996?**

15 Who was the French goalkeeper who saved a penalty to take his team through to the 1996 semi-finals?

 ## Quiz 16 European Championships

1   Which Croat player, who would later become familiar to Premiership spectators, was sent off in their quarter-final against Germany in 1996?

2   Which future Premiership player handled the ball to give Germany a penalty in their 1996 quarter-final against Croatia?

3   Who scored the Czech Republic's winner against Portugal in the 1996 quarter-Finals?

4   Which English referee took part in Euro '96?

5   Who scored Germany's equaliser in their Euro '96 semi-final with England?

6   Which English player hit the post in their 1996 semi-final defeat at the hands of Germany?

7   Who was the German keeper who saved Gareth Southgate's penalty in the 1996 semi-final penalty shoot-out?

8   Who converted Germany's final penalty to take them through to the 1996 Final?

9   Which French player's penalty was saved in the 1996 shoot-out against the Czech Republic?

10 Who scored the deciding penalty in the semi-final tie between the Czech Republic and France in 1996?

11 What was the attendance for the Euro '96 Final at Wembley?

12 Who brought down Patrick Berger in the 1996 Final for the Czech penalty?

13 Which German striker scored twice in the Euro '96 Final?

14 Which team finished the 1996 tournament top of the Fair Play charts?

15 Which two countries have been chosen as hosts for the 2000 European Championships.

1 **Igor Stimac** 2 Nikola Jerkan 3 **Karel Poborsky** 4 David Ellery 5 **Stefan Kuntz**
6 Darren Anderton 7 **Andreas Kopke** 8 Andreas Moller 9 **Reynald Pedros**
10 Miroslav Kadlec 11 73,611 12 Matthias Sammer 13 Oliver Bierhoff 14 England
15 Holland and Belgium

Quiz 17 European Championships

1   By what name were the European Football Championships formerly known?

2   How often are the European Championship Finals held?

3   In which year was the European Championship first contested?

4   Who were the first champions, winning the Cup for the only time in their entire history as a nation?

5   Which is the only nation to have won the European Championship more than once?

6   Who is the secretary of the French Football Federation after whom the European Championship trophy was named?

7   Which three countries have won the European Championship on their home soil?

8   Who was the goalkeeper for Czechoslovakia when they beat West Germany on penalties in the 1976 Final in Belgrade?

9   Which two neighbouring countries met for the first time in September 1978 in a qualifying match for the 1980 European Championship Finals?

10   Who scored both West Germany's goals in their 2-1 victory over Belgium in the 1980 European Championship Final?

11   Which Danish international broke his leg in the opening match of the 1984 Finals?

12   Who won the 1988 European Championship, beating the USSR 2-0 in the Final?

13   Who was captain of the 1988 European Champions?

14   1992 European Champions Denmark originally failed to qualify for the Finals but were brought in eight days before the tournament began to fill the gap created by the expulsion of which country?

15   Which Brondby and future Arsenal player scored the opening goal for Denmark in the 1992 Final against Germany?

1 **The European Nations' Cup** 2 *Every four years* 3 1960 4 The USSR 5 **West Germany (twice)** 6 Henri Delaunay 7 **Spain** (1964), **Italy** (1968) **and France (1984)** 8 Igor Viktor 9 **Northern Ireland and the Republic of Ireland** 10 Horst Hrubesch 11 **Allan Simonsen** 12 Holland 13 **Ruud Gullit** 14 Yugoslavia 15 **John Jensen**

 ## Quiz 18 European Championships

1 Who scored the goal for Sweden that finally put paid to England's hopes in the 1992 European Championship Finals?

2 Which member of the Scotland squad in the 1992 European Championship Finals in Sweden was born in Sweden?

3 In which four Swedish cities were European Championship Finals matches played in 1992?

4 In which of these cities was the 1992 Final played?

5 Who was the captain of winners Germany in Euro '96?

6 Who scored Germany's match-winner in the Final against the Czech Republic?

7 What was historic about this goal?

8 Who took the first four kicks for England in their penalty shoot-outs against both Spain and Germany?

9 Who took England's fifth penalty against Germany?

10 After Gareth Southgate's famous England miss, who scored the winning spot-kick for Germany?

11 Who was the leading scorer in Euro '96, with five goals in the tournament?

12 Which club was he playing for at this stage of his career?

13 Who scored three goals for Croatia during their first appearance in the Finals of an international tournament?

14 Three other players – one Bulgarian, one Dane and one German – scored three goals in Euro '96. Name them.

15 Apart from England, which other country took part in two penalty shoot-outs in Euro '96?

---

15 France
12 Blackburn Rovers 13 Davor Suker 14 Hristo Stoichkov, Brian Laudrup and Jürgen Klinsmann
Pearce, Paul Gascoigne 9 Teddy Sheringham 10 Andreas Möller 11 Alan Shearer
tional had been settled by the 'Golden Goal' method 8 Alan Shearer, David Platt, Stuart
4 Gothenburg 5 Jürgen Klinsmann 6 Oliver Bierhoff 7 It was the first time an interna-
1 Tomas Brolin 2 Richard Gough 3 Stockholm, Gothenburg, Malmo and Norrkoping

Quiz 19 European Championships

1 **Which outfield player saved on the line with his hands in the Scotland v Holland group match in Euro '96?**

2 Which club was he playing for at this stage of his career?

3 **Whose penalty for France was saved in the semi-final shoot-out against the Czech Republic?**

4 When Germany and the Czech Republic met during the group stage of Euro '96, ten players were shown the yellow card. Who was the English referee who booked them?

5 **At which grounds were the quarter-Finals of Euro '96 played?**

6 Who scored Scotland's only goal of Euro '96?

7 **Which Englishman scored against his own club keeper in Euro '96?**

8 Which member of the Italian squad for Euro '96 played his club football in the USA?

9 **Who scored from the penalty spot to give the Czech Republic the lead in the Euro '96 Final against Germany?**

10 Who had been fouled in the penalty area?

11 **Give the name and/or the nationality of the referee who pointed to the spot?**

12 Who was the French goalkeeper, man of the match in the quarter-final victory over Holland?

13 **Which country won the Euro '96 tournament Fair Play Award?**

14 At the time of Euro '96, for which Italian club was star Bulgarian striker Hristo Stoichkov playing club football?

15 **Where will the Finals of the 2000 European Championship be held?**

1 John Collins 2 Celtic 3 Reynald Pedros 4 David Ellery 5 Anfield, Old Trafford, Villa Park and Wembley 6 Ally McCoist 7 Paul Gascoigne against fellow Rangers player Andy Goram (Scotland) 8 Roberto Donadoni 9 Patrik Berger 10 Karel Poborsky 11 Pierluigi Pairetto (Italy) 12 Bernard Lama 13 England 14 Parma 15 Belgium and Holland

Quiz 20

Cup Winners' Cup

1 Which Italian team were the first winners of the Cup Winners' Cup in 1961?

2 Which British club did they beat, in the only Cup Winners' Cup Final to have been played over two legs?

3 Which was the first English team to participate in the Cup Winners' Cup?

4 Which was the first English team to win the Cup Winners' Cup?

5 Which three teams have won Cup Winners' Cup Finals in their home cities?

6 Who became the first German winners of the Cup Winners' Cup when they beat Liverpool in the 1966 Final?

7 Which member of this German team created a Cup Winners' individual goal-scoring record, with 14 goals in 1965-66?

8 Who, in 1969, became the first Eastern European club to win the Cup Winners' Cup?

9 Which club reached three consecutive Cup Winners' Cup Finals in the 1970s?

10 Which Dutch international scored twice for this club in both the 1976 and 1977 Cup Winners' Cup Finals?

11 What was unusual about the atmosphere during the second leg of West Ham United's 1981 Cup Winners' Cup match against Castilla of Spain?

12 The 1981 Cup Winners' Cup Final was the only one ever to have been contested by two teams from Eastern Europe – name them.

13 Which manager has led two British clubs to Cup Winners' Cup victory?

14 Which Italian Serie B club reached the Cup Winners' Cup semi-final in 1988?

15 Which Belgian team won the 1988 Cup Winners' Cup in their first season in European competition?

1 Fiorentina 2 Rangers 3 Wolverhampton Wanderers 4 Tottenham Hotspur
5 West Ham United (1965), Anderlecht (1976), Barcelona (1982) 6 Borussia Dortmund
7 Lothar Emmerich 8 Slovan Bratislava 9 Anderlecht 10 Robbie Rensenbrink
11 The match was played behind closed doors because of crowd trouble in the first
leg 12 Dynamo Tbilisi (USSR) and Carl Zeiss Jena (East Germany) 13 Alex Ferguson
(Aberdeen and Manchester United) 14 Atalanta 15 Mechelen

Quiz 21

Cup Winners' Cup

1 **Who scored both goals for Sampdoria in their 2-0 victory over Anderlecht in the 1990 Cup Winners' Cup Final?**

2 Who scored both goals for Manchester United in their 2-1 victory over Barcelona in the 1991 Cup Winners' Cup Final?

3 **Which Spanish club knocked holders Manchester United out of the 1991-92 Cup Winners' Cup in the second round?**

4 One of Werder Bremen's goals in their 1992 Cup Winners' Cup Final victory over Monaco was scored by Wynton Rufer. Which country did he play for at international level?

5 **Who played for Parma against Antwerp from his native Belgium in the 1993 Cup Winners' Cup Final?**

6 In which city was the 1994 Cup Winners' Cup Final between Arsenal and Parma played?

7 **Name the Real Zaragoza player who scored in every round of the 1994-95 Cup Winners' Cup?**

8 Which Welsh international scored Arsenal's goal in their 2-1 defeat by Real Zaragoza in the 1995 Cup Winners' Cup Final?

9 **Whose shot from the halfway line won the 1995 European Cup Winners' Cup Final?**

10 Which English club reached the semi-finals of the 1996-97 Cup Winners' Cup?

11 **Which Brazilian scored the only goal of the 1997 Final for Barcelona against Paris St Germain?**

12 Name any of the three teams from the former East Germany that played in Cup Winners' Cup Finals.

13 **Which seven English teams have won the Cup Winners' Cup?**

14 Which club has won the Cup Winners' Cup most often?

15 **In which city has the Final been played most often?**

Quiz 22

European Cup

1 **As what did the early stages of the European Cup become known in 1991?**

2 In which season had the European Cup first been held?

3 **Which Spanish team were the first winners of the trophy?**

4 As holders of the trophy, this team automatically entered the competition the following season. When were they eventually knocked out?

5 **Before the adoption of the league system, what was the lowest number of matches required to win the European Cup?**

6 Where was the first European Cup Final held?

7 **The attendance at this match was a mere 38,000. Which ground holds the record for the highest European Cup gate – 135,000 for the Real Madrid v Eintracht Frankfurt Final in 1960?**

8 Which team has won the European Cup most often?

9 **Benfica have played in seven European Cup Finals. How many times have they won the trophy?**

10 What outstanding feat in the European Cup has been achieved by all the following teams: AC Milan, Ajax, Bayern Munich, Benfica, Internazionale, Liverpool, Nottingham Forest and Real Madrid?

11 **Which is the only team to have won the European Cup more often than its own domestic Championship?**

12 To date, there has only ever been one European Cup match between teams from the same city. Which were the clubs involved in this local derby in the 1958-59 semi-finals?

13 **Who was the Spanish international who played in European Cup Finals for both Barcelona and Inter Milan in the 1960s?**

14 Who scored both AC Milan's goals when they won the Cup in 1963 and also played for Juventus when they lost the 1973 Final to Ajax?

15 **Velibor Vasovic appeared in the European Cup Finals of 1966 and 1969 and finished on the losing side on both occasions. Which teams did he play for?**

Quiz 23

European Cup

1 In 1967, who became the first British team to win the European Cup?

2 Who did they beat in the Final?

3 **Who scored the goals in their 2-1 victory?**

4 Who scored for the opposition from the penalty spot?

5 **Where was the 1967 Final played?**

6 Which was the first English team to take part in the European Cup?

7 **Who was manager of Manchester United when they won the European Cup in 1968?**

8 Who were their opponents in the Final?

9 **Where was the 1968 Final played?**

10 In which year did Liverpool become the next British team to win the European Cup?

11 **Who scored for Liverpool in their 3-1 victory over Borussia Moenchengladbach in Rome?**

12 Borussia Moenchengladbach's goal was scored by Danish international Alan Simonsen. For which English League club did he later play?

13 **Which German international was twice a loser to Liverpool in European Cup Finals?**

14 In 1979, who became the first Swedish team to reach the Final of the European Cup?

15 **Who scored on his European Cup debut in the 1979 Final?**

CARLING 10,000 FOOTBALL FACTS & QUESTIONS

Quiz 24

European Cup

1 **Who was the first Englishman to manage a European Cup-winning side?**

2 Which team won the only European Cup Final to date to have gone to a replay?

3 **Which England international played against Nottingham Forest in the 1980 European Cup Final?**

4 Which was the last team to win the European Cup in their first ever season in the competition?

5 **After English teams had won the European Cup for six years in succession, which German club interrupted their domination of the tournament in 1983?**

6 Which was the only Eastern European or Iron Curtain team ever to win the European Cup?

7 **With which two clubs did Dutch international star Ronald Koeman win European Cup medals?**

8 Which Dutchman scored the winning goal for AC Milan in the 1990 European Cup Final?

9 **Which England International played for Marseille in the 1991 European Cup Final?**

10 Which two British clubs played each other in the European Cup in 1992?

11 **Why did the second leg of Leeds United's 1992 first round tie against Stuttgart have to be replayed?**

12 Which French international played in three consecutive European Cup Finals in 1993, 1994 and 1995?

13 **Who scored twice for AC Milan in the 1994 European Cup Final?**

14 Before Borussia Dortmund in 1997, which was the last team to win the European Cup Final in their own country?

15 **Who scored for Juventus in their 1997 European Cup Final defeat by Borussia Dortmund?**

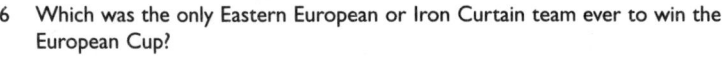

 **Quiz 25**

1 Originally known as the Inter-Cities Fairs Cup, when was the UEFA Cup given its present name?

2 What was the special significance of the tie between Dunfermline Athletic and Dinamo Zagreb in the 1966-67 Fairs Cup?

3 **Who, in 1968, became the first English winners of the Fairs Cup?**

4 Which English team won the trophy in the year it was renamed the UEFA Cup?

5 **Who scored twice for Liverpool in two UEFA Cup Finals?**

6 Who, in 1976 and 1977, became the only team ever to win the European Cup the year after winning the UEFA Cup?

7 **In 1979-80, all four UEFA Cup semi-finalists came from the same country. Which?**

8 And which two contested the Final?

9 **Who won this Final on the away goals rule, after the two legs finished level at 3-3?**

10 Which two English clubs won the Cup during the 1980s?

11 **Name the Scot who scored 14 goals for an English club in the 1980-81 UEFA Cup.**

12 Who, in 1985 and 1986, became the last team to retain the UEFA Cup?

13 **Who, in 1987, became the only Scottish club to reach the UEFA Cup Final?**

14 Who beat them in the Final of the competition?

15 **Which two Italian teams contested the 1990 Final?**

Quiz 26

1 **Which German international scored 10 goals for Roma in their 1990-91 UEFA Cup campaign?**

2 Whose six goals helped Inter Milan win the 1990-91 UEFA Cup?

3 **Name the Englishman who scored against Liverpool for Kuusysi Lahti of Finland in the 1991-92 UEFA Cup.**

4 Who scored in both legs of Norwich City's victory over Bayern Munich in the 1993-94 UEFA Cup?

5 **In 1994, who became the first Austrian team to reach the UEFA Cup Final?**

6 Who scored all five goals for Juventus in one leg of their 1994-95 match against CSKA Sofia?

7 **Who scored for winners Parma in both legs of the 1994-95 Final against Juventus?**

8 Who scored a hat-trick for Leeds United in their 1995 UEFA Cup match against Monaco?

9 **Which English team reached the quarter-Finals of the competition in 1995-96?**

10 Who, in 1996, became the first French club to reach the UEFA Cup Final?

11 **Which German team beat them 5-1 on aggregate to win the competition for the first time in their distinguished history?**

12 In the 1996-97 UEFA Cup, which German team did Brondby of Denmark beat 8-1 on aggregate after losing the home leg 3-1?

13 **Who won the UEFA Cup in 1997?**

14 Who did they beat 4-1 on penalties in the Final after the match had finished 1-1 at the end of extra time?

15 **Name the six English clubs that have won the Inter-Cities Fairs or UEFA Cup a total of nine times to the end of 1997.**

CARLING 10,000 FOOTBALL FACTS & QUESTIONS

 ## Quiz 27   **European Football**

1   Apart from Athens and Thessaloniki, which is the only other city in Greece to have been home to winners of the Greek League Championship?

2   In which Austrian city do FC Tirol play their home games?

3   In which European nation does the football season usually run from April to October?

4   In which Italian city do Atalanta play their home matches?

5   In which Russian city do Zenit play their home matches?

6   In which Swiss city do Servette play their home matches?

7   Name the Atletico Madrid goalkeeper who kept a clean sheet for 1,275 minutes (more than 14 games) in March 1991.

8   To what did Dinamo Zagreb change their name in 1991?

9   Under Communism, what was the name of the Polish police team?

10   What is the real forename of the German goalkeeper universally known as 'Sepp' Maier?

11   What nationality is Jean-Marc Bosman, of the European Court's famous 1995 'Bosman ruling'?

12   What, to English-speakers at least, is the more familiar Flemish name of the Belgian club known in French as FC Malines?

13   Which Ajax star of the '70s was Holland's first full-time soccer professional?

14   Which are the two leading football clubs in Munich?

15   Which Austrian international striker has played club football for Torino (Italy), Seville (Spain) and FC Koln (Germany)?

THE WORLD CUP

 **Quiz 1**   **World Cup**

1 **By the end of the 20th century, how many World Cups will have been held altogether?**

2 Before the start of the 1998 tournament, how many different countries had won it?

3 **How many times has the host nation won the World Cup?**

4 Which country had won it four times before the start of the 1998 Finals?

5 **Which two countries had won it three times?**

6 Which two countries had won it twice?

7 **Which country had won it once?**

8 Which is the only country to have competed in all the 20th century's World Cup Finals tournaments?

9 **In which year did the holders not defend the trophy?**

10 Which team has held the World Cup for longest (1934-50)?

11 **In which year did England first take part in the World Cup?**

12 In which World Cup did all four British nations – England, Northern Ireland, Scotland and Wales – make the Finals?

13 **In how many World Cup Finals have Scotland failed to progress past the first round?**

14 Which is the only country to have won the World Cup outside their own continent?

15 **Which countries will co-host the World Cup in 2002?**

CARLING 10,000 FOOTBALL FACTS & QUESTIONS

 **Quiz 2**   World Cup

1 Two pairs of brothers have played together in World Cup winning teams. One was the Charltons in 1966 – who was the other?

2 Who are the only two players to have scored in the Final of two World Cups?

3 **Who is England's leading scorer in World Cup matches?**

4 Who are the only men to have both played for and managed a World Cup winning side?

5 **Who is the oldest player to score in the Finals of the World Cup?**

6 Who, in 1970, became the first player to score in every round of the World Cup Finals?

7 **Who scored 13 goals in the 1958 Finals, the highest total ever?**

8 In which year was the number of teams in the World Cup Finals increased from 16 to 24?

9 **What was the name of the Chilean goalkeeper who – in an attempt to have the qualifying match against Brazil abandoned – pretended to have been hurt by an object thrown from the crowd and was subsequently banned for life?**

10 In which World Cup Finals were substitutes first allowed?

11 **Which two countries have hosted the World Cup Finals twice?**

12 Where were the 1986 Finals originally scheduled to have taken place?

13 **Which four European countries have reached a World Cup Final but never won the tournament?**

14 Who is the only man to have played in World Cup Finals for different countries?

15 **Which country was eliminated on goal difference from three World Cup Finals in succession?**

---

1 Fritz and Ottmar Walter (West Germany 1954) 2 Pele (Brazil) in 1958 and 1970 and Paul Breitner (West Germany) in 1974 and 1982 3 Gary Lineker 4 Franz Beckenbauer (West Germany) and Mario Zagalo (Brazil) in 1990 6 Jairzinho (Brazil) 7 Just Fontaine (France) 8 1982 9 Roberto Rojas 10 1970 11 Mexico in 1970 and 1986 and France in 1938 and 1998 12 Colombia 13 Czechoslovakia, Holland, Hungary and Sweden 14 Luis Monti (Argentina in 1930 and Italy in 1934) 15 Scotland in 1974, 1978 and 1982

 Quiz 3 World Cup

1 **Which international body organised this and all subsequent World Cups?**

2 In which year was this international body formed?

3 **Of the 13 participants in the first World Cup Finals, which were the only four European nations?**

4 Name the seven South American countries that took part

5 **Which two other nations played in the 1930 tournament?**

6 Which two teams met in the first ever World Cup match, on July 13, 1930?

7 **In the group match between Argentina and Mexico, a record number of penalties were awarded – how many?**

8 Who were the four semi-finalists?

9 **Who did the hosts meet in the Final on July 30, 1930?**

10 How did the Finalists resolve a disagreement over which ball to play with?

11 **Who was the captain of Uruguay?**

12 Name the Uruguayan centre forward who had the lower part of an arm missing.

13 **Who presented the World Cup to Uruguay at the end of the Final, which they won 4-2?**

14 Who was the tournament's leading scorer, with eight goals for Argentina?

15 **Where were all 18 matches in the 1930 World Cup Finals played?**

CARLING 10,000 FOOTBALL FACTS & QUESTIONS

Quiz 4

World Cup

1 **Who was the manager of victorious host nation Italy?**

2 Often described in newspapers as 'The Father of Italian Football', on which pre-First World War English club did the Italian manager try to model his team's style of play?

3 **Who did Italy beat by the record score of 7-1 in the first round?**

4 Who scored the first goal for Czechoslovakia in the Final?

5 **Which Argentine-born left winger then equalised for Italy?**

6 For which Italian club had he played since 1929?

7 **Who then scored the winner for Italy in extra time?**

8 Who was the goalkeeper captain of Italy?

9 **Who was the goalkeeper captain of Czechoslovakia?**

10 Which European nations had been beaten in the semi-finals?

11 **In which two Italian cities were the semi-finals played?**

12 Which were the only two South American nations to appear in the 1934 World Cup Finals?

13 **In 1934, who became the first African nation to appear in the World Cup Finals?**

14 What was the nationality of John Langenus, the 1930 World Cup Final referee, who officiated in one match in 1934 and famously described the tournament as 'a sporting fiasco'?

15 **At the end of the 1934 World Cup Final in Rome, who presented the Jules Rimet trophy to the winners?**

1 **Vittorio Pozzo** 2 Manchester United 3 The USA 4 Antonin Puc 5 **Raimondo Orsi** 6 Juventus 7 **Angelo Schiavio** 8 Giampiero Combi 9 **Frantisek Planicka** 10 Austria and Germany 11 **Milan and Rome** 12 Argentina and Brazil 13 **Egypt** 14 Belgian 15 **Benito Mussolini**

 **Quiz 5** World Cup

1 **Which South American country wanted to host the 1938 tournament and refused to take part when they were turned down in favour of France?**

2 Which country qualified in 1937 but by the time of the Finals had ceased to exist as a separate national entity?

3 **The withdrawal of which Asian country left the way open for the Dutch East Indies to appear in the Finals?**

4 What was the name of the manager of Germany?

5 **Who was the tournament's leading scorer – a Brazilian, with eight goals in the tournament, including four in against Poland?**

6 Which Pole also scored four goals in this match?

7 **Which Swede then scored another four goals in the quarter-Finals?**

8 Which Hungarian was the second highest scorer, with seven goals in the tournament?

9 **The players of which nation refused to give the Nazi salute during the national anthems before their first round match with Germany?**

10 To which country had Germany lost 6-3 in Berlin only a few weeks before the start of the World Cup Finals?

11 **What was the name of the Brazilian coach who decided to rest his star players in the semi-final, which they lost to Italy?**

12 Who did Italy beat 4-2 in the World Cup Final in Paris on June 19, 1938?

13 **Which two Italians scored twice in this match?**

14 Giuseppe Meazza was one of only two survivors of Italy's previous World Cup triumph in 1934. On his death in 1979, which famous Italian football stadium was renamed in his honour?

15 **Which Caribbean island reached the quarter Finals after beating Romania in the first round?**

 ## Quiz 6

World Cup

1 **Where were the 1950 World Cup Finals held?**

2 How many countries took part in the Finals?

3 **Who won the tournament?**

4 Which future England manager played for his country in the match versus the USA?

5 **Who scored the USA's goal in their shock victory over England?**

6 Who was the England manager?

7 **Where was the match played?**

8 Who scored England's goals in their 2-0 victory over Chile?

9 **Who beat England 1-0 in their third group match?**

10 Which team of amateurs beat the holders, Italy, 3-2 and finished above them in their group?

11 **What tragic event in 1949 had seriously weakened the Italian challenge?**

12 Which teams contested the deciding match in the Final Pool?

13 **Which Brazilian was the leading scorer in the 1950 tournament, with nine goals?**

14 For which Rio de Janeiro club did he play?

15 **Who was the World Cup winning captain?**

1 **Brazil** 2 Thirteen 3 **Uruguay** 4 Alf Ramsey 5 **Larry Gaetjens** 6 Walter Winterbottom
7 **Belo Horizonte** 8 Stan Mortensen and Wilf Mannion 9 **Spain** 10 Sweden
11 **The Superga air crash, in which the entire Torino team had been killed**
12 Brazil and Uruguay 13 **Marques Menezes Ademir** 14 Vasco da Gama 15 **Obdulio Varela**

Quiz 7

World Cup

1   **Where were the 1954 World Cup Finals held?**

2   Ante-post favourites Hungary began their Finals campaign with a 9-0 defeat of which Asian country?

3   **What was the name of Scotland's first World Cup manager, who resigned during the course of the tournament after his team lost 1-0 to Austria?**

4   Who then trounced Scotland 7-0?

5   **With which European nation did England draw 4-4 at the group stage of the tournament?**

6   What was the final score in the quarter-final between Brazil and Hungary, the so-called 'Battle of Berne'?

7   **Who knocked out the hosts, beating them 7-5 in the quarter Finals?**

8   Who beat England 4-2 in the quarter Finals?

9   **Which country inflicted Uruguay's first ever World Cup defeat?**

10   Which great Hungarian made his first appearance of the tournament in the Final and scored the opening goal?

11   **Where was the Final played?**

12   Who was the tournament's leading scorer, with 11 goals for Hungary?

13   **Who scored the goals in the Final that brought West Germany back from 2-0 down and made them World champions?**

14   Who was captain of the winning team?

15   **Which German club did he play for?**

1 **Switzerland** 2 South Korea 3 **Andy Beattie** 4 Uruguay 5 **Belgium** 6 Hungary 4 Brazil 2
7 **Austria** 8 Uruguay 9 **Hungary** 10 Ferenc Puskas 11 **The Wankdorf Stadium, Berne**
12 Sandor Kocsis 13 **Morlock and Helmut Rahn (2)** 14 Fritz Walter 15 **Kaiserslautern**

Quiz 8

World Cup

1 **Which Englishman was manager of 1958 hosts and beaten finalists Sweden?**

2 Who knocked Wales out in the quarter Finals?

3 **Which 17-year-old scored the only goal of this game, his first in World Cup Finals?**

4 For which English League club did Wales' World Cup goalkeeper Jack Kelsey play?

5 **Which Arsenal left half was captain of Wales?**

6 Which Frenchman scored 13 goals in the Finals, a record?

7 **Who was captain of Northern Ireland?**

8 Who was manager of Northern Ireland?

9 **Which future manager of Northern Ireland played for them on the wing in this tournament?**

10 Who knocked Northern Ireland out in the quarter Finals?

11 **Which two players scored twice for Brazil in their 5-2 victory over Sweden in the Final?**

12 Which future manager of Brazil scored the other goal?

13 **To which Spanish club did Brazil midfield star Didi transfer in the year after he had made his name in the World Cup?**

14 Which nation did Didi subsequently manage in the 1970 World Cup Finals?

15 **Which nation finished equal second with England at the group stage and then beat them 1-0 in the play-off for a place in the quarter Finals?**

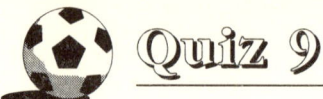

Quiz 9

World Cup

1 In which country were the 1962 World Cup Finals held?

2 Who was the tournament's leading scorer, with five goals for beaten semi-finalists Yugoslavia?

3 **Who was England's captain in the 1962 World Cup?**

4 Who scored for England in their 3-1 victory over Argentina in the group stage of the Finals?

5 **Immediately before the first goal, which England debutant's shot had been handled on the line?**

6 For which English club was he playing at the time?

7 **Who scored two goals for Brazil in their 3-1 quarter final victory over England?**

8 England's consolation goal was scored by Gerry Hitchens. For which European team was he playing club football?

9 **At which English club had he started his career?**

10 Who was the English referee who sent off two Italians during their 2-0 defeat by Chile in the so-called 'Battle of Santiago'?

11 **Which Chilean – a striker in more than one sense – broke the nose of Italy's Humberto Maschio and finished the tournament as his country's leading scorer with four goals?**

12 What was the name of the so-called 'White Pele' who came on as a substitute for the black one after he pulled a muscle in the group match against Czechoslovakia?

13 **Which Brazilian scored two goals and was then sent off in his country's 4-2 semi-final victory over Chile?**

14 Who did Brazil beat in the Final to retain the trophy?

15 **Which three players scored for Brazil in this match?**

1 Chile 2 Drazen Jerkovic 3 **Johnny Haynes** 4 Ron Flowers (penalty), Bobby Charlton and Jimmy Greaves 5 **Alan Peacock** 6 Middlesbrough 7 **Garrincha** 8 Inter Milan 9 **Aston Villa** 10 Ken Aston 11 **Leonel Sanchez** 12 Amarildo 13 **Garrincha** 14 Czechoslovakia 15 **Amarildo, Zito and Vava**

 ## Quiz 10 — World Cup

1 **Who scored the first goal of the tournament in the group match between Brazil and Bulgaria?**

2 Who scored England's first goal of the tournament in their second group match against Mexico?

3 **Name the captain of Argentina who was sent off in the quarter-final against England**

4 Who scored both goals for England in their 2-1 victory over Portugal in the semi-final?

5 **Which England defender punched the ball off the goal line to give away a penalty in the match against Portugal?**

6 Who did West Germany defeat in the other semi-final?

7 **Who scored West Germany's goals in the Final against England?**

8 Who was Tofik Bakhramov?

9 **Who was the tournament's top scorer, with nine goals?**

10 Who was the youngest member of England's World Cup winning team?

11 **Name the captain of West Germany in 1966 who won 72 caps but never a World Cup?**

12 At home in Germany, which Bundesliga club did he play for?

13 **What sort of animal was 1966 mascot World Cup Willie?**

14 How many matches did Jimmy Greaves play for England in the 1966 World Cup Finals?

15 **Three of Geoff Hurst's four goals in the competition were scored in the Final. Against which other country did he score?**

1 Pele 2 Bobby Charlton 3 **Antonio Rattin** 4 Bobby Charlton 5 **Jack Charlton**
6 The USSR 7 **Haller and Weber** 8 The Russian linesman who ruled that Hurst's disputed goal
for England had crossed the line 9 Eusebio **(Portugal)** 10 Alan Ball 11 **Uwe Seeler**
12 Hamburg 13 **A lion** 14 Three 15 **Argentina**

Quiz 11

World Cup

1   **Which Leeds United striker made his England debut in the group match against Czechoslovakia?**

2   Who scored Brazil's goal in their group game against England?

3   **Who was captain of Brazil in the 1970 World Cup?**

4   Who was leading scorer in the 1970 World Cup?

5   **Which European country topped its group with the following match statistics:**
Played 3 Won 1 Drawn 2 Lost 0 Goals For 1 Goals Against 0?

6   In which Mexican city did England play their group matches?

7   **In which city did England play their quarter final match against West Germany?**

8   Who scored for England to put them 2-0 up in this match?

9   **Name the England right back who supplied the crosses for both these goals.**

10 Who scored for West Germany to make it 2-1?

11 **England manager Sir Alf Ramsey then took off Bobby Charlton and Martin Peters. Who took their places?**

12 Who equalised for West Germany?

13 **Who scored the winner in extra time?**

14 Apart from West Germany, who were the other three semi-finalists?

15 **Which Brazilian star was almost blind in one eye?**

Quiz 12

World Cup

1 Which European nation was edged out of a place in the 1974 World Cup Finals by Holland, despite being undefeated in the qualifying matches and conceding not a single goal?

2 Who supplanted Sir Stanley Rous as President of FIFA three days before the World Cup Finals opening ceremony?

3 Which Englishman refereed the 1974 World Cup Final in Munich?

4 Which West German gave away a penalty in the Final by tripping Johan Cruyff of Holland?

5 Who became the first player to score from the penalty spot in a World Cup Final?

6 And who became the second, when West Germany equalised later in the first half?

7 Who scored the winner for West Germany?

8 Who was the Dutch captain in the 1974 World Cup Finals?

9 Who was the manager of Holland?

10 Who was manager of World Cup winners West Germany?

11 Who was their captain?

12 Who was the leading scorer in the 1974 World Cup Finals, with seven goals for third-placed Poland?

13 Who was manager of Scotland, the only British nation to qualify for the Finals?

14 Who was Scotland's World Cup captain?

15 Who won the first meeting between East and West Germany?

1 **Belgium** 2 Joao Havelange 3 **Jack Taylor** 4 Uli Hoeness 5 **Johan Neeskens**
6 Paul Breitner 7 **Gerd Muller** 8 Johan Cruyff 9 **Rinus Michels** 10 Helmut Schoen
11 **Franz Beckenbauer** 12 Grzegorz Lato 13 **Willie Ormond** 14 Billy Bremner
15 **East Germany, 1-0**

Quiz 13

World Cup

1 **Which Scotland player failed a drugs test after the opening match against Peru and was sent home in disgrace?**

2 For which English League club was he then playing?

3 **Who was Scotland's manager?**

4 Who was Scotland's first-choice goalkeeper?

5 **For which Scottish League club was he then playing?**

6 Which Scotsman had a penalty saved in their match against Peru?

7 **For which English League club was he then playing?**

8 Which Argentine player scored two goals in the Final?

9 **Name the substitute who scored Holland's goal to take the Final into extra time.**

10 Who was Argentina's manager?

11 **Which two countries – one Asian, the other African – made their first appearances in the World Cup Finals in 1978?**

12 Who was the tournament's leading scorer, with six goals for World Cup winners Argentina?

13 **Which great veteran – a star of the 1970 World Cup – scored five goals in the tournament for quarter finalists Peru?**

14 Which winger scored five goals in the tournament for Holland?

15 **To which Dutchman's protective arm shield did the Argentine players object at the start of the Final?**

Quiz 14

World Cup

1 How many teams beat England in the 1982 World Cup Finals?

2 Name the German goalkeeper involved in the infamous incident in the 1982 semi-final which left a French forward unconscious

3 **And who was the French forward?**

4 Which Hungarian became the first ever substitute to score a hat trick in the World Cup Finals?

5 **Who scored Italy's three goals in the Final against West Germany?**

6 Who scored West Germany's goal in the Final?

7 **Who scored Northern Ireland's goal when they beat the hosts Spain in the 1982 World Cup?**

8 For which English League club was he playing at the time?

9 **Which Italian was leading scorer in the 1982 World Cup?**

10 Who was manager of Italy?

11 **Who was the captain of Brazil?**

12 Who, in 1982, became the oldest player to win the World Cup?

13 **Which Northern Ireland forward was the youngest player in the 1982 World Cup Finals?**

14 Which side became the first ever to be eliminated from the World Cup Finals on penalties?

15 **Who scored the fastest ever goal in World Cup Finals after 27 seconds of the England versus France group match?**

1 None 2 Harald Schumacher 3 Patrick Battiston 4 Laszlo Kiss v El Salvador 5 Paolo Rossi, Allesandro Altobelli and Marco Tardelli 6 Paul Breitner 7 Gerry Armstrong 8 Watford 9 Paolo Rossi 10 Enzo Bearzot 11 Socrates 12 Dino Zoff (Italy) 13 Norman Whiteside 14 France 15 Bryan Robson (England)

Quiz 15

World Cup

1   All but one of England's seven goals in the 1986 tournament were scored by Gary Lineker. Who scored the other?

2   Which England player was sent off in the group game against Morocco?

3   **Name the two Manchester United players in the England squad.**

4   Who were the two Manchester United players in the Scotland squad?

5   **Name the Manchester United player in the Northern Ireland World Cup squad.**

6   Who were the two Manchester United players in the Denmark squad?

7   **Which Uruguayan player was sent off after less than a minute of the match against Scotland?**

8   Who scored Portugal's goal in their 1-0 group victory over England?

9   **Who played for Northern Ireland v Brazil on his 41st birthday?**

10   Who scored four goals in Spain's 5-1 demolition of Denmark?

11   **Which neighbouring European countries were the losing semi-finalists in the 1986 World Cup?**

12   The World Cup Final reached 2-2 – Brown and Valdano scored first for Argentina; Rummenigge and Voller equalised for West Germany. Who scored Argentina's winning goal?

13   **For which French club side was he then playing?**

14   Who was the manager of England?

15   **In which city did England play their matches in the so-called Group of Sleep?**

 **Quiz 16** World Cup

1 From which Puccini opera did the Italia 90 theme song Nessun Dorma come?

2 For which team did Roger Milla play in the 1990 World Cup?

3 **Which two players were sent off in the West Germany v Holland second round match?**

4 Which was the first African nation to reach the World Cup quarter-Finals?

5 **Who scored for the Republic of Ireland in their 1-1 draw with England in the group stage?**

6 Who scored for England in their 1-1 draw with the Republic of Ireland in the group stage?

7 **Who did the Republic of Ireland beat in a penalty shoot-out to clinch their place in the quarter-Finals?**

8 Who scored for England against Belgium in the last minute of extra time to take them through to the quarter Finals?

9 **Who scored West Germany's goal in their 1-1 semi-final draw with England?**

10 Off which England defender was the shot cruelly and crucially deflected?

11 **Who scored England's goal in their 1-1 semi-final draw with West Germany?**

12 Who missed England's last penalty in the semi-final shoot-out?

13 **Who scored West Germany's goal in their 1-0 victory over Argentina in the 1990 World Cup Final?**

14 Who was captain of West Germany?

15 **Who was leading goalscorer in the 1990 World Cup, with six goals for Italy?**

Quiz 17

World Cup

1 **Name the Colombian captain who scored an own goal in the 1994 World Cup and was shot dead on his return home.**

2 Which Argentine player was sent home after failing a random drugs test?

3 **What was historic about the USA v Switzerland match at the Silverdome, Detroit?**

4 Who scored for the Republic of Ireland in their 1-0 victory over Italy?

5 **Which country won its first World Cup Finals match in its sixth appearance in this stage of the tournament?**

6 Name the Russian and the Bulgarian who were the tournament's joint top scorers, with six goals each

7 **Who knocked Romania out of the World Cup on penalties in the quarter-final?**

8 Who knocked out the holders, West Germany, in the quarter Finals?

9 **Which three Italians missed penalties in the Final shoot-out?**

10 What were the names of the two goalkeepers in the Final?

11 **What relation are Roberto and Dino Baggio of Italy?**

12 Where was the 1994 World Cup Final held?

13 **Which Brazilian was awarded the Golden Ball as the outstanding player of the tournament?**

14 What was the name of Brazil's World Cup-winning captain?

15 **What was the nationality of referee Kurt Rothlisberger, who mistakenly denied Belgium a penalty against Germany?**

15 Swiss
Pagliuca (Italy) **11 None** 12 The Pasadena Rose Bowl, Los Angeles **13 Romario 14** Dunga
8 Bulgaria 9 Franco Baresi, Daniele Massaro and Roberto Baggio 10 Taffarel (Brazil) and
indoors 4 Ray Houghton **5 Bulgaria 6** Oleg Salenko and Hristo Stoichkov **7 Sweden**
1 Andres Escobar 2 Diego Maradona **3 It was the first World Cup match to be played**

 ## Quiz 18

World Cup

1   Where was the opening match of the 1998 World Cup Finals played?

2   Which Brazilian scored the first goal of the tournament?

3   Which Scot was the first player to be booked in the tournament?

4   Who gave away the penalty from which Scotland equalised against Brazil?

5   Who scored for Scotland from the spot kick?

6   Which Scot scored an own goal to give Brazil a 2-1 victory in the opening match?

7   How many of members of the Norwegian starting line-up in the game against Morocco had played in the English Premiership in 1997-98?

8   Who scored both goals for Chile in their 2-2 draw with Italy in the opening match of Group B?

9   Who opened the scoring in this match for Italy?

10 Who then equalised for Italy from the penalty spot with five minutes remaining?

11 In which city did the hosts, France, play their opening match?

12 Danish captain Michael Laudrup won his 100th international cap against Saudi Arabia. Which of his teammates was winning his 101st?

13 Who was the first player to be sent off in the 1998 World Cup Finals?

14 During Mexico's 3-1 victory over South Korea, which Mexican stunned the world by gripping the ball between both feet and jumping over a tackle?

15 Which Dutchman was sent off for elbowing Lorenzo Staelens in the chest during Holland's 0-0 draw with Belgium in Group E?

 **Quiz 19**   **World Cup**

1   Who was the manager of Argentina at the 1998 World Cup Finals?

2   Who scored for Argentina in their 1-0 win over Japan in the opening match of Group H?

3   Who scored Jamaica's first ever goal in the World Cup Finals?

4   Who took the free kick from which Alan Shearer scored England's first goal in their 2-0 victory over Tunisia in Group G?

5   Who was standing in an offside position when Paul Scholes scored England's second goal against Tunisia?

6   Who scored for Scotland in their 1-1 draw with Norway?

7   Which English-based Norwegian fouled Gordon Durie right on the edge of the penalty area, an offence which some thought was committed inside the box?

8   Who walked out of the Colombia squad after less than a week of the tournament?

9   Which French player was sent off in their 4-0 defeat of Saudi Arabia?

10 Which referee sent off two players in the Belgium v Mexico group match?

11 Who scored both goals for Belgium in their 2-2 draw with Mexico?

12 Who did Holland beat 5-0 in Group E?

13 Who scored a ten-minute hat trick in Argentina's 5-0 defeat of Jamaica?

14 How many players were sent off altogether in the two matches played on 'Red Thursday', June 18, 1998?

15 During the course of the 1998 tournament, which German broke the record for the number of minutes played in the World Cup?

 ## Quiz 20 — World Cup

1 Who became the first team to go out of the World Cup Finals on the golden goal?

2 Who scored twice for Brazil as they beat Chile 4-1 in the round of 16?

3 Which Dane scored against Nigeria 16 seconds after coming on as substitute?

4 Who missed a penalty for Yugoslavia against Holland?

5 Whose twice-taken penalty was enough to take Croatia past Romania in the second round?

6 Name the Danish referee of the Argentina v England match.

7 Who moved to right back after David Beckham had been sent off?

8 Which England player had a goal disallowed in the dying seconds of normal time against Argentina?

9 Where was the Argentina v England match played?

10 Which German was sent off in their quarter final match against Croatia?

11 Who scored Holland's last-minute quarter final winner against Argentina, thus becoming the leading scorer in his country's history?

12 Which Italian missed the last kick in their quarter-final penalty shoot-out against France?

13 Who scored two goals for Brazil in their quarter final against Denmark?

14 Who scored for Holland in both the quarter final and the semi-final?

15 What was the name of the Paraguay goalkeeper who took long-range shots from free kicks?

1 **Paraguay** 2 Cesar Sampaio 3 **Ebbe Sand** 4 Predrag Mijatovic 5 **Davor Suker** 6 Kim Milton Nielsen 7 **Alan Shearer** 8 Sol Campbell 9 **St Etienne** 10 Christian Worns 11 **Dennis Bergkamp** 12 Luigi Di Biagio 13 **Rivaldo** 14 Patrick Kluivert 15 Jose Chilavert

Quiz 21

World Cup

1 Who scored straight after half-time to give Brazil the lead in their semi-final against Holland?

2 Who scored both goals for France in their semi-final victory over Croatia?

3 Which Frenchman was sent off in the semi-final against Croatia?

4 Which Croatian defender did the French player appear to hit?

5 What was the score in the third place play-off between Holland and Croatia?

6 Who was passed fit to play only 45 minutes before kick-off in the World Cup Final?

7 For which club does French goalkeeper Fabien Barthez play football?

8 Who was the captain of France?

9 Who was the captain of Brazil?

10 Who was the manager of Brazil?

11 Who was the manager of France?

12 Which Frenchman was sent off in the World Cup Final?

13 Who scored twice for France in the World Cup Final?

14 Who won the Golden Boot as the competition's leading scorer, with six goals in the tournament?

15 Where will the 2002 World Cup Finals be held?

1 Ronaldo 2 Lilian Thuram 3 **Laurent Blanc** 4 Slaven Bilic 5 **Holland I Croatia 2**
6 Ronaldo 7 **AS Monaco** 8 Didier Deschamps 9 **Dunga** 10 Mario Zagalo
11 **Aimé Jacquet** 12 Marcel Desailly 13 **Zinedine Zidane** 14 Davor Suker (Croatia)
15 **Japan and South Korea**

Quiz 22

World Cup

1   The United States finished in third place in which World Cup?

2   Who failed a routine drugs test in the 1994 World Cup and as a result was expelled from the competition?

3   This Colombian player scored an own goal when playing the United States in the 1994 World Cup. What was his name and what happened when he returned home?

4   Which two past winners failed to qualify for the 1994 World Cup Finals?

5   Name the three countries to make their World Cup debut in the 1994 Finals.

6   Who was Brazil's captain in the 1970 World Cup?

7   Which manager received a one-match touchline ban and a £10,000 fine from FIFA in the 1994 Finals?

8   In the World Cup campaigns of 1990 and 1994 Ireland have played nine games. How many did they actually win?

9   The United States played Brazil in the second round of the 1994 World Cup. What was the score?

10 Who beat USA 7-1 in the 1934 World Cup?

11 Wales missed out on qualifying for the 1994 World Cup. Who was their manager at the time?

12 Altogether there were 52 games played in the 1990 World Cup. How many players were sent off?

13 Which captain has led two losing teams in the World Cup Finals?

14 Which team beat the defending champions Argentina in the opening match of the 1990 World Cup Finals?

15 Who was the top goalscorer of the 1990 World Cup?

 **Quiz 23** World Cup

1 Who was Cameroon's famous centre-forward in the 1990 Finals?

2 **West Germany beat Holland 2-1 in the second round of the 1990 Finals. During the game which Dutch player was sent off for spitting?**

3 Dutch manager Leo Beenhakker went on to manage which international team in the 1994 World Cup?

4 **In the 1990 World Cup who won the Fair Play award?**

5 Who became the first man to captain and manage a World Cup winning side?

6 **How many players were there left on the pitch at the end of the 1990 World Cup Final?**

7 In 1990 Scotland qualified but once again failed to get past the first phase. How many times had this happened before?

8 **What nationality was the referee in the England v Argentina 'Hand of God' 1986 quarter-final?**

9 Ray Wilkins was sent off when England played Morocco in their second game of the 1986 Finals. What for?

10 **Who returned from a two-year suspension to become the top goalscorer in the 1982 World Cup?**

11 In the 1982 semi-final West German keeper Harald Schumacher knocked unconscious which French defender in a now infamous challenge?

12 **After this incident what action did the referee take?**

13 Two Ipswich Town players played a major role in the English 1982 World Cup team. Who were they?

14 **Who captained the French team in the 1982 Finals?**

15 How many games did England lose before being eliminated from the 1982 World Cup?

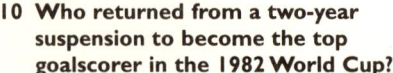

14 **Michel Platini – check** 15 None
12 **He awarded West Germany a goal kick** 13 Mick Mills and Paul Mariner
7 7 8 **Tunisian** 9 For throwing the ball at the referee 10 **Paulo Rossi** 11 Patrick Battiston
1 Roger Milla 2 **Frank Rijkaard** 3 Saudi Arabia 4 **England** 5 Franz Beckenbauer 6 20

 Quiz 24

World Cup

1 How many goals did England concede before being eliminated from the 1982 World Cup?

2 Northern Ireland progressed to the second phase of the 1982 World Cup. When were the other occasions they had for the Finals?

3 **Argentina had to beat Peru by four goals to reach the 1978 World Cup Final, they won 6-0. Where was the Peruvian goalkeeper Quiroga born?**

4 Which Scottish player failed a random drugs test in the 1978 Finals and was sent home?

5 **What was used for the first time in the 1974 World Cup Finals?**

6 Which player has appeared in five World Cup tournaments?

7 **The fastest goal in a World Cup final was scored by who in 1974?**

8 England failed to qualify in 1974 thanks to which team?

9 **Name the Dutch captain for the 1974 Finals?**

10 Who was the top goalscorer in the 1970 World Cup?

11 **England, Wales, Scotland and Northern Ireland were not eligible to participate in the first World Cup in Uruguay 1930 – why?**

12 England made their World Cup debut in which tournament?

13 **In the 1950 World Cup England lost 1-0 to a team of rank outsiders, who were they?**

14 What did Brazil get to keep after winning the 1970 World Cup?

15 **Who scored the only goal of the 1990 World Cup Final?**

 # Quiz 25

World Cup

1   Who refused to shake hands with the President of FIFA after the 1990 World Cup Final?

2   Which team did Alf Ramsey brand 'animals' in the 1966 World Cup?

3   Who scored England's two goals against Portugal in the 1966 World Cup semi-final?

4   Which country has withdrawn from the World Cup on four occasions?

5   In 1966 which team were pelted with rotten fruit on their return from England?

6   What was the name of the dog who found the stolen Jules Rimet trophy in 1966?

7   Who was captain of the England 1962 World Cup team?

8   How old was Pele when he made his World Cup debut for Brazil in 1958?

9   Who was the first person to score a goal in the World Cup Finals?

10 What was stolen from the Olympic Stadium in Rome on 8 July after the 1990 World Cup?

11 What was the name of the Italian 1990 World Cup mascot?

12 What fruit was the 1982 Spanish World Cup mascot based on?

13 In 1974 West Germany had two children as their World Cup mascots. What were their names?

14 How many times has the host nation won the World Cup?

15 Why did Uruguay refuse to defend their World Cup title in Italy in 1934?

CARLING 10,000 FOOTBALL FACTS & QUESTIONS

Quiz 26

World Cup

1 Which team has held the World Cup the longest?

2 In which World Cup was Britain represented by all four Home Countries?

3 Who were the first country to hold both the European Championship and the World Cup at the same time?

4 What has been the highest score in a World Cup Finals match?

5 Who holds the individual goal scoring record in a World Cup tournament?

6 Who was the manager of the 1974 Dutch World Cup squad?

7 The 1986 World Cup Final was held in which stadium?

8 Who won the Most Exciting Team award at the 1994 World Cup?

9 Who won the Fair Play award at the 1994 World Cup?

10 Which two ex-England players recently backed Japan's failed bid for the 2002 World Cup?

11 How many countries played in the 1998 World Cup?

12 Who called the Polish keeper Jan Tomaszewski a 'clown' before the England v Poland 1974 World Cup qualifier?

13 Where did the draw for the 1994 World Cup Finals take place?

14 Who were the first team to qualify for the 1994 World Cup?

15 What did all the 15 penalties awarded in open play in 1994 have in common?

15 They were all converted

Lineker 11 32 12 Brian Clough 13 Ceasars Palace, Las Vegas 14 Mexico
in 1958 6 Rinus Michels 7 Azteca Stadium 8 Brazil 9 Brazil 10 Sir Bobby Charlton and Gary
2 Sweden 1958 3 West Germany 4 Hungary 10 El Salvador 1 1982 5 Just Fontaine (France)
1 Italy. They won it in 1938, then war broke out so they held onto it until 1950

 **Quiz 27** **World Cup**

1 In the 1994 World Cup the referees and linesmen's kit came in which three colours?

2 **Up to the 1994 Finals, which is the only country to have played in every World Cup tournament?**

3 For the first time in the World Cup Finals what was awarded for a win in a group match in 1994?

4 **The 1994 World Cup mascot 'Striker' was a dog created by whom?**

5 Who won the Golden Ball award for best player in the 1994 World Cup?

6 **Who said: 'I don't know how we do it sometimes.' When England reached the 1990 World Cup semi-finals?**

7 Scotland lost 1-0 to which unfancied team in their first match at the 1990 World Cup?

8 **Who is England's top scorer in all World Cup matches?**

9 Scotland's manager resigned after the 1986 Finals – who was he?

10 **Who scored in the Republic of Ireland's shock defeat of Italy in the 1994 World Cup?**

11 Who scored the goal in England's shock defeat by the United States in the 1950 World Cup tournament?

12 **Who scored the 1000th World Cup goal in 1978?**

13 Which was the first black African country to qualify for the World Cup Finals?

14 **Why did the English referee Jack Taylor delay the start of the 1974 World Cup Final?**

15 In the 1970 World Cup what was Bobby Moore accused of stealing in Bogota, Colombia?

Quiz 28

World Cup

1 **Who are currently the only two players to have scored in more than one World Cup Finals?**

2 Who is the oldest player to have won a World Cup winners' medal?

3 **Which African country have qualified for both World Cup Finals that have been held in Mexico?**

4 What could Argentina and Uruguay not agree on before the start of the 1930 World Cup Final?

5 **Spain entered the 1938 World Cup, why did they not compete?**

6 In the 1970 World Cup match between England and Brazil who scored Brazil's winning goal?

7 **In 1970 England lost to West Germany in the quarter-Finals, but who scored the two English goals?**

8 Which World Cup tournament was the first to be televised?

9 **Who was the first player to score in every game of a World Cup tournament?**

10 Which country was eliminated from the 1974 World Cup on goal difference without losing a game?

11 **Who was Argentina's chain-smoking manager in the 1978 World Cup?**

12 Who is the youngest player ever to have played in the World Cup?

13 **Who was Brazil's philosophical captain in the 1982 World Cup?**

14 Alf Ramsey was an England player in which World Cup?

15 **What was the average age of the England World Cup winning squad in 1966?**

---

15 Twenty-six and a half years

12 **Norman Whiteside – Northern Ireland** 13 Socrates 14 1950 World Cup

8 **Switzerland** 1954 9 Jairinho, Brazil 1970 10 **Scotland** 11 Cesar Luis Menotti

outbreak of the Spanish Civil War 6 Jairinho 7 Martin Peters and Alan Mullery

aged 40 – Italy 3 **Morocco** 4 They couldn't agree on which ball to use 5 **Because of the**

1 Pele in 1958 and 1970, Paul Breitner (West Germany) 1974 and 1982 2 Dino Zoff

Quiz 29

World Cup

1   **What is the highest recorded attendance at a World Cup Finals match?**

2   Gary Lineker scored a hat-trick in England's last group game in the 1986 Finals. Against which country?

3   **Lineker scored six of England's seven goals in the 1986 Finals. Who got the other one?**

4   When Argentina beat England in 1986 which England player was the last to touch the ball before Diego Maradona scored his 'hand of God' goal?

5   **Which club did Gary Lineker join after the 1986 Finals?**

6   Who scored Argentina's winning goal in the 1986 Final?

7   **Which Chilean goalkeeper feigned injury against Brazil in the qualifying round tie for Italia '90, and was banned from international football for life?**

8   Who scored the only goal for Cameroon in the opening game of the 1990 Finals against Argentina?

9   **How many players did Cameroon finish that game with?**

10 Who is the oldest player to score in a World Cup Finals match?

11 **Who scored England's winning goal against Egypt to help them through to the second round of the 1990 Finals?**

12 Who scored the Republic of Ireland's winning penalty in the shoot-out against Romania in the 1990 Finals?

13 **Who did Andreas Brehme's shot deflect off to open the scoring for Germany in the 1990 semi-final against England?**

14 The opening game of the 1994 Finals was played at Soldier Field. What city is the stadium in?

15 **How many European teams qualified for the quarter-Finals in 1994?**

Quiz 30

World Cup

1 **Who was the first player banned for drug taking by FIFA in a World Cup?**

2 Who finished top of England's qualifying group in the lead up to the 1990 World Cup?

3 **England drew with the Republic of Ireland in the 1990 World Cup, who scored the goals?**

4 In the 1990 World Cup who replaced David Seaman after he had broken his thumb in training?

5 **Which was the first African country to reach a World Cup quarter-final?**

6 Who presented the Jules Rimet trophy to the Italian captain Combi after his team had won the 1934 World Cup?

7 **In the 1994 qualifiers San Marino lost nine games and drew one. Who was the draw against?**

8 Why did India withdraw from the 1950 World Cup?

9 **Who were the first team to win the World Cup outside of their own continent?**

10 In their opening game of the 1990 World Cup Holland, the favourites, were held to a 1-1 draw, by who?

11 **In the same group the Republic of Ireland also drew 1-1 with Holland, who scored the goals?**

12 Who did Italy beat in the 1934 World Cup Final?

13 **Why were Nigeria disqualified from the 1974 World Cup?**

14 How many players did Brazil use in the 1962 World Cup?

15 **Allan Clarke made his international debut against which team in the 1970 World Cup?**

1 Haiti's Ernest Jean-Joseph, 1974 2 Sweden 3 Sheedy and Lineker 4 Dave Beasant
5 Cameroon 6 Mussolini 7 Turkey 8 FIFA had told them they would not be allowed to play
barefoot 9 Brazil in 1958 10 Egypt 11 Ruud Gullit and Niall Quinn 12 Czechoslovakia
13 After crowd trouble at a home fixture against Ghana which led to the match being
abandoned 14 12 15 Czechoslovakia

Quiz 31

World Cup

1 Peter Shilton's World Cup Finals debut was against which team in 1982?

2 **Ex-England manager Bobby Robson played in which World Cup?**

3 In which tournament and against which team did Gordon Banks play his last World Cup game?

4 **Who missed a late goalscoring chance for England against Brazil in the 1970 Finals?**

5 Who managed the 1982 World Cup winning Italian team?

6 **How long did it take Bryan Robson to score England's first goal in the 1982 tournament against France?**

7 Who finished third in the 1982 World Cup?

8 **Having successfully qualified for the 1950 World Cup why did the Scottish team refuse to go?**

9 What was the nationality of the linesman who awarded England's third goal in the 1966 World Cup Final?

10 **North Korea beat which team to progress to the quarter-Finals in the 1966 World Cup?**

11 Which German defender has scored in two World Cup Finals?

12 **Which two Dutch brothers played in the 1978 World Cup Final?**

13 In the match for third place in the 1970 World Cup who did West Germany beat 1-0?

14 **The first penalty to be awarded in a World Cup Final was in which tournament?**

15 Which Dutch player had his arm bandaged in the 1978 World Cup Final against Argentina?

1 France 2 1958 3 Brazil 1970 4 Jeff Astle 5 Enzo Bearzot 6 27 seconds 7 Poland
8 Because they did not win the qualifying group 9 Russian 10 Italy 11 Paul Breitner
12 Willie and Rene Van de Kerkhof 13 Uruguay 14 1974 15 Rene Van de Kerkhof

CARLING 10,000 FOOTBALL FACTS & QUESTIONS

Quiz 32

World Cup

1   Who held Scotland to a 1-1 draw in a first round match during the 1978 World Cup?

2   What was unusual about the two goalkeepers in the 1978 World Cup Final?

3   **In the 1982 World Cup which team drew all three of their first round matches?**

4   In the 1982 World Cup who beat the hosts 1-0 in the first round?

5   **Who scored the goal?**

6   Which team were threatened with expulsion from the 1986 World Cup tournament for persistant foul-play?

7   **Which two teams were in the third place play-off in the 1986 World Cup – and what was the score?**

8   What position did Alf Ramsey play in the 1950 World Cup squad?

9   **In England's second game in the 1986 World Cup against Morocco, what injury did Bryan Robson sustain?**

10   Who qualified for the 1950 World Cup without having to play a single game?

11   **Which city hosted the first World Cup Final in 1930?**

12   Played 6, lost 6, goals for 1, goals against 22 – the worst record in the World Cup Finals. Which team is this?

13   **Up to the end of the 1994 Finals, Brazil have the best record in the World Cup followed by the Germans. Who are third?**

14   Who was the eccentric Colombian goalkeeper in the 1990 World Cup?

15   **In which World Cup match did Chelsea's Peter Bonnetti earn his seventh and last England cap?**

1 Iran 2 Jan Jongbloed wore number eight shirt and Ubaldo Fillol wore the number seven
3 Italy and Cameroon 4 Northern Ireland 5 Gerry Armstrong 6 Uruguay
7 Belgium and France. France won 4-2 8 Right-back 9 Shoulder injury 10 Brazil
11 Montevideo 12 El Salvador 13 Italy 14 Rene Higuita 15 The quarter-final against West
Germany-1970

Quiz 33

World Cup

1   Billy Wright captained England through how many World Cup Finals campaigns?

2   **Up to 1994, how many Finals matches have New Zealand played?**

3   Who was the youngest player in the England World Cup Final team of 1966?

4   **In England's 1970 World Cup quarter-final against West Germany Sir Alf Ramsey made a critical substitution when the German's pulled a goal back, what was it?**

5   In the 1978 World Cup, Scotland beat Holland 3-2 in a first round group match. Who scored for the Scots?

6   **In the same group which two unfancied teams did the Scots lose to and draw with?**

7   Who did the West Germans put six past in a first round group match of the 1978 World Cup?

8   **Who was the first player to be sent off in a World Cup Final?**

9   Which England player announced his retirement after the third place play-off in the 1990 World Cup?

10   **Italy, Spain, Holland and Sweden all applied to stage the first World Cup. Why did FIFA ultimately choose Uruguay?**

11   In the 1938 World Cup which country received a bye through to the second round due to Germany's invasion of Austria?

12   **Who was the Russian goalkeeper in the 1958 World Cup?**

13   Why did Gordon Banks miss the 1970 World Cup quarter-final against West Germany?

14   **Patented by the Dutch, 'Total Football' made its debut in which World Cup?**

15   The Soviet Union failed to qualify for the 1974 World Cup after drawing with Chile 0-0 in Moscow and refusing to play the return leg. Why did the Russians refuse to play in Chile?

SEASON BY SEASON

Quiz 1

Season 1899-1900

1 **Who were the first Champions of the 20th century, scoring a record number of goals (77) in the course of the 34-match season?**

2 Who was their – and the League's – leading scorer, with 27 goals?

3 **Who was their versatile captain?**

4 Which Yorkshire team made the running for most of the season before being pipped at the post on the last day of the season?

5 **Which team from the smallest habitation ever to have been represented in English top-flight football was relegated from the First Division, never to return?**

6 Which two teams bounced straight back up to the First Division, winning promotion from Division Two the year after they had both been relegated?

7 **Which team left the League for ever, after finishing bottom of Division Two with one victory, 18 goals for and 100 against in 34 matches?**

8 Which small Lancashire club heralded the dawn of their finest era by winning the FA Cup for the first time, beating non-League Southampton 4-0 in the Final?

9 **Which three First Division sides had Southampton put out on their way to the Final?**

10 Which non-League side from London did Southampton beat in a semi-final that went to a replay?

11 **The first match – a 0-0 draw – had been played at Crystal Palace. Where in Berkshire was the replay, which Southampton won 3-0?**

12 Which Derby-winning racehorse owner talked Scotland into playing their match against England at Parkhead in his racing colours?

13 **Playing in primrose and pink had no ill-effect on the Scots, who won the match 4-1. Who was the Queens Park amateur who scored a hat trick?**

14 Rangers won the Scottish Championship, winning all but three of their 20 matches. Which was the only team they failed to beat at home or away?

15 **Celtic retained the Scottish FA Cup. Who did they beat 4-3 in the Final, after trailing 3-1 at half time?**

1 Aston Villa 2 Bill Garratt 3 John Devey 4 Sheffield United 5 Glossop North End
6 Bolton Wanderers and The Wednesday 7 Loughborough Town 8 Bury 9 Everton,
Newcastle United and West Bromwich Albion 10 Millwall Athletic 11 Reading
12 Lord Rosebery 13 R.S. McColl 14 Celtic 15 Queen's Park

 **Quiz 2**   **Season 1900-1901**

1 Tottenham Hotspur became the first non-League club to win the FA Cup. Which Yorkshire club did they beat 3-1 in the Final replay, after the first match had been drawn 1-1?

2 Who was the triumphant Spurs manager?

3 The first match had been played at Crystal Palace – where was the replay held?

4 When had the FA Cup Final last gone to a replay?

5 What was the name of the Spurs centre forward who became the first man to score in every round of the Cup?

6 How many times in the 20th century did Spurs win the Cup in a year ending with the number one?

7 Who won their first League Championship, and went on to take the title 17 more times during the 20th century?

8 Who was their star Scottish international centre half?

9 Which two former League champions were relegated to the Second Division?

10 Who was the First Division's leading scorer, with 24 goals for 12th-placed Derby County?

11 Which founder member of the Football League won the Second Division title and promotion to the First Division for the first time?

12 Against which nation did Scotland record their highest ever international victory – 11-0?

13 In Scotland, who won the League Championship for the third year in succession?

14 Who were runners-up in both the Scottish League and FA Cup?

15 Who lifted the Scottish FA Cup, after a 4-3 victory in the Final?

Quiz 3

Season 1901-1902

1 In which stadium were 25 people killed and hundreds injured when a stand collapsed during an international match?

2 What was the new maximum wage for professional footballers in England?

3 Sunderland won the League Championship for the fourth time – when had they last been champions?

4 Of the current Sunderland squad, two had played in the previous Championship-winning team. One was their Scottish international goalkeeper – what was his name?

5 The other survivor was the centre forward, another Scot who had been capped for his country while at Rangers – what was his name?

6 The First Division's leading scorers were James Settle and Fred Priest, each with 18 goals. Which teams did they play for?

7 Who won the FA Cup for the second time, beating Southampton 2-1 in the Final replay after the first match had been drawn 1-1?

8 Which great England cricketer played at right back for Southampton in the FA Cup Final?

9 Which Midlands team won the Second Division title with a record number of points (55)?

10 This was the last season in which there was a League club called Newton Heath – to what did they change their name the following season?

11 What was historic about the Home International between England and Scotland at Villa Park?

12 Rangers won the League; who won the Scottish Cup for the second time in their history?

13 Who were runners-up in both the Scottish First Division and the FA Cup?

14 Which Glasgow club won promotion from the Second Division, only to go down again the following season and out of the League altogether in 1911?

15 Which other club was promoted in readiness for the following season, when the Scottish First Division was increased from 10 clubs to 12?

---

1 **Ibrox Park, Glasgow** 2 **£4 a week** 3 **1895** 4 **Ted Doig** 5 **Jimmy Millar** 6 **Everton** and Sheffield United respectively 7 **Sheffield United** 8 C.B. Fry 9 **West Bromwich Albion** 10 Manchester United 11 It was the first international in which all the players on both sides were professionals 12 Hibernian 13 Celtic 14 Port Glasgow Athletic 15 Partick Thistle

 ## Quiz 4

Season 1902-1903

1 What was spotted for the first time at football grounds all around the country?

2 The Wednesday won the League Championship, the first of four times that they achieved this feat. Who was their centre forward and leading scorer, with 12 goals?

3 Who was the local Sheffield hero who had an outstanding season at centre half?

4 Who won the FA Cup for the second time in their history, winning the Final by the all-time record margin of 6-0?

5 For only the second time in the history of the FA Cup, the winners did not concede a single goal throughout the tournament. Which other club had previously achieved this feat?

6 Who were the beaten Cup Finalists, the third time they had lost at this stage since 1896?

7 Which Midlands' team were runners-up in the League and semi-finalists in the FA Cup?

8 The other beaten FA Cup semi-finalists were a London club – then non-League – with strong North British links, taking many of their players from the Docklands factory of Scottish jam and marmalade maker Morton & Co – who were they?

9 Who was the First Division's leading scorer, with 31 goals for fifth-placed Liverpool?

10 Why was Roker Park closed for a week after Sunderland lost 1-0 at home to The Wednesday?

11 Which three teams shared the Home International Championship?

12 Who won the first of their four Scottish League Championships, the others coming in 1948, 1951 and 1952?

13 Who were runners-up in Scotland, their best position in the League until they finally won it in 1962?

14 Rangers won the Scottish FA Cup after the Final had gone to a second replay. Who did they beat 2-0 after the two previous matches had ended 1-1 and 0-0?

15 Which three Scottish internationals also formed the backbone of the Sunderland defence?

 **Quiz 5**   **Season 1903-1904**

1 **The Wednesday won their second League Championship in succession. Who was their secretary-manager?**

2 Who came second in the League and won the FA Cup?

3 **Which Second Division team did they beat 1-0 in the all-Lancashire Final?**

4 Name the great Welsh international who scored the winning goal in the 1904 FA Cup Final.

5 **What was the name of the winning team's manager?**

6 Which Lancashire team was relegated from the First Division despite having scored one more goal (49) than the Champions?

7 **Who was the First Division's leading scorer, with 20 goals for 14th-placed Derby County?**

8 Who became the first side from south of the River Trent to win promotion to the First Division?

9 **Who won the Scottish League Championship for the only time in their history?**

10 The Scottish First Division had been increased from 12 clubs to 14. Who were the two newcomers?

11 **Who scored two goals for Rangers in the Scottish FA Cup Final?**

12 Who then scored a hat-trick to make the final score Celtic 3 Rangers 2?

13 **For which established centre forward had the hat-trick hero been a last-minute replacement?**

14 Who was the Celtic manager who made this controversial selection?

15 **What is the unique link between this year's English and Scottish FA Cup winners?**

 ## Quiz 6   Season 1904-1905

1 **Newcastle United won the League Championship for the first time in their history. Which Midlands side stopped them winning the double by beating them in the Final of the FA Cup?**

2 Name the centre forward who scored both goals in their 2-0 victory in the Final at Crystal Palace?

3 **In addition to making up the champions' formidable half-back line, what was the other link between Newcastle's Andy Aitken, Alex Gardner and Peter McWilliam?**

4 Who was the Newcastle United centre forward?

5 **Who, in February 1905, became the first £1000 player, when he moved from Sunderland to Middlesbrough?**

6 With which Yorkshire club had he started his career?

7 **How many times did he play for England?**

8 Who was the First Division's leading scorer, with 23 goals for 13th-placed Sheffield United?

9 **Which Lancashire club were runners-up in the League and beaten semi-finalists in the FA Cup?**

10 After finishing seventh in the First Division, to what did Small Heath change their name?

11 **Where did they finish the following season (1905-06)?**

12 Celtic and Rangers finished joint top of the Scottish First Division, with both clubs on 41 points. Which club had the better goal average?

13 **Which club won the Scottish title after a play-off?**

14 Who came third in the League and won the Scottish FA Cup for the second time in their history?

15 **Who did they beat 3-1 in the Final?**

Quiz 7   Season 1905-1906

1   **What was unprecedented about Liverpool's second League title?**

2   Who was their goalkeeper, an early-season purchase from Second Division Chesterfield Town, against whom they had netted six the previous season?

3   **Which old stager did he replace in goal?**

4   Who was Liverpool's Scottish centre half?

5   **Who was their leading scorer, with 22 League goals?**

6   Whose place did he take at centre forward when the first choice broke his wrist on the opening day of the season at Woolwich Arsenal?

7   **The joint leading scorers in the First Division were 'Bullet' Jones and Albert Shepherd, with 26 goals apiece. Which teams did they play for?**

8   Which Lancashire club won the FA Cup for the first time in their history?

9   **Who lost in the Final for the second year running?**

10 Who scored the only goal of the match?

11 **Which West Country won the Second Division Championship and very nearly went on to win the First Division the following year?**

12 Which great name – eventually seven-time Championship winners – won promotion to the First Division as runners-up?

13 **Celtic won the Scottish Championship, while the runners-up in the League had the consolation of winning the FA Cup – who were they?**

14 In the Final, they beat the holders of the trophy 1-0. Who scored the winning goal?

15 **Which other team finished above fourth-placed Rangers in the Scottish First Division?**

 **Quiz 8**   **Season 1906-1907**

1 **Who won the League Championship for the second time?**

2 Which was the only team to take a point off them at home this season?

3 **Who were runners-up, their highest ever position in the Football League, and the highest achieved to date by a team from south of the River Trent?**

4 Who was their most distinguished player, dominating the defence at centre half despite appearing overweight and being only 5 feet 4 inches tall?

5 **Which club became the first southern team ever to lead the First Division, although they faded later in the season and finished in seventh place?**

6 Who was the League's leading scorer, with 30 goals for third-placed Everton?

7 **Which lowly Southern League club from London knocked Newcastle United out of the FA Cup, beating them 1-0 at St James's Park in the first round?**

8 Which two 'W's were beaten semi-finalists in the Cup?

9 **Which Yorkshire club won the FA Cup for the second time in their history, beating Everton 2-1 in the Final?**

10 Who bounced straight back as Second Division Champions after having been relegated in 1906?

11 **Which London club came second and thus won promotion to the First Division for the first time in their history?**

12 Wales became the first country other than England and Scotland to win the Home International Championship outright. Who scored in their goal in the 1-1 draw with England at Craven Cottage?

13 **Which Lancashire club did he play for?**

14 Celtic won the Scottish League Championship for the seventh time, their third title in succession. They also became the first team to do the double – who did they beat 3-0 in the Scottish FA Cup Final?

15 **Who scored Celtic's goals in this match?**

13 **Manchester City** 14 Heart of Midlothian 15 Orr (penalty) and Somers (2)

9 **The Wednesday** 10 Nottingham Forest 11 **Chelsea** 12 William 'Lot' Jones

6 Sandy Young 7 **Crystal Palace** 8 West Bromwich Albion and Woolwich Arsenal

1 **Newcastle United** 2 Sheffield United 3 **Bristol City** 4 Billy Wedlock 5 **Woolwich Arsenal**

 **Quiz 9**   **Season 1907-1908**

1 Manchester United won the first of seven League Championships – who was their captain?

2 What was the famous habit of their great right winger, Billy Meredith?

3 How many times did Meredith play for Wales?

4 Enoch West, the League's leading scorer, netted 27 times in the season – for which club?

5 Wolverhampton Wanderers won the FA Cup for the second time in their history – who did they beat 3-1 in the Final?

6 Which Wolverhampton Wanderers player became the only clergyman to appear in an FA Cup Final?

7 The vicar opened the scoring; his goal was followed three minutes later with another by George Hedley. With which team had Hedley twice won the Cup before?

8 Which London Second Division team reached the semi-final of the Cup?

9 Which south-coast non-League side were the other beaten semi-finalists?

10 In their first ever international on foreign soil on June 6, England won 6-1 – who were their opponents?

11 Before moving on to their next destination, they played the same country again. What was the score in this match?

12 Which two other countries did England beat on their summer tour?

13 North of the border, Celtic won their fourth Championship on the trot, scoring 86 goals in 34 League games. But who were the runners-up who became the first Scottish team to score a century, with an all-time record 102 goals?

14 Who did Celtic beat 5-1 in the Scottish FA Cup Final?

15 Which teams shared the Home International Championship, drawing 1-1 with each other and beating the other two nations?

Quiz 10

Season 1908-1909

1 Newcastle United won the League Championship for the third time this century. What was the amazing scoreline in their home fixture with Sunderland, who finished third?

2 Who were the two main goalscorers in this game?

3 **Who was the League's leading goalscorer, with 38 goals for runners-up Everton?**

4 Which new trophy – introduced for the first time this year – was played for between Manchester United, the 1908 League Champions, and Queens Park Rangers, winners of the Southern League?

5 **Who equalled West Bromwich Albion's record First Division victory with a 12-0 defeat of already relegated Leicester Fosse on April 21?**

6 When did Leicester Fosse change their name to Leicester City?

7 **Which other team was relegated, only to bounce straight back as Division Two champions in 1910?**

8 Manchester United won the FA Cup – which west country team did they beat 1-0 in the Final?

9 **Who scored the only goal of the match?**

10 Celtic won their fifth consecutive Scottish League Championship – what happened in the Scottish FA Cup?

11 **Which founder member of the Scottish League won the Second Division before going out of the League for ever in 1915?**

12 Who won the Olympic soccer gold medal?

13 **Who did they beat 2-0 in the Final?**

14 Who scored the goals?

15 **Where in London was the Olympic Final played?**

---

1 **Newcastle United** 1 **Sunderland 9 (nine)** 2 Billy Hogg (four) and George Holley (three) 3 **Bert Freeman** 4 The FA Charity Shield 5 **Nottingham Forest** 6 1919 7 **Manchester City** 8 Bristol City 9 **A. Turnbull** 10 The trophy was withheld after the crowd rioted during the Final replay between Celtic and Rangers 11 **Abercorn** 12 The United Kingdom, represented by England 13 **Denmark** 14 F.W. Chapman (South Notts) and Vivian Woodward (Tottenham Hotspur) 15 **White City**

 Quiz 11   Season 1909-1910

1 Who won the League Championship for the first time in 10 years, but the sixth time in their history?

2 Who was the First Division's leading scorer, with 25 goals for Liverpool, the runners-up?

3 Who eventually won the FA Cup for the first time after reaching the semi-final the previous year and appearing in three out of four previous Finals?

4 Who did they beat 2-0 in the Final replay, after the first match had been drawn 1-1?

5 Who was their centre forward who scored both goals?

6 Who was their right half and captain?

7 What was historic about the second goal in this match?

8 Where was the replay held?

9 Playing for England in an amateur international against Holland, who became the first player to score a double hat trick for the second time?

10 In Scotland, Celtic won the Championship for the sixth year in a row. Who were runners-up, for the second time in three years?

11 Who finished bottom of the Scottish First Division and then went out of the League?

12 Who knocked Celtic out of the Scottish FA Cup in the semi-final?

13 Who won the Scottish Cup for the first time, beating Clyde 2-1 in the second replay?

14 Who scored the winning goal?

15 Who won the Home International Championship outright for the first time in 10 years?

 # Quiz 12   ## Season 1910-1911

1 Of the 20 teams in the First Division, eight were from Lancashire – name them

2 Which of them won the First Division for the second time in four years?

3 Who was their manager?

4 Who was still their captain?

5 Which Midlands club did they beat into second place by one point?

6 Who was the Champions' leading scorer, with 19 goals?

7 And who chipped in with a further 18?

8 But who was the League's leading scorer, with 25 goals for eighth-placed Newcastle United?

9 Who won their first major honour by beating Newcastle 1-0 in the FA Cup Final replay after the first match had been drawn 0-0?

10 The first match had been at Crystal Palace – where was the replay held?

11 Which ex-Rangers Scottish international scored the winner?

12 Who was the winning manager?

13 After five consecutive Scottish League titles, Celtic finished a lowly fifth. Who were the Champions?

14 Celtic had the consolation of victory in the Scottish FA Cup – who did they beat in the Final?

15 Who scored the goals in their 2-0 victory?

1 Blackburn Rovers, Bury, Everton, Liverpool, Manchester City, Manchester United, Oldham Athletic, Preston North End 2 Manchester United 3 Ernest Magnall 4 Charlie Roberts 5 Aston Villa 6 Enoch West 7 Alec Turnbull 8 Albert Shepherd 9 Bradford City 10 Old Trafford 11 Jimmy Speirs 12 Peter O'Rourke 13 Rangers 14 Hamilton Academical 15 Quinn and McAteer

Quiz 13

Season 1911-1912

1 **Who won the League Championship for the first time and were beaten semi-finalists in the FA Cup?**

2 The joint top scorers in the League were Harry Hampton, George Holley and Dave McLean, with 25 goals each. Which teams did they play for?

3 **Who became the first Second Division team to win the FA Cup?**

4 Who did they beat 1-0 in a replay after the first match had been drawn 0-0?

5 **The first game was at Crystal Palace. Where was the replay?**

6 Name the inside right who scored the winning goal in the last minute of extra time.

7 **What change was made to the playing conditions as a result of the length of time it had taken to get results in the last three FA Cup Finals?**

8 Which non-League club reached the semi-finals of the FA Cup?

9 **Which Lincolnshire club finished bottom of Division Two and then disappeared for ever from the Football League?**

10 Who won the Olympic football gold medal in Stockholm?

11 **Who did they beat in the Final?**

12 Who won the Scottish League Championship for the second year running?

13 **Who won the Scottish FA Cup for the second year in succession?**

14 Who scored the goals in their 2-0 Final victory?

15 **Who came third in the League and were runners-up in the Cup?**

1 **Blackburn Rovers** 2 Aston Villa, Sunderland and The Wednesday respectively 3 **Barnsley** 4 West Bromwich Albion 5 **Bramall Lane** 6 Harry Tufnell 7 **In future years, there would be extra time in the first Final if the scores were level after 90 minutes** 8 Swindon Town 9 Gainsborough Trinity 10 England 11 **Denmark** 12 Rangers 13 **Celtic** 14 McMenemy and Gallacher 15 **Clyde**

Quiz 14

Season 1912-1913

1 **Who won the League Championship for the fifth time and lost in the Final of the FA Cup?**

2 Who won the FA Cup for the fifth time and finished second in the League?

3 **Who was the right half who scored the only goal of the Final with a header from a corner?**

4 What happened to Final referee A. Adams after the match?

5 **Who was the First Division's leading scorer, with 30 goals for third-placed Wednesday?**

6 Which Lancashire team reached the semi-final of the Cup and won promotion from the Second Division?

7 **Which Sheffield United centre forward scored both goals for Ireland in their 2-1 victory over England in the Home International in Belfast?**

8 Which Sunderland and future Arsenal inside forward won the first of his six England caps and scored the opening goal in this game?

9 **With which other players did he make one third of England's so-called 'Sunderland Triangle'?**

10 Who was the Huddersfield Town inside left who went off with a knee injury in the first half, reducing the Irish to 10 men?

11 **Who moved their ground, changed their name and were relegated from the First Division, all in the same season?**

12 Who won the Scottish League for the third year in succession?

13 **Which two teams made their first appearances in the Scottish FA Cup Final?**

14 Who won the Cup, with a 2-0 victory?

15 **Where was the Final played?**

 Quiz 15 **Season 1913-1914**

1 Blackburn Rovers won the League Championship for the second time in three years. Who were runners-up and semi-finalists in the FA Cup?

2 Who was the English First Division's leading scorer, with 31 goals for third-placed Middlesbrough?

3 Which Lancashire club was relegated from the First Division after having been promoted the previous year and relegated the year before that?

4 Which other Lancashire club won the FA Cup – its first major honour – beating yet another (Liverpool) 1-0 in the Final?

5 Where was the Final played?

6 Who was the victorious captain?

7 Which monarch presented him with the Cup?

8 Who won the Home International Championship for the first time?

9 On their way to the title, they beat England 3-0 away. Where was this match played?

10 Who was the leading scorer in the Scottish First Division, with 21 goals for double-winners Celtic?

11 Celtic created a Scottish First Division record for the fewest League goals against in a season – how many did they concede in their 38 matches?

12 How many times had Celtic now won the Scottish League and the Cup in the same season?

13 Who did they beat 4-1 in the replayed Final of the Scottish FA Cup, after the first match had been drawn 0-0?

14 Which two players scored twice in this game?

15 Who won the Second Division but were not promoted because of the following season's reorganisation of the Scottish League?

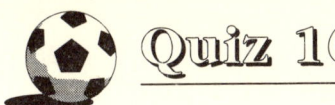

Quiz 16

Season 1914-1915

1 Who won the League Championship for the second time in their history and retained the title for five years because of the intervention of the First World War?

2 Who was their leading scorer, with 35 goals in the season?

3 Who were runners-up, the highest position in their history, one point behind the winners?

4 Why was Oldham Athletic's game against Middlesbrough abandoned?

5 How did the War with Germany cause the FA Cup second round replay at Lincoln between Bradford City and Norwich City to be played behind closed doors?

6 Who won the FA Cup, beating Chelsea 3-0 in the Final?

7 Who scored the goals?

8 Who was the victorious captain who won his second FA Cup winner's medal after having played for Barnsley in their 1912 victory?

9 Where was the 1915 FA Cup Final played?

10 By what name is this match more commonly known, because of the large number of servicemen in the crowd of 49,557?

11 Who presented the Cup and made a speech about the need to serve King and country?

12 In Scotland, there was no FA Cup for five years after 1914 because of the War. However, the League continued right through without interruption. Who won it in 1915, 1916, 1917 and 1919?

13 And who pipped them by a point for the 1918 title?

14 In the Scottish Division B, there was a tie on points and the Championship was decided by a three-way play off. Which were the teams involved?

15 Which team was promoted?

---

1 Everton 2 Bobby Parker **3 Oldham Athletic** 4 Because Billy Cook of Oldham refused to leave the field when sent off **5 Because the ground was next door to a munitions factory, and there was thought to be a danger of an explosion** 6 Sheffield United 7 **Simmons, Kitchen and Fazackerley** 8 George Utley 9 **Old Trafford** 10 The Khaki Cup Final 11 **Lord Derby** 12 Celtic 13 **Rangers** 14 Cowdenbeath, Leith Athletic and St Bernard's 15 None of them: only the top division as previously constituted played for the rest of the War

Quiz 17

Season 1919-1920

1 The First Division was enlarged to 22 clubs. How many teams had previously been in the top flight of English football?

2 Which two clubs were promoted after finishing first and second in Division Two in 1915, before the First World War brought League football to a halt?

3 To help make up the numbers, one club was not relegated from the First Division, despite having finished next to last in 1915 – which club?

4 Which was the other new member of the First Division, promoted despite having finished only fifth in Division Two in 1915?

5 The First Division's bottom club in 1915 was relegated. This was much to their consternation, because the last time the number of clubs in the First Division had been increased, in 1905, no one had been relegated. Which was the club?

6 Which Second Division club was thrown out of the League in October 1919 after the discovery of irregularities in their payments to players during the War and their subsequent refusal to produce accounts for the previous two years?

7 Among the club officials punished by the Football League was former manager George Cripps. Which other former manager – later to win the Championship with two clubs – was also banned?

8 Who took over their place in the Second Division and the 10 points they had gained before their expulsion?

9 Who won the League Championship with a record number of goals scored (104)?

10 Who was their leading individual scorer, with 37 goals?

11 Who won the FA Cup for a record sixth time, beating Huddersfield Town 1-0 in the Final?

12 Who scored the winning goal in extra time?

13 From where had he been bought for £250 earlier in the season?

14 Kilmarnock won the Scottish FA Cup for the first time. Which team – who came bottom of the First Division – did they beat 3-2 in the Final?

15 The Scottish First Division was also increased to 22 clubs. Who won the first Championship in the new format with a record 71 points?

---

1 **Twenty** 2 Derby County and Preston North End 3 Chelsea 4 Arsenal 5 Tottenham Hotspur 6 Leeds City 7 **Herbert Chapman** 8 Port Vale 9 **West Bromwich Albion** 10 Fred Morris 11 **Aston Villa** 12 Bill Kirton 13 **Disgraced Leeds City** 14 Albion Rovers 15 **Rangers**

Quiz 18   Season 1920-1921

1 Burnley won the first of their two League Championships – when was their next title?

2 From September 4, Burnley went 30 matches without defeat, a League record. Who finally beat them on March 26?

3 The League was increased from two divisions to three. Of the teams that played in the first ever Third Division, which is the only one to have gone on to win the League Championship?

4 Who were the first Champions of the Third Division?

5 The First Division's top scorer was Joe Smith, with 38 goals in the season. Who did he play for?

6 Who won promotion to the First Division in their first season in the Football League?

7 Which newly-promoted First Division team won the FA Cup?

8 Which Second Division team did they beat 1-0 in the Final?

9 Who was the winning captain and goalscorer?

10 Which member of the 1910 Newcastle United team now became the first man to have played in and then managed a Cup-winning team?

11 In the Third Division, the 0-0 draw at Old Trafford on May 7 between Stockport County and Leicester City was watched by fewer paying spectators than any other first class match in the history of the game. How many turned up?

12 Who joined the League as replacements for Lincoln City, who failed to win re-election after finishing next to bottom of the Second Division in 1920?

13 In Scotland, Rangers won the Championship; who were the only club to beat them in the League all season?

14 Who was the League's leading scorer for the second season running, with 43 goals for fifth-placed Motherwell?

15 Who won the Scottish FA Cup for the only time, beating Rangers 1-0 in the Final?

CARLING 10,000 FOOTBALL FACTS & QUESTIONS

 **Quiz 19**　　　　　**Season 1921-1922**

1　**Who won the English League Championship for the third time in their history?**

2　Who was their manager?

3　**Who were relegated for the first time under their present name?**

4　Their manager stayed in place for long enough to see them back into the First Division at the start of the 1925-26 season. Name him.

5　**Eighth-placed Middlesbrough had the League's leading scorer, with 31 goals. What was his name?**

6　How many new clubs joined the League when the old Third Division was enlarged and divided into Northern and Southern sections?

7　**Of these new clubs, how many have since won the League Championship, the Premiership or the FA Cup?**

8　Who won the FA Cup, beating Preston North End 1-0 in the Final?

9　**Who scored the winner from the penalty spot?**

10　Where was the match held?

11　**In Scotland, who were runners-up in both League and FA Cup?**

12　Who beat them 1-0 in the Cup Final, the only major honour in their long history?

13　**Who scored their winner at Hampden Park on April 15, in front of 75,000 people?**

14　For the first time, the Scottish League was divided into two divisions: who were the first champions of the new lower division?

15　**At the end of the season, which three clubs became the first to be relegated from the Scottish First Division?**

Quiz 20

Season 1922-1923

1   The players' maximum wage was reduced by £1 from its 1921-22 level. What was the new rate?

2   Liverpool won the League title for the second year running. Who was their Northern Ireland international goalkeeper?

3   **Liverpool then entered the longest period in their history without a League title. When did they next win it?**

4   Who were runners-up in 1923, six points behind the champions?

5   **Which player for the second placed team was the First Division's leading scorer, with 30 goals?**

6   Which London team won promotion to the First Division for the first time in its history?

7   **Who was their centre forward who won the first of his five England caps in this year?**

8   Who was their England international goalkeeper?

9   **Who was their manager?**

10   Which three other teams from the capital did they join in the top flight?

11   **Who beat them 2-0 in this year's FA Cup Final, the first to be played at Wembley?**

12   Who scored the goals?

13   **What is this Final commonly known as?**

14   Who was the leading scorer in Scotland, with 30 of Heart of Midlothian's 51 goals in the season?

15   **Who is the leading scorer in Scottish League history, with 410 goals in a 408-game career which began in this year?**

1 £8 a week 2 Elisha Scott 3 1947 4 Sunderland 5 **Charlie Buchan** 6 West Ham United
7 **Vic Watson** 8 Ted Hufton 9 **Syd King** 10 Arsenal, Chelsea and Tottenham Hotspur
11 **Bolton Wanderers** 12 David Jack and Jack Smith 13 **The White Horse Final**
14 John White 15 **Jimmy McGrory** (Celtic and Clydebank)

Quiz 21

Season 1923-1924

1 **Who won the first of three successive League Championships?**

2 Who was their captain?

3 **Who did they edge into second place on goal average?**

4 Who was the First Division's leading scorer, with 28 goals for Everton?

5 **What made the Second Division game between Manchester United and Oldham Athletic unforgettable for Latics' full back Sam Wynne?**

6 Who won the FA Cup, beating Aston Villa 2-0 in the Final?

7 **Who, at 41 years and 8 months, became the oldest player ever to appear in an FA Cup Final?**

8 What was the score in the England v Scotland game, the first international to be played at Wembley?

9 **Wales won the Home International Championship for the second time and made their first clean sweep of three victories. Which Plymouth Argyle player scored from the penalty spot in their 1-0 victory over Northern Ireland in Belfast?**

10 In the Wales v Scotland match – which the home side won 2-0 – both captains – Fred Keenor (Wales) and Jimmy Blair (Scotland) – played for the same club. Which?

11 **What was the venue for the England v Wales match, which Wales won 2-1?**

12 The Scottish League launched a Third Division. Of the 16 original members, how many were still in existence in 1998?

13 **Which now defunct club were the first Champions of this division?**

14 Rangers won the Scottish Championship. Who was the League's leading scorer, with 38 goals for Dundee?

15 **Who won the Scottish FA Cup, beating Hibernian 2-0 in the Final?**

---

1 **Huddersfield Town** 2 Clem Stephenson 3 **Cardiff City** 4 Bill Chadwick 5 **He scored twice for both sides** 6 Newcastle United 7 **Walter Hampson (Newcastle United)** 8 England 1 Scotland 1 9 **Moses Russell** 10 Cardiff City 11 **Ewood Park, Blackburn** 12 Four – Brechin City, East Stirlingshire, Montrose and Queen of the South 13 **Arthurlie** 14 Dave Halliday 15 **Airdrieonians**

 Quiz 22 **Season 1924-1925**

1 **Which Midlands team were runners-up to Huddersfield Town in the English First Division?**

2 Which Huddersfield player became the first footballer to score direct from a corner (this was the first season in which it was permissible to do so)?

3 **Who were Huddersfield's opponents in this match on October 11?**

4 And who scored the first FA Cup goal from a corner, enabling Cardiff City to scrape through a fourth round tie against Leicester City?

5 **Who was the First Division's leading scorer, with 31 goals for tenth-placed Manchester City?**

6 Which south coast Second Division side lost 2-0 to Sheffield United in the semi-final of the FA Cup?

7 **Who did Sheffield United beat 1-0 in the Final?**

8 Who scored the winning goal in that match?

9 **Who won the Scottish League Championship?**

10 Willie Devlin was the leading scorer in Scotland, with 33 goals for the fifth-placed club. Which?

11 **Which now defunct Dumfries club won promotion from the Scottish Third Division?**

12 Celtic won the Scottish FA Cup, beating Dundee 2-1 in the Final. Who scored the Celtic equaliser by somersaulting into the net with the ball held between his feet?

13 **What was his nickname?**

14 This was Celtic's eleventh FA Cup triumph. Whose record of ten victories did they overtake?

15 **At the end of the season, which other law was altered leading to a glut of goals in succeeding years?**

played to him was reduced from three to two
number of players that had to be between the attacker and the ball when it was
Wanderers 12 Patsy Gallagher 13 The **Mighty Atom** 14 Queens Park 15 **Offside:** the
6 Southampton 7 **Cardiff City** 8 Fred Tunstall 9 **Rangers** 10 Cowdenbeath 11 **Nithsdale**
1 **West Bromwich Albion** 2 Billy Smith 3 **Arsenal** 4 Willie Davies 5 **Fred Roberts**

 **Quiz 23** Season 1925-1926

1 Who did Herbert Chapman succeed as manager of Arsenal?

2 When Chapman signed Charlie Buchan from Sunderland, the fee was £2000 plus how much per goal?

3 How much more did this cost Arsenal in the first year?

4 Huddersfield Town became the first club ever to win the League Championship three years in a row. Who took over from Herbert Chapman as their manager at the start of the season?

5 Which of Chapman's last signings for Huddersfield (from Aberdeen) scored 16 goals from outside right in his first season south of the border?

6 Which Huddersfield player created a new club scoring record, with 35 goals in the League?

7 Who was the League's leading scorer, with 43 goals in the season for twelfth-placed Blackburn Rovers?

8 Which team became the first to reach the FA Cup Final and be relegated from the First Division in the same season?

9 Who won the FA Cup?

10 Which future Arsenal star scored the only goal of the match?

11 Celtic won the Scottish League title but lost in the Final of the FA Cup. Who beat them 2-0 to win the competition for the first time?

12 Who were runners-up in the Scottish League for the fourth year running?

13 Bobby Skinner set a British scoring record with 53 goals for the Division Two champions in Scotland. Who were they?

14 Why was the Scottish Third Division not completed?

15 Which team topped the Third Division table but were not promoted and then left the League altogether?

Quiz 24

Season 1926-1927

1 **Who won the League Championship for the first time in 18 years?**

2 Who was their Scottish captain, scorer of 36 goals in the season?

3 **Who was their secretary-manager?**

4 On January 22, live commentary on a football match was broadcast on radio for the first time. Which teams were involved?

5 **What was the famous catchphrase popularised – if not actually originated – by this and subsequent broadcasts?**

6 The FA Cup left England for the only time when Cardiff City beat Arsenal in the Final. Who scored the only goal of the game?

7 **What was the name of Arsenal's Welsh international goalkeeper who was widely thought to have been at fault with the goal?**

8 Cardiff City were one of six Welsh clubs in the Football League at the time. Name the other five.

9 **Which two Second Division clubs from the south of England were beaten FA Cup semi-finalists?**

10 Which member of The Wednesday team was the First Division's leading scorer, with 37 goals?

11 **Who scored 59 of Middlesbrough's 122 goals as they romped to the Second Division title?**

12 Which Celtic player was Scotland's leading scorer with 49 goals despite missing five of their 38 games through injury?

13 **Despite scoring 101 goals, Celtic finished third behind champions Rangers and which other club?**

14 Which great Evertonian scored both goals for England in their 2-1 victory over Scotland?

15 **When was the last time England had won at Hampden Park?**

Quiz 25   Season 1927-1928

1   Who scored the all-time record number of goals in a season – 60 – for League Champions Everton?

2   How many of the club's 42 League games did he play in?

3   Which other Lancashire club won the FA Cup?

4   Which Yorkshire club were runners-up in both the League and the Cup?

5   Which London club scored a League record 127 goals while winning the Third Division (South)?

6   What was the score when Scotland's 'Wembley Wizards' played England in the Home International Championship at Wembley?

7   Who scored a hat-trick in this match?

8   Who was the Scottish outside left – known as 'The Wee Blue Devil' – who put over the crosses for three of the goals?

9   Who was the Scotland captain in this match?

10 Which Scottish team won their first League and Cup double?

11 Who were runners-up in both the Scottish League and FA Cup?

12 Which Celtic player was the First Division's top scorer?

13 Of this player's 47 goals, a record eight came in one game, a 9-0 victory over which Fife team?

14 Jim Smith scored 66 goals in the season, a British record. Which team did he help to win the Scottish Second Division title?

15 For two Scottish Second Division clubs, this was to be the last full season of existence. Which two?

 ## Quiz 26   **Season 1928-1929**

1   Who, on August 25, became the first two teams to wear numbered shirts in a League game?

2   For which great Arsenal player, now retiring, was David Jack a replacement?

3   Where did Arsenal buy David Jack from?

4   What was the record-breaking transfer fee?

5   The First Division was won by The Wednesday, who then changed their name to Sheffield Wednesday during the close season. Who was their captain?

6   Name the Wednesday manager who had bought this player from Spurs.

7   Who won the FA Cup for the third time this decade, beating Portsmouth 2-0 in the Final?

8   On May 15, England suffered their first-ever defeat on foreign soil. Who beat them 4-3?

9   Who was the First Division's leading scorer, with 43 goals for fourth-placed Sunderland?

10 Rangers won the Scottish Championship, but who beat them 2-0 in the FA Cup Final?

11 Which Rangers player became the first man to be sent off in an FA Cup Final?

12 For which team did Scotland's leading scorer Evelyn Morrison – with 43 goals in the season – play?

13 Who scored a record five goals for Scotland in their 7-3 win over Northern Ireland in Belfast?

14 This player had begun his international career in 1924 while with Airdrieonians. For which English First Division club was he now playing?

15 Scotland won the Home International Championship with three wins out of three. What was historic about Alex Cheyne's goal in their 1-0 win over England at Hampden Park?

Quiz 27

Season 1929-1930

1 **Sheffield Wednesday retained the League Championship; who was the season's leading scorer, with 42 goals for seventh-placed West Ham United?**

2 Who were runners-up in the League under George Jobey, equalling their previous best in 1895-96?

3 **Who won the FA Cup for the first time, beating Huddersfield Town 2-0 in the so-called Graf Zeppelin Final in which the German airship passed over Wembley on the afternoon of the match?**

4 Who was their manager, who had previously been the manager of the runners-up?

5 **Who scored the goals in the Final?**

6 From which club did Arsenal buy Alex James?

7 **How much was the record fee for which he was transferred?**

8 How many caps did James win for Scotland?

9 **Five days before the FA Cup Final, Arsenal were involved in the highest scoring draw in League history, 6-6 away to whom?**

10 Who won promotion to the Second Division after having finished second in Division Three (South) in six of the previous eight seasons?

11 **Rangers won the Scottish Championship, but the First Division's leading scorer – with 38 goals – played for third-placed Aberdeen. What was his name?**

12 Rangers also won the FA Cup; who did they beat 2-1 in the Final replay, after the first match had been drawn 0-0?

13 **Which now defunct team won the Second Division title?**

14 England beat Scotland 5-1 at Wembley to win the Home Championship outright for the first time since the First World War. Which Sheffield Wednesday player scored twice in this game on his international debut?

15 **Which Arsenal player was England captain in this match?**

Quiz 28

Season 1930-1931

1 Arsenal became the first London club to win the Championship. How many goals did they score in the 42-game season?

2 Who was their leading scorer, with 38 goals in the season?

3 Name the Arsenal inside right who contributed another 31 goals...

4 ...And the left winger who scored a further 28.

5 Amazingly, Arsenal were not the top scorers in the First Division that year – that title went to the runners-up. Who were they?

6 Who was their – and the League's – leading scorer, with 49 goals?

7 Which team became the first to win the FA Cup and promotion from the Second Division in the same season?

8 In the semi-final, they beat the team who beat them into second place in the Second Division. Who?

9 Who were the runners-up in the FA Cup?

10 Who scored both the winning side's goals in the Final?

11 Rangers won the Scottish League Championship, but the highest scorer, with 44 goals, played for fifth-placed Heart of Midlothian. Name him.

12 Who did Celtic beat 4-2 in the replayed Final of the Scottish FA Cup, after the first match had been drawn 2-2?

13 In May, which country became the first to defeat Scotland on foreign soil?

14 Which other team did Scotland lose to on this tour?

15 Who did Scotland beat 3-2 in the final match of their 1931 summer tour?

Quiz 29

Season 1931-1932

1 **Who won the First Division Championship?**

2 What was the real name of Dixie Dean, their leading scorer that season with 44 goals?

3 **Why was he called Dixie?**

4 How many goals did Dean score for England in his 16 international appearances between 1927 and 1933?

5 **Who were runners-up in both the League and the FA Cup?**

6 Who scored both Newcastle United's goals in their 2-1 Cup Final victory?

7 **What has the Newcastle equaliser come to be known as?**

8 Which Third Division club became the first to resign from the Football League during the course of a season?

9 **Who bounced straight back up to the First Division after having been relegated in 1931?**

10 Which Newcastle and England player made his name during the Home Internationals as perhaps the first exponent of the long throw-in?

11 **Motherwell won the Scottish League Championship for the only time in their history. When was the last time it had been won by anyone other than Celtic or Rangers?**

12 And who had won it then?

13 **Which Motherwell player set a Scottish League scoring record, with 52 goals in the season?**

14 Who were runners-up to Rangers in the Scottish FA Cup, going down 3-0 in a replay after the first match had been drawn 1-1?

15 **Name the Celtic and Scotland goalkeeper who died from head injuries after throwing himself at the feet of a Rangers player during the Old Firm match at Ibrox on September 5.**

---

1 **Everton** 2 William Ralph Dean 3 **Because of his dark complexion** 4 Eighteen 5 **Arsenal** 6 Jack Allen 7 **The Over-The-Line Goal** 8 Wigan Borough 9 **Leeds United** 10 Sam Weaver 11 1904 12 Third Lanark 13 **Bill McFadyen** 14 Kilmarnock 15 **John Thomson**

 **Quiz 30**   **Season 1932-1933**

1 **Who won the English League Championship, the first of three consecutive titles?**

2 Who were the so-called Wünderteam, who played against England at Stamford Bridge?

3 **Which former Bolton Wanderers player was their national coach?**

4 What was the score in this match?

5 **Who won the FA Cup, beating Manchester City 3-0 in the Final?**

6 Who scored the goals?

7 **Who pulled off one of the great shocks of FA Cup history when they beat Arsenal 2-0 in the third round?**

8 Who scored for the Third Division club?

9 **Which Arsenal player never played for the club again after giving away a penalty in this match?**

10 Which team finished runners-up in both the Scottish League and FA Cup?

11 **Who was their leading scorer for the second season running, with 45 goals?**

12 How many times did he play for Scotland?

13 **Who won the Scottish Championship, despite winning one fewer game and scoring one fewer goal than the runners-up?**

14 Which two clubs were expelled from the Scottish League in November 1932 for inability to meet match guarantees?

15 **In which year had they both joined the League?**

1 **Arsenal** 2 Austria 3 **Jimmy Hagan** 4 England 4 Austria 3 5 **Everton** 6 Stein, Dean and Dunn
7 **Walsall** 8 Alsop and Sheppard (penalty) 9 **Tommy Black** 10 Motherwell
11 **Bill McFadyean** 12 Twice 13 **Rangers** 14 Armadale and Bo'ness 15 1921

 **Quiz 31**   **Season 1933-1934**

1   Who took over as Arsenal manager after the untimely death of Herbert Chapman from pneumonia while watching his third team play at Guildford on January 6, 1934?

2   What had been his previous job?

3   Who was his first purchase?

4   Where did he get him from?

5   Who won the FA Cup, beating Portsmouth 2-1 in the Final?

6   Who was the winning goalkeeper?

7   Who scored both the winning team's goals?

8   Which future President of FIFA refereed the Final?

9   Who was the First Division's leading scorer for the second season running, with 35 goals for fourth-placed Derby County?

10 Who was top scorer, with 41 goals, for Scottish double winners Rangers?

11 Who won the home International Championship for the second year running?

12 Who came 20th in the Second Division, the lowest league position in their distinguished history, which already included two Championships, and avoided relegation to the Third Division (North) by only one point?

13 Who were runners-up to Arsenal in the First Division?

14 Who was their manager, a former captain and one of their most distinguished players?

15 Who did Rangers beat 5-0 in the Scottish FA Cup Final?

1 **George Allison** 2 Broadcaster and Arsenal Managing Director 3 **Ted Drake** 4 Southampton
5 **Manchester City** 6 Frank Swift 7 **Freddy Tilson** 8 Stanley Rous 9 **Jack Bowers**
10 Jimmy Smith 11 **Wales** 12 Manchester United 13 **Huddersfield Town**
14 Clem Stephenson 15 **St Mirren**

 # Quiz 32   Season 1934-1935

1. **Which future manager of Chelsea scored 42 goals in the season for Arsenal?**

2. Arsenal won the Championship for the third year in succession, a feat previously achieved by one team only. Which?

3. **Which country were the opposition in the so-called Battle of Highbury, which England won 3-2?**

4. Which Manchester City outside left missed a penalty in this match and then scored the first in open play?

5. **Which great Stoke City player scored the second on his second international appearance?**

6. The third goal was scored by Ted Drake – how many other Arsenal players were in the England side?

7. **Who scored both goals for the opposition?**

8. Who scored two goals for Sheffield Wednesday in their 4-2 Cup Final victory over West Bromwich Albion? (He also scored in every round of the competition that year.)

9. **Which Lancashire club lost to West Brom in the semi-finals but had the consolation of promotion as runners-up in Division Two?**

10. Which London club won the Second Division, thus gaining promotion to the top flight for the first time in their history?

11. **Who was their legendary manager?**

12. Which London club was relegated from the First Division after having been promoted in 1933, and coming third in Division One in 1934?

13. **Who was their manager until they were relegated?**

14. Rangers did the double for the fourth time. Who did they beat in the Scottish FA Cup Final?

15. **Which Heart of Midlothian player was Scotland's top scorer, with 38 goals?**

 **Quiz 33** **Season 1935-1936**

1 Sunderland won the League Championship – what was the nickname given to this team?

2 Who was their manager?

3 One of the stars of this team was the great inside forward known to everyone as 'Raich' Carter. What was his real Christian name?

4 Which member of the championship-winning side was nicknamed 'The Mighty Atom'?

5 For which two countries did he play at international level?

6 Who was the First Division's leading scorer, with 39 goals for West Bromwich Albion?

7 Arsenal won the FA Cup, beating Sheffield United 1-0 in the Final. Who scored the goal?

8 Which two founder members of the Football League were relegated together from the First Division for the first time in their history?

9 Who equalled the First Division scoring record with seven goals against Aston Villa on December 14?

10 Who, in 1888, was the only other player to have scored seven in a First Division match?

11 On Boxing Day, 1935, in a Third Division (North) game, who scored a record nine goals for Tranmere Rovers in their 13-4 win over Oldham Athletic?

12 Then, on April 13, 1936, in the Third Division (South), who broke this record when he scored 10 goals in Luton Town's 12-0 defeat of Bristol Rovers?

13 Who scored 50 goals in the season for Scottish champions Celtic?

14 Who scored eight goals for Morton in their Division Two game against Raith Rovers on April 18?

15 Who were runners-up to Rangers in the Scottish FA Cup?

1 The Bank of England 2 Johnny Cochrane 3 Horatio 4 Patsy Gallagher 5 Northern Ireland and the Republic of Ireland 6 Ginger Richardson 7 Ted Drake 8 Aston Villa and Blackburn Rovers 9 Ted Drake (Arsenal) 10 James Ross for Preston North End v Stoke City 11 Robert 'Bunny' Bell 12 Joe Payne 13 Jimmy McGrory 14 John Calder 15 Third Lanark

CARLING 10,000 FOOTBALL FACTS & QUESTIONS

Quiz 34

Season 1936-1937

1 **Who were First Division Champions?**

2 What unwanted feat did they achieve the following season?

3 **Which London club became the first Third Division side to reach the semi-finals of the FA Cup?**

4 Name this team's player manager who scored both goals in their 2-0 sixth round victory over high-flying Manchester City.

5 **Who created a new First Division scoring record, with 375 goals in his career?**

6 In Division Three, two players scored 55 goals in the season. One played for Mansfield Town in the Third Division (North). Name him

7 **The other 55-er played for Luton Town in the Third Division (South). Who was he?**

8 How many goals did this player score on his only appearance for England, an 8-0 victory over Finland during the summer tour?

9 **Who scored a hat-trick on his home ground as England beat Hungary 6-2 at Highbury?**

10 The First Division's leading scorer was Freddie Steele, with 33 goals. Which team did he play for?

11 **Who won the FA Cup for the first time, beating Preston North End 3-1 in the Final?**

12 Who was their captain?

13 **Which Scottish international centre forward scored in the Final for Preston North End?**

14 Who won the Home International championship, winning all three games?

15 **In Scotland, Rangers won the League and Celtic the FA Cup. Who were runners-up in both competitions?**

Quiz 35

Season 1937-1938

1 **Who won the League Championship?**

2 How many times had they won it before?

3 **Who was the First Division's leading scorer, with 28 goals for 14th-placed Everton?**

4 Which team scored the most goals in the First Division – 80, three more than the champions?

5 **In the FA Cup Final, in which Preston North End beat Huddersfield Town 1-0, two things happened that had never happened before in this fixture at Wembley. What?**

6 Name the Scottish international inside right who scored the Preston winner.

7 **How many times did he play for Scotland?**

8 In Scotland, Celtic won the League. Who won the FA Cup for the first time, and became the only Second Division club ever to win the trophy?

9 **Who did they beat 4-2 after extra time in the Final replay after the first match had been drawn 1-1?**

10 Which team took the Cup winners to two replays in the semi-final only two years before going out of the Scottish League for ever?

11 **The Scottish First Division's leading scorer was Andy Black, with 40 goals in the season. Which team did he play for?**

12 Which Fife team won the Scottish Second Division scoring a British record 142 goals in 34 games?

13 **What was the score in the controversial Germany v England international in Berlin at the start of which the England players gave the Nazi salute?**

14 Adolf Hitler did not attend the match. Which two leading Nazis were guests of honour?

15 **Which West Ham United player scored for England in this game with a 25-yard drive?**

---

1 **Arsenal** 2 Four 3 **Tommy Lawton** 4 **Manchester City**, who were relegated 5 It was the first Final that went to extra time, and the first to be settled by a penalty (the last kick of the match) 6 George Mutch 7 **Once** 8 East Fife 9 **Kilmarnock** 10 St Bernard's 11 **Heart of Midlothian** 12 Raith Rovers 13 **Germany 3 England 6** 14 Josef Goebbels and Hermann Goering 15 Len Goulden

Quiz 36

Season 1938-1939

1   Which Tottenham Hotspur player equalled the England scoring record with five goals against Northern Ireland at Maine Road?

2   Who was the First Division's leading scorer, with 35 goals for League Champions Everton?

3   Who won the FA Cup, beating Wolverhampton Wanderers in the Final, and held the trophy for longer than any other club, because of the outbreak of the Second World War?

4   Who was the winning manager with the lucky spats?

5   Which former Wolves player, transferred only two months previously, scored one of the goals in their 4-1 victory?

6   Which Wolves player had moved to Arsenal earlier in the season at a cost of £14,000?

7   Which Highbury legend was he bought to replace?

8   Who was the leading scorer in Scotland, with 34 goals for League Champions Rangers?

9   Who won the Scottish FA Cup for the first time?

10   Who scored with his hand to help Italy draw 2-2 with England in Turin?

11   Who scored the England goals?

12   In the Second Division, Blackburn Rovers were champions and Sheffield United were promoted as runners-up. Who did United beat into third place by one point?

13   Which game on January 2 had the highest-ever attendance – 118,567 – at a British football match?

14   Who was relegated to the Third Division (North) after suffering more defeats in a season – 31 out of 42 games played – than any other team in the history of the Second Division?

15   Who were the leaders of the First Division – played three, won three – on September 3, 1939 when the League was suspended because of the outbreak of the Second World War?

CARLING 10,000 FOOTBALL FACTS & QUESTIONS

 **Quiz 37**   **Season 1946-1947**

1 Which Yorkshire team won Division Three (North) with a record number of points (72), a record number of wins (33), a record number of away wins (18) and a record number of away points (37)?

2 Which London club won the FA Cup for the only time in their history?

3 **Who scored their winning goal in extra time in the Final?**

4 Which Lancashire team were runners-up in both the Cup and Division Two, but had the consolation of promotion?

5 **Liverpool won the League Championship, Manchester United were second. Which team came third and had the highest scorer – Dennis Westcott, with 37 goals in the season?**

6 England's end of season tour began with a 1-0 defeat in Switzerland. They then travelled west and defeated which country 10-0?

7 **Who won his first cap in this game and scored four goals?**

8 Which other England player scored four goals in this match?

9 **Who scored six goals on his debut for Newcastle United in their record 13-0 Second Division victory over Newport County?**

10 From which other Second Division club had Newcastle United bought him for £13,000?

11 **The sale of whom to Liverpool earlier that season for the same amount had helped Newcastle to finance the deal?**

12 This player finished the season with 24 goals in the First Division. Which other Liverpool player was joint top scorer?

13 **The four top teams in Scottish Division A were also the semi-finalists in the FA Cup. Name them.**

14 Who went on to win the Scottish Cup for the first time in their history?

15 **Top scorer in the Scottish First Division was Bobby Mitchell, with 22 goals. Which team did he play for?**

Quiz 38   Season 1947-1948

1 **Arsenal won the League Championship for the sixth time. Who was their leading scorer, with 33 goals?**

2 Runners-up in the League, Manchester United had the consolation of winning the FA Cup. Who did they beat 4-2 in the Final?

3 **Which member of the losing side scored in every round of the competition, a total of 10 goals?**

4 Which Third Division side sensationally bought England centre forward Tommy Lawton from Chelsea for £20,000 – £5,000 more than the previous highest transfer fee?

5 **Where did Manchester United play their home matches?**

6 Who did First Division Sunderland buy from Second Division Newcastle United for £20,050?

7 **Which Blackpool player made every one of England's goals in their 5-2 victory over Belgium in Brussels?**

8 And which three players scored them?

9 **Which Manchester City player – the first goalkeeper to captain England – kept a clean sheet for his country in the 4-0 defeat of Italy in Turin?**

10 And which three players scored the goals in this match?

11 **Who won the Scottish League Championship?**

12 Which Falkirk player was the First Division's leading scorer, with 20 goals?

13 **Who won the Scottish FA Cup, beating Morton 1-0 in a replay after the first game had finished 1-1?**

14 Who won the Scottish League Cup, beating Falkirk 4-1 in a replay after the first match had been drawn 0-0?

15 **What other distinction did the same team achieve this season?**

---

1 Ronnie **Rooke** 2 Blackpool 3 Stan **Mortensen** 4 Notts County 5 **Maine Road**
6 Len Shackleton 7 **Stanley Matthews (Blackpool)** 8 Tommy Lawton (Chelsea) (2), Stan Mortensen (Blackpool), Tom Finney (Preston North End) (2) **9 Frank Swift** 10 Stan Mortensen (2), Tommy Lawton and Tom Finney 11 **Hibernian** 12 Archie Aikman 13 **Rangers** 14 East Fife
15 **They won the Scottish Second Division title**

 **Quiz 39**   **Season 1948-1949**

1   Which team became the first to rise from the Third Division and win the League Championship?

2   Who was their manager?

3   **Who came second in the First Division for the third year in a row?**

4   Which Second Division side reached the FA Cup Final?

5   **Which future England manager missed playing for them in the Final because of illness?**

6   Who scored both goals in Wolverhampton Wanderers' 2-0 victory over them in the FA Cup Final?

7   **The First Division's leading scorer was Willie Moir, with 25 goals. For which team did he play?**

8   Which team was knocked out of the FA Cup in the fourth round in the mist on the sloping pitch of Southern League Yeovil?

9   **Which future manager of Queens Park Rangers was the only Yeovil player in this match with League experience?**

10   Who beat Yeovil 8-0 in the FA Cup fifth round?

11   **Who scored five of their goals?**

12   Which Newcastle United legend scored on his debut for England in their 3-1 defeat against Scotland at Wembley?

13   **Rangers won the Scottish Championship, but who was the First Division's leading scorer, with 30 goals for runners-up Dundee?**

14   Rangers also won the Scottish FA Cup: who did they beat in the Final?

15   **Rangers completed the treble by winning the League Cup – who did they beat in the Final of this competition?**

1 **Portsmouth** 2 Bob Jackson 3 **Manchester United** 4 Leicester City 5 **Don Revie** 6 Jesse Pye 7 **Bolton Wanderers** 8 Sunderland 9 Alec Stock 10 Manchester United 11 **Jack Rowley** 12 Jackie Milburn 13 **Alec Stott** 14 Clyde 15 **Raith Rovers**

 Quiz 40   **Season 1949-1950**

1 Portsmouth won the League Championship on goal average ahead of which Midlands club?

2 Name the First Division's leading scorer, who netted 25 times for third- placed Sunderland

3 Who, famously, ignored the Arsenal captain's instruction to stay back, went up for a corner and headed the equaliser in their FA Cup semi-final against Chelsea?

4 Who was the Arsenal captain and 1950 Football Writers' Player of the Year?

5 Who scored both goals for Arsenal in their 2-0 FA Cup Final win over Liverpool?

6 Which great England Test cricketer won a Cup winner's medal in this match?

7 Who was manager of Liverpool?

8 Which London team on the verge of greater things won the Second Division Championship?

9 Who became the youngest player to win a cap for Wales when he played against Northern Ireland aged 18 years 71 days?

10 Who was captain of the Republic of Ireland team that beat England for the first time away at Goodison Park?

11 Which Scottish team won its first major honour, winning the League Cup, a trophy they were to retain the following year?

12 Which Heart of Midlothian player was Scotland's leading scorer, with 30 goals?

13 Which Chelsea player scored England's goal in their 1-0 Home International victory over Scotland at Hampden?

14 Which of the Home nations qualified for the World Cup Finals in Brazil?

15 Which of the Home nations actually took part?

Quiz 41

Season 1950-1951

1   **What was the name given to the style of play that brought Tottenham Hotspur the League Championship for the first time in their history?**

2   Who was Spurs' manager?

3   **Which future Spurs manager played for them at right-half?**

4   Which future Ipswich and England manager played for them at right back?

5   **Who were runners-up in the First Division?**

6   Who became the oldest player to make his England debut, appearing in the match against Wales at the age of 38 years and 2 months?

7   **What was the surname of Alec and David, the father and son who played together for Stockport County in their 2-0 Division Three (North) defeat of Hartlepool on the last day of the season?**

8   Who won the FA Cup, beating Blackpool 2-0 in the Final?

9   **Who scored both goals in the Final (and had also scored in every previous round that season)?**

10 Which team of Oxbridge graduates won the FA Amateur Cup, beating Bishop Auckland 2-1 in the Final in front of 100,000 at Wembley?

11 **Which Lancashire team won the Second Division Championship two years after relegation from the top flight?**

12 In the match against Scotland at Wembley, which England player had to go off after a clash of heads with Billy Liddell?

13 **What was the final score in this match?**

14 Who won the Scottish Championship, finishing 10 points ahead of second placed Rangers?

15 **Who won the Scottish League Cup and were runners-up to Celtic in the FA Cup?**

Quiz 42

Season 1951-1952

1. **Who won the Championship for the first time in 41 years after finishing second four times since the War?**

2. Which was the first English club to install floodlights? (They played their first game under them this season – a 6-1 victory over Hapeol of Tel Aviv.)

3. **In the FA Cup Final, Newcastle United beat Arsenal 1-0. What were the names of the opposing captains, who had served together in the Army during the War?**

4. Which Chilean scored the winning goal in the Cup Final, to add to the 33 which had made him the League's top scorer?

5. **Who was the Newcastle United manager who told his defeated opponents: 'We have won the Cup, but the glory is yours'?**

6. Who scored 46 goals in 32 games as Sheffield Wednesday won the Second Division title?

7. **Whose record for the number of England caps did Billy Wright of Wolverhampton Wanderers break when he made his 42nd international appearance against Austria in Vienna?**

8. How many caps did Wright eventually win altogether?

9. **Who scored two of England's goals in their 3-2 victory in this international match?**

10. Which Sheffield Wednesday player scored the other goal?

11. **What had been the score in that season's previous meeting between England and Austria at Wembley?**

12. What nickname did the press give to Austrian centre half Ernst Ocwirk?

13. **Which member of the so-called 'Famous Five' was Scotland's leading scorer, with 27 goals for champions Hibernian?**

14. Who won the Scottish FA Cup for the first time in their history?

15. **Which of the Home Nations celebrated its centenary by beating the Rest of the UK 3-2?**

 **Quiz 43**　　　**Season 1952-1953**

1   **Which manager led Arsenal to their seventh Championship (then a record)?**

2   Which Lancashire team did they edge out at the last on goal average?

3   **The runners-up had the First Division's leading scorer, with 24 goals. Name him.**

4   Which goalkeeper retired at the age of 43 after serving Everton since 1929 – the longest ever career (24 years) with a single club?

5   **By what name will this season's FA Cup Final forever be known?**

6   Which teams played in it, and what was the result?

7   **In this match, who became the first man ever to score a hat-trick in the FA Cup Final?**

8   Who scored the last goal in this match and became the first South African to win an FA Cup winners' medal?

9   **Who scored in every round of the FA Cup, including the Final?**

10   Which First Division team conceded three own goals at home on Boxing Day in a 5-4 defeat by West Bromwich Albion?

11   **The career of which rising Sheffield Wednesday star was cruelly ended at the age of 23 when he had to have a leg amputated after challenging the opposition goalkeeper in a League game against Preston North End?**

12   Rangers did the double in Scotland, but won the League only on goal average. Who were runners-up?

13   **And who did Rangers beat in the FA Cup Final after a replay?**

14   Who won the Scottish League Cup, beating Kilmarnock 2-0 in the Final?

15   **The Scottish First Division had joint top scorers, both with 30 goals in the season. One was Lawrie Reilly of Hibernian. Who was the other?**

---

1 **Tom Whittaker** 2 Preston North End 3 **Charlie Wayman** 4 Ted Sagar 5 **The Matthews Final** 6 Blackpool 4 Bolton Wanderers 3 7 **Stan Mortensen (Blackpool)** 8 Bill Perry 9 **Nat Lofthouse (Bolton Wanderers)** 10 Sheffield Wednesday 11 **Derek Dooley** 12 Hibernian 13 Aberdeen 14 Dundee 15 **Charlie Fleming (East Fife)**

 **Quiz 44**   **Season 1953-1954**

1 **Wolverhampton Wanderers won the League Championship for the first time. What name was given to their style of play?**

2 Who was manager of Wolves?

3 **The defeat of which two European clubs in friendly matches led the Wolves manager to claim that his team were 'Champions of the World'?**

4 Which competition is believed to have been set up as a result of this hype?

5 **Which other Midlands team were runners-up in the League?**

6 Who was the League's leading scorer, with 29 goals in the season for third-placed Huddersfield Town?

7 **Which Lancashire team were relegated after finishing bottom of the First Division and did not return until 1962?**

8 Which Third Division (North) team created records by conceding the fewest goals ever (21) in a season, keeping the greatest number of clean sheets (30), and suffering the fewest defeats (three)?

9 **Who achieved the unique feat of winning a Cup winners' medal in three countries when he played for Derry City in Northern Ireland after winning the Scottish Cup with Celtic in 1937 and the English FA Cup with Manchester United in 1948?**

10 What was the score in the historic game in which Hungary inflicted the first defeat ever suffered by England against overseas opposition at Wembley?

11 **Which Hungarian scored a hat-trick in this match?**

12 What was the score in the return fixture in Budapest six months later?

13 **Who scored two goals in both games?**

14 Who did West Bromwich Albion beat 3-2 in the Final of the FA Cup?

15 **In Scotland, Celtic won the League and the FA Cup. Who won the League Cup, beating Partick Thistle 3-2 in the Final?**

1 **Kick and rush** 2 Stan Cullis 3 **Spartak Moscow (USSR)** and Honved **(Hungary)**
4 The European Cup 5 **West Bromwich Albion** 6 Jimmy Glazzard 7 **Liverpool**
8 Port Vale 9 **Jimmy Delaney** 10 England 3 Hungary 6 11 **Nandor Hidegkuti**
12 Hungary 7 England 1 13 **Ferenc Puskas** 14 Preston North End 15 **East Fife**

Quiz 45

Season 1954-1955

1 **Chelsea won the League Championship for the only time in their history. Who was their manager?**

2 Who beat them 6-5 on their own pitch?

3 **Which Chelsea amateur scored a hat-trick in this match?**

4 Which West Bromwich Albion forward was the First Division's leading scorer, with 27 goals?

5 **Which three teams tied on 54 points at the top of the Second Division?**

6 Who set a Second Division scoring record, with seven goals in Blackburn Rovers' 8-3 victory over Bristol Rovers?

7 **Which Third Division side reached the semi-final of the FA Cup?**

8 Who won the FA Cup, beating Manchester City 3-1 in the Final?

9 **Who scored the first goal after only 45 seconds?**

10 Which future Cup-winning manager of Sunderland played a blinder in the winners' defence?

11 **Who won the Scottish League Championship for the first time in their history?**

12 Who won the Scottish FA Cup, beating Celtic 1-0 in a replay after the first match had been drawn 1-1?

13 **Heart of Midlothian won the League Cup, beating Motherwell 4-0 in the Final. Who was their leading scorer, with 21 goals?**

14 In the Home International Championship, Scotland lost to England by a record score of 7-2. Which Wolverhampton Wanderers forward scored four of the England goals?

15 **In which year had Scotland beaten England by the same score?**

1 **Ted Drake** 2 Manchester United 3 **Seamus O'Connell** 4 Ronnie Allen 5 **Birmingham City, Luton Town and Rotherham United** 6 Tommy Briggs 7 **York City** 8 Newcastle United 9 **Jackie Milburn** 10 Bob Stokoe 11 **Aberdeen** 12 Clyde 13 **Willie Bauld** 14 Dennis Wilshaw

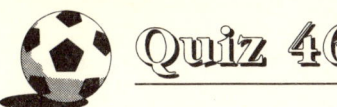 ## Quiz 46   **Season 1955-1956**

1 **Name the Manchester City goalkeeper who broke his neck in the FA Cup Final but played on and collected a winner's medal.**

2 Who were their opponents in the Final?

3 **Which future England manager played at centre forward for City?**

4 Who was the leading scorer in the First Division, with 32 goals for Bolton Wanderers?

5 **Who won the first ever European Cup, the first of five consecutive victories in this tournament?**

6 Which French team did they beat 4-3 in the Final in Paris?

7 **Who scored a hat-trick for the winning side?**

8 What was his nationality?

9 **Who were Britain's sole representatives in the competition?**

10 Who scored a hat-trick in England's 4-2 victory over Brazil at Wembley?

11 **What was historic about the First Division match between Portsmouth and Newcastle United at Fratton Park on February 22, 1956?**

12 Who won the First Division by a record margin, finishing 11 points ahead of the runners-up?

13 **Who came second and third, both with 49 points?**

14 Who beat Celtic 3-1 in the Scottish FA Cup Final?

15 **Who won the Scottish League Cup, beating St Mirren 2-1 in the Final?**

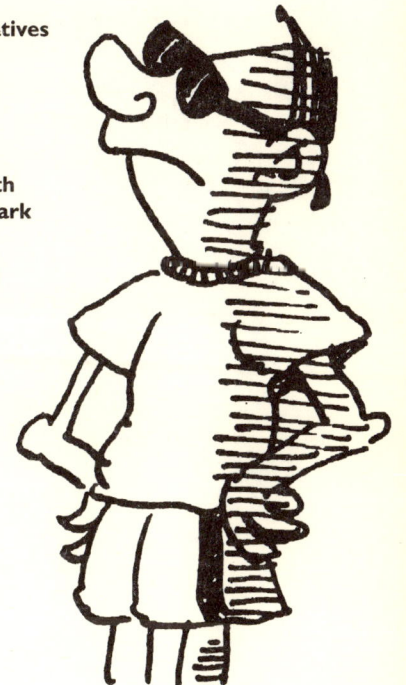

Quiz 47

Season 1956-1957

1 **Which Leeds United forward was the First Division's leading scorer, with 38 goals?**

2 Manchester United won the League Championship, but who denied them the double by beating them 2-1 in the Final of the FA Cup?

3 **Who was the winning team's manager?**

4 Name the United goalkeeper who had to go off with concussion, returning later to play on the wing.

5 **Who took his place in the Manchester goal?**

6 Who scored United's goal?

7 **Who was the Manchester United captain?**

8 Which Third Division (South) club knocked Wolverhampton Wanderers out of the FA Cup in the 4th round?

9 **Who scored the only goal of this game?**

10 Which First Division opponents did the same team knock out in the 5th round of the 1957 FA Cup?

11 **Which team won the Second Division Championship for the second time in three years?**

12 Which great Englishman became the first European Footballer of the Year?

13 **Who knocked Manchester United out of the European Cup?**

14 In Scotland, Rangers won the League Championship – who won the FA Cup, beating Kilmarnock 2-1 in a replay after the first game had been drawn 1-1?

15 **Scotland's leading scorer was Hugh Baird, with 33 goals. Which team did he play for?**

1 John Charles 2 Aston Villa 3 Eric Houghton 4 Ray Wood 5 Jackie Blanchflower 6 Tommy Taylor 7 Roger Byrne 8 Reg Cutler 9 Bournemouth 10 Tottenham Hotspur 11 Leicester City 12 Stanley Matthews (Blackpool) 13 Real Madrid 14 Falkirk 15 Airdrieonians

 **Quiz 48** **Season 1957-1958**

1 **Who won the English League Championship?**

2 Which team was relegated from the English First Division for the first time since 1890?

3 **Who were Champions of the Second Division?**

4 Which Tottenham Hotspur player was the First Division's leading scorer, with 36 goals?

5 **Name the eight Manchester United first team members who were killed in the Munich air crash on February 6.**

6 Manchester United were returning from a European Cup match against the Champions of Yugoslavia – who were they?

7 **Despite the tragedy, Manchester United reached the Final of the FA Cup. Which four survivors played at Wembley?**

8 They lost 2-0 to Bolton Wanderers. Who scored both the goals?

9 **Which Welsh international was the leading scorer in the Italian League, with 28 goals in 34 games for Juventus?**

10 In the last season of the Third Division North and South, who won their respective sections?

11 **Who beat Rangers 7-1 in the Final of the Scottish League Cup?**

12 Who won the Scottish League Championship for the first time in the 20th century, scoring a record number of goals (132) in the process?

13 **With 28 goals apiece, the joint top scorers both played for the Champions. What were their names?**

14 Who won the Scottish FA Cup for the third time, beating Hibernian 1-0 in the Final?

15 **Barcelona won the first Inter-Cities Fairs Cup. Who did they beat 8-2 on aggregate in the Final?**

---

1 Wolverhampton Wanderers 2 Sunderland 3 West Ham United 4 Bobby Smith 5 Roger Byrne, Geoff Bent, Eddie Colman, Duncan Edwards, Mark Jones, David Pegg, Tommy Taylor, Billy Whelan 6 Red Star Belgrade 7 Bobby Charlton, Harry Gregg, Bill Foulkes and Dennis Viollet 8 Nat Lofthouse 9 John Charles 10 Scunthorpe United and Brighton and Hove Albion 11 Celtic 12 Heart of Midlothian 13 Jimmy Murray and Jimmy Wardhaugh 14 Clyde 15 A combined team called London

Quiz 49

Season 1958-1959

1   Who became Scotland's youngest international, winning his first cap at the age of 18 years 236 days?

2   Who was he then playing for?

3   Who won the English League Championship, for the third time in five years?

4   Which Chelsea and England star was the First Division's leading scorer, with 32 goals?

5   Who won the English FA Cup, having won it once before in 1898?

6   Who were the runners-up?

7   Which future manager of Northern Ireland was on the losing side?

8   Who scored the opening goal and then broke his leg in the 32nd minute?

9   Which Third Division side reached the semi-final?

10   With 42 goals, which MIddlesbrough centre forward was the Second Division's leading scorer for the second season running?

11   In Scotland, Rangers won the League Championship. Who won the FA Cup for the second time in their history?

12   Who did Heart of Midlothian beat 5-1 in the Scottish League Cup Final?

13   Who, on April 11, became the first player to win 100 England caps in a match against Scotland at Wembley?

14   England won this game 1-0. Who scored the goal?

15   Which former Tottenham Hotspur player became the manager of the club, in succession to Jimmy Anderson?

1 Denis Law 2 Huddersfield Town 3 **Wolverhampton Wanderers** 4 Jimmy Greaves
5 **Nottingham Forest** 6 Luton Town 7 **Billy Bingham** 8 Roy Dwight (Nottingham Forest)
9 **Norwich City** 10 Brian Clough 11 **St Mirren** 12 Partick Thistle 13 **Billy Wright**
(**Wolverhampton Wanderers**) 14 Bobby Charlton (Manchester United) 15 Bill Nicholson

 **Quiz 50**   Season 1959-1960

1 **Which player scored all the goals in the English Football League's 5-0 defeat of the Irish League in Belfast?**

2 Which Midlands First Division club became the first to score 100 goals in three consecutive seasons?

3 **Which emerging player – later a Liverpool star – scored a hat-trick in less than three minutes for Motherwell in a Scottish League Cup tie against Hibernian?**

4 Against which Cheshire club did Tottenham Hotspur record their highest-ever victory – 13-2 – in an FA Cup 4th round replay?

5 **Who were their four scorers?**

6 The European Cup Final between Real Madrid and Eintracht Frankfurt led to a record result. What was the score?

7 **And there was also a record attendance – 135,000. Where was the match played?**

8 Which Lancashire club won the League Championship for the second time in their history?

9 **When had they previously won it?**

10 Which Manchester United player was the First Division's leading scorer, with 32 goals?

11 **Who won the FA Cup, beating Blackburn Rovers 3-0 in the Final?**

12 Who won the first European Nations Cup, beating Yugoslavia 2-1 in the Final in Paris?

13 **In Scotland, which team did the League and League Cup double?**

14 Who was their leading scorer, with 42 goals?

15 **Which Real Madrid star was European Footballer of the Year?**

CARLING 10,000 FOOTBALL FACTS & QUESTIONS

Quiz 51

Season 1960-1961

1 **Tottenham Hotspur did the double for the first time this century. Which two clubs had previously done it?**

2 Jimmy Greaves was the First Division's leading scorer, with 41 goals for Chelsea. To which Italian club was he soon to move?

3 **Which Yorkshire team were runners-up to Spurs in the League?**

4 Which East Midlands team were runners-up to Spurs in the FA Cup?

5 **Which Midlands team were the first winners of the new League Cup competition?**

6 Which five leading clubs declined to take part in the inaugural League Cup?

7 **Who won the Fourth Division Championship in their first season in the League?**

8 Who became England's first £100-a-week footballer?

9 **Real Madrid – who had won the European Cup in each of the five years it had been contested – finally lost a tie. Who beat them?**

10 Who knocked English Champions Burnley out of the European Cup in the quarter-final?

11 **Who was Burnley's manager?**

12 Which Italian team beat Birmingham City 4-2 on aggregate in the Final of the Inter-Cities Fairs Cup?

13 **With 42 goals, the leading scorer in the Scottish First Division was Alex Harley, who played for a club which, by 1967, had ceased to exist. Which club?**

14 Who won the Scottish FA Cup for the first time in their history, beating Celtic 2-0 in a replay after the first game had been drawn 0-0?

15 **Meanwhile, the Scottish League and League Cup were both won by a Rangers team inspired by recent signing Jim Baxter. Where had he been bought from?**

---

1 Preston North End and Aston Villa 2 AC Milan 3 Sheffield Wednesday 4 Leicester City 5 Aston Villa 6 Arsenal, Sheffield Wednesday, Tottenham Hotspur, West Bromwich Albion and Wolverhampton Wanderers 7 Peterborough United 8 Johnny Haynes (Fulham and England) 9 Barcelona 10 FC Hamburg 11 Harry Potts 12 AS Roma 13 Third Lanark 14 Dunfermline Athletic 15 Raith Rovers

Quiz 52

Season by Season

1 Which prolific scorer and manager of the future moved from Middlesbrough to Sunderland for £45,000?

2 Which team resigned from the Football League on March 6 because of financial problems?

3 Which team would replace them in the Fourth Division, with effect from the start of the 1962-63 season?

4 Who won the League Championship only a year after being promoted from the Second Division?

5 Who was their – and the First Division's – leading scorer, with 33 goals in the season?

6 Tottenham Hotspur only just failed to repeat their feats of the previous season – they slipped to third in the League, but had the consolation of retaining the FA Cup. Which Lancashire team did they beat 3-1 in the Final?

7 And where had the Cup runners-up finished in the League?

8 How far did Tottenham go in the European Cup?

9 Who knocked them out of the competition?

10 Which foreign-based Hungarian scored a hat-trick in the 1962 European Cup Final?

11 Who won the European Cup Winners' Cup Final, beating Fiorentina 3-0 in a replay after the first game had been drawn 1-1?

12 Which Fourth Division Lancashire team did Norwich City beat 4-0 on aggregate to win the League Cup?

13 Who won the Scottish League Championship for the first time in their history?

14 Who was their – and Scotland's – leading scorer, with 24 goals?

15 Which member of this Championship-winning side went on to greater fame with Arsenal?

 # Quiz 53   Season 1962-1963

1   **Who did Manchester United bring back to Britain from Torino for a record fee of £115,000?**

2   Who, with 37 goals, was the First Division's leading scorer, a position he would occupy the following season and the season after that?

3   **Who won the League Championship for the sixth time but the first time since 1939?**

4   Who was their manager?

5   **Manchester United won the FA Cup. Which club were runners-up for the third time in their history?**

6   Whose legal action against Newcastle United led to the end of the fixed wage for footballers?

7   **Tottenham Hotspur became the first British side to win a European trophy when they beat Atletico Madrid 5-1 in the Cup Winners' Cup Final in Rotterdam. Name any of the three Spurs scorers**

8   Who did Alf Ramsey succeed as England manager?

9   **Who was Ramsey's first new cap?**

10   What was the result of his first game in charge, against France in Paris in the European Nations Cup?

11   **Who won the League Cup, their first major honour, beating Aston Villa 3-1 on aggregate in the Final?**

12   The European Cup Final was held at Wembley for the first time. Who did AC Milan beat 2-1 in this match?

13   **Who won the Second Division Championship?**

14   Which 48-year-old scored his first goal of the season in the game in which they clinched the Second Division title?

15   **In Scotland, Rangers won the League Championship and the FA Cup. Who won the League Cup?**

---

1 **Denis Law** 2 Jimmy Greaves (Tottenham Hotspur) 3 **Everton** 4 Harry Catterick 5 **Leicester City** 6 George Eastham 7 **Jimmy Greaves (2), John White and Terry Dyson** (2) 8 Walter Winterbottom 9 **Ron Henry (Tottenham Hotspur)** 10 5-2 to France 11 **Birmingham City** 12 Benfica 13 **Stoke City** 14 Stanley Matthews 15 Heart of Midlothian

Quiz 54

Season 1963-1964

1 **Who did West Ham United beat 3-2 in the Final to win the FA Cup for the first time in their history?**

2 Who scored the West Ham goals?

3 **Who, at 17 years 345 days, became the youngest player to appear in an FA Cup Final?**

4 The previous Boxing Day, West Ham United had suffered their record defeat, 8-2 at home to which Lancashire club?

5 **Apart from the score, what was unusual about the Home International in which England beat Northern Ireland 8-3?**

6 Which Lancashire team won the First Division Championship?

7 **Which Yorkshire team won the Second Division Championship, heralding the dawn of an era?**

8 Who became the first Fourth Division side to reach the 6th round of the FA Cup?

9 **Which Bradford Park Avenue player scored the fastest first class goal on record, timed at four seconds after the kick-off, against Tranmere Rovers?**

10 Which Tottenham Hotspur and Northern Ireland star announced his retirement after failing to overcome a persistent knee injury?

11 **Who did Spurs manager Bill Nicholson buy from Fulham for £72,500 to replace him?**

12 What was unusual about the Finals of the Inter-Cities Fairs Cup in both this and the following year?

13 **What was unusual about the European Cup Winners' Cup Final between Sporting Lisbon and MTK Budapest?**

14 Which great goalkeeper was voted European Footballer of the Year?

15 **Which future Tottenham Hotspur star was top scorer in the Scottish First Division, with 32 goals for Dundee?**

---

1 **Preston North End** 2 John Sissons, Geoff Hurst and Ron Boyce 3 **Preston's Howard Kendall** 4 Blackburn Rovers 5 **It was the first game at Wembley to be played under floodlights** 6 Liverpool 7 **Leeds United** 8 Oxford United 9 **Jim Fryatt** 10 Danny Blanchflower 11 **Alan Mullery** 12 They were one-off matches, rather than two-legged affairs 13 **It was the first of these Finals to go to a replay** 14 Lev Yashin (Dynamo Moscow and USSR) 15 Alan Gilzean

Quiz 55   Season 1964-1965

1 **Who won their first Scottish League title, beating Heart of Midlothian 2-0 in the last match of the season and thus edging the Edinburgh side into second place on goal average?**

2 Name the highest British goalscorer of all time, with 434 League goals in his career, who retired this year after spending his last season as player-manager of Shrewsbury Town.

3 **There were joint top scorers in the English First Division, both with 29 goals. One was Jimmy Greaves (Tottenham Hotspur); the other played for Blackburn Rovers – name him.**

4 Who won the 1965 League Championship?

5 **Who won the FA Cup?**

6 Who scored their goals in their 2-1 Final victory?

7 **Who were runners-up in both the League and the FA Cup?**

8 Who became the first footballer to be knighted?

9 **How old was he when he played his last match?**

10 West Ham United won the European Cup Winners' Cup. Who did they beat 2-0 in the Final at Wembley?

11 **Who scored both goals?**

12 Which Tottenham Hotspur and Scotland international was killed at the age of 27 after being struck by lightning while playing golf?

13 **Name the England international who retired this year after making a record number of League appearances – 764 – for his only club, Portsmouth.**

14 Which Manchester United and Scotland star was voted European Footballer of the Year?

15 **Which Rangers player was the leading goalscorer in the Scottish First Division?**

Quiz 56

Season 1965-1966

1 On the opening day of the season, who became the first ever substitute in an English League match, when he came on for Charlton Athletic against Bolton Wanderers in Division Two?

2 On December 4, 1965, who became the first Tottenham Hotspur player to be sent off since October 27, 1928?

3 Liverpool won the League Championship. Who was their leading scorer – for the fifth year running – with 30 goals?

4 Everton won the FA Cup, beating Sheffield Wednesday 3-2 in the Final. Who scored the Toffeemen's goals?

5 And who scored for Wednesday?

6 Which former Wolverhampton Wanderers and England star left Arsenal, where he had been manager for four years?

7 In the last two-legged League Cup Final, which London team did West Bromwich Albion beat 5-3 on aggregate?

8 Whose record did Liverpool equal when they won their seventh English League title?

9 Who was the Liverpool captain?

10 Who beat Liverpool 2-1 after extra time in the Final of the European Cup Winners' Cup?

11 Who did Real Madrid beat 2-1 in the Final to win the European Cup for the sixth time in its 11-year history?

12 Which two Spanish teams contested the Final of the Inter-Cities Fairs Cup?

13 Which two English teams had they knocked out in the semi-finals?

14 There were joint top scorers in the Scottish First Division, both with 31 goals in the season. One played for Celtic, the other for Dunfermline Athletic. Name either.

15 Who was voted European Footballer of the Year, even before his outstanding contribution to the 1966 World Cup?

1 Keith Peacock 2 Frank Saul 3 Roger Hunt 4 Mike Trebilcock (2) and Derek Temple
5 Jim McCalliog and Dave Ford 6 Billy Wright 7 West Ham United 8 Arsenal
9 Ron Yeats 10 Borussia Dortmund 11 Partizan Belgrade 12 Barcelona and Real Zaragoza
13 Chelsea and Leeds United 14 Joe McBride and Alex Ferguson 15 Eusebio

 ## Quiz 57 Season 1966-1967

1 Which Third Division side won the League Cup in the first year the Final was held at Wembley?

2 Which First Division side did they beat?

3 Who scored the three goals that brought them victory after going 2-0 down?

4 Who was their manager?

5 Who sensationally knocked Rangers out of the Scottish FA Cup in the first round?

6 Who was the manager of Celtic, who won the European Cup, the Scottish League Championship, the FA Cup, the League Cup and the Glasgow Cup?

7 Who won the English First Division Championship?

8 Who was the leading scorer in the First Division, with 37 goals for 19th-placed Southampton?

9 Tottenham Hotspur beat Chelsea 2-1 in the first all-London FA Cup Final. Who scored the goals?

10 Who were the only two survivors of Tottenham's previous Cup-winning side in 1962?

11 Who became the first 6-figure British footballer when he moved from Blackpool to Everton for £110,000 in August 1966?

12 Where in the First Division table did Blackpool finish the season?

13 Which German club beat Rangers 1-0 after extra time in the Final of the European Cup Winners' Cup?

14 Who won the Second Division Championship and promotion to the top flight for the first time in their history?

15 Who became the first country to beat England after their World Cup triumph?

1 Queens Park Rangers 2 West Bromwich Albion 3 Roger Morgan, Rodney Marsh and Mark Lazarus 4 Alec Stock 5 Berwick Rangers 6 Jock Stein 7 Manchester United 8 Ron Davies 9 Jimmy Robertson and Frank Saul for Spurs, Bobby Tambling for Chelsea 10 Jimmy Greaves and Dave Mackay 11 Alan Ball 12 Bottom 13 Bayern Munich 14 Coventry City 15 Scotland

 **Quiz 58**   **Season 1967-1968**

1 **From which club did Tottenham Hotspur buy Martin Chivers, for a British record fee of £125,000?**

2 Manchester City won their second League Championship. When had they previously won it?

3 **They were managed by Joe Mercer and coached by Malcolm Allison. Who was their captain?**

4 Who won the FA Cup, beating Everton 1-0 in extra time in the Final?

5 **The First Division had joint leading scorers, with 28 goals apiece. One was George Best of Manchester United. The other played for Southampton – name him.**

6 In the semi-final of the European Championships in Italy, who became the first English player ever to be sent off in a full international?

7 **Manchester United won the European Cup, beating Benfica 4-1 after extra time in the Final. Who scored United's goals?**

8 And who equalised for Benfica late in the second half of normal time?

9 **Who was the leading scorer in Scotland, with 32 goals for Celtic?**

10 How many Celtic players were sent off in the third, play-off, match for the World Club Championship against Racing Club (Argentina) in Montevideo?

11 **Leeds United won the Inter-Cities Fairs Cup – which Hungarian side did they beat 1-0 on aggregate in the Final?**

12 Name the 1967 European Footballer of the Year who played for the Hungarians in this match.

13 **Who overtook Jimmy Greaves as England's all-time leading scorer when he netted his 45th international goal in the 3-1 victory over Sweden at Wembley on May 22?**

14 Which British team reached the semi-final of the Cup Winners' Cup, losing 4-3 on aggregate to SV Hamburg?

15 **Who was their manager?**

Quiz 59

Season 1968-1969

1 **Which Scottish team knocked West Bromwich Albion out in the quarter-final of the European Cup Winners' Cup?**

2 They themselves lost in the semi-final to the Czech club that went on to win the competition. Who?

3 **Tommy Docherty managed three clubs in six weeks. Which three?**

4 When they were relegated from the Third Division, which team had gone full circle – from Fourth to First and back to Fourth again – in nine years?

5 **Who won the League Championship for the first time?**

6 Who was their leading scorer, with only 14 League goals?

7 **Who was the First Division's leading scorer, with 27 goals for Tottenham Hotspur?**

8 Which English team won the Inter-Cities Fairs Cup?

9 **Which Hungarian team did they beat 3-0 and 3-2 in the Final?**

10 Who scored the winner in Manchester City's 1-0 FA Cup Final victory over Leicester City?

11 **What other blow did Leicester suffer in the same season?**

12 Third Division Swindon Town won the League Cup, beating Arsenal 3-1 in the Final. Who scored two of the goals?

13 **Who won the Second Division Championship and went quickly on to much higher things?**

14 Who took over from Sir Matt Busby when he retired as manager of Manchester United?

15 **Who scored six goals in West Ham United's record 8-0 victory in a First Division match against Sunderland on October 19?**

1 **Dunfermline Athletic** 2 Slovan Bratislava 3 Rotherham United, Queens Park Rangers **and Aston Villa** 4 Northampton Town 5 **Leeds United** 6 Mick Jones 7 **Jimmy Greaves** 8 Newcastle United 9 **Ujpest Dozsa** 10 Neil Young 11 **Relegation from the First Division** 12 Don Rogers 13 **Derby County** 14 Wilf McGuinness 15 **Geoff Hurst**

 **Quiz 60**   **Season 1969-1970**

1   **Who scored on his 100th international appearance for England in a 3-1 Home International victory over Northern Ireland?**

2   Cambridge United were elected members of the Football League. Which Yorkshire team went out to make room for them?

3   **Which World Cup star – not a Briton – scored his 1000th goal in first-class football?**

4   Which World Cup star did Tottenham Hotspur buy from West Ham United?

5   **Which great international player went in the other direction as part of the deal?**

6   On his return from a month's suspension, George Best scored six goals for Manchester United in their 8-2 FA Cup 5th round victory over who?

7   **Who knocked Leeds United out in the semi-final of the 1970 European Cup?**

8   Who then beat them in the Final?

9   **What was historic about the FA Cup Final between Chelsea and Leeds United?**

10 Who eventually scored the winner for Chelsea?

11 **The two FA Cup Finalists came second and third in the First Division. Who were the Champions?**

12 Who scored two goals for Aberdeen in their shock 3-1 victory over Celtic in the Scottish FA Cup Final?

13 **Which team won the Second Division championship, to the delight of Prime Minister Harold Wilson, their most famous fan?**

14 Who was their manager?

15 **Despite being the First Division's leading scorer with 25 goals, which West Bromwich Albion forward will forever be remembered for one he missed against Brazil later the same year?**

 **Quiz 61**   Season 1970-1971

1 **Which Fourth Division side knocked First Division leaders Leeds United out of the FA Cup in the fifth round?**

2 Rangers won their first trophy for four years when they beat Celtic 1-0 in the Final of the League Cup. Who was their goalscorer – the youngest player ever to appear in a Scottish cup final?

3 **Arsenal did the League and FA Cup double. Which was the last team to have achieved this feat?**

4 Who was the Arsenal manager?

5 **Who did Arsenal beat 2-1 in the FA Cup Final?**

6 Who won the European Cup Winners' Cup, beating Real Madrid 2-1 in a replay after the first match had been drawn 1-1?

7 **Which other English club had they beaten in the semi-final?**

8 Who won the Inter-Cities Fairs Cup, beating Juventus on away goals after the two legs had finished 2-2 and 1-1, in the last year before the competition's name was changed to the UEFA Cup?

9 **Why was the first leg of the Inter-Cities Fairs Cup Final against Juventus abandoned?**

10 Which other English club had the victors beaten in the semi-final?

11 **Which other English club reached the quarter-Finals of the same competition?**

12 Which two founder members of the Football League were relegated to the Third Division for the first time in their history?

13 **For the second year in succession, a West Bromwich Albion forward was the First Division's leading scorer (with 28 goals). Who was he?**

14 Who was Celtic's – and Scotland's – leading scorer, with 22 goals?

15 **Who won the European Cup, the first of three successive triumphs in this competition?**

Quiz 62　　　　　Season 1971-1972

1　**Who won the Scottish League Cup, their first trophy since 1921?**

2　Leeds United won the 100th FA Cup Final, beating Arsenal 1-0.
　　Who scored the winner?

3　**Which outfield player saved a penalty for West Ham United in the second replay of their epic League Cup semi-final with Stoke City?**

4　Stoke won that game and then beat Chelsea 2-1 in the Final, to win the first major trophy in their 109-year history. Who scored for them at Wembley?

5　**Who won the English League Championship for the first time in their history?**

6　Which midfielder did Leeds United nearly buy from West Bromwich Albion before pulling out at the last minute when a medical revealed that he had a hole in his heart?

7　**To which club did the player subsequently move?**

8　Which Manchester City player was the First Division's leading scorer, with 33 goals?

9　**Who scored eight goals for Chelsea in their 21-0 aggregate defeat of Jeunesse Hautcharage (Luxembourg) in the European Cup Winners' Cup?**

10　Which non-League side knocked Newcastle United out of the FA Cup?

11　**Who scored the goals in their 2-1 home victory after a 2-2 draw at St James' Park?**

12　Later that season, the same side won election by one vote to the Football League. Who did they replace in the Fourth Division?

13　**After their 1963 Cup Winners' Cup victory, Tottenham Hotspur became the first English club to win two different European competitions when they won the UEFA Cup. Which other English club did they beat in the Final?**

14　Which former England star, recalled from Fulham where he had been on loan, scored Spurs' goal in the second leg of the UEFA Cup Final?

15　**Which ex-Motherwell striker scored a hat trick for Celtic in their 6-1 defeat of Hibernian in the Scottish FA Cup Final?**

 **Quiz 63**   **Season 1972-1973**

1 Sunderland became the first Second Division side to win the FA Cup since who?

2 Who scored the goal in their 1-0 Final victory over Leeds United?

3 **Which Leeds player was making a record fifth appearance in the FA Cup Final?**

4 Who went down to the Third Division for the first time in their distinguished history, which included three League Championships?

5 **Who was the First Division's leading scorer, with 28 goals for sixth-placed West Ham United?**

6 Which Italian team beat Leeds United 1-0 in the European Cup Winners' Cup Final in Salonika (Greece)?

7 **Celtic won the Scottish Championship but were beaten in the Finals of both cups. By which two teams?**

8 Which great hero of the 1966 and 1970 World Cups lost the sight in his right eye in a road accident on October 22?

9 **Tottenham Hotspur goalkeeper Pat Jennings saved two penalties in a League match at Anfield. Who took them?**

10 Liverpool won both the League Championship and the UEFA Cup. Which German team did they beat in the Final of the latter competition?

11 **Kevin Keegan scored two goals in their 3-0 victory in the first leg. Which defender scored the other?**

12 Which star of the 1966 World Cup won the Golden Boot for being Europe's leading scorer with 40 goals?

13 **Which other '66 hero hung up his boots, finishing as his club's leading scorer for the season, albeit with only 6 goals?**

14 Who made his 100th international appearance for England in the game against Scotland at Hampden Park?

15 **Name one of the scorers in England's 5-0 victory in this match.**

Quiz 64

Season 1973-1974

1. **This was the first season in which promotion and relegation became three up and three down. Which was the first First Division club to be relegated after finishing 20th?**

2. And which was the first club to be promoted to the top flight after finishing third in the Second Division?

3. **Who won the Second Division Championship by 15 points, a record margin?**

4. Who became the first Welsh player to be sent off in an international match (versus Poland)?

5. **Which Third Division team reached the semi-finals of the FA Cup?**

6. Which three First Division sides had they beaten en route?

7. **What was historic about the FA Cup 3rd round match between Cambridge United and Oldham Athletic on January 6?**

8. Which Southampton player was the First Division's leading scorer?

9. **After the dismissal of Sir Alf Ramsey, who briefly became manager of England?**

10. Which East German club won the European Cup Winners' Cup?

11. **Wolverhampton Wanderers won the League Cup, beating Manchester City 2-1 at Wembley. Name one of their goalscorers.**

12. Joao Havelange became President of FIFA. Who did he succeed?

13. **Which Dutch club beat Tottenham Hotspur in the Final of the 1974 UEFA Cup?**

14. Who won the first of four successive European Cups?

15. **Celtic were Champions for the ninth year running and also won the FA Cup. Who was their – and Scotland's – leading scorer?**

1 **Southampton** 2 Carlise United 3 **Middlesbrough** 4 Trevor Hockey (Aston Villa)
5 **Plymouth Argyle** 6 Burnley, Queens Park Rangers and Birmingham City 7 **It was the first Sunday game** 8 Mick Channon 9 **Joe Mercer** 10 FC Magdeburg 11 **Ken Hibbitt and John Richards** 12 Sir Stanley Rous 13 **Feyenoord** 14 Bayern Munich 15 **Dixie Deans**

 **Quiz 65**   **Season 1974-1975**

1 After a close title race in which the leadership of the First Division changed hands 21 times, who won the Championship for the second time in four seasons?

2 Who was their leading scorer, with 15 goals in the season?

3 **Who was the First Division's leading scorer, with 21 goals for 15th-placed Newcastle United?**

4 Against which country did the same player equal Willie Hall's England record of five goals in an international match?

5 **West Ham United won the FA Cup for the second time in eleven years – which Second Division side did they beat 2-0 in the Final?**

6 Who scored two goals for West Ham in the quarter-final, the semi-final and the Final?

7 **From which Lancashire club had West Ham bought him during the winter of 1974?**

8 Who beat Leeds United 2-0 in the Final of the European Cup?

9 **In which European capital was the match played?**

10 Aston Villa won the League Cup – which Second Division club did they beat 1-0 in the Final?

11 **It was third time lucky for the Villa manager, who had previously lost in the League Cup Final with Norwich City and Manchester City – name him.**

12 In Scotland, there were joint leading scorers, both with 20 goals. One was Willie Pettigrew of Motherwell. The other was a Dundee United player who later became more famous at Aston Villa, Wolverhampton Wanderers, Everton and on Sky TV – name him.

13 **Rangers won the Scottish League Championship, bringing to an end Celtic's record run of nine titles in a row. Which Rangers player was voted Scottish Footballer of the Year?**

14 Which Soviet club won the European Cup Winners' Cup, beating Ferencvaros of Hungary 3-0 in the Final?

15 **Which great player, now with Barcelona after moving from his native country, was European Footballer of the Year?**

Quiz 66

Season 1975-1976

1 **Who scored the only goal of the FA Cup Final in which Southampton beat Manchester United?**

2 Who won both the League Championship and the UEFA Cup?

3 **Who resigned as manager of Preston North End?**

4 Who knocked English champions Derby out of the European Cup, coming back from a 4-1 first leg defeat to win the return 5-1 after extra time?

5 **Which striker did Derby sell to FC Bruges for £130,000?**

6 Who won the European Cup Winners' Cup, beating West Ham United 4-2 in the Final?

7 **Which star of the winning side later went to play for the losers?**

8 When Aston Villa drew 2-2 with Leicester City on March 20, who scored all four goals?

9 **Rangers won the Scottish League Championship, the FA Cup and the League Cup. Who was their captain?**

10 Who won the European Cup, beating St Etienne (France) 1-0 in the Final, and the World Club Championship, beating Cruzeiro (Brazil) 2-0 on aggregate?

11 **Name the goalkeeper who was the star of Czechoslovakia's victory over West Germany in the Final of the 1976 European Championship in Yugoslavia.**

12 Which Norwich City striker was the First Division's leading scorer?

13 **Name three of the seven other clubs he played for in a career that lasted from 1966 to 1980.**

14 Which Celtic striker was top scorer in the Scottish First Division, with 24 goals?

15 **Who became only the third Fourth Division club to reach the semi-finals of the English FA Cup?**

1 **Bobby Stokes** 2 Liverpool 3 **Bobby Charlton** 4 Real Madrid 5 **Roger Davies** 6 Anderlecht 7 **Francois Van der Elst** 8 Villa's Chris Nicholl 9 **John Greig** 10 Bayern Munich 11 **Igor Viktor** 12 Ted MacDougall 13 Liverpool, York City, Bournemouth, **Manchester United, West Ham United, Southampton, Blackpool** 14 Kenny Dalglish 15 **Bradford City**

Quiz 67

Season 1976-1977

1　**What new accessories did referees show for the first time?**

2　Who joined Second Division Fulham and scored within two minutes of making his debut?

3　**Who played his 1000th League game and then retired on May 14?**

4　Which Southampton, Hereford United and England winger retired after a record 824 League appearances?

5　**Which Southern League team was elected to the Football League?**

6　Who did they replace in the Fourth Division?

7　**What did Wales do on May 31 for the first time in their history?**

8　Who awarded himself his 48th Republic of Ireland cap on March 30?

9　**League Champions Liverpool won the European Cup for the first time. Who did they beat in the Final in Rome?**

10　The final score in this match was 3-1 – who netted for Liverpool?

11　**The English First Division had joint top scorers, both with 25 goals. One played for Arsenal, the other for Aston Villa – name them.**

12　Aston Villa eventually won the League Cup after extra time in the second replay. Who were the runners-up?

13　**Who did the double in Scotland?**

14　Who denied them a clean sweep by beating them 2-1 after extra time in the Scottish League Cup Final?

15　**Who became the first player ever to win Cup medals with both Celtic and Rangers?**

11 Malcolm Macdonald and Andy Gray 12 Everton **13 Celtic** 14 Aberdeen **15 Alfie Conn**
Moenchengladbach 10 Terry McDermott, Tommy Smith, Phil Neal (penalty)
6 Workington Town **7 Beat England at Wembley** 8 Player manager Johnny Giles **9 Borussia**
1 Red and yellow cards 2 George Best **3 Bobby Moore** 4 Terry Paine **5 Wimbledon**

 **Quiz 68**   **Season 1977-1978**

1 How much did Liverpool pay Celtic when they bought Kenny Dalglish on August 10?

2 Don Revie quit as England manager to coach which Middle Eastern country?

3 Scotland qualified for the World Cup Finals in Argentina by beating Wales 2-0 in the last group match. The game was played on neutral territory – where?

4 Scotland's first goal in this match was scored by Don Masson from the penalty spot after the referee thought he saw a Welsh player handle the ball, but television replays revealed that it was really a Scot – who?

5 Nottingham Forest won the English Championship in their first season back in the First Division. Which of their players – ex-Birmingham City and widely regarded as a wild man – was voted PFA Player of the Year?

6 Which club finished in the bottom four of the Fourth Division, thus having to apply for re-election only two seasons after having been in the Second Division?

7 How many Liverpool players were in the England team that faced Switzerland in Ron Greenwood's first match in charge of the national side?

8 Which non-league club reached the fifth round of the FA Cup?

9 Ipswich Town won the FA Cup, beating hot favourites Arsenal 1-0 in the Final. Who scored the goal?

10 Liverpool retained the European Cup, beating FC Bruges 1-0. Who scored the winner?

11 Nottingham Forest also won the League Cup, beating Liverpool 1-0 in the replayed Final after the first match had been drawn 0-0. Which future England international kept goal for Forest?

12 Which established international goalkeeper did he replace, and why?

13 European Footballer of the Year was Allan Simonsen, of Borussia Moenchengladbach and Denmark. For which English team did he subsequently play?

14 Which Everton player, formerly with Birmingham City, was the First Division's leading scorer?

15 In Scotland, Rangers did the treble (League, FA Cup and League Cup). Who was their leading scorer, with 25 goals?

CARLING 10,000 FOOTBALL FACTS & QUESTIONS

Quiz 69

Season 1978-1979

1 Which two members of Argentina's World Cup-winning squad did Tottenham Hotspur manager Steve Burkinshaw buy only 15 days after the Final?

2 Which other member of the Argentina team later went to Birmingham City?

3 Who became Britain's first £1 million player, when he went from Birmingham City to Nottingham Forest?

4 The First Division's leading scorer was Frank Worthington. For which of his 11 League clubs was he then playing?

5 Who was banned from football for 10 years for bringing the game into disrepute in 1977?

6 Who scored Arsenal's winner in their 3-2 FA Cup Final victory over Manchester United?

7 Who knocked Liverpool out of the 1979 European Cup in the second round?

8 Who scored Nottingham Forest's winner in their 1-0 European Cup Final victory over Malmo?

9 Who was the Forest captain?

10 On November 29, which Forest player became the first black footballer to win a full England cap in the game against Czechoslovakia at Wembley?

11 Which team began their rise to prominence by winning promotion from the Fourth Division for the first time in their history?

12 Who was their manager at this time?

13 For which team did the Scottish First Division's leading scorer, Andy Ritchie, play?

14 Who won the 1979 Scottish FA Cup in a second replay after two 0-0 draws?

15 Who were the runners-up?

12 Dario Gradi 13 Morton 14 Rangers 15 Hibernian
Forest 8 Million-pound Trevor Francis 9 John McGovern 10 Viv Anderson 11 Wimbledon
Wanderers 5 Former England manager Don Revie 6 Alan Sunderland 7 Nottingham
1 Osvaldo Ardiles and Ricardo Villa 2 Alberto Tarantini 3 Trevor Francis 4 Bolton

Quiz 70

Season 1979-1980

1   **Who became the first Israeli to play in the English First Division when he made his debut for Liverpool at home to Aston Villa?**

2   How did he mark the occasion?

3   **Second Division West Ham United won the FA Cup, beating Arsenal 1-0 in the Final. How many times had they won it before?**

4   Who scored the only goal of the match?

5   **Nottingham Forest retained the European Cup when they beat SV Hamburg 1-0 in the Final in Madrid. Who scored the goal?**

6   Which England striker was on the losing side?

7   **Which English First Division team had he already contracted to join the following season?**

8   This same English team already had the First Division's leading scorer, with 23 goals in 1979-80 – what was his name?

9   **Northern Ireland won the Home International Championship outright – when had they last achieved this feat?**

10   What was unprecedented about the European Cup Winners' Cup Final in which Arsenal lost to Valencia?

11   **Who briefly became Britain's most expensive footballer when Manchester City manager Malcolm Allison bought him for £1,437,500 from Wolverhampton Wanderers?**

12   Who shortly afterwards broke this record when Wolverhampton Wanderers bought him from Aston Villa for £1,469,000, and then scored the winning goal in the League Cup Final?

13   **Who was the wheeler-dealer manager of Wolves?**

14   Name the Ipswich Town goalkeeper who saved a League record of eight penalties in the season, including two in the same match, out of 10 faced?

15   **What unusual distinction was achieved by Colin Garwood, who played 24 matches for Portsmouth before being transferred to Aldershot, for whom he appeared in 16 games?**

Quiz 71   Season 1980-1981

1 **Which club won their seventh League Championship, their first for 71 years?**

2 Who was their captain?

3 **Who was their manager?**

4 Who won the League Cup for the first time in their history, beating West Ham United 2-1 in a replay?

5 **After the first game had been drawn 1-1, West Ham manager John Lyall was quoted as saying 'We have been cheated', to which the match referee responded angrily 'No one calls me a cheat'. Who was the referee?**

6 In British soccer's biggest ever transfer swap, Arsenal gave striker Clive Allen – who had been on their books for only 62 days – and goalkeeper Paul Barron to Crystal Palace in return for whom?

7 **Who broke the record for the number of League appearances by a player at a single club when he played his 765th game for Swindon Town on October 18?**

8 Name the Scotsman, the Dutchman and the Englishman – all from Ipswich Town – who took the first three places in the PFA Player of the Year poll.

9 **Ipswich won the UEFA Cup Final 5-4 on aggregate (won 3-0 at home; lost 4-2 away). Which Dutch team did they beat?**

10 Who scored a goal and an own goal in the 100th English FA Cup Final between Tottenham Hotspur and Manchester City?

11 **Which West Country Third Division side reached the FA Cup 6th round despite having been drawn away in all but one of their ties?**

12 Who beat Liverpool on January 31, thus becoming the first team to win away at Anfield for three years, 10 days – an all-time record run that included a total of 85 matches?

13 **Who scored the goal in Liverpool's 1-0 defeat of Real Madrid in the European Cup Final?**

14 Which England international played for the Spanish side in this match?

15 **In Scotland, who won the FA Cup and finished runners-up in the League Cup?**

---

13 Alan Kennedy 14 Laurie Cunningham 15 **Dundee United**
9 **AZ 67 Alkmaar (Holland)** 10 City's Tommy Hutchison 11 **Exeter City** 12 Leicester City
6 Kenny Sansom 7 **John Trollope** 8 John Wark (winner), Frans Thijssen and Paul Mariner
1 **Aston Villa** 2 Dennis Mortimer 3 **Ron Saunders** 4 Liverpool 5 **Clive Thomas**

 ## Quiz 72

Season 1981-1982

1 **Which former Liverpool manager died on September 29 1981, at the age of 67?**

2 Who was manager of the current Liverpool side which won its fifth League title in seven seasons, its thirteenth in all, and the League Cup for the second year in succession?

3 **Which Southampton player was the First Division's leading scorer, with 26 goals?**

4 Who became the first paid director of a Football League club when appointed by Fulham on November 19?

5 **Who became the first club apart from Celtic and Rangers to win the Scottish FA Cup since 1970?**

6 Who did Manchester United manager Ron Atkinson buy from West Bromwich Albion?

7 **The fee was a British transfer record. How much was it?**

8 Tottenham Hotspur retained the English FA Cup, beating Queens Park Rangers 1-0 in a replay after the Wembley Final had been drawn 1-1. Who scored the winning goal?

9 **This goal was scored from the penalty spot. How many previous spot kicks had there been in FA Cup Finals?**

10 How many had been scored from?

11 **Which Spurs player was PFA Footballer of the Year?**

12 Which German team did Aston Villa beat 1-0 in the European Cup Final?

13 **Who scored the winning goal in the Final in Rotterdam?**

14 Which member of the winning team was playing in only his second competitive first class match?

15 **Name the European Footballer of the Year who played on the losing side.**

---

1 Bill Shankly 2 Bob Paisley **3 Kevin Keegan 4** Malcolm Macdonald **5 Aberdeen 6** Bryan Robson **7 £1.7 million 8 Glenn Hoddle 9 Five 10** All of them **11 Steve Perryman 12** Bayern Munich **13 Peter Withe 14** Goalkeeper Nigel Spink **15 Karl-Heinz Rummenigge**

 ## Quiz 73 — Season 1982-1983

1 In the dying moments of extra time in the FA Cup Final, with the score at 2-2, which Brighton and Hove Albion player hesitated in front of goal, allowing Manchester United's keeper to make a crucial save?

2 Brighton's sad season ended with them being relegated from the League's top flight. When had they been promoted to it?

3 Swansea City also went down, after a stay of only two seasons. By the last day of the season, the third relegation spot was a straight fight between Manchester City and Luton Town, who played each other at Maine Road. Who scored the only goal of the game?

4 Liverpool won their 14th League Championship by an 11-point margin. Who were the runners-up?

5 In winning the Scottish FA Cup, how did Aberdeen join a club of which only Celtic and Rangers were members?

6 Which other major trophy did Aberdeen win?

7 Who did they beat in the Final in Gothenburg?

8 Who won the Scottish Championship for the first time in their history?

9 Which team were runners-up in both the Scottish FA Cup and the Scottish League Cup?

10 Whose report recommended – among other things – a reduction in the size of the English First Division from 22 to 20 clubs?

11 On July 7, the FA appointed Bobby Robson England manager in succession to Ron Greenwood. Which League club had Robson run until then?

12 Who took over as manager of Robson's old club?

13 Which French international, playing for Juventus (Italy) won the first of three consecutive European Footballer of the Year awards?

14 Who lifted the Milk Cup for Liverpool after their 2-1 victory over Manchester United in the Final?

15 Which future Chelsea star gained the extraordinary distinction of scoring four goals in a match and yet finishing on the losing side, as Reading went down 7-5 to Doncaster Rovers in the Third Division?

 # Quiz 74 ### Season 1983-1984

1 Which businessman made an unsuccessful £10 million takeover bid for Manchester United?

2 Who won the Scottish FA Cup?

3 What happened in this Final for the third year running?

4 Who scored a famous goal for England when they beat Brazil for the first time ever in a friendly at the Maracana Stadium, Rio de Janeiro?

5 This season marked the end of the Home International Championship. Who were the last winners?

6 Which Third Division side from Staffordshire reached the semi-finals of the Milk Cup?

7 Which West Country Third Division side reached the semi-finals of the FA Cup?

8 Who became only the third player to score 100 League goals in both Scotland and England?

9 Who came second in the Scottish First Division and were runners-up in both the Scottish FA Cup and the League Cup?

10 Which Italian team did Liverpool beat in the Final of the European Cup?

11 Where was the match played?

12 The score was 1-1 after extra time, and then Liverpool won 4-2 on penalties. This was the famous occasion when Bruce Grobelaar did his knocking-knees routine to put the penalty taker off. Who missed?

13 Tottenham Hotspur won the UEFA Cup, beating Anderlecht of Belgium in the Final on penalties. Who was Spurs' heroic goalkeeper in this match?

14 Whose last game as Spurs' manager was the UEFA Cup Final?

15 Who was the manager of France when they won the European Championship for the first time?

CARLING 10,000 FOOTBALL FACTS & QUESTIONS

 **Quiz 75**   **Season 1984-1985**

1   After crowd trouble at Parkhead, where were Celtic forced to play the home leg of their Cup Winners' Cup tie against Rapid Vienna?

2   Which team won the Second Division Championship, thus gaining promotion to the First Division for the first time in their history?

3   Which ex-Chelsea player returned to Stamford Bridge with Sunderland and scored two goals which helped to knock his old team out of the Milk Cup in the semi-final?

4   Which goalkeeper completed 472 League appearances, a record?

5   Which Manchester United defender became the first player ever to be sent off in an English FA Cup Final?

6   Who scored the winner in the Final against Everton?

7   Which English team won the home leg of their UEFA Cup tie with Partizan Belgrade 6-2 and then lost 4-0 in Yugoslavia, thus going out on away goals?

8   Which two great tragedies cast a shadow over the world of football?

9   English clubs were banned from European competitions: when were they re-admitted?

10   What unprecedented – and partly unwanted – double did Norwich City achieve in 1985?

11   Who won the League Championship and the European Cup Winners' Cup?

12   Where was the European Cup Winners' Cup Final played?

13   Which Austrian team were the Cup Winners' Cup runners-up?

14   Who scored the winning team's three goals in the Final?

15   Which great Austrian international scored a consolation goal for the losers?

1 **Old Trafford, Manchester** 2 Oxford United 3 **Clive Walker** 4 Pat Jennings (Tottenham Hotspur and Arsenal) 5 **Kevin Moran** 6 Norman Whiteside 7 **Queens Park Rangers** 8 The Bradford fire and the Heysel Stadium riot 9 **1990 for all clubs except Liverpool, who were readmitted in 1991** 10 They won the Milk Cup and were relegated from the First Division in the same season 11 **Everton** 12 The Feyenoord Stadium, Rotterdam 13 **Rapid Vienna** 14 Andy Gray, Trevor Steven and Kevin Sheedy 15 **Franz Krankl**

Quiz 76

Season 1985-1986

1 Which great manager suffered a fatal heart attack during Scotland's World Cup qualifying match with Wales at Ninian Park?

2 Who won the Milk Cup?

3 Which club announced plans to ban away fans from its stadium?

4 Who won the Double?

5 What was unique about the season's Merseyside FA Cup Final?

6 Who was the only member of the Liverpool Cup Final team to have been born in England?

7 Who became the first Australian to score in an FA Cup Final?

8 Which Third Division team created a League record by winning their first 13 games of the season?

9 Who became the first Scotsman to win 100 international caps?

10 Which London club came third in the First Division, the highest League position in their history?

11 Who became the first Iron Curtain winners of the European Cup?

12 Spain had clubs in the Finals of all three main European club competitions – the European Cup, the Cup Winners' Cup and the UEFA Cup. Name them.

13 Which was the only one of the three to win their competition?

14 Who became manager of Rangers?

15 Which Scottish team suffered a double disappointment, finishing runners-up to Celtic in the First Division on goal difference, and losing 3-0 to Aberdeen in the Final of the Scottish FA Cup?

1 Jock Stein 2 Oxford United 3 Luton Town 4 Liverpool 5 It was the first time Liverpool and Everton had met at this stage of the competition 6 Republic of Ireland international Mark Lawrenson (born in Preston) 7 Craig Johnston (Liverpool) 8 Reading 9 Kenny Dalglish 10 West Ham United 11 Steaua Bucharest (Romania) 12 Barcelona, Atletico Madrid, Real Madrid 13 Real Madrid won the UEFA Cup 14 Graeme Souness 15 Heart of Midlothian

CARLING 10,000 FOOTBALL FACTS & QUESTIONS

 ## Quiz 77   ### Season 1986-1987

1 What happened to Graeme Souness in his first match as player manager of Rangers, away to Hibernian?

2 Which four-times winner of the FA Cup, now languishing in the Fourth Division, was knocked out in the First Round by non-league Chorley?

3 Which two London teams attempted to merge?

4 Which team became the first champions of the GM Vauxhall Conference to win promotion to the Fourth Division of the Football League?

5 Which Fourth Division team did they replace?

6 Which Portuguese team won both the European Cup and the World Club Championship?

7 Which team were runners-up in both the UEFA Cup and the Scottish FA Cup?

8 What happened to English Divisions One and Two at the end of the season?

9 The bottom two clubs in the First Division were Manchester City and Aston Villa. Which was the extra team relegated from the First Division to accommodate this change?

10 Which Tottenham striker was both the First Division's leading scorer, with 33 goals, and the players' Player of the Year?

11 Apart from Spurs, this player was on the books of seven other clubs in a career that ran from 1978 to 1994. Name the clubs, all but one of which were in London.

12 Which one of these did he never actually play a match for?

13 Who won the League Championship for the ninth time in their history and the second time in three years?

14 Which team were runners-up in both the League and the League Cup?

15 Who won the FA Cup for the first time in their history?

 ## Quiz 78   **Season 1987-1988**

1 **Which company became the sponsors of the Football League in its centenary year?**

2 Who, on April 9, became – at 17 years and 240 days – the youngest player ever to score a First Division hat trick?

3 **Who won the FA Cup after being in the League for only 10 years?**

4 Who did they beat 1-0 in the Final?

5 **Who scored the winning goal?**

6 Who missed a penalty for the opposition?

7 **For the first time, four teams were relegated from the First Division – Portsmouth, Watford, Oxford and which London club?**

8 What was unique about the circumstances of their relegation?

9 **Which team took their place?**

10 Which Welsh club lost its status as a member of the Football League?

11 **Which re-elected team filled the gap created by their demise?**

12 Who won the Littlewoods (League) Cup?

13 **They beat the holders 3-2 in the Final. Who were they?**

14 Who took a penalty in this match for the eventual losers?

15 **Who saved it?**

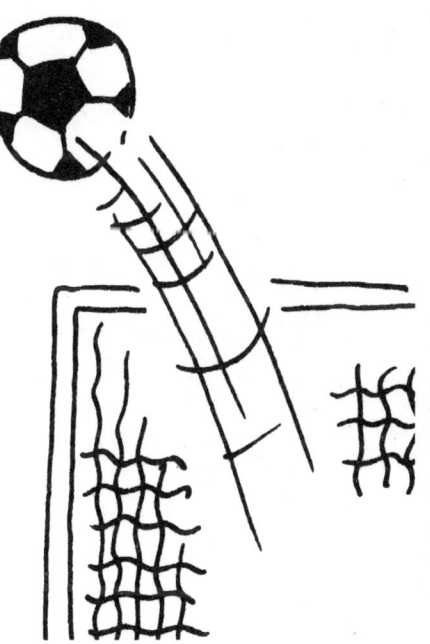

Quiz 79

Season 1988-1989

1 Who, on July 7, became Britain's first £2 million footballer?

2 Which club sold him?

3 Which club bought him?

4 Whose transfer from Newcastle United to Liverpool had been the previous British record?

5 On August 18, Liverpool bought Ian Rush for a reported £2.8 million from the European club to which they had sold him only 12 months previously for £3.2 million. Which club?

6 Rush had not enjoyed himself abroad. What, according to reports, did he say Italy was like?

7 By the end of the season, the Championship rested on the result of the final match between Liverpool and Arsenal at Anfield. If Liverpool won, drew or lost 1-0, they would retain the title. Any worse defeat, and Arsenal themselves would win. What was the final score?

8 Who scored the goals?

9 Who took the indirect free kick from which the first goal was headed in?

10 The scorer of the first goal was the First Division's leading scorer for the whole season. How many goals did he score: 23, 33 or 43?

11 The leading scorer in European football, Dorin Mateut of Dinamo Bucharest, scored how many: 33, 43 or 53?

12 Which former England manager died on May 26?

13 On October 22, three brothers appeared on the same side in a First Division match, the first time this had happened since the Carrs of Middlesbrough in 1920. What were their names?

14 How was the format of the play-offs changed?

15 Which London club was promoted from the Second Division through the play-offs?

Quiz 80

Season 1989-1990

1 Who tried, unsuccessfully, to buy Manchester United in a £20 million takeover deal?

2 Who beat Sunderland 1-0 on May 28 to win the Second Division play-off Final?

3 What happened to the victors 10 days later?

4 What was unprecedented about the Scottish FA Cup Final in which Aberdeen beat Celtic?

5 Aberdeen also won the Scottish League Cup. Which team had last performed this Cup double, and in which year?

6 In the English FA Cup Final, Manchester United drew 3-3 with Crystal Palace. When was the last time six or more goals had been scored in this fixture?

7 Which game-changing 104-page document was published on January 29, 1990?

8 Who were the English Second Division champions?

9 When had they last been in the First Division?

10 What were they destined to achieve two years later?

11 Bobby Robson announced his intention to resign as manager of England after the 1990 World Cup Finals to take up the same position with which club?

12 Which three Italian clubs made a clean sweep of the European cups?

13 Which English Second Division team reached their first FA Cup semi-final since 1913 and their first ever League Cup Final?

14 Who became the Republic of Ireland's all-time leading scored when he netted twice in the 3-0 win in Malta on June 2?

15 Which team was promoted to the Fourth Division of the English Football League only a year after having been relegated from it?

1 Ken Knighton 2 Swindon Town 3 They were relegated to Division Three because of financial irregularities dating from 1985, although they played the following season in the Second Division 4 It was the first Scottish Cup Final to be decided on penalties 5 Aberdeen themselves, in 1986 6 1953 7 The Taylor Report 8 Leeds United 9 1981-82 10 They were to win the First Division Championship 11 PSV Eindhoven (Holland) 12 AC Milan (European Cup), Sampdoria (Cup Winners' Cup) Juventus (UEFA Cup) 13 Oldham Athletic 14 Frank Stapleton (Arsenal) 15 Darlington

 **Quiz 81**　　　Season 1990-1991

1   **Who won the First Division Championship?**

2   Who resigned unexpectedly as manager of Liverpool after his team had drawn 4-4 with Everton in an FA Cup fifth round replay on February 22?

3   **Who became manager of Liverpool on April 16, 1991?**

4   Who had been caretaker manager during the intervening period?

5   **Who won the Scottish FA Cup, beating Dundee United 4-3 after extra time in the Final?**

6   When had they last won it?

7   **What was unusual about the relationship between the managers of the two Scottish FA Cup finalists?**

8   Which Dundee United player was voted Scottish Footballer of the Year?

9   **In the English FA Cup Final, into whom did Paul Gascoigne launch the infamous tackle which led to him (Gascoigne) being stretchered off?**

10 Which club became the first to win promotion on a shoot-out, when they beat Blackpool 5-4 on penalties after their Fourth Division play-off Final had ended 2-2 after extra time?

11 **Which group of islands entered its first ever European Championship qualifiers?**

12 They were not allowed to play home games at home because UEFA banned them from using artificial pitches. Where in Sweden did they play their first home match?

13 **Who were their opponents in this match?**

14 What was the score?

15 **On June 5, Wales beat West Germany 1-0 in their European Championship qualifying match at Cardiff Arms Park. Who scored?**

1 **Arsenal** 2 Kenny Dalglish 3 **Graeme Souness** 4 Ronnie Moran 5 **Motherwell** 6 1952
7 **They were brothers – Tommy McLean (Motherwell) and Jim McLean (Dundee United)** 8 Maurice Malpas 9 **Gary Charles (Nottingham Forest)** 10 Torquay United
11 **The Faroes** 12 Landskrona 13 **Austria** 14 Faroe Islands 1 Austria 0 15 Ian Rush

Quiz 82

Season 1991-1992

1 **Which Arsenal striker scored the goal when England beat Turkey 1-0 at Wembley in the European Championship qualifier?**

2 Which was the first Division One team ever to be knocked out of the FA Cup on penalties?

3 **Who did they lose to?**

4 This was the final season of the old Football League before the new Premiership. Who were the last First Division Champions?

5 **One member of this team was winning his second Champion's medal, having won one with Arsenal the previous year. Name him.**

6 What was this player's connection with the 1958 Munich air disaster in which eight members of the Manchester United team were killed?

7 **Which Rangers player won the Golden Boot as the leading scorer in European club football?**

8 Who won the European Championship without having qualified for it in the first place?

9 **Which country did they replace?**

10 In which country were the European Championship Finals held?

11 **Which Everton and former Manchester United Northern Ireland international was forced to retire at the age of 26?**

12 In the FA Cup Final, what was unusual about the awards ceremony?

13 **And why did this not work?**

14 Which two teams contested this Final?

15 **Which team was expelled from the Football League?**

 ## Quiz 83   ### Season 1992-1993

1 **Who was sent off for the first time in his career in his 971st League game while player manager of Plymouth Argyle?**

2 After starting the season with 11 wins off the reel, Premiership Newcastle United suffered their first defeat at home to which First Division club?

3 **Who was paid £1,500 by a film company but fined £20,000 by the FA for his starring role in the notorious video 'Soccer's Hard Men'?**

4 Which former England captain and all-time great died on February 24, 1993?

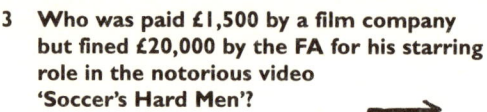

5 **Brian Clough retired. Which two clubs had he led to the League Championship?**

6 Which other two clubs had he also managed?

7 **Ian Rush became Liverpool's all-time leading scorer. Whose record did he beat with his 287th goal for the club?**

8 Which team resigned from the Football League?

9 **Which team achieved an unprecedented double by winning both the Coca-Cola Cup and the FA Cup?**

10 Who did they beat in both the Coca-Cola Cup Final and the FA Cup Final?

11 **Who broke his arm during the team's Coca-Cola victory celebrations when he fell off Tony Adams?**

12 The FA Cup Final went to a replay: when was the last time this had happened?

13 **This was the first season in which the old First Division became the FA Premier League, and the first champions were Manchester United. Who was the team captain?**

14 Who was the club captain?

15 In their previous Championship year, 1967, Manchester United had been managed by Matt Busby. Now they were managed by Alex Ferguson. How many managers had they had in the intervening period, and what were their names?

---

1 Peter Shilton 2 Grimsby Town **3 Vinnie Jones (Wimbledon)** 4 Bobby Moore
5 Derby County and Nottingham Forest 6 Leeds United and Brighton and Hove Albion
7 Roger Hunt 8 Maidstone United **9 Arsenal** 10 Sheffield Wednesday **11 Steve Morrow**
12 1990, Manchester United v Crystal Palace **13 Steve Bruce** 14 Bryan Robson **15 Five – Wilf McGuinness, Frank O'Farrell, Tommy Docherty, Dave Sexton, Ron Atkinson**

Quiz 84

Season 1992-1993

1 Which team won promotion to the Football League from the GM Vauxhall Conference?

2 Which team came bottom of the Third Division and were therefore relegated to the GM Vauxhall Conference?

3 Which country had a team in the Final of each of the three main cup tournaments – the European Cup, the Cup Winners' Cup and the UEFA Cup?

4 Name the clubs.

5 Two of the three won – which lost?

6 The losers had the consolation of having one of their players voted European Footballer of the Year for the third time in his career. He was a Dutch international. Name him.

7 Who had been the last Dutchman to win the award?

8 Which three teams were the first to be relegated from the Premiership?

9 Which three teams were the first to be promoted to it?

10 Which team came third in the First Division but missed out in the play-offs?

11 Who was sacked as chief executive of Tottenham Hotspur on May 14, 1993?

12 Which strangely tonsured one-hit wonder was voted the Football Writers' English Footballer of the Year?

13 Which team did he then play for?

14 Which Aston Villa and Republic of Ireland defender was the PFA Footballer of the Year?

15 The season ended with Manchester United qualifying for the European Cup and Arsenal for the Cup Winners' Cup. But as Arsenal had done the Cup double, which English team took the Coca-Cola Cup winner's place in the UEFA Cup?

 Quiz 85   Season 1993-1994

1   In the Third Division on October 16, 1993, which team became the first to have both their original and their substitute goalkeepers sent off in the same match?

2   Who were their opponents in that game?

3   In July 1993, who did Rangers buy from Dundee United for a then British record fee of £4 million?

4   In 1993-94, Kidderminster Harriers of the GM Vauxhall Conference reached the fifth round of the FA Cup. Which League teams did they beat in the third and fourth rounds?

5   Who eventually knocked Kidderminster out, 1-0 in the fifth round?

6   In 1993, who won the Welsh Cup and qualified for Europe with a Final victory over Cardiff City, 22-times winners of the trophy?

7   What was the score in this historic match?

8   Who did Blackburn Rovers sign from Southampton for £2 million, then a British record for a goalkeeper?

9   In the second year of the Premiership, Manchester United became the fourth team in the 20th century to win the Championship and FA Cup in the same season. Who were the other three double winners, and when?

10 Who won the GM Vauxhall Conference?

11 Why were they not promoted to the Third Division?

12 Who thus escaped relegation from the Football league, despite having come bottom of the Third Division?

13 Which Newcastle striker was the Premiership's leading scorer?

14 Which Blackburn Rover was the PFA Footballer of the Year?

15 Rangers won the Scottish League Championship. When was the last time they had not done so?

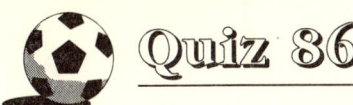

Quiz 86

Season 1993-1994

1 **Who scored the goal with which Arsenal beat Parma 1-0 in the European Cup Winners' Cup Final in Copenhagen?**

2 Arsenal's Ian Wright and John Jensen were awarded Winners' medals. Why was this odd?

3 **Who scored the goals when England lost 2-0 to the USA in Foxboro, Massachusetts?**

4 Who scored Holland's goals in their 2-0 victory over England in the World Cup qualifying game in Rotterdam?

5 **When Ronald Koeman committed his famous foul on the edge of the Dutch penalty area, which England player was through on goal?**

6 In which Italian city was the San Marino v England World Cup qualifying match played?

7 **Who scored the first goal after 10 seconds' play?**

8 Who scored four goals in England's 7-1 victory?

9 **Which three teams were relegated from the Premiership?**

10 Who were promoted to the Premiership as champions of Division One?

11 **Which other team won automatic promotion to the Premiership by finishing second in Division One?**

12 Although Millwall came third in the First Division, which team was promoted to the Premiership in their place through the play-offs?

13 **Which team did Manchester United beat 4-0 in the FA Cup Final?**

14 Who scored two penalties in this match?

15 **When was the last time the FA Cup Final had been won by the same score?**

1 **Alan Smith** 2 Neither of them was in the team on the night, and Wright was ineligible through suspension 3 **Thomas Dooley and Alexei Lalas** 4 Ronald Koeman and Dennis Bergkamp 5 **David Platt** 6 Bologna 7 **San Marino's Davide Gualtieri** 8 Ian Wright (Arsenal) 9 **Sheffield United, Oldham Athletic, Swindon Town** 10 Crystal Palace 11 **Nottingham Forest** 12 Leicester City 13 **Chelsea** 14 Eric Cantona 15 1983, when **Manchester United** beat **Brighton and Hove Albion** in a replay after the first game had ended 2-2

Quiz 87

Season 1994-1995

1 **Who was the manager of FA Premier League Champions Blackburn Rovers?**

2 Which other team had he previously managed to a League title?

3 **Which other two managers had previously won the English League with two different clubs?**

4 When had Blackburn Rovers last been English League Champions?

5 **Who was the great benefactor who financed Blackburn's transformation from Second Division obscurity to title-winners?**

6 To which club did Blackburn Rovers pay £5 million for Chris Sutton?

7 **Which World Cup star scored seven goals in his first six games for Tottenham Hotspur?**

8 Which was his last club before moving to White Hart Lane?

9 **Which star of the 1992 European Championship scored his first goal for Arsenal after 98 appearances?**

10 What was the record Premiership victory achieved by Manchester United on March 4 in their home game against Ipswich Town?

11 **Which Canadian international was the hapless Ipswich Town goalkeeper that day?**

12 Which former Aston Villa full back was sent off on his debut for Everton?

13 **Liverpool won the Coca-Cola Cup, beating Middlesbrough 2-1 in the Final. Who scored both their goals?**

14 Who won the FA Cup, beating Manchester United in the Final?

15 **Who scored the only goal of the game?**

1 Kenny Dalglish 2 Liverpool 3 Herbert Chapman (Huddersfield Town and Arsenal) and Brian Clough (Derby County and Nottingham Forest) 4 1914 5 Jack Walker 6 Norwich City 7 Jurgen Klinsmann 8 AS Monaco 9 John Jensen 10 Manchester United 9 Ipswich Town 0 11 Craig Forrest 12 Earl Barrett 13 Steve McManaman 14 Everton 15 Paul Rideout

 Quiz 88   **Season 1994-1995**

1 **Who was the leading scorer in the FA Premiership, with 34 goals in 42 games?**

2 Which London club were beaten semi-finalists in both the Coca-Cola and the FA Cups?

3 **Name the four teams relegated from the top flight as the Premiership began to reduce itself in size.**

4 Middlesbrough were Champions of the First Division – who were the runners-up?

5 **But which club was promoted with Middlesbrough in their stead after beating the League's second-placed team in the play-off final at Wembley?**

6 Who won the GM Vauxhall Conference but were not promoted to the Third Division because their ground was not up to the standard now required by the Football League?

7 **Which team were thus saved from relegation despite finishing bottom of the Third Division?**

8 Which Turkish team knocked Aston Villa out of the UEFA Cup?

9 **Which Newcastle United and former Charlton Athletic midfielder scored on his international debut for England against Romania?**

10 In Scotland, Rangers won their seventh Premier title in a row and Celtic finished fourth – who were runners-up?

11 **Who beat Celtic 6-5 on penalties in the Final of the Scottish League Cup?**

12 Celtic won the Scottish FA Cup, beating Airdrieonians 1-0 in the Final. Which Dutchman scored the goal?

13 **For which Dutch club had this striker played immediately before moving to Glasgow?**

14 Which two clubs came into the new Scottish Third Division?

15 **Who won the first ever Scottish Third Division Championship?**

 **Quiz 89**   **Season 1995-1996**

1   Manchester United did the double, winning the **FA Carling Premiership** for the third time in the four years of its existence and the FA Cup. Who were runners-up in the Premiership?

2   Who were the beaten finalists in the FA Cup?

3   **Who scored the only goal of the Final?**

4   On New Year's Day 1996, who became the youngest player to appear in the Premiership when he kept goal for West Ham United against Manchester City at the age of 17 years 3 days?

5   **Dutch international striker Dennis Bergkamp went to Arsenal. From which Italian club was he transferred?**

6   Who scored on his Middlesbrough debut after a close season transfer from Tottenham Hotspur?

7   **Which three clubs were relegated from the Premiership?**

8   Who won the First Division Championship?

9   **Which other club was promoted automatically after finishing second in the First Division?**

10 Who came third in the First Division but failed to win promotion after losing in the play-offs?

11 **Which was the third promoted team?**

12 Who became the first Italian to play in the Premiership when he joined Nottingham Forest from Torino?

13 **Who made his Premiership debut at the age of 34 when he played for Queens Park Rangers in December?**

14 Which Geordie defender did Southampton buy from Galatasaray in Turkey?

15 **Aston Villa beat Leeds United 3-0 in the Coca-Cola Cup Final. Who scored their goals?**

Quiz 90   Season 1995-1996

1 **Which Dutch team knocked Everton out of the European Cup Winners' Cup?**

2 Which English team did best in Europe, reaching the quarter Finals of the UEFA Cup?

3 **Who won the GM Vauxhall Conference, but were not promoted to the Third Division because their ground facilities were held to be sub-standard by the Football League?**

4 Which club were thus spared relegation despite finishing bottom of the Third Division?

5 **This is the year in which Manchester United changed out of their grey away strip at half time because their players complained they couldn't see each other. Who were they playing?**

6 In this season, Wimbledon officials started talking about the possibility of a move to Dublin. Who is their Chairman?

7 **Which UEFA restriction on the composition of teams was outlawed as a result of the so-called 'Bosman Ruling' by the European Court of Justice?**

8 Which goalkeeper scored in a UEFA Cup match in September?

9 **At which English Premiership ground did Holland beat the Republic of Ireland in a play-off for Euro '96?**

10 Name the visiting goalkeeper who saved with a 'scorpion kick' during the England v Colombia international in September

11 **Which 1996 film starring Sean Bean told the story of a Sheffield United trainee hopeful?**

12 Rangers made it eight Premiership titles in a row and also won the Scottish FA Cup. Which two players scored the goals in their 5-1 Final defeat of Heart of Midlothian?

13 **Who scored a hat trick against Aberdeen in the match in which Rangers clinched the title and was voted Player of the Year by both the Scottish PFA and the Scottish Football Writers' Association?**

14 Who won the Scottish League Cup, beating Dundee 2-0 in the Final?

15 **Which new club replaced Meadowbank Thistle in the Scottish League and won the Third Division in their first season?**

 Quiz 91   **Season 1996-1997**

1 **Manchester United won the FA Carling Premiership for the fourth time in five years. Who was their leading scorer, with 19 goals?**

2 For the second year running, the Premiership's leading scorer was Alan Shearer, with 25 goals for his new club, Newcastle United. Who ran him a close second, with 23 goals in the League, and outscored him 30 to 28 in all competitions?

3 **Which team were runners-up in both the FA and Coca-Cola Cups and were relegated from the Premiership?**

4 Which other two teams went down with them?

5 **Which two teams won automatic promotion to the Premiership from the First Division?**

6 The third team promoted was Crystal Palace, who won the play-off final – which club had finished third in the Second Division League table?

7 **Who won the Coca-Cola Cup, beating Middlesbrough 1-0 in a replay after the first match had been drawn 1-1?**

8 Who scored the winning goal?

9 **Where was the replay held?**

10 Which Second Division club reached the FA Cup semi-final?

11 **After only 43 seconds, who scored the fastest ever goal in an FA Cup Final as Chelsea beat Middlesbrough 2-0?**

12 Whose record – a goal after 45 seconds for Newcastle United against Manchester City in 1955 – did he beat?

13 **Who scored Chelsea's second goal in that match?**

14 Who did former Dutch international Ruud Gullit succeed in May 1996 as player-manager of Chelsea?

15 **Which two February signings scored 13 goals between them in the remainder of the season and lifted West Ham United to Premiership safety?**

 **Quiz 92**   **Season 1996-1997**

1   **Who left his job as manager of Newcastle United in mid-season when his team were second in the Premiership?**

2   Which French club knocked Newcastle United out of the UEFA Cup in the quarter-final?

3   **Which French club knocked Liverpool out of the Cup Winners' Cup in the semi-final?**

4   Middlesbrough had three points deducted for cancelling a Premiership fixture without sufficient notice – which club were they due to have played?

5   **Macclesfield Town won the GM Vauxhall Conference to gain entry to the Football League for the first time. Which former Manchester United and Northern Ireland star was their manager?**

6   Which team did they replace in the Third Division of the Football League?

7   **Which club retained its League status only by drawing 1-1 with Hereford United on the last day of the season?**

8   Which London team reached the semi-finals of the Coca-Cola and FA Cups?

9   **In Scotland, Rangers won the Premier League for the ninth year in succession, thus equalling Celtic's record of 1966-1974. They also won the League Cup – which two internationals scored twice in their 4-3 Final victory over Heart of Midlothian?**

10 Who won the 1997 Scottish FA Cup, beating Falkirk 1-0 in the Final?

11 **In which year had these two teams previously faced each other in the Final?**

12 Who knocked Celtic out of the UEFA Cup in the first round?

13 **Which Welsh club did Aberdeen beat in the first round of the UEFA Cup?**

14 Which Danish club knocked Aberdeen out in the second round of the UEFA Cup?

15 **Which clubs contested the relegation/promotion play-off between the Scottish Premiership and the First Division?**

 **Quiz 93**   Season 1996-1997

1   Which Czech star of Euro '96 did Liverpool sign for £3.25 million from Borussia Dortmund?

2   At the start of the season, what serious illness kept Andy Cole out of contention for a Manchester United first team place?

3   Which entrepreneur from the music business bought Queens Park Rangers for £10 million?

4   Which Celtic player was sent off during their UEFA Cup qualifying match against KC Kosice in Slovakia?

5   Which controversial goalkeeper signed a one-year contract with Plymouth Argyle?

6   Which Liverpool defender was fined £2000 by the FA for exceeding 45 disciplinary points in the previous season?

7   Who did Manchester United sell to Leeds United for £4.5 million?

8   Who became Director of Football at Portsmouth?

9   Who was sacked after 61 weeks as manager of Arsenal?

10 Of which club had his successor, Arsene Wenger, previously been the coach?

11 Wenger's first signings were fellow Frenchmen Remi Garde on a free transfer from Strasbourg and Patrick Viera for £3.5 million – from where?

12 Who resigned as manager of Barnet to become England goalkeeping coach?

13 Which club bought striker Niall Quinn from Manchester City for £1.3 million?

14 Who scored the first goal of the season in a 1-0 win for Manchester City over Ipswich Town in the Nationwide First Division?

15 Who scored a hat-trick on his debut for Middlesbrough?

1 **Patrik Berger** 2 Pneumonia 3 **Chris Wright** 4 Simon Donnelly 5 **Bruce Grobelaar** 6 Neil Ruddock 7 **Lee Sharpe** 8 Terry Venables 9 **Bruce Rioch** 10 Grampus Eight (Japan) 11 **AC Milan** 12 Ray Clemence 14 Steve Lomas 15 Fabrizio Ravanelli 13 **Sunderland**

 ## Quiz 94   Season 1996-1997

1 **Which former Gunner scored a hat-trick for Nottingham Forest in their opening game, a 3-0 victory at Coventry City?**

2 Still on the opening day of the season, who scored for Manchester United against Wimbledon with a shot from inside his own half?

3 **Which Tottenham Hotspur player broke his leg in their 2-0 victory at Blackburn Rovers?**

4 Which former Liverpool star was now player manager of Swansea City?

5 **Who did Barry Town beat in the UEFA Cup to become the first League of Wales side to reach the first round proper of a European competition?**

6 Who left Blackburn Rovers on August 21, 1996?

7 **Which Yorkshire club were the early leaders in the FA Carling Premiership, with three wins out of three?**

8 Who resigned on August 26 as manager of Manchester City?

9 **Who took over from Tony Adams as captain of England?**

10 What was the score in England's opening World Cup qualifying match, away to Moldova?

11 **Who resigned as player-manager of Queens Park Rangers and then played for Wycombe Wanderers the following week?**

12 Who was sent off for the 12th time in his career as Wimbledon beat Tottenham Hotspur 1-0?

13 **Who robbed Sheffield Wednesday of their hundred per cent record, with a 2-0 victory at Hillsborough on September 7?**

14 Who was sacked after eight years in charge of Leeds United?

15 **Who took over as manager of Queens Park Rangers?**

Quiz 95   Season 1996-1997

1   **Which former England international signed for Falkirk?**

2   Who took over as manager of Leeds after 19 months out of the game?

3   **Which Yorkshire First Division club was the last team in England to lose its hundred per cent League record, with a 3-1 home defeat by Queens Park Rangers?**

4   Who had four men sent off in their 3-0 defeat at Ibrox Park?

5   **In which country was new Rotherham United manager Danny Bergara born?**

6   Which former Arsenal No 1 became No 2 at Queens Park Rangers?

7   **Which Swedish club knocked Aston Villa out of the UEFA Cup?**

8   Which Arsenal midfielder was recalled to the England squad two years after confessing to alcoholism and drug dependence?

9   **Which Arsenal and England defender now admitted alcoholism?**

10   Who was sacked as manager of Wycombe Wanderers, after only 15 months in charge?

11   **Which club had he previously managed?**

12   Which Nationwide Third Division club knocked First Division Manchester City out of the Coca-Cola Cup, with a 5-1 aggregate victory?

13   **Which German club knocked Arsenal out of the UEFA Cup?**

14   Who resigned as manager of Hibernian after 10 years in charge?

15   **The life, love and drinking habits of which England player were the subject of a controversial television documentary?**

1 **Chris Waddle** 2 George Graham 3 **Barnsley** 4 Heart of Midlothian 5 **Uruguay**
6 Bruce Rioch 7 **Helsingborg** 8 Paul Merson 9 **Tony Adams** 10 Alan Smith
11 **Crystal Palace** 12 Lincoln City 13 **Borussia Moenchengladbach** 14 Alex Miller
15 Paul Gascoigne

 **Quiz 96**   **Season 1996-1997**

1 At which **Nationwide Third Division** club were there three pitch invasions during October?

2 Which Celtic striker scored two goals for Holland in their 3-1 defeat of Wales in the World Cup qualifiers?

3 **Which Manchester United striker broke his ankle in a collision with Liverpool's Neil Ruddock?**

4 Who took over as manager of Manchester City, six weeks after they sacked the previous incumbent?

5 **Which nation didn't turn up for their World Cup qualifying match against Scotland?**

6 A year after fouling Tottenham's Jurgen Klinsmann, whose arm movements got him into even hotter water at White Hart Lane?

7 **From which Italian club did Sheffield Wednesday buy Benito Carbone for £3 million?**

8 Which striker – then with Arsenal – was the first Premiership player to be suspended this season after accumulating 21 disciplinary points?

9 **Which Dutchman did Southampton buy for £1.3 million from Galatasaray (Turkey)?**

10 In which Cental American country were 00 people killed at a football match due to overcrowding?

11 **Which Rangers player was sent off as his team lost 4-1 to Ajax?**

12 Who beat Manchester United 5-0 in the Premiership?

13 **Which Aston Villa coach took over as manager of Nationwide Second Division Wycombe Wanderers?**

14 Which Chelsea director was killed in a helicopter crash on the way back from his team's Coca-Cola Cup match at Bolton Wanderers?

15 **Who resigned as manager of Blackburn Rovers?**

1 **Brighton and Hove Albion** 2 Pierre van Hooijdonk 3 **Andy Cole** 4 Steve Coppell
5 **Estonia** 6 Mark Bosnich (Aston Villa) 7 **Internazionale** 8 John Hartson
9 **Ulrich van Gobbel** 10 Guatemala 11 **Paul Gascoigne** 12 Newcastle United
13 John Gregory 14 Matthew Harding 15 **Ray Harford**

 **Quiz 97**   **Season 1996-1997**

1 **Who beat Manchester United 6-3 in the Premiership?**

2 Which Red Devil was shown a red card in this match?

3 **Who inflicted Manchester United's first ever home defeat in European competition?**

4 Who took over as manager of Coventry City as Ron Atkinson was moved upstairs?

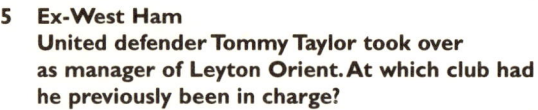

5 **Ex-West Ham United defender Tommy Taylor took over as manager of Leyton Orient. At which club had he previously been in charge?**

6 Who was fined by Liverpool for refusing to play in the Reserves?

7 **Who became captain of Wales?**

8 What was the score in England's World Cup victory away to Georgia?

9 **Who scored a hat-trick in Holland's 7-1 defeat of Wales?**

10 Who missed a penalty for Rangers in their Premier League match at Celtic Park?

11 **And who missed a penalty for Celtic in the same match?**

12 Who became part-time manager of the Australian national soccer team?

13 **Which Scotland international did Queens Park Rangers buy from Chelsea for £2.5 million?**

14 Which other Chelsea player did Queens Park Rangers take on loan?

15 **Which Sheffield Wednesday player was banned by FIFA until December 6 because of claims by Udinese, one of his previous clubs, that they had prior claims on his services?**

 **Quiz 98** **Season 1996-1997**

1 **Which former Chelsea star scored the goal for non-League Woking that knocked First Division Millwall out of the FA Cup?**

2 Which Dutch winger who cost Arsenal £2.3 million joined Benfica on loan?

3 **For what was Faustino Asprilla booked during Newcastle United's UEFA Cup quarter-final against Metz?**

4 Which former Liverpool and Southampton star was sacked as manager of Brighton and Hove Albion?

5 **From which Norwegian club did Tottenham Hotspur buy Steffen Iversen for £2.7 million?**

6 After thinking seriously about a move to Leeds United, to which club did Liverpool and former Wimbledon defender John Scales actually transfer for £2.6 million?

7 **Which Portuguese international retired while at West Ham?**

8 Who did Blackburn Rovers announce would be their next manager, with effect from the following June?

9 **Which Nationwide Second Division team knocked West Ham United out of the Coca-Cola Cup?**

10 Who resigned as manager of Nottingham Forest?

11 **Who took over as caretaker manager?**

12 For which team did Peter Shilton make his 1000th League appearance on December 22?

13 **Which club sacked two managers – Colin Murphy and Steve Thompson – and then appointed two more – Gary Strodder and Tony Agana?**

14 Which Premiership club announced plans to become a public company?

15 **Who took over as Manchester City manager, the previous occupant having resigned after only 33 days 'for health reasons'?**

 ## Quiz 99   ### Season 1996-1997

1   **Who scored his 200th League goal in Arsenal's 2-0 victory over Middlesbrough on New Year's Day 1997?**

2   Which Nationwide First Division side knocked Southampton out of the FA Cup in a third round match on an icy pitch?

3   **For which club was Ian Culverhouse playing when he achieved the unwanted distinction of being sent off after only 52 seconds – sooner than anyone else in the history of the FA Cup?**

4   Which of the season's sacked managers became the first Technical Director of the FA?

5   **From which Italian club did Tottenham Hotspur sign Swiss international defender Ramon Vega for £3.7 million?**

6   Onto which club did West Ham United manage to offload Romanian midfielder Ilie Dumitrescu for £1 million?

7   **Which other Romanian did West Ham United return to sender – Espanol (Spain)?**

8   From which club did Leeds United sign Robert Molenaar for £1 million?

9   **Which former England captain – a star with West Bromwich Albion, Manchester United and Middlesbrough – finally gave up playing on his 40th birthday?**

10   Who, on January 14, became manager of Newcastle United?

11   **And, six days later, which Portuguese defender became his first signing for his new club?**

12   Who did Middlesbrough buy for £2.7 million from Inter Milan?

13   **Who announced his intention to play for Arsenal next season in the morning and got dropped in the evening by his present club, Paris St Germain?**

14   From which Nationwide First Division club did Leicester City sign Matt Elliott for £1.6 million?

15   **Which Scottish manager was banned from the touchline for a year after making remarks to officials after a local derby?**

 ## Quiz 100   Season 1996-1997

1   Name the owner of the Pizza Express restaurant chain who bought a 97% stake in Peterborough United for about £1 million.

2   Who bought twenty-five per cent of Rangers for £40 million?

3   Who bought fifty-one per cent of Portsmouth for one pound?

4   Which Portuguese scored for West Ham United in their FA Cup third round match on a frozen pitch at Second Division Wrexham?

5   And who scored a last minute winner for Wrexham in the replay at Upton Park?

6   Which former England international scored the winner for Bradford City as they beat Everton 3-2 at Goodison Park in the FA Cup third round?

7   Recovering rapidly from his illness while at Maine Road, who became part-time assistant to Dave Bassett at Crystal Palace?

8   To which Italian club did unsettled Andrei Kanchelskis move from Everton?

9   Who was sacked as manager of Plymouth Argyle after leading them to promotion in the previous season?

10   Who took over as manager of West Bromwich Albion?

11   Who was sacked as manager of First Division Millwall as part of a cost-cutting exercise?

12   Which former Everton player resigned as manager of Oldham Athletic?

13   Whose goal for Italy inflicted England's first ever World Cup defeat at Wembley?

14   Who was the England goalkeeper beaten at the near post?

15   Who did Blackburn Rovers buy from Odense for £2.5 million?

 ## Quiz 101   Season 1996-1997

1 **Which referee awarded Chelsea a controversial penalty in extra time in their FA Cup fifth round replay with Leicester City?**

2 Who took over as general manager of Nottingham Forest?

3 **Who did Manchester United beat 4-0 at Old Trafford in the Champions' Cup quarter-final?**

4 Who did Nottingham Forest buy from Celtic to get them out of trouble?

5 **Who did Blackburn Rovers announce would be their next manager after the last appointment said he was very sorry but he wouldn't be coming after all?**

6 Of which team was he previously manager?

7 **For which Italian club did Queens Park Rangers striker Daniele Dichio sign?**

8 Who refereed the Premiership clash at Highbury in which Liverpool were awarded a penalty despite the protestations of Robbie Fowler that he had not been fouled?

9 **Which former Leeds United and Scotland forward left his job as manager of Bristol City by mutual consent?**

10 Which former England forward left his job as manager of his old club, Everton, by mutual consent?

11 **Who took over as caretaker player-manager at Goodison?**

12 Which Liverpool season ticket holder is chairman of Everton?

13 **Who did Celtic buy from Aston Villa for £2.4 million?**

14 Which Swiss World Cup referee was banned for life for attempted bribery, partly through the evidence of Eric Cantona?

15 **Who announced his retirement from international football after winning 99 caps for Wales?**

1 **Mike Reed** 2 Dave Bassett 3 **FC Porto** 4 Pierre van Hooijdonk 5 **Roy Hodgson** 6 Inter Milan 7 **Sampdoria** 8 Gerald Ashby 9 **Joe Jordan** 10 Joe Royle 11 **Dave Watson** 12 Peter Johnson 13 **Tommy Johnson** 14 Kurt Rothlisburger 15 **Neville Southall**

Quiz 102

Season 1996-1997

1 Faced with the prospect of playing their last four matches in nine days, which Premiership club applied to have the season extended?

2 The manager of which club – then second in the Premiership – described the idea as ridiculous?

3 For the second leg of their Cup Winners' Cup semi-final against Paris St Germain, who did Liverpool drop for the first time in his long and distinguished career?

4 Which Chesterfield player had what looked like a good goal disallowed in their FA Cup semi-final against Middlesbrough?

5 Why did UEFA warn that, after 1997-98, they would let no more English Coca-Cola Cup winners into the UEFA Cup?

6 Who returned as chairman of Watford after a seven-year absence?

7 Who was PFA Footballer of the Year?

8 Who was the Football Writers' Footballer of the Year?

9 Who was sacked as manager of Celtic?

10 Who were Sunderland's opponents in the last ever match at Roker Park, and what was the result?

11 Who was the captain of the Luton Town youth team signed by Arsenal for £1 million?

12 How much did Aston Villa pay Liverpool for Stan Collymore?

13 Whose move from West Ham United to Everton for £4.25 million created a new Premiership transfer record?

14 Who became the first player in the 20th century to win four FA Cup winner's medals?

15 Which player announced his retirement on May 18, six days before his 31st birthday?

---

13 **Slaven Bilic** 14 Mark Hughes (Chelsea) 15 Eric Cantona (**Manchester United**)
9 Tommy **Burns** 10 Sunderland 3 Everton 0 11 **Matthew Upson** 12 £7 million
6 Elton John 7 **Alan Shearer (Newcastle United)** 8 Gianfranco Zola (Chelsea)
wanted the Premiership reduced from 20 clubs to 18 and the League refused
1 **Manchester United** 2 Arsenal 3 John Barnes 4 Jonathan Howard 5 Because UEFA

Quiz 103   **Season 1997-1998**

1 **Why was Scotland's international scheduled for Saturday September 6 postponed?**

2 Which Blackburn player scored two goals for Scotland in their 4-1 defeat of Belarus in a World Cup qualifier?

3 **Which Chelsea player scored the winner for Norway against Azerbaijan in a World Cup qualifier?**

4 Which Arsenal player scored two goals for England in their 4-0 World Cup victory over Moldova?

5 **Which Arsenal player captained England in their World Cup qualifier away to Italy?**

6 Who was the captain of Italy?

7 **Who was the manager of Italy?**

8 Who had he replaced after Euro '96?

9 **Which Italian was sent off during the 0-0 draw with England?**

10 Which club chairman said 'I have never believed in managers' after sacking Mervyn Day?

11 **Who were Chelsea's opponents in the first round of the European Cup Winners' Cup?**

12 Who scored off his backside for Chelsea in the second leg of this tie?

13 **In the Premiership in September, which teams drew 3-3, three of the goals coming controversially in time added on at the end of the match?**

14 Which former Chelsea central defender did West Ham United buy from Blackburn Rovers for £2.3 million?

15 **Which Danish central defender did West Ham United sell to Celtic for £1.4 million?**

Quiz 104

Season 1997-1998

1 **Why was West Ham United's Rio Ferdinand dropped from the England squad for the game against Moldova?**

2 Who bought Fulham of the Nationwide Second Division?

3 **Which other going concern in West London did he already own?**

4 To which French club was Fabrizio Ravanelli eventually transferred from Middlesbrough for £5 million?

5 **Who did Liverpool meet in the first round of the UEFA Cup?**

6 Which defender scored both goals for Newcastle United in their 2-2 draw away to Dynamo Kiev in the Champions' League?

7 **Who did Sheffield Wednesday buy from Molde in his native Norway for £800,000?**

8 Who did Bolton Wanderers buy for a club record £3.5 million?

9 **Which Arsenal player missed an away match in Greece because of his fear of flying?**

10 Which Nationwide First Division team knocked Manchester United out of the Coca-Cola Cup in the third round?

11 **In September, which chairman said of which recently deceased fellow director: 'He left bitterness and wounds'?**

12 Who scored for PSV Eindhoven as they beat Newcastle United 1-0 in the Champions' League?

13 **With which Spanish team did Aston Villa draw 0-0 in the UEFA Cup second round first leg?**

14 Who beat Liverpool 3-0 in the UEFA Cup second round first leg?

15 **Who resigned as manager of Swansea City only 13 days after taking over?**

---

1 Because he had been convicted of a drink-driving offence 2 Mohamed al Fayed 3 **Harrods** 4 Olympique Marseille 5 **Celtic** 6 John Beresford 7 **Petter Rudi** 8 Dean Holdsworth 9 **Dennis Bergkamp** 10 Ipswich Town 11 **Ken Bates of Matthew Harding (Chelsea)** 12 Wim Jonk 13 **Athletic Bilbao** 14 Strasbourg 15 **Micky Adams**

Quiz 105

Season 1997-1998

1 **Which three other clubs were in Manchester United's Champions' League group?**

2 Which three other clubs were in Newcastle's Champions' League group?

3 **Who was sacked in October as manager of Northern Ireland?**

4 Name the Northern Ireland assistant manager, who also got the boot.

5 **Name the player bought by Liverpool from Columbus Crew.**

6 What was the score in the snowy first leg of Chelsea's Cup Winners' Cup second round tie in Tromso (Norway)?

7 **Which Villa striker accused one of his team-mates of being, not 'Stan the man' but 'the wrong man'?**

8 Which Arsenal defender was sent off in the Premiership match against Aston Villa for handling the ref?

9 **Who scored a hat trick in Manchester United's 7-0 Premiership defeat of Barnsley?**

10 Which Bolton Wanderers defender was sent off in their match at West Ham United on October 18?

11 **Why, according to John Hartson of West Ham United, is referee Mike Reed like an ancient Greek poet?**

12 Who announced in October his intention to leave Rangers at the end of the 1997-98 season?

13 **Which Manchester United player scored the Republic of Ireland's goal in their 1-1 draw with Belgium in the first leg of the World Cup qualifying play-off?**

14 And which six other nations were paired in the other three play-offs?

15 **Who were Derby County's Premiership visitors on the night the floodlights went out during the match?**

Quiz 106

Season 1997-1998

1 Which was the second Premiership match of the season to be abandoned through floodlight failure?

2 Who scored the goals that took Aston Villa through 2-1 in the second leg of their second round UEFA Cup tie with Athletic Bilbao?

3 Who hit a Champions' League hat-trick for Manchester United in their 3-1 win at Feyenoord?

4 In November, who was appointed manager of Brentford in succession to David Webb?

5 What was the score in the second leg of Chelsea's Cup Winners' Cup second round tie with Tromso?

6 Who hit whom during the Chelsea v West Ham United Premiership match at Stamford Bridge?

7 Who was given a vote of confidence by the board of Manchester City?

8 Who was sacked as manager of Queens Park Rangers?

9 Who did Crystal Palace buy from Juventus for £1.7 million?

10 Ron Atkinson took over as manager of Sheffield Wednesday – who had just been sacked?

11 Where had Atkinson first been a manager, between December 1971 and November 1974?

12 Where was Atkinson's first League manager's job, from November 1974 to January 1978?

13 Which Scot took over as manager of Benfica?

14 Who scored for the Republic of Ireland in their 2-1 defeat in the second leg of the World Cup qualifying play-off against Belgium in Brussels?

15 Who was the manager of Belgium?

---

1 **West Ham United v Crystal Palace** 2 Ian Taylor and Dwight Yorke 3 **Andy Cole**
4 Micky Adams 5 Chelsea 7 Tromso 1 6 Eyal Berkovic hit John Moncur (both West Ham players)
7 **Manager Frank Clark** 8 Bruce Rioch 9 **Michele Padovano** 10 David Pleat 11 **Kettering**
12 Cambridge United 13 **Graeme Souness** 14 Ray Houghton 15 Georges Leekens

 Quiz 107   **Season 1997-1998**

1 **Who scored the only goal of the World Cup qualifying play-off second leg that enabled Italy to go through to the Finals at the expense of Russia?**

2 For which Italian Serie A club was he playing at the time?

3 **In November, it was widely reported that the world's richest man was interested in buying Everton – who was he?**

4 Which Nationwide First Division team knocked Leeds United out of the Coca-Cola Cup at Elland Road?

5 **Who took over as coach of Tottenham Hotspur after the departure of Gerry Francis?**

6 With which Swiss club had he previously held the same position?

7 **What was the name of the fitness coach he tried but failed to bring with him to England?**

8 Who scored Barnsley's goal in their Premiership win at Anfield?

9 **Which Romanian team beat Aston Villa 2-1 in the first leg of their third round UEFA Cup tie?**

10 Who scored Villa's valuable away goal?

11 **In an Internet poll of half a million people in 110 countries, who was voted the best footballer of all time?**

12 Which British player was runner-up?

13 **Which Englishman came third?**

14 Which Dutchman came fourth?

15 **Which former England captain was fifth?**

 # Quiz 108   Season 1997-1998

1 In December, which manager left West Bromwich Albion to take over the reins at Queens Park Rangers?

2 By winning 6-1 at White Hart Lane, which team inflicted Tottenham Hotspur's worst home defeat since 1935?

3 Who scored Aston Villa's goals in their 2-0 UEFA Cup third round second leg victory against Steua Bucharest to take them through 3-2 on aggregate?

4 Who scored the goal for Juventus that beat Manchester United in their Champions League game in Turin?

5 Name the former Leeds United and Scotland star who died on December 7.

6 In December, Coventry City fans may have been surprised to see someone other than Steve Ogrizovic in their goal – who was his replacement?

7 Who scored his first goal for Southampton after 10 years as a regular (against Leicester City)?

8 Who missed his third penalty in succession for Manchester United during their 1-0 Premiership victory over Aston Villa?

9 Which Unibond League team knocked Lincoln City out of the FA Cup to earn a crack at Premiership opposition in the third round?

10 Which former Newcastle player scored the winning goal for Manchester United on his return to St James's Park?

11 Which Premiership match was the scene of the season's third floodlight failure?

12 Which Romanian international did Coventry City buy for £3.25 from Grasshopper Zurich?

13 Who came back to Spurs after having left in 1994?

14 In which Scottish Third Division match was the referee hit by a coin thrown from the crowd?

15 Which ailing Yorkshire team did Leyton Orient beat 8-0 in a Third Division match, thus equalling their highest ever score?

1 Ray Harford 2 Chelsea 3 Ian Taylor and Dwight Yorke 4 Filippo Inzaghi 5 Billy Bremner 6 Magnus Hedman 7 Francis Benali 8 Teddy Sheringham 9 Emley 10 Andy Cole 11 Wimbledon v Arsenal 12 Viorel Moldovan 13 Jurgen Klinsmann 14 Montrose v Arbroath 15 Doncaster Rovers

Quiz 109

Season 1997-1998

1 **Which old Preston North End hero was the only sporting knight in the New Year's Honours List?**

2 From which Spanish club did Everton acquire French international striker Mickael Medar?

3 **Which BBC radio programme celebrated its 50th anniversary on Saturday January 3, 1998?**

4 Now on Radio Five Live, which station had it previously been on?

5 **Who scored for Emley at West Ham in the FA Cup third round?**

6 Who missed a penalty for West Ham United in their Coca-Cola Cup quarter-final against Arsenal?

7 **Name the four Coca-Cola Cup semi-finalists.**

8 Which Rangers star announced in March that he would be joining Chelsea at the end of the season?

9 **Who finally moved from Middlesbrough to Tenerife?**

10 Which former England striker moved from Sheffield United to Benfica?

11 **When the draw for the qualifying matches of Euro 2000 was announced, who came out in England's group?**

12 Who was drawn in Northern Ireland's group?

13 **Who was drawn in the Republic of Ireland's group?**

14 Who was drawn in Scotland's group?

15 **Who was drawn in the same group as Wales?**

 **Quiz 110** **Season 1997-1998**

1 Which goalkeeper scored in the penalty shoot-out in which his team knocked Watford out of the FA Cup?

2 Which club announced plans for a permanent move to Wembley?

3 Which Liverpool player was widely reported in January to be on the brink of a move to Barcelona?

4 In a Carling Net website poll, who was voted the most popular British football commentator?

5 Uwe Rosler missed a penalty for Manchester City in their FA Cup fourth round tie at home to West Ham United. Which club in the former East Germany did he come from?

6 Which club sacked manager Chris Kamara?

7 To which club did he go two weeks later?

8 Who did he replace there?

9 In the FA Cup fourth round, Newcastle United drew 1-1 at Stevenage Borough. Who scored for the Premiership club?

10 Who equalised for the underdogs from the Vauxhall Conference?

11 Which Aston Villa player allegedly spat at his own club's fans?

12 Which Queens Park Rangers striker moved to West Ham United?

13 A couple of weeks later, which two Northern Ireland internationals made the same journey across London in the opposite direction?

14 Who bought Andy Hinchcliffe from Everton for £3 million?

15 How did Marco Negri sustain the eye injury that left him unfit to play for Rangers?

1 Kevin Pressman (Sheffield Wednesday) 2 Arsenal 3 Steve McManaman 4 John Motson
5 Dynamo Dresden 6 Bradford City 7 Stoke City 8 Chic Bates 9 Alan Shearer
10 Giuliano Grazioli 11 Savo Milosevic 12 Trevor Sinclair 13 Ian Dowie and Kevin Rowland
14 Sheffield Wednesday 15 Playing squash

Quiz 111   Season 1997-1998

1   **During which Nationwide First Division match on February 2 was a linesman attacked and knocked unconscious by a spectator?**

2   Who was named as the English referee for the forthcoming World Cup?

3   **Who was named as the Scottish referee for the forthcoming World Cup?**

4   What is the name of Derby County's new stadium?

5   **What was the name of their old stadium?**

6   Which Englishman was appointed manager of Northern Ireland?

7   **Which former Scotland international is his assistant?**

8   Who became the youngest England international this century when he won his first cap against Chile at the age of 18 years and 59 days?

9   **Who scored both goals in Chile's 2-0 victory in this match?**

10   Who was the manager of Chile?

11   **In the fifth round of the FA Cup, who won at Villa Park for the first time ever?**

12   Who was appointed the new manager of Rangers?

13   **Which was his previous club?**

14   From which Italian club did Middlesbrough buy Marco Branca?

15   **Who scored Middlesbrough's first goal in the second leg of their Coca-Cola Cup semi-final against Liverpool?**

---

1 **Portsmouth v Sheffield United** 2 Paul Durkin 3 Hugh Dallas 4 Pride Park
5 **The Baseball Ground** 6 Lawrie McMenemy 7 Joe Jordan 8 Michael Owen (Liverpool)
9 **Marcelo Salas** 10 Nelson Acosta 11 **Coventry City** 12 Dick Advocaat
13 **PSV Eindhoven** 14 Internazionale 15 **Paul Merson**

 **Quiz 112**   **Season 1997-1998**

1 **After a 2-1 Arsenal victory over Chelsea in the first game, what was the score in the Coca-Cola Cup semi-final second leg at Stamford Bridge?**

2 Which Arsenal player was sent off in the second game?

3 **What upheaval had Chelsea suffered in the fortnight between the two legs?**

4 What is the name of the Aston Villa chairman?

5 **Who took over from Brian Little as manager of Aston Villa?**

6 Of which Nationwide Second Division club had he previously been manager?

7 **What is his unusual method of attracting his players' attention during the course of a match?**

8 At about the same time, which sponsor announced its intention not to take up an option to continue having its name on the front of Villa's shirts?

9 **Of which electronics company are they a subsidiary?**

10 Who scored two goals for Barnsley in their FA Cup fifth round replay victory over Manchester United?

11 **Frank Clark's November vote of confidence was followed in February by the sack. Who took his place as manager of Manchester City?**

12 Which millionaire businessman announced plans to buy Crystal Palace?

13 **Which leading Italian club was said to be a major part of this deal?**

14 Who was sacked as manager of Brighton and Hove Albion?

15 **Who was appointed to replace him?**

 # Quiz 113   Season 1997-1998

1   **In March, who won the African Cup of Nations?**

2   Who were the runners-up?

3   **Where was the tournament played?**

4   Who scored the only goal of the UEFA Cup quarter-final first leg match in which Atletico Madrid beat Aston Villa?

5   **Which former Brighton and Liverpool forward was one of Spanish television's top commentators at the game?**

6   What injury prevented Juninho from playing in this match for Atletico?

7   **Who left his job as manager of Sheffield United four days before their FA Cup sixth round tie against Coventry City?**

8   Who scored the only goal in Arsenal's Premiership victory at Old Trafford?

9   **Who scored both goals in Chelsea's 2-1 Cup Winners' Cup quarter final win over Real Betis?**

10   Who scored a goal and gave a way a penalty in the FA Cup sixth round match between Arsenal and West Ham United?

11   **Which two German-speakers had a public row in the Tottenham tunnel?**

12   Who walked out on Birmingham City but came back to them a couple of days later?

13   **Who did Newcastle United buy for £2 million from Olympiakos?**

14   Which Liverpool player did Stan Collymore accuse of making racist remarks to him during Aston Villa's visit to Anfield?

15   **Which two Chelsea players scored twice in their 6-2 defeat of Crystal Palace at Stamford Bridge in the Premiership?**

---

1 **Egypt** 2 South Africa 3 **Ouagadougu, Burkina Faso** 4 Christian Vieri (penalty) 5 **Michael Robinson** 6 A broken leg 7 **Nigel Spackman** 8 Marc Overmars 9 **Tore Andre Flo** 10 Ian Pearce (West Ham United) 11 **Christian Gross and Jurgen Klinsmann** 12 Trevor Francis 13 **Nicos Dabizas** 14 Steve Harkness 15 Gianluca Vialli and Tore Andre Flo

Quiz 114   Season 1997-1998

1 **Who stepped down as chairman of Manchester City?**

2 In their FA Cup sixth round replay against Arsenal, which three West Ham players failed to score in the penalty shoot-out?

3 **Who scored for Aston Villa's two goals in the second leg of their UEFA Cup quarter-final against Atletico Madrid?**

4 Who scored Atletico's goal to send the Spanish club through on away goals?

5 **Who knocked Manchester United out of the European Cup?**

6 After a 0-0 draw in the away leg, United drew 1-1 at home – which French international scored after four minutes for the visitors?

7 **And who equalised for United early in the second half?**

8 What was the score in the second leg of Chelsea's Cup Winners' Cup quarter-final against Real Betis?

9 **Which Nationwide Third Division club was served with a winding-up order by the Inland Revenue?**

10 Which two directors of Newcastle United resigned after tabloid press revelations about their behaviour in Marbella?

11 **Who moved from Rangers to Middlesbrough?**

12 Which Tottenham Hotspur player scored in the Switzerland v England friendly international?

13 **Where was this match played?**

14 Name the two Blackburn Rovers players who took part in this match.

15 **How many Barnsley players remained on the pitch at the end of their Premiership match at home to Liverpool?**

1 **Francis Lee** 2 John Harrison, Eyal Berkovic and Samassi Abou 3 **Ian Taylor and Stan Collymore** 4 Jose Luis Caminero 5 **AS Monaco** 6 David Trezeguet 7 **Ole Gunnar Solskjaer** 8 Chelsea 3 Real Betis 1 (Aggregate 5-2) 9 **Chester City** 10 Douglas Hall and Freddie Shepherd 11 **Paul Gascoigne** 12 Ramon Vega for Switzerland 13 **The Wankdorf Stadium, Berne** 14 Flowers (England) and Henchoz (Switzerland) 15 **Eight**

Quiz 115

Season 1997-1998

1 **Chelsea won the Coca-Cola Cup, beating Middlesbrough 2-0 in the Final at Wembley. Who scored the goals?**

2 Dennis Wise was captain, but who collected the Cup for Chelsea?

3 **Which government minister handed him the Cup?**

4 Who made his Middlesbrough debut when he came on as a substitute in the Coca-Cola Cup Final?

5 **With which airline did Leeds United fly home from their Premiership match at Upton Park?**

6 From which airport did they take off?

7 **Who kept Arsenal's title hopes alive by scoring the only goal in their Premiership victory at the Reebok Stadium, Bolton?**

8 In the European Cup semi-final first leg, who scored a hat-trick — including two penalties — for Juventus against AS Monaco?

9 **Who replaced Tim Flowers in goal during Blackburn Rovers' 2-1 Premiership victory over Barnsley?**

10 In the other European Cup semi-final first leg, who scored the goals that gave Real Madrid a 2-0 victory over Borussia Dortmund?

11 **Why was the kick-off in this match delayed for 75 minutes?**

12 Who scored for Vicenza when they beat Chelsea 1-0 in the first leg of the Cup Winners' Cup semi-final?

13 **In the other Cup Winners' Cup semi-final, who scored in the last minute to give Stuttgart a 2-1 victory over Lokomotiv Moscow?**

14 Which Third Division club became the first side to guarantee promotion in March since Middlesbrough went up from Division Two in 1974?

15 **Which former Scotland international and Cup-winner with Newcastle United in 1955 died on March 19, 1998 at the age of 73?**

Quiz 116   Season 1997-1998

1   Outside which Second Division ground was a fan stabbed to death after the game against Fulham?

2   Who scored two goals for Heart of Midlothian in their 3-1 defeat of Falkirk in the semi-final of the Scottish FA Cup?

3   **Who scored for Falkirk?**

4   Who scored the killer blow for Hearts in the 90th minute?

5   **Who was manager of Falkirk?**

6   Which defender headed spectacularly into his own net as Barnsley went down 2-1 at Leeds in the Premiership?

7   **Who scored for Barnsley and was then sent off for two bookable cases of dissent in less than a minute?**

8   Who scored for Arsenal in their 1-0 FA Cup semi-final victory over Wolverhampton Wanderers?

9   **Who was the Littlewoods Man of the Arsenal v Wolves FA Cup semi-final, nominated by Ron Atkinson?**

10 Where was the match played?

11 **Who scored for Newcastle United as they beat Sheffield United 1-0 in the other FA Cup semi-final?**

12 Who was the manager of Sheffield United?

13 **At which neutral venue was this match played?**

14 Who scored the goals for Rangers that knocked Celtic out of the Scottish FA Cup at the semi-final stage?

15 **Hampden Park was under reconstruction, so the two teams drew lots to decide at which of their grounds the semi-final would be played. Who won the draw?**

1 Gillingham 2 Stephane Adam 3 **Kevin McAllister** 4 Neil McCann 5 **Alex Totten**
6 Adrian Moses 7 **Georgi Hristov** 8 Christopher Wreh 9 **Patrick Viera** 10 Villa Park
11 **Alan Shearer** 12 Alan Thompson 13 **Old Trafford** 14 Ally McCoist and Jorg Albertz
15 Celtic – the match was played at Parkhead

Quiz 117

Season 1997-1998

1 Which of Arsenal's foreign legion was PFA Player of the Year?

2 Name the Irish international who was the last Arsenal player to win this award in 1979.

3 Which Manchester United striker was runner-up in the 1998 poll?

4 Who was PFA Young Player of the Year, ahead of Kevin Davies (Southampton) and Rio Ferdinand (West Ham United)?

5 Which folk hero (or villain, depending on your view) moved from Wimbledon to Queens Park Rangers?

6 On Good Friday, April 10, which Second Division side became the second team in England to clinch promotion this season after their closest rivals, Grimsby Town, failed to win at Wycombe Wanderers?

7 Who scored and was then sent off in the Good Friday Premiership match between Manchester United and Liverpool?

8 Which PSV Eindhoven centre back – the Dutch Player of the Year – was linked in early April with a £9 million move to Manchester United?

9 Bob Taylor – the scorer of Bolton Wanderers' winning goal against Blackburn Rovers – was on loan from which Midlands club?

10 A week after their semi-final victories, the FA Cup finalists met in the Premiership, Arsenal beating Newcastle United 3-1 at Highbury. Who scored two goals in this match?

11 Martin Keown missed this match because of an injury to his eye socket – who took his place in the Arsenal defence?

12 Who scored Newcastle's goal – the first Arsenal had conceded in nearly 14 hours of Premiership football?

13 Which club learned on April 11 that they had lost their Football League status?

14 Which two players – one from each side – were sent off in West Ham United's 0-0 draw with Derby County in the Premiership?

15 Which Italian scored a hat-trick for Middlesbrough as they beat Bury 4-0 in the First Division?

---

15 Marco Branca

1 Dennis Bergkamp 2 Liam Brady 3 Andy Cole 4 Michael Owen (Liverpool) 5 Vinnie Jones 6 Bristol City 7 Michael Owen 8 Jaap Stam 9 West Bromwich Albion 10 Nicholas Anelka 11 Steve Bould 12 Warren Barton 13 Doncaster Rovers 14 John Hartson and Stefano Eranio

Quiz 118

Season 1997-1998

1. **Who scored two goals for Arsenal in their 4-1 defeat of Blackburn Rovers at Ewood Park on Easter Monday?**

2. Which former Nottingham Forest striker scored for Watford in the 1-1 draw with Bristol City that assured them of promotion from the Second Division?

3. **Which Brazilian scored both goals for Internazionale as they beat Spartak Moscow 2-1 in the second leg of the UEFA Cup semi-final, winning 4-2 on aggregate?**

4. Who knocked Atletico Madrid, conquerors of Aston Villa, out of the UEFA Cup in the semi-final?

5. **Who came on as substitute and scored the killer goal for Chelsea in their 3-1 victory over Vicenza in the second leg of the Cup Winners' Cup semi-final?**

6. In this match, which Uruguayan made his first appearance for Chelsea in six months after sustaining a career-threatening knee injury?

7. **Who did VfB Stuttgart beat in the other semi-final of the Cup Winners' Cup?**

8. Name the three 'H's who scored for Leeds United in their 3-2 win at Bolton Wanderers in the Premiership on April 18.

9. **Which Manchester United player was sent off during their 1-1 home draw with Newcastle United?**

10. Who notched up their first home win of the season with a 3-1 victory over Derby County on April 18?

11. **Halifax Town assured themselves of the GM Vauxhall Conference title and thus booked their return to the Football League. In which year had they dropped out of it?**

12. Which Tottenham Hotspur player was sent off in their Premiership match at Barnsley on April 18?

13. **Who scored his 23rd and 24th goals of the season for West Ham United in their Premiership victory over Blackburn Rovers?**

14. What was the name of the faith healer summoned to help England in their preparations for their friendly with Portugal?

15. **Who won their first trophy for 18 years when they beat Bournemouth 2-1 after extra time in the Final of the Auto Windscreens Trophy?**

1 Ray Parlour 2 Jason Lee 3 Ronaldo 4 Lazio 5 Mark Hughes 6 Gustavo Poyet 7 Lokomotiv Moscow 8 Haaland, Halle, Hasselbaink 9 Ole Gunnar Solskjaer 10 Crystal Palace 11 1993 12 Ramon Vega 13 John Hartson 14 Eileen Drewery 15 Grimsby Town

Quiz 119

Season 1997-1998

1 **Who scored for Aberdeen in the 1-0 defeat of Rangers which left the losers three points behind Celtic with three matches to play?**

2 In April, for which Juventus and Italy striker were Manchester United reported to have made an £18 million bid?

3 **Which Southampton player staked a claim for a place in the full England World Cup squad with a hat-trick in the 'B' international against Russia at Loftus Road?**

4 Which Reading striker, formerly with West Ham United and Manchester City, announced that he was retiring at the end of the season to go and live with his Norwegian wife and child in Bergen?

5 **Which was the only Premiership club to take six points off West Ham United in 1997-98?**

6 Who came on as a substitute in the second half for Newcastle United at Tottenham, only to leave the field with a ligament injury four minutes later?

7 **What was unusual about the ball used in the Premiership match between Everton and Sheffield Wednesday on April 25?**

8 Who scored his first goal for Chelsea in six years as they beat Liverpool 4-1?

9 **Who scored a hat-trick for Coventry City in their 3-3 draw at Leeds United?**

10 Who scored twice for Leeds in the same match?

11 **Which team won promotion to the Nationwide Second Division in their first year as a member of the Football League?**

12 Which seaside team completed a drop from First to Third Divisions in successive seasons?

13 **Manchester City announced that Uwe Rosler would be returning to Germany at the end of the season. For which Bundesliga club had he signed?**

14 Who was made full-time manager of Wycombe Wanderers after doing the job on a temporary basis since the departure of John Gregory?

15 **Name the club which was the last to have been promoted from last season's First Division and the first to be relegated from this year's Premiership.**

 # Quiz 120   Season 1997-1998

1   As Arsenal edged towards their first Premiership title, which Frenchman scored the only goal – his second for the club – in their victory over Derby County?

2   Which Blackburn Rovers player was shown the red card while on the bench during his team's 2-0 defeat at Coventry?

3   Who scored four of Tottenham Hotspur's goals in their 6-2 victory at Wimbledon?

4   Which Wimbledon defender was sent off in this match for the second time this season?

5   Which team was relegated from the top division for the first time since the Scottish League was founded in 1890?

6   When Attilio Lombardo stood down as acting player-coach of Crystal Palace, who first took over the day-to-day running of team affairs?

7   And who took over from him?

8   Who beat Rangers in their last home match of the season?

9   Dennis Bergkamp was voted the Football Writers' Footballer of the Year. Who, in 1971, was the last Arsenal player to have won this award?

10   Name the Greek international who scored the goal for Leicester City that condemned Barnsley to relegation?

11   Reading played their last match at Elm Park, their home since 1896. What is the name of their new ground?

12   Why is it so called?

13   Which clubs clinched the two automatic promotion places from Division One?

14   Who scored for Tranmere Rovers against Wolverhampton Wanderers in his last match before retirement?

15   Which three clubs were relegated from Division One?

 # Quiz 121   ### Season 1997-1998

1   Which former Norwich and Nottingham Forest forward was found dead in a garage in Shoreditch, East London, at the age of 37?

2   Arsenal clinched the Premiership title by beating Everton in their last home match of the season. Which Arsenal player made his 500th appearance for the club in this game?

3   **Who scored two goals in Arsenal's 4-0 victory over Everton?**

4   Which Nigerian-born 20-year-old scored his first two goals for West Ham United in their 3-3 draw with relegated Crystal Palace?

5   **Who scored twice for Liverpool in their 4-0 Premiership victory over new Champions Arsenal?**

6   Which forward scored for Liverpool in this match and also missed a penalty?

7   **In the UEFA Cup Final, Inter Milan beat Lazio 3-0. Where was the match played?**

8   One player from each side was sent off – name either

9   **What was the name of Inter Milan's coach?**

10 In Newcastle United's Premiership match against Leicester City, who did England captain Alan Shearer allegedly kick when he was down?

11 **Who was sacked as manager of Fulham shortly after leading them to a place in the Second Division play-offs?**

12 Who parted company with First Division Millwall 'by mutual consent' after managing the club since June 1997?

13 **Who scored a penalty for Fulham as they drew 1-1 with Grimsby Town in the first leg of their Second Division play-off?**

14 Who scored for Celtic as they beat St Johnstone 2-0 in their final League match of the season to clinch their first Scottish title since 1988?

15 **Who was Celtic's Dutch coach?**

 ## Quiz 122 — Season 1997-1998

1   Who was the first captain of Celtic to lift the Premier League trophy for 10 years?

2   Who scored a penalty and was sent off in Rangers' last League match of the season at Dundee United?

3   Who scored for Everton in the 1-1 home draw with Coventry City that guaranteed their safety in the Premiership?

4   Which Everton player had a penalty saved in the same match?

5   And who saved it?

6   Which was the only Premiership team beaten at home and away by Crystal Palace in 1997-98?

7   Which Newcastle United player was sent off at Ewood Park in the last match of the season against his previous club?

8   Which Chelsea player scored his first Premiership goal in their 2-0 defeat of Bolton Wanderers at Stamford Bridge?

9   Who scored a penalty in Aston Villa's home win over new Champions Arsenal?

10 Who was the FA Carling Premiership's leading scorer in the 1997-98, with 25 goals in all competitions?

11 A month before the start of the World Cup squad, which member of the England squad was outed as a cigarette smoker?

12 Which former Manchester United and Leeds United striker was appointed manager of Oldham Athletic in place of Neil Warnock?

13 To which Spanish club did Aston Villa sell Yugoslav international Savo Milosevic for £3.5 million?

14 Who was sacked as manager of Second Division Burnley?

15 Who took over as manager of Stoke City?

 **Quiz 123**   **Season 1997-1998**

1   **Where was the European Cup Winners' Cup Final played?**

2   Graeme Le Saux had a calf injury – who took his place at left back for Chelsea in the Cup Winners' Cup Final?

3   **Gianfranco Zola came on as substitute in the 71st minute and scored the winner with his first touch. Which Chelsea forward did he replace?**

4   Which Chelsea player was sent off?

5   **Which VfB Stuttgart player was dismissed in the dying seconds of the match?**

6   To which Chelsea player was the Cup Winners' Cup presented?

7   **This victory made England the country with the greatest number of victories in the history of the Cup Winners' Cup – how many?**

8   Who did Sunderland beat in their First Division play-off semi-final?

9   **Who did Charlton Athletic beat in their First Division play-off semi-final?**

10   Which Fulham player was sent off in the second leg of their Second Division play-off semi-final against Grimsby Town?

11   **Who scored the first goal for Arsenal in the FA Cup Final against Newcastle United?**

12   Who scored the second goal for Arsenal in the same match?

13   **Who was Littlewoods Man of the Match in the 1998 FA Cup Final?**

14   When was the last time Arsenal won the League and Cup double?

15   **Frank McLintock was their captain then – who was their victorious captain now?**

 ## Quiz 124   Season 1997-1998

1 Who scored from the penalty spot for Heart of Midlothian against Rangers after two minutes of the Scottish FA Cup Final?

2 Who had been fouled in the area?

3 Who scored the second Hearts goal after 52 minutes?

4 Who came on as substitute and pulled a goal back for Rangers nine minutes from time?

5 Who was manager of Hearts?

6 When had Hearts last won the Scottish FA Cup?

7 When had Hearts last won anything, and what was it?

8 In which year had Rangers last failed to win a trophy?

9 Which Scottish Third Division team played their last home game at Boghead and start the 1998-99 season at a new stadium in Castle Road?

10 Which former Italian national coach took over from Raddy Antic as coach of Atletico Madrid?

11 Who was appointed the new manager of Millwall?

12 Who bought Georgi Kinkladze from Manchester City?

13 Who offered all the England and Scotland players a week on his private island (Necker – normal price £13,000 a night) if they won the World Cup?

14 When his name did not appear in the England World Cup squad, who said:'I realise that it will probably need Hoddle to go before I get a chance and that might be a long time'?

15 Who took over as manager of Walsall?

Quiz 125

Season 1997-1998

1   Who did Real Madrid beat in the Final of the European Cup?

2   Where was the Final played?

3   What nationality is Predrag Mijatovic, who scored the only goal of the game?

4   Who was the German manager of Real Madrid?

5   How many times had Real previously won the European Cup?

6   In which year had they last won it?

7   Which Premiership club's season tickets became the first to break the £1000 mark?

8   Which Premiership club has the cheapest top-price season ticket in 1998-99, a comparative snip at £295?

9   Who did Colchester United beat in the Third Division Play-Off Final at Wembley?

10 Who scored the only goal of the match, from the penalty spot?

11 When was the last time Colchester United had been out of the lowest division?

12 With which country did England draw 0-0 in their last home game before the World Cup Finals?

13 Who did Grimsby Town beat 1-0 in the Second Division play-off Final to secure a return to the First Division only a year after they had been relegated?

14 Who scored the Grimsby winner?

15 Who is the manager of Grimsby Town?

Quiz 126   Season 1998-1999

1   From which club did Rangers buy Andrei Kanchelskis?

2   Who did Tottenham Hotspur buy from Perugia for £3.5 million?

3   Where did Manchester United get Jesper Blomqvist?

4   At which neutral ground did Rangers play Shelburne in the UEFA Cup?

5   Which Irish club held Celtic to a goalless draw at Parkhead in the Champions' League?

6   Who took over from Littlewoods as sponsors of the English FA Cup?

7   Who became the first English club to go out of Europe, after losing to Samsunspor in the Inter Toto Cup?

8   Who joined Everton from Monaco for £2.5 million?

9   Who became the first Peruvian to play in top-flight English football?

10 From which Dutch club did Sheffield Wednesday get Wim Jonk?

11 Who were double-winning Arsenal's opponents in the FA Charity Shield?

12 Who won the 1998 FA Charity Shield?

13 What nationality is Coventry City's new signing Robert Jarni?

14 Which First Division club drew the opening day's largest crowd - 41,008 for the visit of Queens Park Rangers?

15 Who spent a week at Aston Villa on his way home to Everton?

15 David Unsworth
10 PSV Eindhoven 11 Manchester United 12 Arsenal 13 Croatian 14 Sunderland
6 AXA insurance 7 Crystal Palace 8 John Collins 9 Nolberto Solano (Newcastle United)
1 Fiorentina 2 Marco Tramezzani 3 Parma 4 Tranmere Rovers 5 St Patrick's Athletic

Quiz 127

Season 1998-1999

1 Which broadcasting company made a £625 million takeover bid for Manchester United?

2 **Which broadcasting company made a bid for Arsenal?**

3 In the Premiership, who came from 3-0 down to win at Upton Park?

4 **Who came on as a substitute and scored two late goals to give Aston Villa a 3-2 victory at home to Stromsgodset in the UEFA Cup?**

5 Who scored for Arsenal in their Champions' League draw at Lens?

6 **Which Second Division club knocked West Ham United out of the Worthington Cup?**

7 Who scored his first League goal for Derby County in the 2-1 win at Leicester?

8 **Who inflicted Oxford United's record League defeat, 7-0?**

9 Which Blackburn Rovers player was sent off in the 4-3 home defeat by Chelsea?

10 **Which Chelsea player was sent off in the same match?**

11 Which Third Division team knocked Premiership Sheffield Wednesday out of the Worthington Cup?

12 **Who resigned as manager of Swindon Town?**

13 Which Third Division club had three players sent off during their match at Swansea?

14 **Who scored a hat trick for Aston Villa in the second leg of their UEFA Cup tie against Stromsgodset?**

15 Who scored twice for Arsenal in their 3-0 win at Newcastle?

Quiz 128

Season 1998-1999

1 **Who kicked Eyal Berkovic in the face at Chadwell Heath?**

2 With which Belgian Second Division club did Manchester United announce a 'feeder' arrangement?

3 **Which Finn resigned as manager of Motherwell?**

4 Which was the last club in England to win a League match?

5 **Which Blackburn Rovers player had his nose broken and got sent off against Arsenal?**

6 At whom did Paul Ince make a two-fingered gesture after being sent off in the Sweden v England European Championship game?

7 **Which Premiership manager did Leeds United want to approach when George Graham defected to White Hart Lane?**

8 Who was sold by Newcastle United to Aston Villa for £4 million?

9 **What was the score in the European Champions' League match between Brondby and Manchester United in Denmark?**

10 For how many matches was Paolo Di Canio banned for pushing referee Paul Alcock?

11 **Who booked 12 players in the Leeds United v Chelsea Premiership match?**

12 Which Chelsea player was sent off at the end of their 4-1 defeat of Aston Villa?

13 **Who scored the winner for Wales against Denmark?**

14 Who equalised for Chelsea in the first leg of their Cup Winners' Cup tie against Copenhagen?

15 **Who scored four of Liverpool's five goals against Nottingham Forest?**

Quiz 129 — Season 1998-1999

1 Which Spanish club knocked Aston Villa out of the UEFA Cup 3-2 on aggregate?

2 **Which Italian club knocked Leeds United out of the UEFA Cup?**

3 Name either of the Liverpool players sent off in their 2-2 draw at Valencia in the UEFA Cup.

4 **Which club did Manchester United beat 5-0 at Old Trafford in the Champions' League?**

5 Who scored Chelsea's winner in the Cup Winners' Cup game against Copenhagen and then promptly joined the losers?

6 **Who was sacked as manager of Wolverhampton Wanderers?**

7 In the 3-3 draw at Southampton, which Middlesbrough player was sent off for calling referee Paul Alcock 'useless'?

8 **Who won at Anfield for the first time since 1970?**

9 What number shirt did Pierre Van Hooijdonk wear on his return from self-imposed exile to the Nottingham Forest side?

10 **Who resigned as General Manager of Celtic?**

11 Which Chelsea player's season ended prematurely after a collision with West Ham United goalkeeper Shaka Hislop?

12 **Which French international scored twice on his debut as Rangers won 7-0 at St Johnstone?**

13 Which rock singer joined forces with Kenny Dalglish to make a takeover bid for Celtic?

14 **At Liverpool, who became Gérard Houllier's assistant manager on the departure of Roy Evans?**

15 Who scored a hat trick for Aston Villa in their 4-1 win over Southampton at The Dell?

---

1 Celta Vigo 2 **Roma** 3 Steve McManaman and Paul Ince 4 **Brøndby** 5 Brian Laudrup 6 **Mark McGhee** 7 Phil Stamp 8 **Derby County** 9 40 10 Jock **Brown** 11 Pierluigi Casiraghi 12 **Stephane Guivarc'h** 13 Jim Kerr of Simple Minds 14 **Phil Thompson** 15 Dion Dublin

Quiz 130
Season 1998-1999

1 **Who called Glenn Hoddle 'a coward' and 'a bad communicator'?**

2 Who inflicted Aston Villa's first League defeat of the season?

3 **Who scored two goals for Villa in this game and also missed a penalty?**

4 Who inflicted First Division leaders Sunderland's first League defeat of the season?

5 **Which wing-back was sold to Leicester City over the head of West Ham United manager Harry Redknapp?**

6 Who said 'The books have to be balanced and Harry [Redknapp] knows that as well as I did. He can like it or lump it'?

7 **Who scored the penalty against Newcastle United that gave Everton their first home win since April?**

8 Who was reported to have burst into tears on being told that he was leaving Everton for Newcastle?

9 **Which Arsenal player was sent off in the Champions' League game against Lens?**

10 Which Arsenal defender was accused of feigning injury against Lens in order to get Tony Vareilles sent off?

11 **Who won the Scottish Coca-Cola Cup?**

12 Who did they beat 2-1 in the Final?

13 **Celtic beat Rangers by the biggest margin for 30 years - what was the score?**

14 Name the assistant manager of Sheffield United who was arrested at Loftus Road for swearing.

15 **Who was sacked as manager of Blackburn Rovers?**

Quiz 131   Season 1998-1999

1   Who announced that he was going to step down as Everton chairman because of 'health concerns'?

2   **Which Premiership manager narrowly avoided hot water when he said that his players had 'a nice few bob' on themselves to win the Worthington Cup?**

3   Which West Ham United defender was sent off in his team's 4-0 premiership defeat at Elland Road?

4   **Which Chelsea player was sent off for the third time this season during a goalless draw at Goodison Park?**

5   Which Spanish club knocked Liverpool out of the UEFA Cup?

6   **Which Italian club knocked Rangers out of the UEFA Cup?**

7   Where did Celtic find Mark Viduka?

8   **What nationality is Mark Viduka?**

9   After scoring the winner against Aston Villa at Stamford Bridge, who was described by Chelsea manager Gianluca Vialli as 'a lethal weapon'?

10   **The FA announced that they were going to investigate transfer dealings between Tranmere Rovers and which Premiership club?**

11   Which Manchester United player was sent off during his side's 2-2 draw at White Hart Lane?

12   **Who beat Oxford 7-1 at the Manor?**

13   Who was described by Arsène Wenger as 'an aggressive player on the pitch but very kind off it'?

14   **Who scored Chelsea's equaliser at Old Trafford?**

15   From which First Division club did Coventry City buy John Aloisi for £650,000?

MIXED BAG

CARLING 10,000 FOOTBALL FACTS & QUESTIONS

Quiz 1

Also Known As

Identify the following:

1 **A 1960s goalkeeper known as the Flying Pig**

2 The winger known as the Kosher Garrincha

3 **The Welsh Wizard or the Prince of Wingers**

4 Der Kaiser

5 **Der Bomber**

6 The Ambassador of Football – the England player who objected most strongly to giving the Nazi salute before the match against Germany in Berlin in 1938

7 **Bald Eagle, a successful manager of Oxford United, Queens Park Rangers, Newcastle United and Derby County**

8 Someone known as The Cat when he was at home and the Mexico Fumbler when he was away

9 **Thomas the Book**

10 The Boy, until recently Arsenal's all-time leading scorer

11 **The Tipton Terror**

12 Budgie

13 **The Vulture**

14 Captain Marvel

15 **The Gentle Giant**

15 John Charles (Leeds United and Wales)

14 Bryan Robson (WBA, Manchester United and England) 13 Emilio Butragueño (Real Madrid and Spain)

12 Johnny Byrne (Crystal Palace, West Ham, Fulham and England)

9 Referee Clive Thomas 10 Cliff Bastin 11 Steve Bull (Wolverhampton Wanderers)

5 Gerd Müller 6 Eddie Hapgood 7 Jim Smith 8 Peter Bonetti (Chelsea and England)

3 Billy Meredith (Manchester City and Manchester United) 4 Franz Beckenbauer

1 Tommy Lawrence (Liverpool and Tranmere Rovers) 2 Mark Lazarus (Queens Park Rangers)

 Quiz 2   **Also Known As**

What are the real names of the following Scottish teams?

1 **The Red Lichties (English: Red Lights), after the town's Stevenson-built Bell Rock lighthouse.**

2 The Bairns, from the line:
'*Better meddle wi' the Devil than the Bairns o'* .....

3 **The Sons, as in 'The Sons of the Rock', a name thought to be derived from the hill on which the local castle stands**

4 The Binos

5 **The Jags**

6 The Wee Jags

7 **Bully Wee (a reference to their most famous forward line, the members of which, though short in stature, more than made up for it in toughness)**

8 The Diamonds, after their team strip, white with red diamonds

9 **The Terrors – a name which might be frightening if it were not shared with gentle little Tooting and Mitcham United**

10 The Pars

11 **The Loons**

12 The Honest Men, from Tam O'Shanter, the poem by Burns which contains the lines:
'*Auld ——, wham ne'er a town surpasses,*
For honest men and bonnie lasses.'

13 **The Gers**

14 The Jammies

15 **The Spiders (after the black and white hoops they play in)**

CARLING 10,000 FOOTBALL FACTS & QUESTIONS

Quiz 3

Also Known As

1   Which team is sometimes known as The Addicks, a term originally derived from the haddocks served at the fish and chip shop over which the team first met?

2   Which team is known as the Chairboys, after the furniture-making industry for which their town was famous?

3   Which team takes one of its nicknames from the thrush or throstle on its badge and the other from the baggy shorts once favoured by its players?

4   Who are the Stags?

5   Who were hubristically called 'The Team of the Eighties' by Terry Venables, their manager from 1976-80?

6   Who are variously known as the Colliers or the Tykes?

7   The most famous Irons are West Ham United. With which other team do they share this nickname?

8   Who are the Seasiders?

9   Who are the Seagulls?

10   Who are called the Quakers because of the strength of the Society of Friends in that part of the country?

11   If you shouted 'Allez les verts!', who would you be supporting?

12   Which team are known as the Terriers and have this type of dog on their badge?

13   Who are known as The Lions?

14   Who are called the Imps after a gargoyle in the local cathedral?

15   Who are nicknamed the Bantams because their colours – claret and amber shirts, black shorts and black stockings – are supposed to resemble those of the farm bird?

1 Charlton Athletic 2 Wycombe Wanderers 3 West Bromwich Albion (The Throstles or the Baggies) 4 Mansfield Town 5 Crystal Palace 6 Barnsley 7 Scunthorpe United 8 Blackpool 9 Brighton and Hove Albion 10 Darlington 11 St Etienne 12 Huddersfield Town 13 Millwall 14 Lincoln City 15 Bradford City

Quiz 4

Also Known As

1 For no good reason, many Brazilian players are known only by a single name. What was Eduardo Gonçalves de Andrade better known as in the 1970 World Cup?

2 What was Jairzinho's full name?

3 What are the forenames of the player known only as Falcao?

4 Manoel Francisco dos Santos was universally known as Garrincha. What does Garrincha mean?

5 What is Pele's real name?

6 What was the nickname of Waldir Pereira, the architect of Brazil's triumph in the 1958 World Cup?

7 What was the real name of his midfield partner, Zito?

8 Juninho means 'junior' in Portuguese. What is his full real name?

9 And what does Mrs Emerson fill in under 'Name of Spouse'?

10 What was the full name of Gerson, midfield general and chain-smoker, who contributed enormously to the 1970 World Cup triumph without, as memory tells it, breaking into a run?

11 What is Ronaldo's full name?

12 Who is Artur Antunes Coimbra, a.k.a 'The White Pele'?

13 Which Brazilian was nicknamed The Little Ant?

14 Who was Joe Mercer referring to in the 1970 World Cup when he said that, despite his name, he was 'no cat'?

15 What is the real name of Middlesbrough's Branco?

1 Tostao 2 Jair Ventura Filho 3 Roberto Antonio 4 Little Bird 5 Edson Arantes do Nascimento 6 Didi 7 José Eli Miranda 8 Oswaldo Giroldo Junior 9 Emerson Moises Costa 10 Gerson de Oliveira Nunez 11 Ronaldo Luiz Nazario de Lima 12 Zico 13 Mario Zagalo 14 Brazilian goalkeeper Felix (full name Felix Mielli Venerando) 15 Claudio Ibraim Vaz Leal

CARLING 10,000 FOOTBALL FACTS & QUESTIONS

 **Quiz 5**   **Book That Man!**

Which footballers are the authors and/or subjects of the following books?

1 **'Tales From The Boot Camps'**

2 'Soccer My Battlefield'

3 **'Bonzo'**

4 'From St Tropez to St James'

5 **'Achieving The Goal'**

6 'Goals From Nowhere'

7 **'Never Afraid To Miss'**

8 'The Goal Machine'

9 **'Return Of The Little Villain'**

10 'Call The Doc'

11 **'The Red And The Black'**

12 'Three Of The Best'

13 **'Rock Bottom'**

14 'The Good, The Bad And The Bubbly'

15 **'Heading For Victory'**

 **Quiz 6**   British Clubs in Europe

1   Which two British players have played in European Cup Finals for more than one club?

2   Who were the last two men to manage English clubs to European Cup success?

3   Who scored Manchester United's goal at Old Trafford against Rotor Volgograd in the UEFA Cup in 1995?

4   Who is the last person to score in an European Final for a British club?

5   Name the five clubs that have won the European Cup at Wembley?

6   Who were Nottingham Forest's first opponents in the European Cup?

7   Who is the only British manager to have won the European Cup Winners' Cup with different clubs?

8   Which team did Manchester United play in their first European Cup tie?

9   Which club did Manchester United defeat to reach the 1968 European Cup Final?

10   Which team did Chelsea beat in the final to win the European Cup Winners' Cup in 1971?

11   Which other English team did Chelsea beat in the semi-finals to reach the 1971 European Cup Winners' Cup Final?

12   The 1971 European Cup Winners' Cup Final went to a replay. Who scored in both games of the Final?

13   Which British club beat AC Milan on a toss of a coin in the Inter-Cities Fairs Cup third round in 1966?

14   Which two present day managers played in that tie?

15   Which English club recorded a 21-0 aggregate score over Luxembourg club Jeunesse Hautcharage in the European Cup Winners' Cup in 1971-72?

Quiz 7   British Clubs in Europe

1　**Who were the first British club to play in a European Cup Final?**

2　Which Yugoslavian side knocked Arsenal out of the 1979 UEFA Cup?

3　**Who did Arsenal beat to reach the 1980 European Cup Winners' Cup Final?**

4　Who scored the winning goal in the second leg of that game?

5　**Arsenal were beaten in the 1980 European Cup Winners' Final on penalties. By which Spanish side?**

6　Which England international missed the decisive penalty?

7　**Which Russian club won 5-2 at Highbury to knock Arsenal out of the 1982-83 UEFA Cup?**

8　Which club knocked Arsenal out of the 1972 European Cup on their way to winning to the trophy?

9　**Which English club beat Anderlecht 4-3 on aggregate to win the 1970 Inter-Cities Fairs Cup?**

10　When they defended the Cup the following season, which German club beat them in the fourth round?

11　**In what season did Arsenal make their first appearance in European competition?**

12　Who were they beaten by in the second round?

13　**Who did Arsenal beat to win the 1994 European Cup Winners' Cup?**

14　Who scored the only goal?

15　**In defence of their title, Arsenal lost in the 1995 European Cup Winners' Cup Final. Which Spanish side beat them?**

1 Celtic 2 Red Star Belgrade 3 **Juventus** 4 Paul Vaessen 5 **Valencia** 6 Graham Rix
7 **Spartak Moscow** 8 Ajax 9 **Arsenal** 10 FC Koln 11 1963-64 12 FC Liege
13 **Parma** 14 Alan Smith 15 **Real Zaragoza**

Quiz 8   **British Clubs in Europe**

1   The 1985 European Cup Final between Liverpool and Juventus was marred by crowd violence at the Heysel stadium. But who scored the only goal for the Italian club?

2   **Who resigned as Liverpool manager after that game?**

3   How did Liverpool beat Cologne in the 1965 European Cup quarter-final?

4   **Who scored West Ham's two goals in their 1965 European Cup Winners' Cup Final success?**

5   Where was that Final played?

6   **How many British clubs have competed in European Finals at Wembley?**

7   What round did West Ham reach in the European Cup Winners' Cup in 1980-81?

8   **Who were Manchester United beaten by in the group stages of the 1996-97 Champions League?**

9   Who beat West Ham in the 1976 European Cup Winners' Cup Final?

10   **Who did Everton beat over two legs in the semi-finals of the 1985 European Cup Winners' Cup?**

11   Everton beat which Austrian club in the European Cup Winners' Cup Final of 1985?

12   **Who scored Everton's goals in that Final victory?**

13   Which Scottish side beat Everton in the 1962-63 UEFA Cup?

14   **Which English club did Inter Milan beat on their way to winning the 1964 European Cup?**

15   Who captained Everton to their European Cup Winners' Cup success in 1985?

WAY OUT

---

1 Michel Platini 2 **Joe Fagan** 3 On a toss of a coin 4 **Alan Sealey** 5 Wembley
6 **Three. Manchester United, Liverpool & West Ham** 7 Quarter-Finals 8 **Juventus (twice)
and Fenerbahce** 9 Anderlecht 10 **Bayern Munich** 11 Rapid Vienna 12 **Andy Gray, Trevor
Steven & Kevin Sheedy** 13 Dunfermline 14 **Everton** 15 Kevin Ratcliffe

Quiz 9

British Clubs in Europe

1 **Which England international goalkeeper had to be taken off after only eight minutes of the 1982 European Cup Final?**

2 Which youngster replaced him?

3 **Manchester United reached the semi-finals of the European Cup in 1957. Which legendary team beat them?**

4 Manchester United were beaten the following year again in the semi-finals. Who inflicted defeat this time?

5 **When Manchester United beat Benfica to win the European Cup in 1968, who scored twice for United?**

6 On defending the European Cup in 1969, Manchester United were beaten in the semi-finals. By who?

7 **Which two English teams met in the European Cup Winners' Cup second round in the 1963-64 season?**

8 Who won the tie?

9 **Which Italian club beat Manchester United in the 1984 European Cup Winners' Cup semi-final?**

10 Who scored Manchester United's other two goals in the 1968 European Cup Final?

11 **Who scored for Celtic in their memorable European Cup Final success in 1967?**

12 Who was Celtic's victorious captain on that day?

13 **Which Manchester United striker missed the 1968 European Cup Final through injury?**

14 Which former European Footballer of the Year played against Manchester United in the 1968 European Cup Final?

15 **Who were nicknamed 'The Lisbon Lions' after their European Cup success?**

Quiz 10   British Clubs in Europe

1   How many European Cup Finals have Celtic appeared in?

2   **Who has scored twice in European Cup Finals for Celtic?**

3   Which Dutch side beat Celtic in the European Cup Final of 1970?

4   **Which English side were beaten by Bayern Munich in an European Cup Final?**

5   Which brothers played in the Leeds side that played in the 1975 European Cup Final?

6   **Which club played in five European Cup Finals in the 1960s, winning twice?**

7   Which Dutchman won the UEFA Cup in 1981 for Ipswich and had a brother that won the European Cup in 1972?

8   **Which Spanish club did Leeds beat to reach the 1975 European Cup Final?**

9   Which former Wales manager played for Leeds in the 1975 European Cup Final?

10 **Which English side beat Real Madrid 4-1 in the European Cup second round first leg, only to be beaten 6-5 on aggregate?**

11 Who scored a hat-trick in that first leg, and also scored in the return?

12 **Which English side won the European Cup at the first attempt?**

13 Who scored the winning away goal for Nottingham Forest against Cologne in the 1979 European Cup semi-final, second leg?

14 **Which former Nottingham Forest manager played for the club in the 1979 European Cup Final?**

15 Who scored the only goal for Nottingham Forest in the 1979 European Cup Final?

1 Two (1967, 1970) 2 **Tommy Gemmell** 3 Feyenoord 4 **Leeds** 5 Eddie and Frank Gray
6 **Benfica** 7 Arnold Muhren 8 **Barcelona** 9 Terry Yorath 10 **Derby** 11 Charlie George
12 **Nottingham Forest** 13 Ian Bowyer 14 **Frank Clark** 15 Trevor Francis

Quiz 11   British Clubs in Europe

1 **Which Brazilian, who would later play in the Premiership, scored for Genoa against Liverpool in the 1992 UEFA Cup?**

2 Who did Nottingham Forest beat in the 1980 European Cup semi-finals?

3 **Who scored the winning goal for Nottingham Forest in the 1980 European Cup Final?**

4 Which England captain played against Nottingham Forest in the 1980 European Cup Final?

5 **Which English club did Rangers beat in the European Cup Winners' Cup semi-final in 1961?**

6 Which Italian club beat Rangers in the 1961 European Cup Winners' Cup Final?

7 **What round did Scottish club Dunfermline reach in the 1962 European Cup Winners' Cup?**

8 Rangers lost to who in the 1963 European Cup Winners' Cup?

9 **Rangers reached the 1967 European Cup Winners' Cup Final. Who did they play?**

10 Which British club reached the European Cup Winners' Cup semi-final in 1968?

11 **Which Scottish team reached the semi-finals in the same competition a year later?**

12 Which English club won the European Cup Winners' Cup in 1970?

13 **Who were their scorers in the Final?**

14 Which Scottish club won the European Cup Winners' Cup in 1972?

15 **Who did they beat in the Final?**

---

1 **Branco** 2 Ajax 3 **John Robertson** 4 Kevin Keegan 5 **Wolves** 6 Fiorentina
7 **Quarter-Finals** 8 Tottenham 9 **Bayern Munich** 10 Cardiff City 11 **Dunfermline**
12 Manchester City 13 **Neil Young and Francis Lee (pen)** 14 Rangers
15 Dynamo Moscow

Quiz 12 British Clubs in Europe

1 Leeds reached the European Cup Winners' Cup Final in 1973. Who beat them in the Final?

2 **Which Irish team reached the 1974 European Cup Winners' Cup quarter-Finals before being beaten by Borussia Moenchengladbach?**

3 Who were England's representatives in the 1973-74 European Cup Winners' Cup?

4 **Which Hungarian side knocked Liverpool out of the 1975 European Cup Winners' Cup on their way to the Final?**

5 Who did West Ham beat in the 1976 European Cup Winners' Cup semi-final?

6 **Who scored twice for West Ham in the second leg of that semi-final?**

7 Who beat West Ham in the 1976 European Cup Winners' Cup Final?

8 **Which English club did Anderlecht beat in the 1977 European Cup Winners' Cup quarter-Finals?**

9 Which English team beat Porto 5-2 in the second leg of the 1978 European Cup Winners' Cup second round, but still lost 6-5 on aggregate?

10 **Which English side lost on away goals to Barcelona in the quarter-Finals of the 1979 European Cup Winners' Cup?**

11 Who played in European Cup Winners' Cup Finals for Chelsea and Arsenal?

12 **Which British club played in consecutive Fairs Cup Finals in the 1960s?**

13 Which British club were the first to reach an European club final?

14 **Which three British clubs were in the 1966 UEFA Cup quarter-Finals?**

15 Leeds played in consecutive Fairs Cup Finals in the 1960s. Which years?

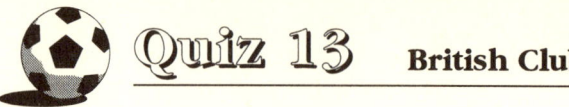

Quiz 13   British Clubs in Europe

1 On reaching the two Finals, Leeds beat Scottish clubs in both semi-finals. Who were they?

2 Which European trophy did Newcastle win in 1969?

3 Which two English clubs contested the 1972 UEFA Cup Final?

4 Which Premiership manager played for Tottenham in the 1972 UEFA Cup Final?

5 Who beat Tottenham on away goals to reach the 1973 UEFA Cup Final?

6 Who beat Tottenham in the 1974 UEFA Cup Final?

7 Aston Villa were beaten by Barcelona in the UEFA Cup quarter-Finals in 1978. But who scored their consolation goal at the Nou Camp?

8 Which Midlands club reached the UEFA Cup quarter-Finals in 1979?

9 Which two Ipswich players scored in both legs of the 1981 UEFA Cup Final?

10 Which English club lost in the 1959 European Cup first round?

11 Which English club did Barcelona beat 9-2 on aggregate in the 1960 European Cup?

12 What English team reached the quarter-Finals of the European Cup in 1961?

13 Who was in goal for Manchester United when Barcelona beat them 4-0 in the Champions League in 1994-95?

14 Which other British club were beaten by Bayern Munich in the 1995-96 UEFA Cup?

15 Which club did Real Zaragoza beat to reach the 1995 European Cup Winners' Cup Final?

1 Kilmarnock and Dundee 2 Fairs Cup 3 Tottenham and Wolves 4 Joe Kinnear 5 Liverpool 6 Feyenoord 7 Brian Little 8 W.B.A 9 John Wark and Frans Thijssen 10 Wolves 11 Wolves 12 Burnley 13 Gary Walsh 14 Raith Rovers 15 Chelsea

 ## Quiz 14   British Clubs in Europe

1   Who did Newcastle lose to in the second round of the 1995 UEFA Cup?

2   Which club of Swedish part-timers beat Blackburn in the first round of the 1994-95 UEFA Cup?

3   To qualify for the 1992-93 Champions League, the English champions faced the Scottish champions. Who won the tie?

4   What was the aggregate score?

5   Rangers missed out on qualifying for the European Cup Final of 1993 by one point in the group stage. Who topped the group?

6   Who scored twice for Manchester United in their 1991 European Cup Winners' Cup Final victory over Barcelona?

7   English clubs were allowed back into European competitions in 1990-91. Why did they not have a representative in the European Cup?

8   Which Premiership striker played in the 1992 European Cup Final?

9   Who did Arsenal lose to in the European Cup second round in 1991-92?

10   How many group matches did Blackburn win in the 1995-96 Champions League?

11   Who scored a hat-trick for Blackburn in the 1995-96 Champions League?

12   Which German, Romanian and Italian side were in Rangers' Champions League group in 1995-96?

13   Who beat Celtic on their way to winning the 1996 European Cup Winners' Cup?

14   Nottingham Forest lost in the UEFA Cup quarter-Finals in 1996 to Bayern Munich 7-2 on aggregate. What was the score after the first leg in Germany?

15   Who, in 1993-94, became the first British side to beat Bayern Munich in an European competition in Germany?

---

1 Athletico Bilbao 2 **Trelleborgs** 3 Rangers 4 **4-2** 5 Marseille 6 **Mark Hughes**
7 Because Liverpool were banned for another three years 8 **Gianluca Vialli (Sampdoria)**
9 Benfica 10 **One** 11 Mike Newell 12 **Borussia Dortmund, Steaua Bucharest and Juventus**
13 Paris St Germain 14 **Munich 1-2 to Munich** 15 Norwich City

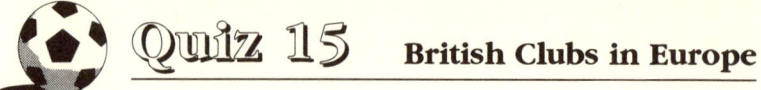

Quiz 15   British Clubs in Europe

1   **Who scored the two goals when Norwich beat Bayern Munich in the UEFA Cup second round, first leg in 1993-94?**

2   Who scored both Inter Milan goals in their 2-0 aggregate victory over Norwich in 1994 UEFA Cup third round?

3   **Which Italian club did Arsenal beat on their way to the 1994 European Cup Winners' Cup Final?**

4   Who did Manchester United lose to on away goals in the 1994 European Cup second round?

5   **Rangers also lost on away goals in the second round of the 1994 European Cup. Who to?**

6   When was the last European final to be played at Wembley?

7   **Manchester United's lost their first Champions League match of the 1996-97 season. Who to?**

8   Who scored the only goal?

9   **Who did Arsenal lose to in the first round of the 1996-97 UEFA Cup?**

10   Who were the only two British clubs to reach the second round of the UEFA Cup in 1996-97?

11   **Who scored Manchester United's first goal in the 1996-97 Champions League?**

12   Which former West Ham forward scored twice for Ajax in Rangers' 4-1 Champions League defeat in 1996-97?

13   **Who was sent-off for Rangers in that match?**

14   What was the score in Liverpool's second round, second leg tie against FC Sion?

15   **Who knocked Newcastle out of the 1997 UEFA Cup?**

Quiz 16   British Players Abroad

1   Who was the first professional player to move from an English club to Italy?

2   Which were the first Italian club to buy a player from England?

3   Who was the first player to transfer from Scotland to Italy, with a move from Hibernian to Juventus?

4   Who moved from English football to AC Milan in June 1961?

5   Who moved from English football to Torino in 1961?

6   Who moved from Aston Villa to Italy in 1961 for £85,000?

7   Who was the first person to move from England to Germany?

8   Who moved from WBA to Real Madrid in 1979?

9   Which player moved from Manchester City to Werder Bremen in 1979?

10   How much did Liam Brady cost Juventus when he left Arsenal in 1980?

11   Trevor Francis moved to which foreign club for £900,000?

12   Who was the first £1m player to move abroad from a British club?

13   Which two players moved from English clubs to AEK Athens in 1983?

14   Which club did Mark Hateley move from when he joined AC Milan?

15   How much did Ray Wilkins cost AC Milan when he joined them in 1984?

CARLING 10,000 FOOTBALL FACTS & QUESTIONS

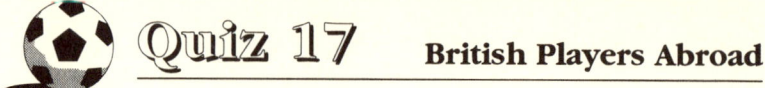

Quiz 17 — British Players Abroad

1 **Which two players moved from Aston Villa to Bari in 1985?**

2 How much did Ian Rush cost Juventus when he left Liverpool in 1987?

3 **Which Italian club did Paul Elliott join in 1987?**

4 How much did David Platt cost when he moved to Bari?

5 **How much did Paul Gascoigne cost Lazio when he moved to Italy?**

6 How much did Des Walker cost Sampdoria when he joined them in 1992?

7 **Who played for AC Milan and Verona from 1981?**

8 Which Italian club did amateur centre forward Norman Adcock join in 1945 to become the first ever player to move to play in Europe?

9 **Which British export became the French First Division's top scorer in the 1994 season?**

10 Which former Arsenal championship winner moved to Stabaeck in Norway?

11 **Which two Brits teamed up for the same club in Italy for the 1996-97 season?**

12 Which player joined Reggiana in the 1996-97 season from an English club?

13 **Ted McMinn moved from Rangers to which Spanish side in 1987?**

14 Mick Robinson moved from QPR to which Spanish side in 1987?

15 **Which two British internationals moved abroad in May 1986?**

 **Quiz 18**   British Players Abroad

1   Who moved from Celtic to Nantes in 1987?

2   **Which ex-Manchester United player moved to Kaizer Chiefs in South Africa in January 1988?**

3   How much did Steve Archibald cost Barcelona when he moved from Tottenham?

4   **Which club did Mark McGhee move to from Aberdeen?**

5   Which club did Andy King join from Everton in 1984?

6   **Which club did Raphael Meade join when he left Arsenal?**

7   Which foreign club did John Richards join in 1983?

8   **Who did Peter Barnes join in 1982 when he moved from Leeds?**

9   Who moved from Liverpool to Lucerne in a free transfer in 1983?

10 **Watford's Gerry Armstrong moved to which foreign club in 1983?**

11 How much was the transfer fee when Graeme Souness moved to Sampdoria?

12 **Eric Black joined which French side when he moved from Aberdeen for £200,000 in 1986?**

13 Dale Tempest joined Lokeren from which English club?

14 **Gary Owen moved to which foreign club from WBA in 1986?**

15 Louie Donowa moved from Norwich to which Spanish club in 1986?

1 Mo Johnston 2 **Gary Bailey** 3 £1,000,000 4 **SV Hamburg** 5 Cabuur 6 **Sporting Lisbon**
7 Marítimo Funchal 8 **Real Betis** 9 David Fairclough 10 **Real Mallorca** 11 £650,000
12 **Metz** 13 Huddersfield 14 **Panionios** 15 La Coruna

Quiz 19 British Players Abroad

1 Tony Woodcock left Arsenal for which German club in 1986?

2 Sammy McIlroy left Manchester City for which foreign club in 1986?

3 Tottenham gave Ally Dick a free transfer to which Dutch team in 1986?

4 Joe Jakub joined which Dutch team for £20,000 in 1986?

5 Garry Brooke moved to which club when he left Norwich in 1987?

6 Murdo McLeod joined which German side in 1987?

7 Which club did Frank Stapleton join on a free transfer to in 1987?

8 George O'Boyle moved from Linfield to which French club in 1987?

9 Which foreign club did Tony Sealey join when he left Leicester in 1987?

10 Dave Swindlehurst joined Anorthosis from which club in 1987?

11 Ex-Norwich player John Devine moved to which club in September 1987?

12 Gary Waddock joined which French club in January 1988 after he left QPR?

13 Which French team signed Ian Wallace when he left Nottingham Forest in 1984?

14 Bob Latchforrd left Swansea on a free transfer to join which club?

15 Which team signed Jim Bett when he left Glasgow Rangers in 1983?

CARLING 10,000 FOOTBALL FACTS & QUESTIONS

Quiz 20 — British Players Abroad

1 Who moved from the Premiership to Malaysia in 1996?

2 Tony Marchi left Tottenham for which foreign side in 1961?

3 John Charles joined which Italian side for £70,000 in 1962?

4 Mick Walsh left QPR for which European team in 1980?

5 How much did Trevor Francis cost Sampdoria when he joined them in 1982?

6 Francois Van Der Elst left West Ham for which side in 1983?

7 Which two Tottenham players from the 1980s moved to France?

8 What are the four Italian teams that Liam Brady played for?

9 Which clubs did David Platt play for in Italy?

10 How many seasons did Denis Law spend in Italy?

11 How many seasons did Trevor Francis spend at Sampdoria?

12 How many games did Jimmy Greaves play in Italy?

13 Who scored 87 goals in six seasons in Italy from 1957-63?

14 Frank Ratcliffe moved from Aldershot to which series B side for the 1949-50 season, where he scored 18 goals in 27 games?

15 In which season did Ian Rush play in Italy?

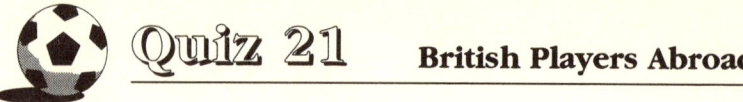

Quiz 21 — British Players Abroad

1 What was the name of the team that Gary Lineker played for in Japan?

2 Which country did Richard Gough leave Rangers to play in after the 1996-97 season?

3 **Which former Watford striker had a spell at French club Nantes?**

4 Which American team did Rodney Marsh play for?

5 **Which team did Charlton's Mike Flanagan play for in America?**

6 Which former Welsh international had a spell at Vancouver Whitecaps?

7 **With which Turkish team did Les Ferdinand have a loan spell with?**

8 Dean Saunders spent a season at which foreign club before moving back to Nottingham Forest?

9 **Dalian Atkinson moved to which foreign club when he left Aston Villa?**

10 Which Scot played for Borussia Dortmund in the 1996-97 season?

11 **Mo Johnston spent the 1996-97 season playing where?**

12 Chris Woods was playing in which country before playing for Southampton in the 1996-97 season?

13 **How many goals did David Platt score in his first season in Italy?**

14 Who moved to Paris St Germain after three years at AC Milan?

15 **Josiah (Paddy) Sloan moved from Sheffield United to which foreign team for the 1948-49 season?**

Quiz 22

Celebrity Fans

Which teams do the following support?

1 **Comedian Tommy Trinder**

2 Comedian Jimmy Tarbuck

3 **Pop group Oasis**

4 Pop singer David Essex

5 **Conservative politicians John Major and David Mellor**

6 Pop star Elton John

7 **Television chef Delia Smith**

8 Television sports presenter Des Lynam

9 **Comedian Frank Skinner**

10 'They Think It's All Over' compere Nick Hancock

11 **Alf Garnett actor Warren Mitchell**

12 Nick Hornby, author of 'Fever Pitch'

13 **Actor Sean Bean (he even has a tattoo to this effect)**

14 Comedian Jasper Carrott

15 **Prime Minister Tony Blair**

 **Quiz 23**   **Celebrity Fans**

Which teams do the following support?

1 **Journalist and television interviewer Michael Parkinson**

2 Actor Kevin Lloyd, best known at the time of his death in May 1998 as Detective Constable Alfred 'Tosh' Lines in 'The Bill'

3 **Leyton-born Manchester United star David Beckham**

4 Liverpool midfielder Jason McAteer

5 **BBC Radio One Breakfast Show presenter Zoe Ball**

6 Newcastle United and England midfielder Robert Lee

7 **1998 World Snooker Champion John Higgins**

8 Classical violinist Nigel Kennedy

9 **Comedian David Baddiel**

10 Comedian Phil Jupitus

11 **Talk show host Clive Anderson**

12 West Ham MP and Sports Minister Tony Banks

13 **King Olaf of Norway**

14 Children's television presenter Kirsten O'Brien

15 **Sporty Spice (Mel C)**

 **Quiz 24**   **Celebrity Fans**

Which teams do the following support?

1 **Eric Morecambe of the celebrated comic double act Morecambe and Wise**

2 Mikhail Gorbachev, the last leader of the USSR

3 **Actor and 'Have I Got News For You' presenter Angus Deayton**

4 Singer and Labour Party member Billy Bragg

5 **Roman Catholic Cardinal Basil Hume**

6 Yorkshire and England fast bowler Darren Gough

7 **Education Secretary David Blunkett**

8 Comedian and cross-dresser Eddie Izzard

9 **Formula One Racing Team boss Eddie Jordan**

10 Time-defying pop singer Engelbert Humperdinck

11 **George Carey, Archbishop of Canterbury**

12 Jim Bowen, the host of television quiz-and-darts show 'Bullseye'

13 **Former World Snooker Champion John Parrott**

14 Johnny Rotten, former lead singer of the Sex Pistols

15 **'Terry and June' star June Whitfield**

1 **Luton Town** 2 Wigan Athletic 3 **Manchester United** 4 West Ham United 5 **Newcastle United** 6 Barnsley 7 **Sheffield Wednesday** 8 Crystal Palace 9 **Coventry City** 10 Leicester City 11 **Arsenal** 12 Blackburn Rovers 13 **Everton** 14 Arsenal 15 **Wimbledon**

Quiz 25

Celebrity Fans

Which teams do the following support/

I **Former world snooker champion Ken Doherty**

2 Leslie Phillips, actor and film star

3 **Actor and film director Lord Richard Attenborough**

4 Former England cricket captain Mike Atherton

5 **Actor Neil Pearson, star of 'Drop The Dead Donkey' and 'Between The Lines'**

6 Richard Whiteley, host of the television quiz show 'Countdown'?

7 **Journalist and Labour MP Roy Hattersley**

8 Scary Spice (Mel B)

9 **Richard Branson, chairman of the Virgin group of companies**

10 Swedish former Wimbledon champion and London resident Stefan Edberg

11 **Comedian Tim Brooke-Taylor**

12 Former Manchester United and England goalkeeper Alex Stepney

13 **Athlete Steve Cram**

14 Television horse racing commentator Julian Wilson

15 **Champion jockey Walter Swinburn**

Quiz 26

Celebrity Fans

Which teams do the following support?

1. **Russian President Boris Yeltsin**

2. Former Labour leader Michael Foot

3. **Composer Michael Nyman**

4. World champion 10,000 metres runner Liz McColgan

5. **Athlete David Moorcroft**

6. Former World Snooker Champion Steve Davis

7. **Snooker star Jimmy White**

8. John Lloyd, former tennis player and husband of Chris Ever?

9. **Wales Rugby Union and Rugby League international Jonathan Davies**

10. Television racing pundit John McCririck

11. **Former Celtic great Kenny Dalglish**

12. Controversial Liverpool politician Derek Hatton

13. **England's 1998 World Cup referee Paul Durkin**

14. Spanish operatic tenor Placido Domingo

15. **Catalan operatic tenor Jose Carreras**

1 **Spartak Moscow** 2 Plymouth Argyle 3 **Queens Park Rangers** 4 Dundee United
5 **Coventry City** 6 Charlton Athletic 7 **Chelsea** 8 Wolverhampton Wanderers 9 **Chelsea**
10 Newcastle United 11 **Rangers** 12 Everton 13 **Manchester City** 14 Real Madrid
15 **Barcelona**

 **Quiz 27**   **Fathers and Sons**

.Identify the following family firms:

1. **Father and son played for the same club and have the same first name. Dad played twice for England, against Yugoslavia in 1973 and Australia in 1980. Son made England B debut in 1998 v Chile.**

2. Dad played for a London club and later, after ten years picking Cherries, returned to manage it. Son was a Cherry who got thrown into a bigger Pool.

3. **From 1958-1973, Dad played for seven clubs, including Chelsea. Son played for Rangers and 32 times for England (1984-92).**

4. Son played for Southend and Cambridge between 1981 and 1984. Dad scored 220 goals for Spurs and played 57 times for England.

5. **Dad was with Colchester when he hung up his gloves in 1982. Son plays for Spurs and made his England debut against Italy in 1998.**

6. Dad played for Scunthorpe, Liverpool, Tottenham Hotspur and 61 times for England. Son broke into the Spurs first team during the 1997-98 season.

7. **Dad played for Derby, Forest and 43 times for Scotland. Son plays for Forest and made his Scotland debut against Japan in 1995.**

8. An elegant defender, Dad won 27 England caps while with Derby County between 1972 and 1977. Son plays for the club his father currently manages.

9. **The father is the only man to have managed the Champions on both sides of the border. The son now plays for Wolves.**

10. Dad is Scotland's most capped player; Son is currently on loan from Dad's present club to Bury.

11. **Dad was a nine-club man who later managed Wimbledon to their 1988 FA Cup triumph. Son keeps goal for Celtic.**

12. Dad played for Middlesbrough and Sunderland and twice for England in 1962. Son started at Forest and won 14 England caps.

13. **Dad scored 27 goals for Spurs in their double year. Two of his sons played football, and one was 1987 PFA Player of the Year.**

14. Both achieved fame with Manchester City, Dad as a wing half in the '50s, Son on the wing in the '70s. Son was capped 22 times by England.

15. **Dad played for Liverpool and was later their chief scout. Son played for Preston and Bristol Rovers between 1983 and 1993. Both have the same name.**

---

1 **Frank Lampard Senior and Junior** 2 Harry and Jamie Redknapp 3 **Tony and Mark Hateley** 4 Danny and Jimmy Greaves 5 **Mike and Ian Walker** 6 Ray and Stephen Clemence 7 **Archie and Scott Gemmill** 8 Colin and Andy Todd 9 **Alex and Darren Ferguson** 10 Kenny and Paul Dalglish 11 **Bobby and Jonathan Gould** 12 Brian and Nigel Clough 13 **Les and Clive and Bradley Allen** 14 Ken and Peter Barnes 15 Geoff Twentyman Senior and Junior

CARLING 10,000 FOOTBALL FACTS & QUESTIONS

 ## Quiz 28 — Football's Pop Songs

1 **Who, in the words of the song, was:**
   'As strong as a lion and never will give up,
   That's why —— is favourite for the Cup'?

2 Which Cup, and when?

3 **Who recorded this song?**

4 Who had a No 1 hit in 1970 with a song containing the words:
   'Once more we will meet with the best
   Like before we'll be put to the test
   Knowing we'll give all we've got to give for the folks…'?

5 **What was the title of this song?**

6 What was the name of the song sung by Glenn Hoddle and Chris Waddle that reached No 12 in the charts in 1987?

7 **What was the name of their follow-up single, which did nothing?**

8 Who had a hit in 1978 with a song about Scotland's World Cup prospects which contained the couplet:
   'Olé, olé, olé ola,
   We're gonna bring that World Cup back from over thar'?

9 **Who had a 1973 hit with the song 'Nice One Cyril'?**

10 To which Tottenham Hotspur player did this refer?

11 **The catchphrase 'Nice One Cyril' originated in a television advert for a product unconnected with football. What?**

12 The Cyril in the advert had nothing to do with Spurs. Where, in the words used, did the product originate?

13 **Complete the missing line from a 1971 hit (Tune: Rule Britannia):**
   '—— —— ——
   We're proud to say that name
   While we sing this song we'll win the game'?

14 For which World Cup was the England song 'This Time (We'll Get It Right)'?

15 **What was the title of the 1982 Liverpool song in which the talents of John Barnes loomed large?**

 ## Quiz 29 — Football's Pop Songs

1 In which year did 'We All Follow Man United' reach No 10?

2 Which group backed England on the No 1 hit 'World in Motion'?

3 Which group played on the Euro '96 anthem 'Football's Coming Home'?

4 And who were the two comedians who wrote the words?

5 What was the title of Kevin Keegan's 1979 hit single?

6 Which footballer made a version of Lindisfarne's 'Fog on the Tyne'?

7 What was Arsenal striker Ian Wright's single called?

8 In which year did Leeds United have a No 10 hit with a song called - inspirationally – 'Leeds United'?

9 What was the title of the Scotland World Cup squad song that reached No 20 in 1974?

10 Who had a hit in 1985 with a song to the tune of 'Here We Go'?

11 In which year was 'I'm Forever Blowing Bubbles' a hit for West Ham United?

12 Who reached No 5 in 1982 with 'We have A Dream'?

13 In which year did Chelsea have a hit with 'Blue is the Colour'?

14 In which year did Tottenham Hotspur have a No 5 hit with 'Ossie's Dream'?

15 Which is thought to be the only professional football club in Great Britain never to have made a pop record?

1 1985 2 New Order 3 The Lightning Seeds 4 David Baddiel and Frank Skinner 5 Head Over Heels In Love 6 Paul Gascoigne 7 Do The Right Thing 8 1972 9 Easy, Easy 10 Everton 11 1975 12 The Scotland World Cup squad 13 1972 14 1981 15 Crewe Alexandra

Quiz 30

Managers

1 Which manager won three FA Cups in the 1960s with Tottenham?

2 **Which manager won two successive FA Cups in the 1980s with Tottenham?**

3 Who was Southampton's manager when they lifted the FA Cup in 1976?

4 **Who was the coach for Coventry City's victory in the 1987 FA Cup?**

5 Which manager won the FA Cup with Manchester City in 1969?

6 **What was unusual about Preston North End's manager when they won the 1938 FA Cup?**

7 Who was West Ham's manager for their 1975 FA Cup victory?

8 **Who was West Bromwich Albion's manager for their last FA Cup victory in 1968?**

9 Which manager won two FA Cups, nine years apart, and with the same club, in the 1960s and 1970s?

10 **Who managed Nottingham Forest for their FA Cup win in 1959, when they beat Luton Town 2-1?**

11 Which manager took over at Hereford United in August 1995?

12 **Which two managers took control at Rotherham United in September 1994?**

13 At the start of the 1996-7 season, who was the longest serving manager in the first division, having taken over his club in March 1984?

14 **How many Division One teams had player-managers at the start of the 1996-97 season?**

15 Who was appointed Swansea City player-manager in February 1996?

1 Bill Nicholson 2 **Keith Burkinshaw** 3 Lawrie McMenemy 4 **John Sillett** 5 Joe Mercer
6 **There was no manager** 7 John Lyall 8 **Alan Ashman** 9 Bill Shankly 10 **Billy Walker**
11 Graham Turner 12 **Archie Gemmill and John McGovern** 13 John Rudge (Port Vale)
14 9 – **Barnsley, Grimsby, Oldham, Portsmouth, QPR, Reading, Southend, Swindon,
Tranmere** 15 Jan Molby

Quiz 31

Managers

1 Which Premiership club has, at the start of the 1996-97 season, had the most manager changes since the Second World War?

2 Which Nationwide side has, at the beginning of the 1996-97 season, had the most managers since World War Two?

3 Which 1996/7 Premiership manager has on his answerphone: 'I'm sorry I'm not here at the moment. If you are the president of AC Milan, Barcelona or Real Madrid, I'll get back to you'?

4 Which Premiership manager has his birthday on New Year's Eve?

5 Who was the 1995-96 Division One Manager of the Year?

6 With which team did Tony Pullis receive his Division Three Manager of the Year award at the end of the 1995-96 season?

7 Which manager led Plymouth to a promotion in 1996, making it four promotions in seven years, following two with Notts County and one with Huddersfield?

8 Bolton Wanderers manager Charles Foweraker was the first to do what?

9 Which manager took his team to both of the two Rumbelows Cup Finals?

10 Which manager saw his team win the 1995-96 Scottish Coca Cola Cup?

11 Who was the losing manager in the 1995-96 Scottish FA Cup final?

12 For which club was Paul Fairclough the Vauxall Conference Manager of the Year, in 1995-96?

13 Which former Premiership manager was sacked after ten matches as the coach of Mexican club Guadalajara?

14 Who became the shortest serving manager in League history, surviving only three days at Scunthorpe in 1959?

15 Who, in 1984, was named as manager at Crystal Palace, but changed his mind four days later, without signing a contract?

---

1 **Coventry City – 20** 2 Darlington – 25 3 18. Joe Kinnear 4 Alex Ferguson 5 **Peter Reid** 6 Gillingham 7 **Neil Warnock** 8 Win the FA Cup 9 **Alex Ferguson** 10 Roy Aitken (Aberdeen) 11 **Jim Jefferies (Hearts)** 12 Stevenage Borough 13 **Ossie Ardiles** 14 Bill Lambton 15 **Dave Bassett**

Quiz 32

Managers

1 Which League club has had the fewest number of managers, by the end of the 1996-97 season?

2 **Who was the first man to achieve the Championship/FA Cup double as player-manager?**

3 Who was England's longest serving manager?

4 **Which manager won the 1958 and 1959 League championships with Wolves?**

5 Who was the first manager to achieve the League and Cup double at Arsenal?

6 **How many matches was John Toshack manager of Wales?**

7 Who was the first player-manager, in the old First Division, when he played for QPR, 1968-69?

8 **Who is the only manager to win the League Championship with Ipswich Town?**

9 For how long was Brian Clough manager of Leeds United in 1974?

10 **Who was the first manager to win the FA Cup with two different sides?**

11 Name the three managers that have won League Championships with two different clubs.

12 **Who was Coventry City's player-manager in 1990-91?**

13 Who is the longest serving manager in Scottish League football, spending 17 years in charge?

14 **How many trophies did Bob Paisley win with Liverpool?**

15 Which manager coached both Watford and Sheffield United in the 1987-98 season?

1 West Ham 2 **Kenny Dalglish** 3 Walter Winterbottom, 1946-62 4 **Stan Cullis** 5 Bertie Mee (Arsenal, 1971) 6 **One** 7 Les Allen 8 **Alf Ramsey (1961-2)** 9 44 days 10 **Billy Walker (Sheffield Wednesday and Nottingham Forest)** 11 Herbert Chapman (Huddersfield and Arsenal), Brian Clough (Derby County and Nottingham Forest), Kenny Dalglish (Liverpool and Blackburn) 12 **Terry Butcher** 13 Jim McLean (Dundee United, 1971-88) 14 20 (6 **Leagues, 3 European cups, 1 UEFA cup, 1 European Super cup, 6 Charity Shields)** 15 Dave Bassett

Quiz 33

Managers

1 With what club did Aston Villa manager Brian Little spend only 49 days in charge?

2 Which 1996-97 manager has scored the fastest ever first class goal at Wembley?

3 Who was the last Second Division manager to win the FA Cup?

4 Which two 1995-96 Premiership managers have been sent off for England in full internationals?

5 Which British manager took over the Kuwait national side in 1986, and later went on to manage Vitoria Setubal in Portugal?

6 Which British manager coached at Athletico Bilbao in 1987?

7 Which English manager was sacked from his foreign club in September 1987?

8 Which British manager was sacked after only 94 days at Athletico Madrid?

9 Which British manager had spells at Celta Vigo and Athletico Madrid?

10 Who moved from Real Madrid to manage Real Sociedad in 1989?

11 Who moved from Tottenham to take over at Espanol for only 41 days?

12 Which British manager has coached four different teams, in three different countries since 1992?

13 Who went from being the Czech national manager to Aston Villa in 1990?

14 Who left Swedish team Malmo to become coach at Southend in August 1992?

15 Which foreign manager joined the Premiership after leaving WBA in 1992?

Quiz 34   Managers

1 Which ex-Chelsea manager moved to Kuwait to head Al-Arabi Sporting Club?

2 **Who, in 1995, signed a contract to manage Norwegian club FC Start?**

3 Which 1996-97 Premiership manager has led clubs in France and Japan?

4 **Which Premiership manager has coached in Turkey?**

5 Which Englishman managed a country in the 1994 World Cup and helped them qualify for Euro '96?

6 **Which European manager snubbed Blackburn Rovers in 1997?**

7 Who became Celtic's manager in 1993, twenty years after leaving as a player?

8 **Who resigned as Coventry manager in October 1993, ten minutes after 5-1 defeat by QPR?**

9 Which Brit became Zambian manager, two months after the side lost 18 players in an air crash?

10 **Which St. Mirren manager resigned to persue a coaching career in Florida?**

11 Which Brit became coach of Spanish club Seville in May 1986?

12 **Who left Sampdoria to become player-manager at Glasgow Rangers?**

13 Who has managed clubs which include Middlesborough, Millwall, Bolton and Arsenal in recent years?

14 **Who made his move into management by becoming player-manager at Sheffield Wednesday?**

15 Which two men became joint player-coaches at Charlton, in July 1991?

 **Quiz 35**   **Managers**

1 Which manager was released as a player by Monaco, following an ankle injury, in April 1991?

2 Who managed Italy to their 1982 World Cup win?

3 Who was the Argentinian manager when they lifted the World Cup in 1986?

4 Who are the only two men to have won the World Cup as both players and managers?

5 In the 1994 World Cup, who was the manager of the only team to have played in all of the World Cup Finals?

6 Who were the two managers in charge for Holland's 1994 World Cup campaign?

7 Who was the Spanish manager during the 1994 World Cup?

8 Who went from managing Millwall to the Republic of Ireland?

9 Who took England to four successive World Cup Finals?

10 Who was the manager of AC Milan when they lifted the World Club Championship in 1994?

11 Who was in charge when England failed to reach the 1978 World Cup Final?

12 Who was England's manager for the 1982 World Cup?

13 Who took England to a quarter-final and a semi-final in two successive World Cups?

14 Who was manager when England finished third in the European Championships?

15 How many England managers have represented their country at senior level football?

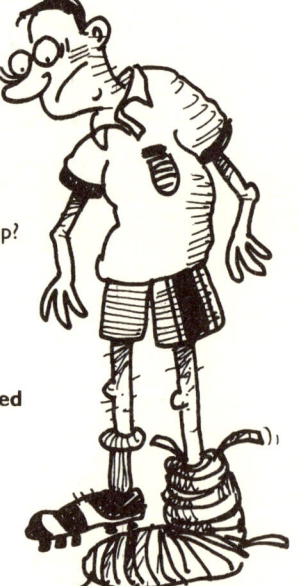

Quiz 36

Managers

1 Who was in charge of England when the World Cup was held in Chile?

2 **Who have been the last three Scottish managers?**

3 Who was Northern Ireland's manager for 13 years, from 1980-93?

4 **Who took over from Roy Hodgson as manager of Switzerland for Euro '96?**

5 Who was the French coach for Euro '96?

6 **Which manager won Euro '96?**

7 Who was the Italian manager that was sacked after Italy's poor results in Euro '96?

8 **Who led Holland in Euro '96?**

9 Which manager won the League Cup three years in a row in the Eighties?

10 **Who was West Ham's manager when they won the 1965 Cup Winners' Cup?**

11 Which two managers have led English sides to two consecutive European Cups?

12 **Who was the manager of the 1995 European Cup champions?**

13 Which acting manager lost out in the 1995 Cup Winners' Cup final?

14 **Who was manager for Everton's 1985 Cup Winners' Cup victory?**

15 Who is the last manager to have won the European Cup with a British side?

CARLING 10,000 FOOTBALL FACTS & QUESTIONS

Quiz 37

Managers

1 **Who was in charge for a British club's last victory in the Cup Winners' Cup?**

2 Who was the manager when a British club last lited the UEFA Cup?

3 **Who was the manager of the last Scottish team to win a European trophy?**

4 Which manager led Chelsea to an FA Cup victory in 1970 and a Cup Winners Cup victory in 1971?

5 **Who was the manager of the British team that beat Inter Milan in the 1994-95 UEFA Cup?**

6 Who was the manager to lead his British club to win the last Fairs Cup, before it became the UEFA Cup?

7 **Who was the losing FA Cup Final manager in 1994?**

8 Who managed the FA Cup Final team that lost to Tottenham in 1982?

9 **Which manager won the 1995 FA Cup?**

10 Who was the losing manager in the 1995 Coca-Cola Cup Final?

11 **Which manager lost in the final of both the FA Cup and League Cup Finals in 1993?**

12 Who was the manager of the Scottish league champions in the 1994/5 season?

13 **Who is the only manager to have led Raith Rovers to a Scottish League Cup success, when they beat Celtic in 1995?**

14 Who was the manager of Celtic when they won the Scottish FA Cup?

15 **Which manager went from Birmingham City to own Peterborough United?**

 Quiz 38   **Managers**

1 Which former Everton player was managing third division Chester City at the start of the 1995-96 season?

2 **Which former England international was in charge at the beginning of the 1995-96 season?**

3 Who moved from Aston Villa to Wolves to Watford, with a period as a national coach in between?

4 **Which ex-england internatioal took over at Portsmouth in February 1995?**

5 Who took Wycombe Wanderers from non-league football to the Second Division for the start of the 1994-95 season?

6 **Who was manager of Oldham Athletic from July 1982 until November 1994?**

7 Who went from the Scottish Premier league to manage Brighton and Hove Albion in 1993?

8 **Who took over as player-manager at Plymouth Argile in March 1992?**

9 Which player-manager won the 1994-95 First division title?

10 **Which manager moved to Leicester and then Wolves after being player-manager at Reading?**

11 Who went from being a player-manager at Barnsley to assistant coach at Premiership Middlesborough?

12 **Which manager rejoined Norwich for his second spell, following an unsuccessful time at Everton?**

13 Who brought Nottingham Forest back into the top division, and then returned to manage Manchester City?

14 **Which former Portsmouth boss took Derby County into the Premiership?**

15 Who did Bryan Robson succeed as Middlesborough manager?

---

1 Kevin Ratcliffe **2 Ray Clemence** 3 Graham Taylor **4 Terry Fenwick** 5 Martin O'Neill **6 Joe Royle** 7 Liam Brady **8 Peter Shilton** 9 Bryan Robson **10 Mark McGhee** 11 Viv Anderson **12 Mike walker** 13 Frank Clark **14 Jim Smith** 15 Lennie Lawrence

 **Quiz 39**   **Managers**

1   **Which FA Cup winning manager took over at Ipswich fron Mick McGiven?**

2   Which Premiership manager won the 1983 Player of the Year award?

3   **Who was the last Scottish manager to beat England in an international?**

4   Which former Liverpool player was Oxford manager when they were relegated in 1988?

5   **Which former international manager was also in charge at Everton?**

6   Which club sacked manager Don O'Riordan the day after his side were beaten 8-1 by Scunthorpe in October 1995?

7   **Which former England captain managed Arsenal btween 1962 and 1966?**

8   Which England legend managed Bolton Wanderers between 1968 and 1970?

9   **Which European Cup winning manager was in charge at Brighton and Hove Albion from 1973 to 1974?**

10 Who managed Bristol Rovers before moving to QPR?

11 **Who was the manager of Fulham in 1968, before moving to coach abroad?**

12 Who was the manager of Leeds United that went on to manage Scotland?

13 **Who was the Leeds United manager before Howard Wilkinson?**

14 What club did Jack Charlton manage before becoming the Republic of Ireland manager?

15 **Who managed Sheffield Wednesday from 1983 to 1988?**

1 **John Lyall** 2 Kenny Dalglish 3 **Jock Stein** 4 Mark Lawrenson 5 **Billy Bingham**
6 Torquay United 7 **Billy Wright** 8 Nat Lofthouse 9 **Brian Clough** 10 Gerry Francis
11 **Bobby Robson** 12 Jock Stein 13 **Billy Bremner** 14 Newcastle United
15 **Howard Wilkinson**

CARLING 10,000 FOOTBALL FACTS & QUESTIONS

Quiz 40

Managers

1 **Before becoming manager of the Republic of Ireland, of which club had Mick McCarthy been in charge from 1992 to 1996?**

2 Before moving to Tottenham Hotspur in 1986, of which club had David Pleat been manager since 1978?

3 **In which year did Brian Clough become the manager of Nottingham Forest?**

4 For which two clubs did Wimbledon manager Joe Kinnear play his football?

5 **From their formation in 1900 to 1998, how many managers have West Ham United had?**

6 Graham Taylor went back to Watford as manager in 1997. When had he left the club?

7 **Huddersfield Town, Notts County, Plymouth Argyle – which manager has won promotion for each of these clubs through the play-offs?**

8 In March 1995, who became Sunderland's 16th manager since the Second World War?

9 **Martin O'Neill took over as manager of Leicester City in December 1995. Where had he briefly worked immediately before?**

10 Name the Derby County manager between 1984 and 1993 who was in charge at Chesterfield from 1976 to 1980

11 **Name the four Rons who have managed West Bromwich Albion**

12 Of which club was Bert Head manager and general manager from 1966-72?

13 **Of which Lincolnshire club was former Everton defender Mike Lyons manager from 1985-87?**

14 The League record for length of service to a single club – 46 years – is held by Fred Everiss. Which club did he manage from 1902-48?

15 **In which month and year did Alex Ferguson take over as manager of Manchester United?**

CARLING 10,000 FOOTBALL FACTS & QUESTIONS

 **Quiz 41**   **Managers**

1   In which year did **Roy Evans** become manager of **Liverpool**?

2   When was John Rudge appointed manager of Port Vale?

3   **Where did Barry Fry go after he left Birmingham City in May 1996?**

4   Where was Glenn Hoddle's first managerial appointment?

5   **Which all-time great cut his teeth in management at Hartlepool United from 1965 to 1967?**

6   Which Dane became manager of Walsall in June 1997?

7   **Which ex-Charlton striker was manager of Gillingham from 1993 to 1995?**

8   Which ex-Chelsea star was appointed player manager of Doncaster Rovers in August 1996?

9   **Which ex-Derby County and Nottingham Forest duo managed Rotherham United from 1994 to 1996?**

10 Which ex-Sunderland manager was in charge of Blackpool in 1978-79?

11 **Which former Arsenal and Republic of Ireland player managed Bradford City between 1991 and 1994?**

12 Which former Chelsea boss was manager of Cambridge United in 1985?

13 **Which former England captain managed Exeter City in 1983-84?**

14 Which former England international was Director of Football at Barnet in 1996 and 1997?

15 **Which former Leeds United and England striker had two spells as manager of Barnsley – 1978-80 and 1985-89?**

CARLING 10,000 FOOTBALL FACTS & QUESTIONS

 ## Quiz 42   **Managers**

1   **Which former Liverpool defender went to manage Oxford United in 1988 but soon fell out with chairman Robert Maxwell?**

2   Which former Manchester United star ran Rochdale in 1983 and 1984?

3   **Which former Norwich City boss became manager of Wigan Athletic in November 1995?**

4   Which former Stoke City defender was manager of Chester City in 1994 and 1995?

5   **Which former West Ham United goalkeeper was manager of Carlisle United from 1996 to 1997?**

6   Which former Wolverhampton Wanderers player and Walsall manager became chief coach at Cardiff City in 1995 and subsequently their Director of Football?

7   **Which future Arsenal manager was in charge at Bolton Wanderers from 1992-95?**

8   Which future Aston Villa boss began his managerial career with Darlington in 1989?

9   **Which future England coach was in charge of Queens Park Rangers from 1980 to 1984?**

10   Which future manager of Birmingham City was in charge at Hillsborough from 1991 to 1995?

11   **Which future Northern Ireland manager was in charge at Southampton from 1973-85?**

12   Which future Nottingham Forest manager managed Blackburn Rovers from 1953-58?

13   **Which goalkeeper managed Plymouth Argyle from 1992 to 1995?**

14   Which Hereford hero ran Wrexham from 1985 to 1989?

15   **Which Lion of Lisbon managed Aston Villa from 1986 to 1987?**

15 Billy McNeill
11 Lawrie McMenemy 12 Johnny Carey 13 Peter Shilton 14 Dixie McNeil
6 Kenny Hibbitt 7 Bruce Rioch 8 Brian Little 9 Terry Venables 10 Trevor Francis
1 Mark Lawrenson 2 Jimmy Greenhoff 3 John Deehan 4 Mike Pejic 5 Mervyn Day

Quiz 43

Managers

1 **Which Liverpool manager was in charge at Huddersfield Town from 1956 to 1959?**

2 Which Munich air crash survivor was manager of Swansea City from 1972 to 1975?

3 **Which of England's 1966 World Cup winning team was manager of Sheffield United in 1981?**

4 Which Shropshire club was managed by Asa Hartford from 1990 to 1991?

5 **Which three Grahams have managed Wolverhampton Wanderers?**

6 Which two England managers were formerly in charge at Ipswich Town?

7 **Which two European Cup winning managers have briefly been in charge at Elland Road?**

8 Which two Liverpool legends have managed Tranmere Rovers since the Second World War?

9 **Which twosome managed Reading from 1994 to 1997?**

10 Which was the only League club Bobby Moore ever managed?

11 **Who became manager of Northampton Town in January 1995?**

12 Who coached Barcelona to the Spanish League title in 1985?

13 **Who has been Newcastle United's longest serving manager since the Second World War?**

14 Who has managed both Brentford and Fulham?

15 **Who has managed Leyton Orient, Luton Town and Queen's Park Rangers?**

1 **Bill Shankly** 2 Harry Gregg 3 **Martin Peters** 4 Shrewsbury Town 5 **Hawkins, Turner and Taylor** 6 Alf Ramsey and Bobby Robson 7 **Brian Clough and Jock Stein** 8 Ron Yeats and John Aldridge 9 **Jimmy Quinn and Mick Gooding** 10 Southend United (1984-86) 11 **Ian Atkins** 12 Terry Venables 13 **Joe Harvey** 14 Bill Dodgin Jr 15 Alec Stock

CARLING 10,000 FOOTBALL FACTS & QUESTIONS

Quiz 44

Managers

1 **Who is the only Doctor to have managed an English First Division League club?**

2 Who is the only man to have managed both Bristol City and Inter Milan?

3 **Who managed Crewe Alexandra from 1972-73 and later led Brighton and Hove Albion to an FA Cup Final?**

4 Who succeeded Jack Charlton as manager of Middlesbrough in 1977?

5 **Who took over as Arsenal manager on the death of Herbert Chapman in 1934?**

6 Who took over from Brian Clough as Derby County manager in 1973?

7 **Who took over from Harry Redknapp when he left Bournemouth for West Ham United in 1992?**

8 Who was appointed Lincoln City manager in October 1995?

9 **Who managed Scunthorpe United for three days in 1959?**

10 Who managed Crystal Palace for four days in 1984?

11 **Who was Danny Wilson's immediate predecessor as manager of Barnsley?**

12 Who was manager of Everton from 1961-73?

13 **Who was manager of Arsenal from 1986 to 1995?**

14 Who was manager of Brighton and Hove Albion when they narrowly escaped relegation from the Football League in 1997?

15 **Who was manager of Burnley when they were last in the First Division in 1975-76?**

 **Quiz 45**   **Managers**

1   Who was manager of Bury when they won the Nationwide Second Division title in 1997?

2   Who was manager of Chelsea when they won the FA Cup in 1970?

3   Who was manager of Coventry City in 1987 when they won the FA Cup?

4   Who was manager of Macclesfield Town when they won promotion to the Football league in 1997?

5   Who was manager of Manchester City in 1968, the last time they won the Championship?

6   Who was manager of Southampton in 1966, when they won promotion to the First Division for the first time in their history?

7   Who was manager of Stoke City when they won the League Cup in 1972?

8   Who was manager of Tottenham Hotspur in their double-winning year?

9   Who was manager of Wycombe Wanderers when they won promotion to the Football League in 1993?

10 Who was sacked by Fulham to make way for Kevin Keegan?

11 Who was the Major who commanded the men of Notts County between 1944 and 1946, Hull City between 1946 and 1948 and Leeds United from 1948 to 1953?

12 Who was West Ham United's third manager, who served his apprenticeship at Colchester United between 1946 and 1948?

13 Who were co-managers of Charlton Athletic from 1991 to 1995?

14 Who, in June 1996, began his second spell as manager of Norwich City?

15 Which manager of Zambia scored the winning goal in an English FA Cup Final?

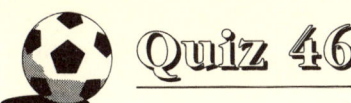

Quiz 46　　Milestones of Football

1　Who was the first 'Footballer of the Year'?

2　Who was the first 'Manager of the Year' in 1966?

3　Which was the first game to be broadcast on 'Match of the Day'?

4　Who were the first team to achieve the 'double'?

5　Who was the first man to hit 60 League goals in a season?

6　Who was the first player in British football to score a 'golden goal'?

7　Which club were the first to concede and score 100 League goals in one season?

8　Who was the first player to notch up a century of England appearances?

9　Who was the first player to notch up a century of Scotland appearances?

10　Who was the first player to notch up a century of Northern Ireland appearances?

11　Where was the first indoor World Cup game?

12　Who were England's opponents for the first all-seated football international at Wembley?

13　Who was the first black player to win a full England cap?

14　Who was the first black player to captain England at full international level?

15　Who was the first man to play in and then manage League Championship-winning teams?

1 Stanley Matthews **2 Jock Stein** 3 Liverpool 3 Arsenal 2 (1964) **4 Preston (1889)**
5 Dixie Dean (1927-28) **6 Iain Dunn (Huddersfield)** 7 Manchester City 8 **Billy Wright**
9 Kenny Dalglish 10 **Pat Jennings** 11 Seattle (USA v Canada in 1976) **12 Yugoslavia**
13 Viv Anderson **14 Paul Ince** 15 Ted Drake

 Quiz 47   Milestones of Football

1   Which club was first to be relegated from the Football League in 1923?

2   In what year were the Division Three North and South replaced by Divisions Three and Four?

3   **In which year was the Premier League created?**

4   Who was the first player to reach 1000 League appearances when he played for Leyton Orient in 1996?

5   **Which Manchester City keeper became the first to play in all four divisions in one season in 1986-87?**

6   Who were the first club to take the FA Cup out of England?

7   **Who is the only man to score a hat-trick in a post-war FA Cup final?**

8   In what year was the hymn 'Abide With Me' introduced as part of the FA Cup Final build-up?

9   **Who was the first guest of honour at the FA Cup Final of 1923?**

10 Who was the first player sent off playing for England?

11 **In what year did Walter Winterbottom become the first official manager of England?**

12 Who was the first manager to win the League Championship with two different clubs when he led both Huddersfield and Arsenal to the title?

13 **Who was the first man to become a player-manager in the top flight when he took over Queens Park Rangers in 1968?**

14 In which year was the first FA Cup Final at Wembley Stadium?

15 **In which year was the first Wembley game played under floodlights?**

1 Stalybridge Celtic 2 1957 3 1992 4 Peter Shilton 5 Eric Nixon 6 Cardiff City in 1927
7 Stan Mortensen 8 1927 9 King George V 10 Alan Mullery 11 1946
12 Herbert Chapman 13 Les Allen 14 1923 15 1955

 ## Quiz 48 **Milestones of Football**

1 Who scored the first 'golden goal' which decided a major international tournament?

2 **In which year was the first penalty scored in a first-class match?**

3 Which clubwas the first in competitive British football to win a game through a penalty shoot-out?

4 **Who became the first player to miss an FA Cup Final penalty at Wembley when he failed to convert in 1988?**

5 Who was the first player to score 200 goals in the Scottish Premier League?

6 **Who were the first British club to play in Europe?**

7 When did the Scottish First Division become the Premier League?

8 **In which year were the first shinguards used?**

9 In which year was professionalism in the game legalised?

10 **In which year did the white ball come into official use?**

11 In which year were substitutes introduced into Football League matches?

12 **The 'three points for a win' system was introduced by the Football League in which year?**

13 When was the 'professional foul' made a sending-off offence?

14 **When was the 'backpass' rule put into operation?**

15 In which year was the numbering of Football League shirts made compulsory?

THE LATEST THING

Quiz 49   Milestones of Football

1 **Two substitutes were permitted in League games from which year?**

2 Who was the first substitute to score in an FA Cup Final?

3 **In which year was the ceiling for footballers' earnings abolished?**

4 Who was the first British footballer to earn £100 a week?

5 **Who became the first sponsors of the Football League in 1983?**

6 Which club was the first to install an artificial pitch, in 1981?

7 **Which year saw the end of artificial turf pitches in the First Division?**

8 According to the original Taylor Report, when were all Premier League and First Division stadia required to become all-seater?

9 **When was the FA's School of Excellence at Lilleshall opened?**

10 Leyton Orient player Terry Howard hit the headlines when he lost his job in Feb 1995. Why?

11 **Which was the first football match to be televised in its entirety?**

12 What was introduced in Jan 1963 after a spell of particularly bad weather?

13 **Who were the first Olympic Games football champions in 1908?**

14 In which year was the first football code of laws compiled?

15 **The foundation of the Football Association occurred in which year?**

 **Quiz 50**   Milestones of Football

1 Who did England play in the first official international in 1872?

2 **The referee's job was made a little easier with what 1878 introduction?**

3 In which year were goal nets introduced?

4 **Which country did England play in the first Wembley international?**

5 In 1935 trials were held for which innovation in football discipline?

6 **Which was the first club to complete a hat-trick of consecutive League titles?**

7 In which year was the first live television transmission of an FA Cup Final?

8 **Who were the first foreign team to beat England in a full international at Wembley?**

9 The last Football League Christmas Day programme was completed in which year?

10 **The system of loan transfers was introduced in which year?**

11 A decision by the PFA in 1978 precipitated which introduction into English football?

12 **A European ban on all English clubs was introduced in which year?**

13 Who, in 1986, became the first club to ban visiting supporters?

14 **The system of play-off matches for promotion and relegation was introduced in which year?**

15 Which English club was the last to revert to grass from artificial pitches?

 # Quiz 51 Moonlighting Footballers

1 **'Fever Pitch' is a book on one fan's obsession with his favourite football club. Which Premiership club does he support?**

2 Which famous actor narrated 'Hero', the official film of the 1986 World Cup?

3 **Which former England international appeared in the film 'When Saturday Comes'?**

4 What was the name of the award winning television drama about the Hillsborough disaster?

5 **Which club was the subject of the documentary 'Yours for a Fiver'?**

6 What was the title of the Cutting Edge television documentary that chronicled Graham Taylor as England manager?

7 **Which international manager wrote the television show 'Hazel'?**

8 Which England international had a hit record with 'Do The Right Thing'?

9 **Which footballers have appeared in adverts for Brut aftershave?**

10 Glenn Hoddle and Chris Waddle had a hit song when they were playing at Tottenham. What was the title of the song?

11 **Ruud Gullit used to be a member of a band. What music did they play?**

12 Which Premiership player appeared in the film 'Le Bonheur Est Dans Le Pre'?

13 **Name the title of the famous play and television programme An Evening with ....**

14 Which Nottingham Forest striker is a singer in a band?

15 **Who wrote the book 'Fever Pitch'?**

 **Quiz 52** **Moonlighting Footballers**

1 Which famous footballer orchestrated the football action in 'Escape to Victory'?

2 Which former England international has advertised Walkers Crisps?

3 The war film 'Escape to Victory' featured a football match between Allied prisoners and West Germany. Who was the manager of the Allies?

4 Which former England captain was in the Allies team in 'Escape to Victory'?

5 What position did Sylvester Stallone's play in 'Escape to Victory'?

6 Which England international writes a weekly article for The Times?

7 Which Croatian footballer had his own column in the Daily Telegraph during Euro '96?

8 Which former Arsenal and England striker occasionally writes for the Daily Telegraph?

9 Which two former Scotland internationals write for The Express?

10 Which England goalscorer wrote for the Observer?

11 Which former England international has a column in the football magazine 'Four-Four-Two'?

12 Which television summariser appeared on a Littlewoods Pools advert in 1997?

13 Which two Premiership players featured in a Nike advertisement in 1996?

14 Which England international has appeared in advertisments for sportswear Adidas?

15 Which Premiership footballer appeared in television adverts for Eurostar?

Quiz 53 Moonlighting Footballers

1 **Which Manchester United and Manchester City players became partners in two lady boutiques?**

2 Which two players from England's 1966 World Cup squad went into partnership in a football kit company?

3 **Which team sung the number one hit 'Back Home' in 1970?**

4 Tottenham's 1981 FA Cup Final song reached number five in the charts. Whose dream were they singing about?

5 **Which nation's World Cup song was titled 'Easy, Easy'?**

6 'Blue is the Colour' was a number five hit for which club in February 1972?

7 **Which England goalkeeper worked as a deck-chair assistant before turning professional?**

8 Which FA Cup winning manager was a clerk in an education office before he took up football?

9 **Which England 1966 World Cup star sung a version of 'You'll Never Walk Alone', but it never reached the charts?**

10 Which former England captain had a number 31 hit with 'Head Over Heels in Love' in June 1979?

11 **Which Spanish singer was once a Real Madrid goalkeeper?**

12 Which Tottenham and Wales striker invested in two butchers shops after finishing his career?

13 **Which French footballer appeared in a Renault advertisement?**

14 Which television commentator supplied the voice-over for that advert?

15 **Highbury was at the centre of which movie?**

CARLING 10,000 FOOTBALL FACTS & QUESTIONS

Quiz 54 — Most Capped Players

1. **Who is the only player to have won an international cap while playing for Hereford United?**

2. Who is Arsenal's most capped player, a full back who played 77 times for England while at Highbury?

3. **Who is the only player to have won an international cap while playing for Hartlepool United?**

4. The Coventry City player with the most international caps (27) has played 37 times for Zimbabwe. Who is he?

5. **With which two clubs was Peter Shilton the most capped player?**

6. Who is Aston Villa's most capped player, making 51 of his 83 international appearances while at Villa Park?

7. **Only one Torquay United player – Rodney Jack – has ever won an international cap. Which country did he represent?**

8. Brentford's most capped player, John Buttigieg, made 63 international appearances for whom?

9. **Although no one has ever won an international cap while playing for Oldham Athletic, the most capped player they have ever had on their books played 54 times for Norway. Name him.**

10. For which English League club was Alan McDonald playing throughout his 52-cap international career with Northern Ireland?

11. **Name the Bermudian who won 18 international caps while playing for Rotherham United.**

12. How many of his 108 England caps did Bobby Moore win while playing for West Ham United?

13. **Watford have two players with the same number of international caps (31). One is John Barnes, who played for England 79 times altogether. The other won all his 31 caps for Wales while at Vicarage Road. Who is he?**

14. Which Nigeria international is Leyton Orient's most capped player?

15. **Which Welshman is Crystal Palace's most capped player?**

Quiz 55

Most Capped Players

1   Bobby Charlton is Manchester United's most capped international player. How many times did he play for England?

2   Stockport County's most capped international player is Martin Nash, who played twice for which country?

3   Who is Leeds United's most capped international, with 54 appearances for Scotland?

4   Gordon Banks won 36 of his England caps while at Stoke City. Where was he when he won the other 37?

5   Who is Leicester City's most capped international, with 39 appearances for Northern Ireland between 1980 and 1986?

6   Eamonn Dunphy, Millwall's most capped player, won all but one of his 23 Republic of Ireland caps while playing at the Den. Which club was he playing for when he played his first international, against Spain in 1966?

7   Who is Wigan Athletic's only international player to date, with a single appearance as a substitute in Northern Ireland's 1997 game against Thailand?

8   Neville Southall is Everton's most capped player. How many times did he play in goal for Wales?

9   Who is Chelsea's most capped player, winning 24 of his 84 England caps while at Stamford Bridge?

10 Name Sunderland's most capped international, who won 38 of his 40 Republic of Ireland caps while at Roker Park between 1958 and 1969.

11 Who is Swansea City's most capped international?

12 How many times did Billy Wright, Wolverhampton Wanderers' most capped player, play for England?

13 In a career spanning 1950-60, who became Newcastle's most capped international, with 40 appearances for Northern Ireland?

14 Nigel Worthington won 66 Northern Ireland caps – two with Stoke City, 14 with Leeds United and 50 with whom, making him their most capped international player?

15 Which Blackburn Rovers player made 41 England appearances between 1902 and 1914?

 Quiz 56   Names of Grounds

Which English Football League teams play at home at the following stadiums?

1 **The City Ground**
2 Craven Cottage
3 **Dean Court**
4 The Dell
5 **The Deva Stadium**
6 Edgeley Park
7 **Elland Road**
8 Ewood Park
9 **Feethams**
10 Filbert Street
11 **Fratton Park**
12 Gay Meadow
13 **Gigg Lane**
14 Glanford Park
15 **Goodison Park**

 **Quiz 57**   **Names of Grounds**

What are the names of the following clubs' grounds?

1 **Arsenal**
2 Bristol Rovers
3 **Colchester United**
4 Coventry City
5 **Crewe Alexandra**
6 Luton Town
7 **Macclesfield Town**
8 Manchester City
9 **Millwall**
10 Peterborough United
11 **Queens Park Rangers**
12 Rotherham United
13 **Scarborough**
14 Sheffield Wednesday
15 **West Bromwich Albion**

1 **The Arsenal Stadium (but popularly Highbury)** 2 The Memorial Ground
3 **Layer Road** 4 Highfield Road 5 **Gresty Road** 6 Kenilworth Road 7 **The Moss Rose Ground**
8 Maine Road 9 **The New Den** 10 London Road 11 **Loftus Road** 12 Millmoor
13 **The McCain Stadium** 14 Hillsborough 15 **The Hawthorns**

Quiz 58   Names of Grounds

Which English Football League teams play at home at the following stadiums?

1 **Molineux**

2 Oakwell

3 **Plainmoor**

4 Portman Road

5 **Prenton Park**

6 Pride Park

7 **The Priestfield Stadium**

8 The Pulse Stadium

9 **The Racecourse Ground**

10 The Recreation Groun

11 **Roots Hall**

12 Sixfields Stadium

13 **Spotland**

14 Springfield Park

15 **St Andrews**

Quiz 59 — Names of Grounds

1   Exeter City and Newcastle United play at grounds with very similar names. What is the key difference between the two?

2   What was the name of Middlesbrough's ground until 1995?

3   What is Sunderland's ground correctly known as?

4   What was the name of Sunderland's old ground, on which they played from 1898-1997?

5   Although almost everyone says that West Ham United play their home games at Upton Park, that is the name of the area in which their stadium is situated. What is the name of the stadium itself?

6   Name the three English League clubs that have played home games at Selhurst Park?

7   With which temporarily exiled club did West Ham United share their home ground during the 1990-91 season?

8   Tottenham Hotspur's ground is universally known as White Hart Lane. In which street is the main entrance?

9   What was the name of Wimbledon's ground when they joined the Football League in 1977-78?

10 What was the name of the ground at which Derby County played their home matches between 1895 and 1997?

11 At which League ground did Brighton and Hove Albion play their home matches in 1997-98?

12 Although it is universally known as Loftus Road, in which street is the main entrance to the Queens Park Rangers ground?

13 What are the names of the three English Football League grounds that are not in England?

14 What is the name of the one Football League ground in England whose team does not play in the English Football League?

15 What was the name of the ground at which Wycombe Wanderers played from 1901 to 1990?

---

1 An apostrophe 'S': the grounds are St James Park (Exeter City) and St James' Park (Newcastle United) 2 Ayresome Park 3 The Stadium of Light 4 Roker Park 5 The Boleyn Ground 6 Crystal Palace, Charlton Athletic and Wimbledon 7 Charlton Athletic 8 Tottenham High Road, London N17 9 Plough Lane 10 The Baseball Ground 11 The Priestfield Stadium, Gillingham 12 South Africa Road, London W12 13 Ninian Park (Cardiff City), The Vetch Field (Swansea City) and The Racecourse Ground (Wrexham) 14 Shielfield Park (Berwick Rangers' ground) 15 Loakes Park

Quiz 60   Names of Grounds

Which Scottish Football League teams play at home at the following stadiums?

1   **The Almondvale Stadium**
2   Bayview Park
3   **Boghead Park**
4   Which two clubs share the Broadwood Stadium
5   **Brockville Park**
6   Burnbrae
7   **The Caledonian Stadium**
8   Cappielow Park
9   **Central Park**
10   The Cliftonhill Stadium
11   **The Cliftonville Stadium**
12   Dens Park
13   **East End Park**
14   Easter Road
15   **Fir Park**

Quiz 61   Scottish League & Cup

1 Who scored Rangers' winning goal in the 1971 Scottish League Cup Final?

2 **What was the score recorded in the 1984 Scottish Cup, which remains a British record this century?**

3 Who was Scotland's Player of the Year in 1996?

4 **Which team beat Celtic 3-1 in the 1970 Scottish Cup Final?**

5 Which Scottish club signed Norwich City's Kevin Drinkell for £500,000 at the start of the 1987-88 season?

6 **Who was voted Scotland's Young Player of the Year in 1981?**

7 Which two teams shared the Division One title in the first season in 1891?

8 **Who won the first Scottish Premier Division in 1976?**

9 Who was voted Player of the Year by the Scottish Football Writers in 1974?

10 **Which former Chelsea star was voted Second Division Player of the Year by the SFA in 1982?**

11 Which Dutchman was voted Premier Division Player of the Year by the SFA in 1989?

12 **Who was the first player since 1972 to score a hat-trick in the Scottish FA Cup Final in 1996?**

13 Where were both Scottish FA Cup semi-finals played in 1996?

14 **Who did Celtic beat in the 1995 Scottish FA Cup Final?**

15 Who won six of the first nine Scottish FA Cup Finals?

1 Derek Johnstone 2 **Stirling Albion 20 Selkirk 0 in 1984** 3 Paul Gascoigne 4 **Aberdeen** 5 Rangers 6 **Charlie Nicholas** 7 Dumbarton and Rangers 8 **Rangers** 9 The Scotland World Cup Squad 10 **Pat Nevin** 11 Theo Snelders 12 **Gordon Durie** 13 Hampden Park 14 **Airdrieonians** 15 Queens Park

Quiz 62   Scottish League & Cup

1 When was the first Rangers-Celtic Scottish FA Cup Final?

2 Who won?

3 Why was the FA Cup withheld in 1909?

4 Which team won the FA Cup four times in five seasons in the early 1980's?

5 Who was voted Scottish Manager of the Year in 1990?

6 Before the end of the 1996-97 season, who was the last Scottish player to be voted Player of the Year by the SFA?

7 What year was it?

8 What was the highest score in the Scottish FA Cup, and still a British record?

9 What year was it in?

10 On that same day Dundee Harp beat which team 35-0 in the Cup?

11 11 goals were scored in the Premier Division game between Celtic and Hamilton in January 1987. What was the score-line?

12 How many goals did Celtic score when the two teams met again in November 1988?

13 Which Scottish team holds the British record score this century?

14 Nine players scored that day. Which player got seven goals?

15 Which Dundee United striker scored five times in the Premier Division against Morton in November 1984?

---

1 1894 2 Rangers (3-1) 3 Because of riots between Rangers and Celtic fans after two drawn matches in the Final 4 Aberdeen 5 Andy Roxburgh (Scotland) 6 Andy Goram 7 1993 8 Arbroath 36, Bon Accord 0 9 1885 10 Aberdeen Rovers 11 8-3 to Celtic 12 Eight 13 Stirling Albion, when they beat Selkirk 20-0 in the Scottish Cup in 1984 14 Davie Thompson 15 Paul Sturrock

Quiz 63   Scottish League & Cup

1   Which Ayr player set a British record of 66 League goals in one season in 1927-28?

2   **When Arbroath beat Bon Accord in the 1885 Scottish Cup, how many goals did John Petrie score?**

3   Who is the Scottish League's top scorer with 410 goals?

4   **Which player scored 338 League goals in a career that started at St Mirren and finished at Clapton Orient?**

5   Which club did Gerry Baker score 10 goals against for St Mirren in the 1960 Scottish Cup first round?

6   **Which team scored 142 goals in just 34 League games in the 1937-38 season?**

7   Which team conceded just 19 goals in 36 Premier Division games in 1990?

8   **Who scored the fastest goal in Scottish Cup history for Aberdeen in 1982?**

9   How many seconds was it?

10 **Which former Motherwell striker, later to play for Liverpool, scored the fastest hat-trick in Scottish history in 1959?**

11 Which Scottish goalkeeper scored for Hibernian in 1988?

12 **Who did he score against?**

13 Which other goalkeeper has scored in a League match?

14 **Which Danish striker scored in 15 consecutive matches for Dundee United in 1964-65?**

15 Which Scottish club went 14 consecutive games without scoring to set a British record?

Quiz 64 — Scottish League & Cup

1 **Which two Scottish teams attracted an attendance of 143,470 in March 1948?**

2 How many people were inside Hampden Park for the 1937 Scottish Cup Final?

3 **135,826 turned up to watch Celtic play an European Cup semi-final in 1970. Which other British team were they playing?**

4 What is the record attendance for a Scottish League Cup Final?

5 **Which two teams were playing?**

6 Who captained Aberdeen to Scottish Cup glory in 1970, and then led Manchester United to FA Cup glory seven years later?

7 **Four players were sent-off when Rangers faced Celtic in the Scottish Cup quarter-final in 1991. Can you name the players?**

8 Which former Scottish international was sent-off 11 times in Scottish matches?

9 **How many times was he sent-off for Scotland?**

10 Which two Hearts players were suspended by the Scottish FA for fighting each other in a 'friendly' game?

11 **Billy McLafferty was banned for eight-and-a-half months and fined £250 by the Scottish FA. Why?**

12 Which club was he playing for at the time?

13 **Which former Rangers striker was banned for 12 games for violent conduct in a game against Raith in 1994?**

14 Which manager was also chairman of the club at the same time, in 1988?

15 **Which club was he at?**

---

1 Rangers and Hibernian 2 146,433 3 Leeds 4 107,609 5 Celtic and Rangers 6 Martin Buchan 7 Terry Hurlock, Mark Walters and Mark Hateley of Rangers and Peter Grant of Celtic 8 Willie Johnston 9 Once 10 Graeme Hogg and Craig Levein 11 Because he had failed to turn up to a disciplinary hearing after being sent-off 12 Stenhousemuir 13 Duncan Ferguson 14 Jim McLean 15 Dundee United

 ## Quiz 65   Scottish League & Cup

1   Sixty six people died when they were trampled near the end of the Rangers-Celtic match in 1971. Where did the tragedy happen.

2   **Which Celtic goalkeeper died after suffering a fractured skull against Rangers in 1931?**

3   How was the 1987 Scottish League Cup Final decided?

4   **Who won the game?**

5   What was the penalty shoot-out score between Aberdeen and Celtic in the 1990 Scottish Cup Final?

6   **Celtic lost the Scottish League Cup Final on penalties. To which side?**

7   Which team won every match in the Scottish League in the 1898-99 season?

8   **Before the 1997-98 season, how many times have Rangers completed the League and Cup double?**

9   Before the 1997-98 season, how many times have Rangers completed the domestic treble?

10 **How many trophies did Celtic win in the 1966-67 season?**

11 Who were the last club to win the Scottish Cup for three years in succession?

12 **When was that?**

13 Before the 1997 Final, who are the three players to be sent-off in Scottish Cup Finals?

14 **Who holds the record for unbeaten matches in the Scottish League?**

15 How many games were they unbeaten?

 **Quiz 66** Scottish League & Cup

1 Who became the first player to score 200 goals in the Premier Division?

2 Which team set a Scottish League record of 40 consecutive home defeats in the 1990s?

3 **Which team collected a total of 67 points out of a possible 72 in the 1963-64 season?**

4 Which Rangers player won nine Scottish Championship medals in 11 years?

5 **Who were the first Scottish club to play in the European Cup?**

6 What season was it?

7 **Which round did they reach?**

8 What season was the first Premier Division played?

9 **Who were the sponsors of the 1996-97 Scottish FA Cup?**

10 What year did the Scottish FA introduce penalty shoot-outs to the Cup Final?

11 **Who provided the shock of the 1995 Scottish Cup by beating Aberdeen 2-0?**

12 Who did Tommy Burns leave to become manager of Celtic?

13 **Which manager was fined £2,000 by the SFA for breach of contract?**

14 When was the Scottish FA formed?

15 **Which two Scottish sides shared Firhill Park for five years?**

Quiz 67 Scottish League & Cup

1 Who became the youngest player in the Scottish League when he played for Queens Park in 1946?

2 How old was he?

3 Who remains the oldest player to earn his first cap for Scotland?

4 How old was he – and who did he play against?

5 Which Scottish club play their home games at Hampden Park?

6 Who were the first Scottish club to have an artificial pitch?

7 Which goalkeeper played for Scotland Under-21's in the afternoon and then turned out for Clyde that same evening?

8 Who were the first Scottish club to issue a Stock Exchange share issue?

9 Which two Scottish clubs have won the European Cup Winners' Cup?

10 Which Scottish club beat Eintracht Frankfurt 5-1 in an UEFA Cup first round, second leg, after losing the first leg 3-0?

11 Which clubs did Alex Ferguson play for?

12 How many Scottish League clubs did Alex Ferguson manage before joining Manchester United?

13 Name them.

14 Who was named Scottish Manager of the Year in 1995?

15 Which goalkeeper was named 1981 Player of the Year?

1 Ronnie Simpson 2 15 3 Ronnie Simpson 4 36 – **against England** 5 Queens Park
6 Stirling Albion 7 Scott Howie **8 Hibernian** 9 Rangers and Aberdeen **10 Kilmarnock**
11 Queens Park, St Johnstone, Dunfermline, Rangers, Falkirk and Ayr United **12 Three**
13 East Stirling, St Mirren and Aberdeen **14 Jimmy Nicholl (Raith)** 15 Alan Rough

Quiz 68   Irish League & Cup

1   **How many times have Moyola Park won the Irish FA Cup?**

2   Who were the Irish League champions in 1982?

3   **In the 1995-96 Irish Premier Division, who finished higher, Glenavon or Glentoran?**

4   Waterford were FAI League Champions for three consecutive seasons. Name the years.

5   **Who was the 1996 Irish Premier Division Player of the Year?**

6   Name the 1996 Smirnoff Irish Premier Division Manager of the Year.

7   **In the replay of the 1996 FAI Cup Final, how many players with the surname Geoghegan played in the Shelbourne side?**

8   Which club were relegated from the Irish Premier Division at the end of the 1995–96 season?

9   **In the 1995-96 FAI Premier Division, which club had three points deducted for fielding players deemed to be 'illegal'?**

10   Who scored the winning goal for Glentoran in last year's Irish Cup Final?

11   **The 1996 Bord Gais FAI League Cup Final between Shelbourne and Sligo Rovers was decided on penalties. Who won and what was the score?**

12   Who were the Irish League Champions in 1976?

13   **How many times have Shamrock Rovers completed the FAI League and Cup double?**

14   Who was the 1995-96 FAI Premier Division's Young Player of the Year?

15   **Who was the 1995-96 Irish Premier Division's top scorer?**

---

1 Once – in 1881 2 Linfield 3 Glentoran 4 1967-68, 1968-69, 1969-70 5 Peter Kennedy (Portadown) 6 Ron McFall (Portadown) 7 Two 8 Bangor 9 U.C.D 10 Glen Little 11 Shelbourne, 4-3 12 Crusaders 13 Six 14 Mick O'Byrne (U.C.D) 15 Gary Haylock (Portadown) with 20 goals

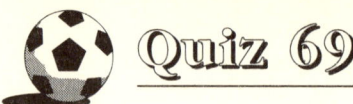

Quiz 69
Welsh League & Cup

1 Which team beat Barry Town on penalties to win the 1996 Welsh Cup?

2 Who won the first Welsh Cup?

3 Who did they beat in the Final?

4 Which team won the Welsh Cup for five consecutive years from 1967?

5 Who did Cardiff City lose the Cup Final to in 1939?

6 Which team appeared in the Cup Final on six occasions in eight years from 1887?

7 When was the last time Aberwystwyth won the Welsh Cup?

8 Which non-league team did Cardiff City beat in the 1992 Cup Final?

9 Cardiff City played in 11 consecutive Cup Finals from 1967. True or False?

10 Who were the Welsh League Champions in 1995?

11 Who did Swansea beat 8-0 in the Welsh Cup quarter-finals in 1995?

12 Bangor City won 12-1 in the fourth round of the 1995 Welsh Cup fourth round. Who were their victims?

13 Shrewsbury lost the 1931 Cup Final 7-0. To who?

14 Which famous non-league side reached the Cup Final twice in the 1980s?

15 Who were the first club to win the Welsh Cup in a penalty shoot-out?

CARLING 10,000 FOOTBALL FACTS & QUESTIONS

Quiz 70 — Songs and Chants

1   Fill in the missing name in the chant of Nottingham Forest, Sheffield Wednesday and England supporters: *You'll never beat —— ——!*

2   Which team is associated with the song 'I'm Forever Blowing Bubbles'?

3   **Which team's signature tune is 'When The Saints Go Marching In'?**

4   On whose terraces might you hear the following lyric, sung to a tune from the film 'Mary Poppins':
'Chim-chiminee, chim-chiminee, chim-chim cheroo,
We've got a kit that's more yellow than blue'?

5   Supporters of which team have adopted – and adapted – the song 'When The Red, Red Robin Comes Bob, Bob, Bobbin' Along'?

6   Although widely used by many supporters, especially those of Manchester United, which club has been linked most closely since their great days of the 1960s with the hymn 'Glory, Glory Hallelujah'?

7   **Complete the following couplet:**
'My name is Edward Ebenezer Jeremiah Brown
I'm a football supporter of —— ——'

8   'On the ball, City – never mind the danger' – which City?

9   **If the football isn't up to much, what do Leicester City fans sing to keep themselves happy?**

10   Where might you hear the song 'Swing Low, Sweet Wheelbarrow'?

11   **Fans of which team sing a version of John Denver's 'Annie's Song' which begins:**
'You light up my senses   Like a packet of Woodbines
Like a gallon of Magnet   Like a good pinch of snuff'?

12   What is the title of the Newcastle United song with the chorus that begins:
'Oh, me lads, you shoulda seen us gannin'?

13   **Which fans sing the following lyric, to the tune of Neil Diamond's 'Daydream Believer' (a '60s hit for The Monkees):**
'We once thought of you as a Scouser dressed in blue
Now you're red and white through and through'?

14   And who are they singing about?

15   **The Liverpool anthem 'You'll Never Walk Alone' is best known as a '60s hit for Gerry and the Pacemakers. But from which musical does it originally come?**

---

15 'Carousel'
11 **Sheffield United** 12 The Blaydon Races 13 **Sunderland** 14 Manager Peter Reid
6 Tottenham Hotspur 7 **Ipswich Town** 8 Norwich 9 **'When You're Smiling'** 10 Notts County
1 **Des Walker** 2 West Ham United 3 **Southampton** 4 Reading 5 **Charlton Athletic**

Quiz 71

Songs and Chants

1 Which team's supporters sing 'Blue Moon'?

2 Which hit by Oasis has more recently been adopted by the same set of fans?

3 Which Tom Jones hit is popular on the terraces at Stoke City?

4 And which other Tom Jones hit then became popular at Port Vale?

5 Which team's anthem is 'Keep Right On To The End Of The Road'?

6 At which ground might you hear the following sung:
'Irene, goodnight, Irene goodnight,
Goodnight, Irene, goodnight Irene
I'll see you in my dreams'?

7 Which team does this describe:
'Here they come, our mighty champions,
Raise your voices to the anthem,
Marching like a mighty army…'?
(Clue: it is sung to the tune 'Men of Harlech'.)

8 Whose fans made up the following words to the tune of 'The Internationale':
'Flying high, up in the sky, we'll keep the blue flag flying high'?

9 Whose fans sing The Dave Clark Five's '60s hit 'Glad All Over'?

10 Where would you be most likely to hear a community singing 'You've Lost
That Loving Feeling', originally a hit for The Righteous Brothers?

11 Which fans sing these lyrics, to the tune of 'John Brown's Body' or
'Glory, Glory Hallelujah':
'Come on the Quaker men, the boys in black and white,
We cheer them every morning, every afternoon and night'?

12 When they play away at grounds with fewer amenities than their own,
whose fans sing this, to the tune of 'When The Saints Go Marching In':
'My garden shed is bigger than this
My garden shed is bigger than this,
It's got a door and a window,
My garden shed is bigger than this'?

13 'I can't help falling in love with you' – who took over this Elvis
Presley song, adding only their team's name at the end?

14 Who did Southampton fans hail as 'The King of Israel' – to the tune of 'The
First Nowel' – until he upped and took himself off to West Ham in 1997?

15 Whose fans sing this, to the tune of 'Yellow Submarine':
'We all follow a black and amber team
A black and amber team
That sometimes play in green'?

11 Darlington 12 Birmingham City 13 Sunderland 14 Eyal Berkovic 15 Hull City
6 Bristol Rovers 7 Wrexham 8 Chelsea 9 Crystal Palace 10 Nottingham Forest
1 Manchester City 2 'Wonderwall' 3 'Delilah' 4 'What's New, Pussycat' 5 Birmingham City

Quiz 72

1　Bristol City's record transfers in and out both involved the same player. They bought him for £500,000 from Arsenal in July 1992 and sold him to Newcastle United for £1.75 million eight months later. Who is he?

2　Crewe Alexandra is a nursery of talent. For which full back did they receive their highest transfer fee – £600,000 – from Liverpool in October 1991?

3　For which Brazilian club did Romario play until June 1996, when Valencia (Spain) bought him for £8 million?

4　For which forward did Blackpool receive their record transfer fee (£750,000) when they sold him to Queens Park Rangers in August 1993?

5　For which forward did Nottingham Forest pay Arsenal £2.8 million in July 1995?

6　For which player did Leeds United pay Charlton Athletic £2.8 million in July 1996?

7　For which player did Liverpool under Graeme Souness pay Coventry City £3.75 million in September 1994?

8　For which Portsmouth player did Tottenham Hotspur pay £2 million in May 1992?

9　For which Wolverhampton Wanderer did Manchester City under Malcolm Allison surprisingly pay £1.15 million in September 1979?

10　From which club did Derby County buy Craig Short in September 1992?

11　From which club did Internazionale buy Dennis Bergkamp for £8 million in June 1993?

12　From which club did Manchester City buy Michael Robinson for £765,000 in June 1979?

13　From which club did Manchester United buy Lee Sharpe for £180,000 in May 1988?

14　From which club did Notts County make their record signing – Tony Agana for £685,000 in November 1991?

15　From which club did Swansea City make their record signing – Colin Irwin for £340,000 in August 1981?

 **Quiz 73**   **Transfers**

1   **From which club did Swansea City receive £375,000 for Des Lyttle in July 1993?**

2   From which club did Wimbledon buy Dean Holdsworth for £720,000 in August 1992?

3   **From which Danish club did Luton Town make their record purchase – £850,000 for Lars Elstrup in August 1989?**

4   From which Dutch club did Barcelona buy Brazilian star Ronaldo for £13.25 million in June 1996?

5   **From which Lancashire club did Aston Villa buy Earl Barrett for £1.7 million in February 1992?**

6   How much did Everton receive for Andrei Kanchelskis when they sold him to sold him to Fiorentina in in February 1997?

7   **How much did Manchester United receive for Paul Ince when they sold him to Internazionale in June 1995?**

8   How much did Newcastle United pay Blackburn Rovers for Alan Shearer in July 1996?

9   **How much did Newcastle United pay ' for Les Ferdinand in June 1995?**

10 How much less than that did they receive from Tottenham Hotspur when they sold him in June 1995?

11 **Impressed by his showing in the 1996-97 FA Cup, which forward did Southampton buy from Chesterfield?**

12 In January 1996, which Dutch club broke the world record for money spent on a Rotherham United player when they bought Mike Jeffrey for £255,000?

13 **In July 1995, which club was paid £3.25 million by Aston Villa for Mark Draper?**

14 In June 1992, who did AC Milan buy from Torino for £13 million?

15 **In June 1995, how much did Liverpool pay Nottingham Forest for Stan Collymore?**

 ## Quiz 74 — **Transfers**

1   **In May 1980, Liverpool paid Chester City £300,000 – more money than they have received in a transfer deal before or since. But it was still a snip for the purchaser – who was the player?**

2   In May 1980, which club learned that £333,333 was the value of Money?

3   **In October 1993, Alen Boksic became the record transfer when he was sold by Marseille for £8.4 million – to which Italian club?**

4   Ipswich Town's record sale and purchase have both involved Tottenham. Who did they sell to the London club for £1.9 million in August 1993?

5   **Who did they buy from Spurs for £1 million in June 1994?**

6   Name the Welsh international striker sold by Derby County to Liverpool for £2.9 million in July 1991.

7   **To which Belgian club did Colchester United pay their record transfer fee – £400,000 – for Dale Tempest in August 1987?**

8   To which club did Manchester City pay £1.5 million for Kevin Horlock in January 1997?

9   **To which club did Stoke City sell Mark Stein in October 1993 for a club record £1.5 million?**

10   To which London club did Newcastle United pay £4 million in June 1995 for Warren Barton?

11   **To which London club did Walsall sell David Kelly in July 1988 for £600,000?**

12   To which Nationwide club did Southampton pay £750,000 for Mickey Evans in March 1997?

13   **To which other Yorkshire club did Sheffield Wednesday pay £2.7 million for Andy Booth in July 1996?**

14   And a month later, who became the seller's record purchase – £1.2 million from Bristol Rovers?

15   **From which club did Wimbledon buy record £1.7 million signing Ben Thatcher?**

Quiz 75

Transfers

1 **Which club's record sale was Darren Peacock to Queens Park Rangers in December 1990?**

2 Which current Aston Villa star moved from Port Vale to Sheffield Wednesday for £1 million in August 1994?

3 **Which current Coventry City star was sold by Lincoln City to Newcastle United in November 1995?**

4 Which former Colchester United player became Wycombe Wanderers' record signing when they bought him from Birmingham City for £140,000 in March 1995?

5 **Which former Queens Park and West Ham United striker was transferred from Derby County to Millwall for £800,000 in December 1989?**

6 Which French star moved from Olympique Marseille to AC Milan for £10 million in June 1992?

7 **Which future Bolton Wanderers star was Cardiff City's record sale when he moved in February 1994 to Sheffield United for £300,000?**

8 Which future captain of Sheffield Wednesday was sold by Wigan Athletic to Coventry City for £329,000 in August 1991?

9 **Which future Chelsea manager moved from Sampdoria to Juventus in June 1992 for a then record £12 million?**

10 Which homesick Oxford boy was Swindon Town's record purchase from West Ham United in August 1994?

11 **Which Italian World Cup star moved from Juventus to AC Milan for £8.5 million in June 1995?**

12 Who did Bolton Wanderers sell for £4.5 million in September 1995?

13 **Which player did Sheffield Wednesday sell to Blackburn Rovers in September 1993 for £2.65 million – a club record?**

14 Who – at £3 million from Internazionale – is Sheffield Wednesday's most expensive purchase?

15 **Which Welsh international full back became Wrexham's record signing when they bought him from Liverpool for £210,000 in October 1978?**

Quiz 76
Transfers

1 Which striker did Sunderland sell to Crystal Palace in September 1991 for £1.5 million?

2 Who did Sunderland buy from Newcastle for £2.5 million in June 1997?

3 Who – at £4 million – is Chelsea's most expensive signing to date?

4 Who – at £2.2 million – is Chelsea's most lucrative sale?

5 Who became the world's most expensive goalkeeper when he moved from Sampdoria to Internazionale for £7.5 million in August 1994?

6 Name the player bought by Barnsley from Nottingham Forest for £1.5 million in May 1991.

7 Who did Leyton Orient sell to Notts County for £600,000 in August 1981?

8 Who is Brighton and Hove Albion's record purchase – £500,000 from Manchester United in October 1980?

9 Who is Brighton and Hove Albion's record sale – £900,000 to Liverpool in August 1981?

10 Who is Cambridge United's record sale – £1 million to Manchester United in August 1992?

11 Who, three months later, became Cambridge United's record purchase – £190,000 from Luton Town?

12 Who is Coventry City's record signing – £3 million from Leeds United in July 1996?

13 Who is Crystal Palace's record sale – £4.5 million to Tottenham Hotspur in June 1995?

14 Who, a month later, became Crystal Palace's record signing – £2.25 million from Millwall?

15 Who is Millwall's record sale – £2.3 million to Liverpool in March 1995?

Quiz 77

Transfers

1   **Who is Norwich City's most expensive signing – £1 million from Leeds United in June 1994?**

2   Who is Oldham Athletic's record signing – £750,000 from Aston Villa in June 1992?

3   **Who is Sheffield United's record purchase – £1.2 million from West Ham United in January 1996?**

4   Who is Sheffield United's record sale – £2.7 million to Leeds United in July 1993?

5   **Who is Tranmere Rovers' record sale – £1.5 million to Sheffield Wednesday in August 1994?**

6   Who is Tranmere Rovers' record purchase – £450,000 from Aston Villa in August 1995?

7   **Who is West Bromwich Albion's record signing – £1.25 million from Preston North End in June 1997?**

8   Who moved from Sampdoria to Parma for £11 million in June 1996?

9   **Who moved from Southampton to Grimsby Town for £300,000 in July 1996, a record for the Nationwide club?**

10 Who paid Aston Villa £5.5 million for David Platt in July 1991?

11 **Who was Luton Town's record sale – £2.5 million to Arsenal in January 1995?**

12 Who, in October 1981, became West Bromwich Albion's most lucrative sale?

13 **Who, in 1957, became the first British player ever to transfer to a foreign club?**

14 Who, in 1961, became Britain's first £100,000 player when he moved from Manchester City to Torino?

15 **Who had previously been transferred from Chelsea to AC Milan for £99,999, because, it was said, 'no one could be worth £100,000'?**

CARLING 10,000 FOOTBALL FACTS & QUESTIONS

 **Quiz 78**   **Transfers**

1   Which former Serie A star left Glasgow Rangers in the
     summer of 1996?

2   **Name the French midfielder who joined Arsenal from AC Milan in
     August 1995?**

3   Which American player has played for Milwall and Leicester?

4   **Who did Egil Ostenstadt sign for in October '96?**

5   Name the Israeli midfielder who also joined Southampton in the same
     month.

6   **Name the Aston Villa player who scored a hat-trick in the World
     Cup Qualifying win against the Faroe Islands.**

7   Which Blackburn player scored Greece's only goal in the 2-1 defeat by
     Demark in a World Cup Qualifying game in October '96?

8   **Name the Croatian defender who helped Croatia to a 4-1 victory
     over Bosnia in the same month.**

9   Which former West Ham player scored two goals in Ajax's 4-1 Champions
     League game against Rangers in 1996?

10   **Name the two foreigners who scored five of Southampton's goals
     in their 6-3 victory against Manchester United.**

11   Which Dutch international scored a hat-trick against Wales in the 7-1 World
     Cup Qualifying win?

12   **From which club did Southampton sign defender Ulrich Van
     Gobbel?**

13   Name the former Inter Milan player who played for Sheffield Wednesday in
     1996-97.

14   **Tottenham added who to their Scandanavian contingent when
     they signed who from Norwegian side Rosenberg in November '96?**

15   How much did he cost?

Quiz 79

Transfers

1 **Name the Norwegian defender who has played for both Leeds and Oldham.**

2 Which Ukrainian joined Coventry for a fee of £800,000 in January 1997?

3 **Who did Middlesbrough sign from Inter Milan during 1996-97?**

4 How much did Middlesbrough pay for him?

5 **At the same time Middlesbrough signed a player from Slaven Bratislava. Who was he?**

6 In February 1997, Blackburn signed a striker from Odense. Who?

7 **Name the goalkeeper who left Bradford to join Middlesbrough**

8 Name the Dutch striker who joined Nottingham Forest for £4.5 million in March 1997.

9 **From which club did he sign?**

10 Name the two Costa Rican players who joined Derby in March 1997.

11 **Name the former Spurs striker who was part of Belgium's 1986 World Cup squad that finished fourth**

12 Name the Brazilian striker that Newcastle bought from Fluminense

13 **Name the Argentinian World Cup winner who had an FA Cup Final song named after him.**

14 Which former Manchester United midfielder was part of the Danish World Cup side that reached the second round of the 1986 tournament?

15 **Name the former Tottenham goalkeeper that played in the 1994 World Cup Finals for Norway.**

1 **Gunnar Halle** 2 Alex Yevtushok 3 **Gianluca Festa** 4 £2.7m 5 **Vladimir Kinder** 6 Per Pedersen 7 **Mark Schwarzer** 8 Pierre Van Hooijdonk 9 **Celtic** 10 Paulo Wanchope and Mauricio Solis 11 **Nico Claesen** 12 Mirandinha 13 **Ossie Ardiles** 14 Jesper Olsen 15 Erik Thorstvedt

Quiz 80

Who Said?

1 Which former Manchester City manager said: 'I'm not a believer in luck, although I do believe you need it'?

2 **Which manager said of his side's FA Cup chances: 'I honestly believe we can go all the way to Wembley.....unless someone knocks us out'?**

3 Which former manager stated: 'I promise results, not promises'?

4 **Which former Aston Villa manager said of chairman Doug Ellis: 'He said he was right behind me, so I told him I'd rather have him in front of me where I could see him'?**

5 Which legendary manager once said: 'Mind, I've been here during the bad times too. One year we finished second'?

6 **Which charismatic manager said: 'John Bond has blackened my name with his insinuations about the private lives of football managers. Both my wives are upset.'**

7 Who said of women in football: 'Women should be in the kitchen, the discotheque and the boutique, but not in football'?

8 **Which former QPR and England striker once said: 'If I had a choice of a night with Raquel Welch or going to a betting shop, I'd choose the betting shop'?**

9 Which former manager said: 'The ideal board of directors should be made up of three men – two dead and one dying'?

10 **Which former manager said: 'Football hooligans? Well, there are ninety-two club chairmen, for a start'?**

 ## Quiz 81

Who Said?

1 **Which former England striker said of Kenny Dalglish: 'He has about as much personality as a tennis racket'?**

2 Who said: 'Trevor Brooking floats like a butterfly, and stings like one too'?

3 **Which commentator said: 'Lukic saved with his foot which is all part of the goalkeeper's arm'?**

4 Which former manager said of Ray Wilkins: 'He can't run, he can't tackle and he can't head the ball. The only time he goes forward is to toss the coin'?

5 **What television commentator said: 'The game is balanced in Arsenal's favour'?**

6 Which commentator stated: 'With the very last kick of the game, Bobby McDonald scored with a header'?

7 **Which international manager once said: 'If history is going to repeat itself, I should think we can expect the same thing again'?**

8 Which former England manager said: 'The first ninety minutes are the most important'?

9 **Which TV commentator said: 'The European Cup is seventeen pounds of silver and it's worth it's weight in gold'?**

10 Which international striker said: 'Moving from Wales to Italy is like going to a different country'?

 **Quiz 82**

Who Said?

1   Which commentator said: 'The ball has broken 50-50 for Keegan'?

2   **Which England international remarked: 'I never predict anything and I never will do'?**

3   Which former Liverpool manager said: 'Without picking out anyone in particular, I thought Mark Wright was tremendous'?

4   **Which former England captain once said: 'If you never concede a goal, you're going to win more games than you lose'?**

5   Name the former Newcastle manager who said: 'There's no job I've ever wanted. This is the only job in football I've ever wanted.'

6   **Which international manager once said: 'It may have just been going wide, but nevertheless it was a great shot on target'?**

7   Which radio commentator said: 'Fifty-two thousand people here at Maine Road tonight, but my goodness me, it seems like fifty-thousand'?

8   **Which former Manchester United manager said: 'Yes, Woodcock would have scored but his shot was too perfect'?**

9   Name the radio commentator who said: 'Ian Rush. Deadly ten times out of ten. But that wasn't one of them.'

10 **Who is the TV commentator who said: 'Oh, he had an eternity to play that ball......but he took too long over it'?**

1 David Coleman 2 Paul Gascoigne **3 Graeme Souness** 4 Bobby Moore **5 Kevin Keegan** 6 Terry Venables **7 Bryon Butler** 8 Ron Atkinson **9 Peter Jones** 10 Martin Tyler

Quiz 83

Who Said?

1   Which former Manchester City and Everton defender once said: 'I can't promise anything but I can promise 100 per cent'?

2   Name the TV commentator who said: 'McCarthy shakes his head in agreement with the referee.'

3   Who said of his side's 4-3 win over Leicester: 'Games like this are probably why Kevin Keegan went grey and Terry McDermott's hair is white'?

4   Which Dutch striker said of an extra £7,000 a week offered to him as: 'Good enough for the homeless but not an international striker'?

5   Which former World Footballer of the Year said of being a substitute: 'At the moment I feel like a Ferrari being driven by a traffic warden'?

6   Which Premiership defender said of coming to England: 'It won't be easy here, and any normal, intelligent person would have stayed at Inter'?

7   Which player said after being sent-off for foul and abusive language: 'Industrial language is part and parcel of the game. If I had been sent off every time I have sworn at an official I'd only have completed 100 games in my career'?

8   Which international striker said of coming to England: 'I did not come here on holiday or to enjoy myself. I came here to play and become a legend in London with Chelsea'?

9   Which manager said of Florin Raducioiu: 'He went missing on the way to the Stockport game because he thought he was going to be sub. He had every chance of playing that night, but he was shopping with his in-laws in Harvey Nichols'?

10 Which manager of Exeter said of his side's chances of beating Aston Villa in the FA Cup: 'I've seen Desert Orchid fall. I've seen Bestie refuse a drink. I've seen Emlyn Hughes buy one. So you never know'?

Quiz 84

Who Said?

1 Which former England international said: 'Playing is like a bug with me. I don't know when I'll be cured. I still get the same buzz. It's a magnificent life, being a professional footballer, and I'm frightened of going too soon'?

2 **Name the former Newcastle manager who said: 'Sir John Hall was a multi-millionaire when I came back to Newcastle. With all the players I've bought, I'm trying to make him just an ordinary millionaire.'**

3 Which former Tottenham manager once said: 'I always tell young managers to pick their best team at the start of the season, write it on a piece of paper and tuck it away in a drawer. Half way through the season, if things are going wrong, look at those names again......because the first team you pick each season is always you best team'?

4 **Who said after Manchester United were knocked out of the European Cup by Galatasaray: 'I just sat at home watching TV – and it wasn't even switched on'?**

5 Which radio commentator said: 'Ray Wilkins sends an inch-perfect pass to no-one in particular'?

6 **Which manager once said: 'Who's want to be a football manager? People like me who are too old to be a player, too poor to be a director and too much in love with the game to be an agent'?**

7 Which goalkeeper said: 'One of the old trainers, John Latimer, said to me: 'Goalkeepers have got to be crackers and daft. You, son, have got the qualities of an international.' I took it as a compliment'?

8 **Who said of living with a footballer: 'I've been married for 17 years and been to 14 clubs, lived in six houses, five hotels and seven rented places. As for John, he is so wrapped up in his job, I've even heard him giving Gerald Sinstadt a TV interview.....in his sleep'?**

9 Which manager said: 'I know we are the team everyone loves to hate. They blame us for everything, from England's failure in the World Cup to the rising price in plums'?

10 **Which former Premiership striker said: 'A goalscorer is paid to get hurt inside the 18-yard box and to die inside the 6-yard box'?**

Quiz 85

Who Said?

1   **Who said after suffering a horrific injury in a challenge with Wimbledon's John Fashanu: 'John Fashanu was playing professional football without due care and attention'?**

2   Which former manager said of Kevin Keegan: 'It was great for the game that Keegan came back to Newcastle. For a long period the club had been not through thick and thin, but through thin and thinner'?

3   **Who said of a Tony Yeboah goal: 'It was in the net in the time it takes a snowflake to melt on a hot stove'?**

4   Who said of Eric Cantona: 'He is so mild-mannered when the volcano inside him isn't erupting'?

5   **Which former Luton manager said of their 3-2 win at Wolves: 'I told my players that Alex Ferguson was here, that they could do themselves a bit of good. He was actually here to watch his lad Darren playing for Wolves, but my lot wouldn't know that, would they?'?**

6   Which former World Cup winning manager said: 'The art of picking a national team is not necessarily to choose the best 11 players in the country, but the 11 who fit together best'?

7   **Who said of John fashanu: 'I think John Fashanu is worth £30 million really. I only said £12 million because it's nearly Christmas'?**

8   Which Premiership striker said after leaving Cambridge United: 'I knew I couldn't take any more when, one day in training, a player shouted 'feet' meaning that's where he wanted the ball – and he was punished by being made to do 40 press-ups'?

9   **Who said of Paul Gascoigne leaving for Lazio: 'I am pleased for him but it's like watching your mother-in-law drive off the cliff in your new car'?**

10   Which Scottish player said on the eve of their vital European Championship tie in Switzerland: 'Our attitude is exactly right. Every player in the squad would give his left arm to play in this game. Well, maybe not the goalkeepers'?

Quiz 86

Who Said?

1 Which TV pundit said: 'Trevor Steven might have scored there if he'd chanced his arm with his left foot'?

2 **Who said on the eve of the 1992 European Championship: 'I expect to win. Let me do the worrying – that's what I'm paid for. You get your feet up in front of the telly, get a few beers in and have a good time'?**

3 Which radio commentator said of the 3,231 fans at a Wimbledon-Luton match: 'The spectators showed the stewards to their seats'?

4 **Which former Sheffield United manager said: 'They've been loyal to me. When I came here, they said there would be no money, and they've kept their word'?**

5 Which veteran striker said: 'It's best being a striker. If you miss five, then score the winner, you're a hero. The goalkeeper can play a blinder, then let one in.....and he's a villain'?

6 **Who replied when asked what an American was doing playing in goal for Millwall: 'Trying to keep the ball out'?**

7 Which former Blackburn manager said: 'If we score more goals than they do, we will win'?

8 **Who said on his first game as Newcastle manager: 'You just sit there, pretend you know what you are doing, and hope you get it right'?**

9 Which legendary England winger said: 'I played in the First Division until I was 50. That was a mistake. I could have gone on for another two years'?

10 **Which former Scotland manager said: 'To me, pressure is being homeless or unemployed, not trying to win a football match'?**

1 **Trevor Brooking** 2 Graham Taylor 3 **Bryon Butler** 4 Dave Bassett 5 Ian Rush 6 Kasey Keller 7 Kenny Dalglish 8 Kevin Keegan 9 Sir Stanley Matthews 10 Andy Roxburgh

 # Quiz 87

Who Said?

1　**Name the veteran manager who said on his return to management at Bristol Rovers: 'It's hard to believe that so many professional in this country haven't been taught how to kick a football correctly.'**

2　Which club owner said of Vinnie Jones' video that showed violence and cheating: 'He must be a mosquito brain to say what he's said'?

3　**Which former Premiership manager said in 1990: 'Ten years from now, Paul Gascoigne might have proved himself the biggest name in football, or he might have blown it. Either way, I will not be surprised'?**

4　Who said of Graeme Souness' decision to leave Rangers to manage Liverpool: 'I believe he is making the biggest mistake of his life. Time will tell'?

5　**Who said on being awarded the OBE in June 1990: 'My wife says it stands for 'Old Big 'Ead'?**

6　'Now the players applaud the crowd at the end of a match. When I was playing, it was the other way round'?

7　**Which legendary manager said of playing youngsters: 'If you don't put them in, you'll never know what you've got'?**

8　Which former Liverpool striker said: 'When my playing career is over, I'll return to Liverpool and stand on the Kop just like I used to when I was a kid'?

9　**Which former QPR manager said: 'I am not difficult to get on with. I am just difficult to get to know'?**

10　Which former England striker said: 'There is no point in looking back in life. I had a marvellous time playing football, travelled the world, played with and against some great players. But I got old. People ask me why I gave up football. I tell them I didn't. Football gave me up'?

Quiz 88

Who Said?

1   Name the former Argentinean manager who said: 'The player who kicks the last penalty either has the key to the hotel or the plane tickets home'?

2   **Which England veteran said in October 1989: 'Every year I play now is an extra. The longer it's gone on, the more I've enjoyed it'?**

3   Which former Wolves manager remarked: 'People say Steve Bull's first touch isn't good, but he usually scores with his second'?

4   **When he was in charge of Derby, who said: 'A mistake is only a mistake when it is done twice'?**

5   Which legendary player said of his first experience of watching England: 'My father took me, as a very young boy, to see the great England, and I went to the match expecting so much. That was the day they lost 1-0 to the U.S.A. in the World Cup'?

6   **Which international goalkeeper said: 'From watching Gordon Banks, I learnt about positioning. From watching Peter Bonetti, I learnt about agility. And from watching Lev Yashin, the great Russian goalkeeper dressed in all black, I learnt about projecting an invincible image'?**

7   Who said on life in Italy: 'The most incredible thing was the way the Juventus players took their minds off a match. Ninety minutes before kick-off, some smoked cigarettes or drank a glass of wine. Everyone seemed to find that normal – except me'?

8   **Who gave this advice to Kenny Dalglish when he signed for Liverpool: 'Don't over-eat and don't lose your accent'?**

9   Which England midfielder said after signing a seven-year contract in November 1991: 'I never seriously thought about going abroad. Knowing I can play out my career with Spurs is brilliant'?

10   **Which England international said: 'I got eight O-levels at school.....zero in every subject'?**

 ## Quiz 89

Who Said?

1 **Which Premiership manager told his team: 'If you have the ball, you command the game. If you kick and rush, it depends on luck'?**

2 Which former England coach said: 'There is nothing you can know about football that cannot be learned from watching Germany. Physically, tactically, technically, mentally, they get it right almost every time'?

3 **Which former legendary manager said once: 'I'm only surprised that people are surprised by surprise results in football'?**

4 Which Premiership manager said: 'You have to remember, a goalkeeper is a goalkeeper because he can't play football'?

5 **Which international manager said of allowing players' wives and girlfriends into the team camp: 'I've nothing against it. Love is good for footballers, as long as it is not at half-time'?**

6 Which Premiership manager had this message on his answerphone: 'I'm sorry I'm not here at the moment. If you are the president of AC Milan, Barcelona or Real Madrid, I'll get back to you'?

7 **Which former manager said: 'Southampton is a very well-run outfit from Monday to Friday. It's Saturday we've got a problem with'?**

8 Who said after his side drew with Newcastle in May 1996: 'Me feel sorry for Kevin Keegan? When he's got Asprilla and Barton and Clark on the bench?'?

9 **Which England captain said after England's 1-1 draw in a friendly against Portugal: 'At least we got a point'?**

10 Which Premiership manager said of his trade: 'Management is a seven-days-a-week job. The intensity of it takes it's toll on your health. Some people want to go on for ever, and I obviously don't. I saw Alan Hansen playing golf three times a week, and it got me thinking'?

 ## Quiz 90

Who Said?

1 Which manager left this message on his answerphone after being sacked by Birmingham: 'Kristine [his wife] has gone shopping and I'm at the job centre, looking for employment. Funny old game, isn't it?'?

2 **Which radio commentator said: 'Barmby stood out like a Pamela Anderson in a sea of Claire Raynors'?**

3 Which fromer England manager said: 'This is a great job – until a ball is kicked'?

4 **Which legendary manager once said: 'The secret of being a manager is to keep the six players who hate you away from the five who are undecided'?**

5 Which England goalscorer said in 1970: 'It's easy to beat Brazil. You just stop them getting twenty yards from your goal'?

6 **Which former European Footballer of the Year said: 'In my life I have had two big vices: smoking and playing football. Football has given me everything, but smoking nearly took it all away'?**

7 Which famous Brazilian said of the difference between South American and European football: 'Our football comes from the heart, theirs comes from the mind'?

8 **Which former Manchester United player once said: 'I could join Alcoholics Anonymous. Only problem is I can't remain anonymous'?**

9 Which Italian defender said of his treatment of Maradona during a match: 'It is not dancing school'?

10 **Which famous Hungarian stated: 'I am grateful to my father for all the coaching he did not give me'?**

Quiz 91

Who Said?

1 **Which former England manager said: 'All managers are frustrated players'?**

2 Which former Newcastle and England star said of his club: 'I have heard of players selling dummies. But this club keeps buying them'?

3 **Which Brazilian remarked in 1982: 'Football became popular because it was an art. But now too many pitches are becoming battlefields'?**

4 Which former manager said: 'I'm as bad a judge as Walter Winterbottom – he gave me only two caps'?

5 **Which Irish player remarked after he swapped shirts with Ruud Gullit in the 1988 European Championship: 'When he gets mine home, he'll wonder who the bloody hell's it is'?**

6 Who said of Italian club Pisa's bid for his son: 'They couldn't afford him even if they threw in the leaning tower'?

7 **Which WBA player said of seeing the Great Wall of China: 'When you've seen one wall, you've seen the lot'?**

8 Which former Aberdeen manager said of signing Charlie Nicholas in 1988: 'He has two arms and legs, same as the rest of our players, but once he finds his feet I'm convinced he'll do well'?

9 **Who said after scoring for Liverpool in 1988: 'As the ball came over I remembered what Graham Taylor said about my having no right foot – so I headed it in'?**

10 Who once said of Paul Gascoigne: 'He is accused of being arrogant, unable to cope with the press and a boozer. Sounds like he's got a chance to me'?

 Quiz 92

Who Said?

1   Which television pundit said of Italian Marco Tardelli: 'He's been responsible for more scar-tissue than the surgeons of Harefield hospital'?

2   **Which charismatic manager said in 1983: 'It's bloody tough being a legend'?**

3   Which manager said: 'One of the main reasons why I never became England manager was because the Football Association thought that I would take over and run the show. They were dead right'?

4   **Juventus owner, Gianni Agnelli, described which England player as being 'a soldier of war with the face of a child'?**

5   Which former England captain said of his drinking days: 'Even after a skinful, I don't have a hangover and can still be up with the others'?

6   **Which manager said in the 1990 World Cup: 'We'll start worrying about the Italians when we sober up tomorrow'?**

7   Which television summariser said in the 1990 World Cup: 'I've just seen Gary Lineker shake hands with Jurgen Klinsmann – it's a wonder Klinsmann hasn't fallen down'?

8   **About which Dutch player was it stated: 'He knows the game from A to Z and if the alphabet had any more letters, he would know those as well'?**

9   Who said to his team before extra-time in a World Cup Final: 'You've done it once, now win it again'?

10 **Which famous club chairman once said: 'I know I'm difficult to deal with. It's because I'm not logical'?**

 **Quiz 93**

Who Said?

1 **Which former Aston Villa manager said: 'I have told my players never to believe what I say about them in the papers'?**

2 Which Scottish manager once remarked: 'They serve a drink in Glasgow called the Souness – one half and you're off'?

3 **Which manager in 1987 described Wimbledon as 'the borstal of football'?**

4 Which former England manager said in 1991: 'A manager can never say always and can never say never'?

5 **Who said when he become the first paid football director: 'Only women and horses work for nothing'?**

6 Which international manager said in Euro '96: 'If I walked on water, my critics would say it was because I couldn't swim'?

7 **Which international defender said on life in English football: 'I came to this country to play football, not to be a kick-boxer, but there seems to be one in every side we play'?**

8 Which England legend said of European football: 'They know on the Continent that European football without the English is like a hot dog without mustard'?

9 **Which legendary European footballer said: 'The failure to understand the physical and mental strains on a professional is behind the widely held belief that footballers are stupid'?**

10 Which manager said of the support on the eve of his team's game with England in Euro '96: 'It's 2,000 of us against 70,000 drunkards'?

1 Graham Taylor 2 **Tommy Docherty** 3 Dave Bassett 4 **Graham Taylor** 5 Doug Ellis
6 **Berti Vogts** 7 Derby County's Igor Stimac 8 **Bobby Charlton** 9 Johan Cruyff
10 **Javier Clemente**

Quiz 94

Who Said?

1   Which TV summariser previewed the Portugal-Czech Republic Euro '96 game by stating: 'I'm looking forward to seeing some sexy football'?

2   **Which former England goalscorer said: 'Football is a simple game where 22 players play against each other and in the end Germany wins'?**

3   Which England international said in 1971: 'Soccer in England is a grey game, played on grey days by grey people'?

4   **Which legendary footballer once said: 'A penalty is a cowardly way to score a goal'?**

5   Which Dutch international once said: 'If I'd wanted to be an individual, I'd have taken up tennis'?

6   **Which former England manager once stated: 'Football is a simple game. The hard part is making it look simple'?**

7   Who told Gareth Southgate after his penalty miss in Euro '96: 'Why didn't you just belt it?'?

8   **Which Scottish player said on the eve of Euro '96: 'For the first match we'll be underdogs, and for the next two we'll be even bigger underdogs – even underpups'?**

9   Which TV summariser said during the England-Spain game in Euro '96: 'Three fresh men, three fresh legs'?

10 **Which international manager said in 1983: 'There's no rapport with referees these days. If you say anything you get booked, and if you don't they send you off for dumb insolence'?**

CARLING 10,000 FOOTBALL FACTS & QUESTIONS

Quiz 95

Who Said?

Who said:

1 **'I'm the best goalkeeper in the country – it's the towns I have trouble in'?**

2 'The moment I saw Middlesbrough I felt it was a strange, terrible place. I had never seen anything like it. It seemed so dark and quiet outside and it was always windy or raining'?

3 **'We've signed five foreigners over the summer. But I'll be on hand to learn them a bit of English'?**

4 'If we played the team of '68, we'd beat them 10-0'?

5 **'The only thing that's ten times better about the current United team is their salaries'?**

6 'I realise now that computer games have affected my performance badly'?

7 **'I'm not a believer in luck, but I do believe you need it'?**

8 'If you want someone to track back as well as do what I do, he would cost about £25 million'?

9 **'If history is going to repeat itself, I should think we can expect the same thing again'?**

10 'I've only taken one penalty before – for Crystal Palace. It was 2-2 in the 90th minute. I hit the post and we went down that year'?

11 **'The Bosman ruling doesn't affect me. I don't have any trouble losing money on transfer fees'?**

12 'English football can end the millennium as it started it – as the greatest football nation in the world'?

13 **'A goalkeeper is a goalkeeper because he can't play football'?**

14 'The trouble is he speaks about as much English as I do'?

15 **And who suggested to whom that he would get into the England team if he let his hair grow?**

Quiz 96

Who Said?

Who said:

1   After scoring six times on his debut for Newcastle United in their 13-0 defeat of Newport County: 'And they were lucky to get nil'?

2   'We don't need people like Vinnie Jones who is just a self-hyped personality – fine for him, but he isn't a good player and no benefit to the game'?

3   '[Lineker] has the charisma of a jellyfish – a jellyfish without a sting'?

4   'You've beaten them once. Now go out and bloody beat them again'?

5   'He [Diego Maradona] is the best one-footed player since Puskas'?

6   'They [Osvaldo Ardiles and Ricardo Villa] can't expect not to be tackled just because Argentina won the World Cup'?

7   'I've got a little black book in which I keep the names of all the players I've got to get before I pack up playing. If I get half a chance they will finish up over the touchline'?

8   'Say nowt, win it, then talk your head off'?

9   'Then my eyesight started to go and I took up refereeing'?

10   'I am amazed by how many vultures there are out there trying to peck my eyes out'?

11   'The last player to score a hat trick in the Cup Final was Stan Mortensen. He even had a Final named after him – the Matthews Final'?

12   'A penalty is a cowardly way to score'?

13   'Football is the opera of the people'?

14   'I was born close to Dracula's castle but I'm no relation. I just like scaring defences'?

15   'Do I not like that'?

Football Facts

Fact Contents

THE COMPETITIONS

FA CUP

FA Cup

Facts

Kennington Oval, Lillie Bridge in London, Fallowfield in Manchester, Goodison Park, Crystal Palace, Old Trafford, Stamford Bridge and Wembley have all hosted the FA Cup Final.

The last time the FA Cup was decided away from Wembley was in 1970 when the replay was played at Old Trafford.

Preston North End hold the record for the biggest win in the competition. They beat Hyde FC 26-0 in the first round proper in 1887.

The first winners of the FA Cup were The Wanderers, in the 1871-72 season.

David Nish became the youngest FA Cup Final captain when he skippered Leicester City in 1969. He was 21 years and seven months old.

The last team to play in an FA Cup Final while not in the top-flight were Sunderland, who lost to Liverpool in 1992.

The first all-Merseyside FA Cup Final was in 1986 when Liverpool beat Everton.

Cardiff City remain the only non-English team to win the FA Cup. They won in 1927.

Queen's Park are the only Scottish side to reach the FA Cup Final. They did so in consecutive years, 1884 and 1885, but lost both games.

 **Facts**

FA Cup

Manchester United have won the FA Cup more times than any other club. They have lifted the trophy nine times.

The highest score in the FA Cup Final was 6-0, when Bury beat Derby County in 1903.

Manchester United have won eight of their nine FA Cups at Wembley.

The last club outside the top flight to win the FA Cup was West Ham in 1980. They were in the Second Division when they won the trophy in 1980.

Tottenham won the FA Cup in 1901 when they were still a Southern League club.

Chesterfield became only the seventh side from the third division to reach the semi-finals of the competition in 1997.

Middlesbrough reached their first FA Cup Final in 1997.

Unfortunately they were beaten by Chelsea.

Cambridge United were the last team to reach the quarter-finals from the old-Fourth Division in 1990.

Since the formation of the competition there have been four replica FA Cup trophies.

Four clubs have reached the FA Cup Final and been relegated in the same season. Manchester City in 1926, Leicester City in 1969, Brighton and Hove Albion in 1983 and Middlesbrough in 1997.

Yeovil Town are the most successful non-league club in FA Cup history. They have won recorded 17 victories over league opposition.

Tottenham Hotspur are the only club to have won the FA Cup as a non-league side, in 1901.

The first semi-final to be staged at Wembley was in 1991 when Tottenham beat Arsenal 3-1.

Up to the end of the 1996-97 season there have been five FA Cup semi-finals at Wembley.

FA Cup

Bobby and Jack Charlton have both played in three FA Cup Finals each, for Manchester United and Leeds respectively.

Denis and Leslie Compton both played in Arsenal's 1950 FA Cup Final win. They also played county cricket for Middlesex and Denis became one of England's finest batsmen.

Jim Standen and Geoff Hurst both played in West Ham's 1964 FA Cup winning team and played first class cricket, Standen for Worcestershire and Hurst for Essex.

Jesper Olsen, Jan Molby, John Jensen, Peter Schmeichel and Jakob Kjeldbjerg are the only Danish players to have played in an FA Cup Final. They have six winners medals between them and Kjeldbjerg is the only one never to collect a winners medal.

Brothers Edward and George Robledo are the only Chileans to have won the Cup. They both played in Newcastle's 1952 triumph, George scored the only goal of the game and played in the Final the previous year as well.

 **Facts**

FA Cup

Jimmy Cochrane (Kilmarnock 1929 and Sunderland 1937) and Alex Ferguson (Aberdeen 1982,1983,1984,1986 and Manchester United 1990,1994,1996) are the only two managers who have led FA Cup-winning teams in both Scotland and England.

Four men have led FA Cup winning teams on three occasions – John Nicholson (Sheffield United 1902,1915,1925), Charles Foweraker (Bolton Wanderers 1923,1926,1929), Bill Nicholson (Tottenham 1961,1962,1967) and Alex Ferguson (Manchester United 1990,1994,1996).

Henry Cursham of Notts County is the highest goalscorer in the history of the FA Cup. He scored 48 goals between 1880 and 1887.

Ian Rush is the highest post-war goalscorer in the competition. He has scored 42 goals (39 for Liverpool, 3 for Chester City) from 1979 to present day.

Rush has also scored the most goals in FA Cup Finals. He scored twice in 1986 and 1989 and once in 1992 to register a record five goals.

The last man to score a hat-trick in an FA Cup Final was Stan Mortensen for Blakpool in 1953. Only two others have achieved the feat – William Townley (Blackburn Rovers 1890) and Jimmy Logan (Notts County 1894).

Only two players have scored in three different Cup Finals – Fred Priest (Sheffield United 1899,1901,1902) and Ian Rush (Liverpool 1986,1989,1992)

Jack Smith is the only player to have scored in both English and Scottish FA Cup Finals. He was on the scoresheet for Kilmarnock in 1920 and for Bolton Wanderers in 1923.

The youngest ever Cup Finalist was James Prinsep, who was 17 years, 245 days when he played for Clapham Rovers in the FA Cup Final of 1879.

David McCreery is the only man to have played in two FA Cup Finals as a teenager. He was an used substitute for Manchester United in 1976 and 1977.

Tottenham's Gary Mabbutt is the last man to score for both teams in an FA Cup Final when he scored both goals in the 1987 Final between Tottenham and Coventry.

FA Cup

The first FA Cup Final to be televised was the 1937 Final between Sunderland and Preston.

The first FA Cup Final to be televised in colour was the 1968 match between West Bromwich Albion and Everton.

The FA Cup has been received in South Africa. Having won the Cup the previous season, Newcastle took the trophy with them when they went on a tour of the country in 1952.

The official record crowd at an FA Cup Final is 126,047 for the 1923 Final between Bolton and West Ham.

The biggest crowd for an FA Cup match other than the Final was for a sixth round tie between Manchester City and Stoke City in 1934. The attendance was 84,569.

The last player to score in every round of the competition in the same season was Chelsea's Peter Osgood in 1970. Others who achieved the feat before him were Sandy Brown (Tottenham 1901), Ellis Rimmer (Sheffield Wednesday 1935), Frank O'Donnell (Preston 1937), Stan Mortensen (Blackpool 1948), Jackie Milburn (Newcastle 1951), Nat Lofthouse (Bolton Wanderers 1953), Charlie Wayman (Preston 1954) and Jeff Astle (West Bromwich Albion 1968).

Three captains missed the FA Cup Final because of suspension in consecutive years in the 1980's. Glenn Roeder missed QPR's replay against Tottenham in 1982, Brighton's Steve Foster missed the Final with Manchester United although he returned for the replay and in 1984 Wilf Rostron was absent from Watford's defeat to Everton.

Manchester United were the first team to win the FA Cup "third-place play-off" between the two losing semi-finalists. They beat Watford in 1970.

The "third-place play-off" was scrapped after only five seasons. Past winners are Manchester United (1970), Stoke City (1971), Birmingham City (1972), Wolves (1973) and Burnley (1974).

The first FA Cup match to be decided on penalties was the 1972 "third-place play-off" between Birmingham City and Stoke City. The Blues won the shoot-out 4-3.

 **Facts**

FA Cup

Southampton reached the FA Cup Final as a non-league club twice in three years. The Saints were a Southern League side when they reached the 1900 and 1902 Finals – they lost both.

The most successful non-league club in recent FA Cup history is Telford United, who reached the fifth round in 1985.

Only four non-league clubs have beaten the Cup holders – Tottenham beat Bury in 1901, Southampton beat Tottenham in 1902, Norwich City beat Sheffield Wednesday in 1908 and Crystal Palace beat Wolverhampton Wanderers in 1909.

The last non-league side to beat a Division One side were Sutton United. They beat Coventry in the third round in 1989.

Since 1948, six First Division sides have been beaten by non-league opposition.

The last amateur player to play in the Cup Final was Bill Slater of Wolves in 1951.

Blackburn Rovers have had the longest unbeaten run in the FA Cup. They went 24 matches undefeated from December 1882 to November 1886.

Six teams have won the League and FA Cup 'double' – Preston (1889), Aston Villa (1897), Tottenham (1961), Arsenal (1971), Liverpool (1986) and Manchester United (1994, 1996).

Manchester United are the only club to have done the 'double' twice (1994 and 1996).

Arsenal are the only club to have won both FA and League Cups in the same season (1993).

Nottingham Forest are the only team to have played FA Cup ties in all four home countries. In 1885 they played Queen's Park in a semi-final replay in Edinburgh. They played Linfield in the first round of 1889. And in 1922 threy lost in the third round at Cardiff City.

Seven Scottish sides have appeared in the FA Cup. They were: Cowlairs, Rangers, Queen's Park, Hearts, Partick Thistle, Third Lanark and Renton.

FA Cup

Three Irish clubs that have appeared in the competition – Cliftonville, Belfast Distillery and Linfield Athletic.

The only FA Cup match to be decided on a toss of a coin was in the 1873-74 season when Sheffield Club won through to the second round at the expense of Shropshire Wanderers.

The first penalty awarded in an FA Cup Final was in the 1910 replay. Albert Shepherd scored for Newcastle against Barnsley.

The first penalty to be awarded in a Wembley Final was in 1938. George Mutch scored the only goal from the spot to give Preston a 1-0 victory over Huddersfield.

 **Facts**   FA Cup

Only three times in the history of FA Cup Finals has a penalty been the only goal of the game – Huddersfield's win over Preston in 1922, Preston's defeat of Huddersfield in 1938 and in 1982 Tottenham's replay win over QPR in 1982.

Charlie Wallace of Aston Villa became the first man to miss a penalty in an FA Cup Final when he sent his spot-kick wide in the 1913 Final.

John Aldridge (Liverpool) and Gary Lineker (Tottenham) are the only two players to have had their penalty kicks saved at Wembley. Aldridge in 1988 and Lineker in 1991.

Manchester City's goalkeeper Bert Trautmann played the last 15 minutes of the 1956 FA Cup Final with a broken neck. City won 3-1.

Ray Wood, Manchester United's goalkeeper, suffered a fractured cheekbone in a collision with Aston Villa's Peter McParland in the 1957 Final. Jackie Blanchflower took over in goal while Wood returned to play on the wing before playing the final minutes back in goal. United lost 2-1.

Nottingham Forest's Roy Dwight scored but then broke his leg in his side's 2-1 Final win over Luton in 1959. Dwight would later become famous for being the uncle of Elton John.

In 1992 Liverpool became the first team to reach the FA Cup Final after winning a penalty shoot-out in the semi-final. They had drew 1-1 and 0-0 with Portsmouth before winning 3-1 on penalties.

The highest score in a semi-final was when Newcastle beat Fulham 6-0 in 1908.

The last non-league side to reach the semi-finals were Swindon Town in 1912.

Five men have been sent-off in semi-finals. The last man to do so was Arsenal's Lee Dixon in 1993.

Millwall, Norwich City, Stoke City and The Swifts have all reached threee FA Cup semi-finals – and lost them all.

Forty two different venues have been used for FA Cup semi-finals.

Everton hold the record for most appearances in the semi-finals – 23.

FA Cup

Facts

The 1980 semi-final between Arsenal and Liverpool is the only to go to a third replay. Arsenal eventually won through.

At the end of the 1992 Final Sunderland were mistakenly awarded the winners medals, despite losing 2-0 to Liverpool.

In 1970 Chelsea's David Webb was refused to collect his winners medal because he was wearing a Leeds shirt he had exchanged after the game and an official believed he was a Leeds player.

The last team to reach the FA Cup Final without conceding a goal was Everton in 1966.

Only two other teams have reached the Final without conceding a goal – Preston in 1889 and Bury in 1903. Both teams went on to win the Cup.

Preston and Bury are the only teams to have won the Cup without conceding a goal in the season's competition.

In Wolves 3-1 defeat of Newcastle United in the 1908 Cup Final, the goalscorers were Kenneth Hunt, George Hedley, Billy Harrison and Jimmy Howie. Amazingly they were the only four players on the pitch with a surname that started with the letter H.

Bob Stokoe has twice beaten Don Revie in Cup Final's. In 1955 Stokoe was a member of the victorious Newcastle side that beat Manchester City, with Revie playing centre-forward. And in 1973, Sunderland, managed by Stokoe, beat Revie's Leeds side.

An hour before the 1960 FA Cup Final Blackburn Rovers' Derek Dougan asked for a transfer. Dougan then went and played for a Rovers side that lost 3-0 to Wolves.

The first FA Cup match to be played under floodlights was between Kidderminster Harriers and Brierley Hill Alliance in a preliminary round in 1955.

Barnsley played a record number of 12 matches on their way to winning the Cup in 1912.

Liverpool's 'Anfield Rap' is the most successful FA Cup Final song recorded. It reched number three in the charts in 1988.

The first FA Cup Final song to hit the top 40 was Arsenal's 'Good Old Arsenal' in 1971. It was in the charts for seven weeks.

 **Facts**

FA Cup

The Wanderers were the first club to win the FA Cup on three occasions – 1872, 1873, 1876.

The first own goal in a Final was scored by Lord Kinnaird, playing for The Wanderers in 1877.

Alexander Bosnor became the first player to score in successive FA Cup Finals. He scored for Old Etonians in the 1875 and 1876 Finals.

The first player to score in successive FA Cup Finals at Wembley was Bobby Johnstone of Manchester City (1955 and 1956).

The 1967 Final between Tottenham and Chelsea was the first at which teams were allowed to name a substitue for the the Final.

The first substitute used in a Final was West Bromwich Albion's Derek Clarke. He replaced John Kaye in the 1968 Final.

Eddie Kelly became the first substitute to score in an FA Cup Final when he scored Arsenal's equaliser in the 1971 Final against Liverpool.

Everton's Stuart McCall beat Ian Rush of Liverpool by two minutes to become the first substitute to score twice in an FA Cup Final. Rush had the last laugh, helping Liverpool win 3-2.

West Bromwich Albion were the first team to win the Cup with eleven English-born players when they received the Cup in 1888.

FA Cup

The first player to play in winning English and Scottish FA Cup sides was Harry Campbell. He won the Scottish Cup with Renton in 1888 and played in the successful Blackburn Rovers that won the FA Cup in 1890.

The first Wembley FA Cup Final goal was scored by David Jack of Bolton in 1923.

The first man to score at Wembley and finish on the losing side was Alex Jackson of Huddersfield in 1928.

The first club to score first and lose at Wembley in a Final was Arsenal in 1932. They lost 2-1 to Newcastle.

David O'Leary ended his 20-year association with Arsenal by winning an FA Cup winners medal in 1993.

The first man to play for and then manage the same club in the FA Cup Final was Stan Seymour. He played for Newcastle in 1924 and managed them in their 1951 and 1952 victories.

King George V was the first reigning monarch to attend an FA Cup Final – in 1914.

The first Wembley FA Cup Final to go to a replay was in 1970 when Chelsea drew 2-2 with Leeds. The replay was played at Old Trafford.

The first FA Cup Final to be replayed at Wembley was the 1981 match between Tottenham and Manchester City.

Manchester United's Kevin Moran became the first player to be sent-off in an FA Cup Final. He was ordered off by referee Peter Willis in the 1985 Final against Everton.

In February 1969, all eight fifth round ties were postponed because of the weather.

The first FA Cup tie to be played on a Sunday was between Cambridge United and Oldham in a third round match in 1974.

The first FA Cup Final to produce gate receipts of £1 million was the 1985 match between Everton and Manchester United.

When Wimbledon won the FA Cup in 1988, Dave Beasant became the first goalkeeper to captain a winning side.

 **Facts**

FA Cup

Beasant also became the first goalkeeper to save a penalty in a Wembley FA Cup Final in the 1988 victory.

The only other goalkeeper to save a penalty in a Wembley FA Cup Final was Nottingham Forest's Mark Crossley, who saved from Tottenham's Gary Lineker in 1991.

The first FA Cup tie to be decided by a penalty shoot-out was the first round match between Rotherham United and Scunthorpe United in 1991. Rotherham won 7-6 in the shoot-out.

The first FA Cup Final where both sets of players wore their names on the back of their shirts was in 1993 between Arsenal and Sheffield Wednesday.

Oldham and Manchester United met twice in four years in FA Cup semi-finals – 1990 and 1994.

Also in the 1993 Final, squad numbers were used rather than the traditional 1-11.

The first black player to captain an FA Cup Final side was Sheffield Wednesday's Viv Anderson in 1993.

Sheffield Wednesday also claimed the second black player to captain a FA Cup Final side when Carlton Palmer led them in the 1993 replay due to Anderson's injury.

The 1993 FA Cup Final was the first occasion where the two team managers collected medals with their sides.

Arsenal became the first Carling Premiership club to win the FA Cup – in 1993.

The last All-London FA Cup Final was in 1982 when Tottenham beat QPR.

The lowest attendance for a semi-final was in 1995 for the replay between Manchester United and Crystal Palace – 17,987. A large number of Palace fans boycotted the match after a fan died before the first game.

Aston Villa's Villa Park has staged the most FA Cup semi-finals – 45.

Sunderland became the first team to win the FA Cup without any international players.

FA Cup

Facts

Ian Rush has played in three FA Cup Finals for Liverpool, and scored in all of them.

H. Lyons was carried off on a stretcher against Doncaster Rovers in a first round replay in 1965, but returned later to score a hat-trick.

In 1987 (Coventry City) and 1988 (Wimbledon), both clubs won the FA Cup in their first Final.

The first winners of the Littlewoods-sponsored FA Cup were Everton in 1995.

The 1923 Final was named the White Horse Final after Billy the horse helped to contain the crowd when they overspilled onto the pitch.

Burnley's Jimmy Robson scored the 100th Cup Final goal in 1962.

Burnley and Tottenham played in three successive FA Cup ties from 1961 to 1963.

Allan Clarke played for Leicester City (1969) and Leeds (1970) in successive FA Cup Finals – and lost them both.

Arsenal and Leeds played in the Centenary Cup Final in 1972.

Mike Trebilcock scored twice for Everton in the 1966 FA Cup Final despite not having his name printed in the official match programme.

Arsenal were the first holders of the FA Cup to lose in the final when they were beaten by Leeds in 1972.

Leicester City were the first club to have their names on the back of their tracksuits before the 1961 FA Cup Final.

Tommy Docherty had lost three FA Cup Finals, once as a player, before managing manchester United to glory in 1977.

Arthur Kinnaird appeared in six FA Cup Finals for Old Etonians, as well as three for The Wanderers.

Bryan Robson captained Manchester United to three FA Cup wins in seven years.

 **Facts**

FA Cup

Arsenal played in five FA Cup Finals in nine years from 1971.

Jimmy Case scored for Liverpool in the 1977 FA Cup Final and in 1983 grabbed the winning goal for Brighton against Liverpool in the fifth round.

At the ripe old age of 20, Manchester United's Norman Whiteside had already scored in two FA Cup Finals (1983 and 1985).

The 100th FA Cup Final was played in 1981 between Tottenham and Manchester City.

Dave Bennett has twice been an FA Cup Finalist. He was a member of the Manchester City team that lost in 1981, and played for Coventry City in 1987. Both games were played against Tottenham.

The last man to play for and then manage the same team in an FA Cup Final was Joe Royle. He played for Everton in the 1968 Final and managed the club to victory in the 1995 Final.

Steve Coppell won the FA Cup in 1977 as a player with Manchester United. As a manger he led Crystal Palace to the 1990 Final but they lost in a replay – to Manchester United.

The last player to score an own goal in an FA Cup Final was Nottingham Forest's Des Walker (1991).

Tottenham's Danny Blanchflower was the first man to captain a team to successive FA Cup Final wins, in 1961 and 1962.

Eric Cantona of Manchester United became the first foreign player to captain an FA Cup Final side when he led out United in the 1996 Final.

Arnold Muhren became the first Dutchman to play in the FA Cup Final when he played, and scored, for Manchester United in 1983.

Chelsea's Ruud Gullit became the first foreign manager to lead a FA Cup Final side when Chelsea reached the 1997 Final.

Glenn Hoddle became the last player-manager to play in an FA Cup Final when he came on as a substitute in Chelsea's 4-0 defeat to Manchester United in 1994.

FA Cup

The last two FA Cup Finals in which a player has scored for both teams have both involved Tottenham. Manchester City's Tommy Hutchinson did it in 1981 and Tottenham's Gary Mabbutt scored for his team as well as Coventry in 1987.

Joe Royle and Howard Kendall both played for Everton in the 1968 FA Cup Final, and later managed the club to Cup success.

There has only been one instance where two pairs of brothers have played in the same Final. In 1876, Hubert and Frederick Heron played for The Wanderers against an Old Etonians team that boasted the Hon. Alfred and The Hon. and Rev. Edward Lyttleton.

 **Facts**

FA Cup

Walton and Hersham's 4-0 win over Brighton in 1973 is the biggest away victory for a non-league side in the competition.

Albert Taylor of Luton scored after just 45 seconds of his senior debut in an FA Cup tie in January 1953.

The 1986 FA Cup Final between Liverpool and Everton was dubbed 'The Friendly Final' because of the atmosphere between both sets of supporters.

Charles Alcock, secretary of the FA, invented the FA Cup in 1871.

Because of an injury crisis at the club Watford had to play Gary Plumley, a wine-bar owner who played part-time football, in goal in their 1987 semi-final against Tottenham. They lost 4-1.

The last FA Cup Final that featured the two clubs that finished first and second in the top division was in 1986 when Liverpool beat Everton to both League and FA Cup.

Ten Mansfield Town players were booked in their third round tie against Crystal Palace in 1963.

Leeds United went 16 matches without a win in the competition between February 1952 and March 1963.

Stoke City are the only founder members of the Football League not to have won the FA Cup.

Cardiff City had to apply for re-election to the Football League in 1934 – just seven years after winning the FA Cup.

In 1933, Everton and Manchester City became the first teams to wear number on the back of their shirts in an FA Cup Final.

Preston North End became the first Football League club to win the FA Cup, in 1889.

Portsmouth won the FA Cup in 1939, but kept the trophy for seven years because of the Second World War.

Nobby Stiles, George Cohen and Martin Peters are the only three memebers of the 1966 World Cup winning team that have not played in an FA Cup Final.

FA Cup

Paul Gascoigne's final game for Tottenham ended with him being carried off on a stretcher after suffering a knee injury after only 16 minutes of the 1991 FA Cup Final.

Non-league side Sutton United beat First Division Coventry City in the third round in 1989, but were beaten by Norwich City 8-0 in the following round.

The last player to be sent-off in an FA Cup semi-final was Middlesbrough's Vladimir Kinder in 1997.

The last player to be named Footballer of the Year and captain his side to FA Cup glory in the same season was Manchester United's Eric Cantona.

Keith Houchen was an FA Cup goalscoring hero for two clubs in the space of two years and both times against North London clubs. He scored the only goal as York City beat Arsenal in 1985, and then scored for Coventry in the 1987 Final against Tottenham.

Up to 1998 there has not been a goalless draw in a Wembley FA Cup Final.

Paul Bracewell is the only player this century to play in three FA Cup Finals against the same club. He played for Everton (1986,1989) and Sunderland in 1992, losing to Liverpool on all three occasions.

Bryan Robson is the last man to captain a winning side and then lead a club to the FA Cup Final. He captained Manchester United to victory in 1983,1985 and 1990 and managed Middlesbrough to the 1997 Final.

Leyton Orient, now in the Third Division, last reached the semi-finals in 1978, but were beaten by Arsenal.

The first man to play in and then manage an FA Cup winning team was Peter McWilliam. He played in Newcastle's 1910 victory and then managed Tottenham to victory in 1921.

Arsenal's Steve Morrow collected a Cup winners medal before the 1993 FA Cup Final. Morrow was injured in the celebrations after the League Cup Final and could not receive his medal.

LEAGUE CUP

League Cup

Facts

The League Cup was founded by Alan Hardaker in 1960. The former League secretary is still part of the competition, his name is given to the Final's Man of the Match trophy.

Aston Villa became the first winners of the League Cup in 1961, when they beat Rotherham United 3-2 on aggregate.

The first six League Cup Finals were played over two legs.

The first League Cup Final to be played at Wembley was in 1967. QPR beat West Bromwich Albion 3-2.

That year also saw the first year of qualification for Europe for the League Cup winners.

Aston Villa became the first team to win the trophy for the second time, when they defeated Norwich City 2-1 in 1975.

Nottingham Forest were the first side to successfully defend the trophy when they beat Liverpool and Southampton in 1978 and 1979 respectively.

In 1982 the League Cup became the Milk Cup and the sponsorship of the Cup began.

Liverpool stamped their authority on League Cup history when they won the competition four times in succession in the early 1980's.

Liverpool's reign was ended in the 1984-85 competition, when eventual winners' Sunderland beat them in the fourth round. Liverpool's undefeated run in the League Cup lasted 41 games.

Everton are the only team out of the original "big five" not to have won the League Cup. They have appeared in two finals, in 1977 and 1984.

Before the start of the 1997-98 season, Aston Villa and Liverpool are the most successful teams in League Cup history. Both have won the trophy five times.

The largest margin of victory in a League Cup Final is currently three goals, shared by Oxford United (1986) and Aston Villa (1996). Both were 3-0 victors.

Facts   League Cup

Before the 1997-98 season, Manchester United have lost three of their four League Cup Finals. Their only victory came in 1992.

In 1987 the Milk Cup became the Littlewoods Cup. The first winners' of the newly named trophy were Arsenal, beating Liverpool 2-1.

Arsenal created another piece of history in the 1987 Final. Liverpool had never lost a game when Ian Rush had scored the first goal, but two goals from Arsenal's Charlie Nicholas put paid to that record.

Luton reached consecutive finals in 1988 and 1989, but failed to retain the trophy they won in 1988 when Nottingham Forest defeated them 3-1.

The name of the Cup changed for the third time in 1991 when it was renamed the Rumbelows Cup. The first winners of the newly sponsored Cup was Sheffield Wednesday when they defeated Manchester United 1-0

Before the 1997-98 season, the last time a League Cup Final went to extra-time was in 1984, when Liverpool beat Everton after a replay.

The top score by a team in a League Cup tie was set by West Ham. They beat Bury 10-0 in the second round, second leg on October 25, 1983. That scoreline was matched by Liverpool in the second round, first leg against Fulham on September 23, 1986.

The record aggregate score was also set by Liverpool in their 13-2 defeat over Fulham in 1986. Other 11-goal aggregate wins: West Ham 12, Bury 1 in 1983 and Liverpool 11, Exeter 0 in 1981.

Oldham Athletic's Frank Bunn set an individual scoring record in the competition when he scored six goals against Scarborough in the 1989 third round.

The 1,987 attendance at the Wimbledon-Bolton second round, second leg tie in 1992 was the lowest for a League Cup tie played at a top division club's ground.

The first £1m gate receipts for a League Cup Final was in 1987 for the Arsenal-Liverpool match.

League Cup

Up to the start of the 1997-98 season, the League Cup has had four sponsors – Milk Cup 1981-86, Littlewoods Cup 1987-90, Rumbelows Cup 1991-92 and Coca-Cola Cup since 1993.

Geoff Hurst set the record for individual League Cup goals. He scored 49 goals (43 for West Ham, 6 for Stoke City) between 1960 and 1975. At the start of the 1997-98 season, Ian Rush was just one goal behind, scoring all his 48 goals for Liverpool.

Clive Allen's 12 goals for Tottenham in 1986-87 was a record by an individual player in a League Cup season.

Kenny Dalglish and Ian Rush have both made six League Cup Final appearances for Liverpool. Rush has won the most winners medals, five.

Port Vale and Nothampton Town both had two players sent-off when they met in a first round, first leg tie on August 18, 1987 to set a League Cup record.

Andrei Kanchelskis became the first player to be sent-off in a Wembley League Cup Final when he was shown the red card for Manchester United against Aston Villa in 1994.

Up to the start of the 1997-98 season, two players have missed League Cup Final penalties at Wembley. Clive Walker (Sunderland) missed in 1985 and Nigel Winterburn (Arsenal) had his saved by Luton's Andy Dibble in 1988.

Aston Villa's Ray Graydon also had his penalty saved by Norwich's Kevin Keelan in the 1975 Final, but he scored from the rebound.

Andy Blair set a League Cup record when he scored a hat-trick of penalties for Sheffield Wednesday against Luton in the fourth round on November 20, 1984.

Facts

League Cup

LEAGUE CUP FINALS
(1961-66 over two legs)
1961   Aston Villa 3, Rotherham United 2 (aet) (0-2a, 3-0h)
1962   Norwich 4, Rochdale 0 (3-0a, 1-0h)
1963   Birmingham City 3, Aston Villa 1 (3-1h, 0-0a)
1964   Leicester City 4, Stoke City 3 (1-1a, 3-2h)
1965   Chelsea 3, Leicester City 2 (3-2h, 0-0a)
1966   West Bromwich Albion 5, West Ham United 3 (1-2a, 4-1h)

AT WEMBLEY
1967 Queens Park Rangers 3, West Browmich Albion 2
1968 Leeds United 1, Arsenal 0
1969 Swindon Town 3, Arsenal 1 (aet)
1970 Manchester City 2, West Bromwich Albion 1 (aet)
1971 Tottenham Hotspur 2, Aston Villa 0
1972 Stoke City 2, Chelsea 1
1973 Tottenham Hotspur 1, Norwich City 0
1974 Wolverhampton Wanderers 2,
       Manchester City 1
1975 Aston Villa 1, Norwich City 0`
1976 Manchester City 2, Newcastle United 1

League Cup

**1977 Aston Villa 0, Everton 0 (aet) (Replay at Sheffield
Wednesday's Hillsborough: 1-1 (aet). Second replay at
manchester United's Old Trafford: 3-2)**
**1978 Nottingham Forest 0, Liverpool 0 (Replay at Manchester
United's Old Trafford: 1-0)**
1979 Nottingham Forest 3, Southampton 2
1980 Wolverhampton Wanderers 1, Nottingham Forest 0
**1981 Liverpool 1, West Ham United 1 (Replay at Aston Villa's Villa
Park: 2-1)**

MILK CUP
1982 Liverpool 3, Tottenham Hotspur 1 (aet)
1983 Liverpool 2, Manchester United 1 (aet)
1984 Liverpool 0, Everton 0 (aet) (Replay at Manchester City's Maine
Road: 1-0)
1985 Norwich City 1, Sunderland 0
1986 Oxford United 3, Queens Park Rangers 0

LITTLEWOODS CUP
1987 Arsenal 2, Liverpool 1
1988 Luton Town 3, Arsenal 2
1989 Nottingham Forest 3, Luton Town 1
1990 Nottingham Forest 1, Oldham Athletic 0
RUMBELOWS CUP
1991 Sheffield Wednesday 1, Manchester United 0
1992 Manchester United 1, Nottingham Forest 0

COCA-COLA CUP
1993 Arsenal 2, Sheffield Wednesday 1
1994 Aston Villa 3, Manchester United 1
1995 Liverpool 2, Bolton Wanderers 1
1996 Aston Villa 3, Leeds United 0
1997 Leicester City 1, Middlesbrough 1 (aet) (Replay at Sheffield
Wednesday's Hillsborough: 1-0)

EUROPEAN CHAMPIONSHIP

European Championship  Facts

European Championship Finals
1960 USSR 2, Yugoslavia 1 (aet) (Paris, France)
1964 Spain 2, USSR 1 (Madrid, Spain)
1968 Italy 1, Yugoslavia 1 (Rome, Italy) (replay: 2-0)
1972 West Germany 3, USSR 0 (Brussels, Belgium)
1976 Czechoslovakia 2, West Germany 2 (aet) (Czechoslovakia
       won 5-3 on penalties) (Belgrade, Yugoslavia)
1980 West Germany 2, Belgium 1 (Rome, Italy)
1984 France 2, Spain 0 (Paris, France)
1988 Holland 2, USSR 0 (Munich, West Germany)
1992 Denmark 2, Germany 0 (Gothenburg, Sweden)
1996 Germany 2, Czech Republic 1 (in overtime) (London,
       England)

The USSR were the first European champions. They beat Yugoslavia 2-1 after extra-time in 1960.

Euro 96 was the 10th European Championship. There have been nine different winners. West Germany won the title in 1972 and 1980, and a united Germany succeded in 1996.

The list of winners are: 1960 – USSR, 1964 – Spain, 1968 – Italy, 1972 – West Germany, 1976 – Czechoslovakia, 1980 – West Germany, 1984 – France, 1988 – Holland, 1992 – Denmark, 1996 – Germany.

West Germany made three successive appearances in the Final, from 1972.

Michel Platini currently holds the record for most goals in the finals. He scored nine in 1984, scoring in every match.

For the first time in the competition's history, the 2000 Championship will be co-hosted. Holland and Belgium were the only applicants and will share the matches.

The trophy is officially named the Henri Delaunay Cup, which is named after the Frenchman who founded the competition.

Seven players were sent-off in Euro 96, equalling the total of dismissals in all of the previous nine finals.

Holland's 1988 semi-final victory over West Germany was particulary special for manager Rinus Michels – he had been in charge of the Dutch when they lost the World Cup Final to the Germans 14 years earlier.

 **Facts**   European Championship

Since winning the first tournament in 1960, the USSR have appeared in three more European Championship Finals – and lost them all.

Up to the 2000 qualifying tournament, three men top the goalscoring charts in the competition's history with 16 goals. Gerd Muller of West Germany scored 12 in qualifying matches and four in the finals, Holland's Marco Van Basten has 11 goals in qualifying and five in finals, and Davor Suker scored once for Yugoslavia in qualifying and 12 for Croatia, plus three in the finals.

Although England were beaten in the 1996 semi-finals, they did win one award – the Fair Play trophy.

Alan Shearer was top goalscorer in the 1996 Championship. He scored five goals in five games. Marco Van Basten is the only other player to score five times in one tournament, in 1988.

West Germany went 32 European Championship matches without defeat (including qualifiers) from October 7, 1967 to November 17, 1982.

The highest score in the tournament was set by Spain on December 21, 1983. They beat Malta 12-1 in a qualifier.

Before Euro 2000 qualifying, only three England players have scored hat-tricks in the Championship, and all in qualifiers – Luther Blissett v Luxembourg in 1984, Gary Lineker in 1988 against Turkey. Malcolm Macdonald scored five goals against Cyprus in 1976.

Germany's Oliver Bierhoff became the first player to score a 'golden goal' in a major Final. His goal five minutes into sudden death gave his country victory over the Czech Republic in 1996.

The USSR reached the 1960 semi-finals after being awarded a walk-over against Spain because General Franco refused his team to play in Communist Moscow.

England first entered the tournament in 1964.

Seventeen teams entered the first tournament in 1960. It was called the European Nations Cup until 1966.

The 1960 Final was played at the Parc des Princes in Paris, which was watched by only 17,966.

European Championship

Facts

England failed to qualify for the 1984 Championship after losing to Denmark 1-0. That goal is the only one the Danes have scored against England at Wembley in five matches.

England scored only two goals in the 1988 Championship in West Germany. Bryan Robson scored in the 1-3 defeat by Holland and Tony Adams netted against USSR, but England suffered the same scoreline as the Dutch game.

Up to the start of the 2000 Championship, no British country have made a Final appearance.

The eight stadiums that hosted matches during Euro 96 were: Wembley, Villa Park (Aston Villa), St James' Park (Newcastle), Elland Road (Leeds), Hillsborough (Sheffield Wednesday), City Ground (Nottingham Forest), Anfield (Liverpool) and Old Trafford (Manchester United).

Holland were the last nation to qualify for Euro 96. They beat the Republic of Ireland in a play-off at Anfield in December 1995.

Royal Mail issued special commemorative stamps for the 1996 Championship. Five football legends were featured: Dixie Dean, Bobby Moore, Duncan Edwards, Billy Wright and Danny Blanchflower.

The first European Championship match was a qualifier between Ireland and Czechoslovakia on April 5, 1958.

England were awarded to host the 1996 Championship because their bid was the only to be registered by the closing date of November 1991.

The Queen presented the trophy to Jurgen Klinsmann after the 1996 Final. The last time she handed over a trophy at Wembley was the World Cup to Bobby Moore in 1966.

For the 1996 European Championship, all the previous winners of the trophy qualified.

England's victory over Scotland in Euro 96 was their first win in the finals since 1980.

San Marino's European qualifying record is abysmal. They have lost all 18 matches.

 **Facts**   European Championship

For the first time in the competition's history, the holders (Denmark) did not have to qualify for the 1996 finals

Denmark caused the biggest shock of the tournament's history when they won in 1992, despite not qualifying. They received a late entry after Yugoslavia were ejected as civil war broke out in the country.

England manager Glenn Hoddle's last playing appearance for his country was in the 1-3 defeat by USSR in the 1988 Championship.

Euro 96 was the biggest tournament in the competition's history. 16 teams competed in the finals for the first time.

Despite being the second highest England goalscorer, Gary Lineker failed to score in his six finals appearances.

Berti Vogts became the first man to win the European Championship as both player and as a manger. He played for the victorious West Germans in 1972 and managed Germany to victory in 1996.

European Championship

Euro 96 was the first top-class tournament to introduce the "Golden Goal" rule.

In 1968 Scotland faced England at Hampden Park in the tournament. 134,000 packed into Hampden Park.

Euro 96 had four countries competing in their first European Championship – Switzerland, Croatia, Turkey and the Czech Republic.

The referee for the first European Championship Final in 1960 was Englishman Arthur Ellis, who later became a presenter on TV game show It's A Knockout.

Germany's Euro 96 captain Jurgen Klinsmann was suspended for the first game of the tournament after picking up a yellow card in his country's final qualifying match.

The official mascot for Euro 96 was a lion named Goaliath.

WORLD CUP

World Cup

Facts

The top scorers for a single match in a World Cup Finals are Hungary. They scored 10 goals against El Salvador in 1982. The final score was 10-1.

The record scoreline in any World Cup match was a qualifying tie in May 1997. Iran beat The Maldives 17-0.

West Germany's Gerd Muller is the highest goalscorer in World Cup finals history. He registered 14 goals – 10 in 1970 and four in 1974.

The next two top scorers are Just Fontaine (France) with 13 goals, and Pele (Brazil) with 12.

Fontaine is the highest goalscorer for a single World Cup finals. He scored 13 goals in six matches of the 1958 tournament.

The first goal scored in the World Cup Finals is credited to France's Louis Laurent against Mexico on July 30, 1930. France went on to win 4-1.

The highest attendance for a World Cup match was 205,000 in Rio de Janeiro in 1950 for Brazil v Uruguay.

Manchester United's Norman Whiteside became the youngest player to appear in the World Cup Finals when he played for Northern Ireland against Yugoslavia on June 17, 1982. He was 17 years 42 days old.

Whiteside beat the previous record, set by Pele in the 1958 tournament, by 195 days.

Brazil's Vava is the only player to have scored in successive World Cup Final's. He scored in 1958 (twice) and in 1962.

The only players, aside from Vava, to have scored in two World Finals are Pele (Brazil, 1958 and 1970) and Paul Breitner of West Germany (1974 and 1982).

Only one player has scored in every match of the Finals. Jairzinho of Brazil scored seven goals in six games in 1970.

Italy's Dino Zoff broke two records when Italy won the World Cup in 1982. He became the oldest player to win a World Cup winners medal and the oldest to captain a winning side at the age of 40.

 **Facts** World Cup

Two goalkeepers have captained their country to World Cup victory – and both are Italian. Giampiero Combi in 1934 and Dino Zoff in 1982.

Geoff Hurst is the only player to score a hat-trick in a World Cup Final. He scored three of England's four goals in their 1966 triumph against West Germany.

The longest unbeaten run in World Cup Finals is 13 games by Brazil. Between 1958 and 1962 they won 11 and drew two before being beaten by Hungary in the 1966 tournament.

Holland's Rob Rensenbrink scored the 1000th goal in World Cup Finals against Scotland in 1978.

The first substitute used in a World Cup Finals match was Anatoly Puzach of USSR against Mexico in 1970.

Brazil used only 12 players when they won the 1962 World Cup, the lowest number used in the tournament's history.

Uruguay's Jose Batista became the quickest dismissal in World Cup history when he was sent-off after only 55 seconds of the match against Scotland in 1986.

Russia's Oleg Salenko is the only man to score five goals in a single World Cup Finals match. His goals helped Russia to a 6-1 victory over Cameroon in 1994.

The highest aggregate match in the World Cup Finals is Austria 7 Switzerland 5 in 1954.

The fastest goal, officially recorded by FIFA, in the Finals is Bryan Robson's 27-second strike for England against France in 1982.

When West Germany won the World Cup in 1954 they produced two goalscoring records for a winning side. Their 25 goals in six matches for an average of 4.16 was a record, as was the 14 goals they conceded.

World Cup

Facts

Before Oleg Salenko's record five goals in a match nine players had scored four goals in a World Cup game. They were Gustav Wetterson (Sweden v Cuba, 1938), Leonidas da Silva (Brazil v Poland, 1938), Ernest Willimowski (Poland v Brazil, 1938), Ademir (Brazil v Sweden, 1950), Juan Schiaffino (Uruguay v Bolivia, 1950), Sandor Kocsis (Hungary v West Germany, 1954), Just Fontaine (France v West Germany, 1958), Eusebio (Portugal v North Korea, 1966) and Emilio Butragueno (Spain v Denmark, 1986).

Pele is the only player to have won the World Cup three times as a player. He won with Brazil in 1958, 1962 and 1970.

The only player to have appeared in five World Cup Finals is Mexico's goalkeeper Antonio Carbajal. He played in 1950, 1954, 1958, 1962 and 1966.

Mario Zagalo has won three World Cups and became the first to win it as both player and manager. He played in the 1958 and 1962 tournaments for Brazil and was manager when they won in 1970.

The only other man to win the World Cup as both player and manager was West Germany's Franz Beckenbauer. He won it in 1974 and was the German manager when they won in 1990. Beckenbauer is the only man to have captained and managed a World Cup winning side.

Beckenbauer has appeared in four World Cup Finals. He played in 1966 and 1974 and managed West Germany in 1986 and 1990. He aslo played in the 1970 tournament.

Bora Milutinovic is the only man to manage three different nations in successive World Cup Finals. He led host nation Mexico in 1986, was in charge of Costa Rica in 1990 and managed USA in 1994.

Two other men have led different countries in successive World Cup Finals. Rudolf Vytlacil was in charge of Czechoslovakia in 1962 and Bulgaria in 1966, while Blagoje Vidinic was manager of Morocco in 1970 and Zaire four years later.

Five countries have won the World Cup in their own country – Uruguay (1930), Italy (1934), England (1966), West Germany (1974) and Argentina (1978).

 **Facts**   **World Cup**

Up to the 1998 finals, Brazil are the only country to win the World Cup outside their continent. They won in Sweden in 1958

Only two countries have hosted the World Cup twice – Italy (1934 and 1990) and Mexico (1970 and 1986).

In the 1930 World Cup Final, Argentina and Uruguay could not decide on which ball to use. So the first half was played with Argentina's ball and the Uruguayan ball was used in the second. Argentina led at half-time but Uruguay eventually won 4-2.

The 1974 World Cup Final was delayed because there were no corner-flags on the pitch.

The 1966 tournament had a special World Cup stamp published for the occasion. The original stamp was to feature the flags of the 16 competing teams but the British government refused to recognise North Korea so instead the official stamp showed various footballers.

World Cup

Facts

One of the most bizarre incidents in World Cup history occurred in 1930. The United States trainer ran on to treat a player, but he tripped and broke a bottle of chloroform. The trainer was carried off unconscious while the player was forced to continue playing without treatment.

Two contrasting fortunes on a special day for famous players in the World Cup Finals. Kazimierz Deyna played his 100th game for Poland in the 1978 Finals but missed a penalty against Argentina in a 2-0 defeat. Italy's Dino Zoff had a better experience. He celebrated his 100th cap with a clean sheet against Poland in the 1982 tournament.

Brazil are the only country to appear in all of the World Cup Finals.

There have been 15 World Cup tournaments and six different winners.

Brazil have won the World Cup more times than any other country. Their win in 1994 was their fourth.

The other countries to win the World Cup are:

**Uruguay (1930, 1950),
Italy (1934, 1938, 1982),
West Germany (1954, 1974, 1990),
England (1966) and
Argentina (1978, 1986).**

Scotland's manager Andy Beattie resigned after Scotland's opening defeat by Austria in the 1954 Finals. They lost their next game 7-0 to Uruguay.

Scotland's Mo Johnston set a Home Countries record when he scored in five qualifying matches during the 1990 qualifying campaign.

Northern Ireland were ordered not to play two of their three group matches in the 1958 Finals because the games were being played on the Sunday. They refused.

The first black African country to reach the Finals was Zaire in 1974.

Haiti's Ernest Jean-Joseph became the first player to be banned by FIFA for drug-taking during the Finals when he was sent home in the middle of the 1974 tournament.

 **Facts** World Cup

In 1990 Walter Zenga set the record for remaining unbeaten in World Cup Finals matches. He had not been beaten for 517 minutes. After five games, he was beaten in the 67th minute by Argentinean Claudio Caniggia in the semi-final.

There has been only one goalless draw in a World Cup Final. The 1994 Final was decided on penalties with Brazil beating Italy.

Ferenc Puskas played for different countries in World Cup Finals. He played for Hungary in 1954 and Spain in 1962.

The original Jules Rimet was stolen in 1966 while on display before the tournament in England and found by a dog called Pickles. Brazil kept the trophy when they won it for the third time in 1970, but it was stolen from a display in Rio and has never been recovered.

Four players share the record for most appearances in Finals matches. Uwe Seeler (West Germany 1958, 1962, 1966, 1970), Wladyslaw Zmuda (Poland 1974, 1978, 1982, 1986), Diego Maradona (Argentina 1982, 1986, 1990, 1994) and Lothar Matthaus (Germany 1982, 1986, 1990, 1994).

The 1994 Finals in the United States were the first to be played outside Europe and South America.

The record average attendance at the Finals was set in 1994 – 68,604.

The record number of yellow cards showed in a single tournament was 227 in 1994. The previous high was 164 in 1990.

The highest number of red cards shown in the Finals was 16 in 1990.

There has been only one missed penalty in a World Cup Final. Antonio Cabrini of Italy missed in the 1982 Final against West Germany, but still collected a winners medal.

The first penalty scored in a Final was by Johan Neeskens in the 1974 defeat by West Germany.

Three goals were scored in the first 12 minutes of the 1954 World Cup Final. Despite taking an early 2-0 lead Hungary were beaten 3-2 by West Germany.

World Cup

Karl-Heinz Rummenigge has captained West Germany to two World Cup Finals – and lost them both.

The United States best World Cup tournament was in 1930, where they finished third.

Two past winners failed to qualify for the 1994 World Cup – England and Uruguay.

Republic of Ireland manager Jack Charlton received a one-match touchline ban and a £10,000 fine in the 1994 Finals after arguing with an official against Mexico.

Roger Milla became the oldest goalscorer in the Finals when he scored for Cameroon against Russia in 1994 at the age of 42. He had also scored four goals in the previous tournament in Italy.

The first player to be sent-off in a World Cup Final was Argentina's Pedro Monzon in 1986 after 65 minutes. He was succeeded by team-mate Gustavo Dezotti 21 minutes later.

Scotland have qualified for the World Cup Finals on seven occasions but have yet to get past the first round.

Paulo Rossi was top-scorer in the 1982 World Cup after returning from a two-year ban for bribery.

Mexico hosted the 1986 World Cup only eight months after 9,500 people died in two earthquakes in the space of 24 hours.

 **Facts**   **World Cup**

West Germany, Brazil and Italy have all appeared in five World Cup Finals.

Two players have scored World Cup Finals hat-tricks and still been on the losing side. Ernest Willimowski scored four in Poland's 6-5 defeat by Brazil in 1938 and Igor Belanov of the USSR scored three in the 4-3 loss to Belgium in 1986.

Alex Ferguson was caretaker-manager for Scotland in 1986 after the shock death of Jock Stein in Scotland's last qualifying match against Wales.

Mexico were banned from the 1990 Finals by FIFA after using over-age players in the World Under-20 tournament.

Cameroon became the first black African country to reach the quarter-finals in 1990.

All 15 penalties awarded in normal time in 1994 were scored.

Both semi-finals in the 1990 Finals were settled by penalty shoot-outs. Argentina beat Italy and West Germany defeated England both by the same score, 4-3.

The first players to be sent-off in a World Cup opening match were Cameroon's Andre Kana-Biyik and Benjamin Massing in 1990. Cameroon still went on to beat holders Argentina 1-0.

The only other player to be sent-off in the opening match was Bolivia's Marco Etcheverry against Germany in 1994.

28 of the 52 matches in Italy 1990 failed to produce a goal.

Johan Neeskens scored the fastest goal in a World Cup Final when he score a penalty for Holland after only two minutes. The first West German player to touch the ball was Sepp Maier when he picked the ball out of the net.

Egypt have withdrawn from the World Cup in 1938, 1958, 1962 and 1966.

The last British player to be sent-off in a World Cup Finals match was England's Ray Wilkins in 1986 against Morocco.

World Cup

Facts

The last time all four Home Countries were in the World Cup Finals was 1958.

West Germany were the first country to be both World Champions and European Champions in the same year. They won the European Championship in 1972 and the World Cup in 1974.

Mexico were the first team to qualify for the 1994 World Cup Final. USA (hosts) and Germany (holders) were exempt from qualification.

Costa Rica made their World Cup debut in Italia '90 and beat Scotland in their first match. They went on to beat Sweden and lose narrowly to Brazil before being beaten by Czechoslovakia in the second round.

Morocco have played in two World Cup Finals – both in Mexico, 1970 and 1986.

Spain withdrew from the 1938 World Cup because of the break-out of civil war in the country.

Scotland were eliminated from the 1974 World Cup despite not losing a game. They won once and drew the other two.

Sir Alf Ramsey was manager of the England side that won the World Cup in 1966, but he has also played in the tournament – for England in 1950.

The World Cup Finals in 2002 will be the first to be hosted by two countries – Japan and South Korea.

Bulgaria had appeared in five World Cup Finals (1962, 1966, 1970, 1974, 1986) and not won a single match.

Bulgaria won their first World Cup Finals match when they beat Greece 4-0 in the 1994 tournament. They went on to reach the semi-finals that year, beating Germany in the quarter-finals.

Famous Italian dictator Benito Mussolini presented the World Cup to Italian captain Giampiero Combi after the 1934 Final.

Czechoslovakia and Hungary have both been beaten in two World Cup Finals. Czechoslovakia in 1934 and 1962, Hungary in 1938 and 1954.

 **Facts** World Cup

Two countries have lost successive World Cup Finals – Holland in 1974 and 1978 and West Germany in 1982 and 1986.

Bobby Robson has appeared in three World Cup Finals for England. He played in 1958 and was manager in 1986 and 1990.

Poland have finished third in two World Cup's – 1974 and 1982.

Despite qualifying in second place, Scotland refused to go to the 1950 World Cup Finals because they did not win the qualifying group.

India withdrew from the 1950 World Cup Finals because FIFA had refused to allow them to play barefoot.

In the 1978 World Cup Final both goalkeepers wore perculiar shirt numbers. Argentina's Ubalodo Fillol wore number seven and Jan Jongbloed of Holland wore number eight.

Uruguay were threatened with expulsion from the 1986 Finals because of persistent foul play.

The first World Cup Final was staged in Montevideo, Uruguay.

Billy Wright was England captain in three World Cup Finals – 1950, 1954, 1958.

Scotland were confident of first round progress when they were drawn against Peru, Iran and Holland in the 1978 Finals. However, they lost to Peru, drew with Iran and beat Holland but not by enough goals to go through to the second stage.

Uruguay were chosen as the host country for the first World Cup Finals because they were Olympic champions and that they also promised to underwrite the costs of the competing nations.

In a play-off match to decide who went through to the Finals of 1974, the Soviet Union refused to play their second leg in Chile because the National Stadium had been used as a prison during Chile's civil war.

World Cup

Facts

Colombia were originally named as host nation for the 1986 Finals, but they had to withdraw because of financial difficulties. Mexico took their place.

Mexico became the first country to host the Finals twice. The 1970 and 1986 tournaments were played there.

Peru beat Bulgaria in the 1970 Finals just two days after 66,794 people had died in a Peruvian earthquake.

 **Facts**   **World Cup**

The first goalless draw in the World Cup Finals was between England and Brazil in 1958.

The first extra-time goal in a Final was in 1934 when Italy beat Czechoslovakia. The scorer was Italy's Angelo Schiavio.

Berne, in Switzerland, is the smallest city to have hosted a World Cup Final (1954).

Two sets of brothers have won the World Cup. Fritz and Ottmar Walter for West Germany in 1954 and England's Bobby and Jack Charlton in 1966.

Luis Monti is the only player to play in two World Cup Final's for different nations. He played for Argentina in 1930 and for Italy in 1934.

Italian Vittorio Pozzo is the only man to win two World Cup's as manager.

Vicente Feola, the 1966 Brazilian manager, stayed in Europe for a month after his country's elimination in England for safety reasons.

Poland's Laszlo Kiss was the first substitute to score three times in a World Cup Finals match against El Salvador in 1982.

All games in the first World Cup Finals in 1930 were played in Montevideo.

Argentina have reached four World Cup semi-finals – and won all of them.

Portugal players had been on strike at the start of the 1986 World Cup Finals because of a dispute over bonuses. They settled their differences and beat England in their first match.

Hungary hold an incredible international record. Between 1950 and 1956 they lost only once in 48 internationals. Their only defeat was in the 1954 World Cup Final to West Germany.

World Cup

Pedro Cea of Uruguay was the first player to score in both Olympic and World Cup Final's.

Argentina have won the World Cup twice, but have also lost both opening games when they were holders. They were beaten by Belgium in 1982 and Cameroon in 1990.

Tunisia have played in just one World Cup, and despite being eliminated in the first round they boast a win against Mexico and a draw with West Germany.

The Dutch East Indies (now Indonesia) have played only one game in the Finals – a 6-0 defeat by Hungary in 1938.

Jan Tomaszewski, Poland's goalkeeper in the 1974 Finals, became the first man to save two penalties in the same tournament.

England were eliminated from the 1982 Finals without losing a game. They beat France, Czechoslovakia and Kuwait in the group stages but lost out on goal difference after goalless draws against West Germany and Spain.

Only six of the 15 tournaments have seen the host nation not reach the semi-finals. They are France (1938), Switzerland (1954), Mexico (1970), Spain (1982), Mexico (1986) and USA (1994).

Of the 16 competing teams in the 1934 Finals 12 were from Europe. The others were Argentina, USA, Brazil and Egypt.

Cuba's last appearance in the World Cup Finals was in 1938. They lost to Sweden 8-0 in the quarter-finals.

Hungary scored 27 goals in just five matches in the 1954 Finals, but still lost in the Final to West Germany.

West Germany's defeat of Hungary in the 1954 Final was a repeat of an earlier group match. On that occasion Hungary won 8-3.

 **Facts**

World Cup

Three European teams made up the 1994 semi-finals. Italy beat Bulgaria and Sweden lost to Brazil.

England were the first Home Countries to play in the World Cup, in 1950.

Despite losing twice to Mexico, 6-0 and 6-2, USA still qualified for the 1950 Finals, and beat England 1-0 in one of the biggest shocks in World Cup history.

Gary Lineker is England's top goalscorer in World Cup Finals history. He has scored 10 goals in just 11 games.

Lineker finished the 1986 World Cup as top goalscorer, the first British player to have done so.

Chilean goalkeeper Roberto Rojas was banned from international football for life when he claimed he was hit by a firecracker during Chile's important 1990 World Cup qualifying match against Brazil which they had to win. The game was abandoned with Brazil winning 1-0, but it was later discovered that Rojas had faked the injury and Brazil were awarded a 2-0 victory.

Seven of the eight quarter-finalists in the 1994 World Cup were European.

The last time two British countries reached the quarter-finals was in 1958. Northern Ireland and Wales both lost.

After being eliminated in 1938, Norway had to wait for 56 years before reaching the Finals again, losing in the first round in 1994.

Two-time winners Argentina had to beat Australia in a play-off to qualify for the 1994 Finals.

Joe Jordan is the only Scotsman to have scored in three successive World Cup Finals – 1974, 1978, 1982.

Against El Salvador in 1970, Mexico's Juan Basaguren became the first substitute to score in a World Cup Finals match.

The 1998 World Cup

Facts

The 1998 World Cup Finals were held in France, which thus became the second country to host the tournament twice (the other was Mexico in 1970 and 1986). The French had previously hosted the tournament in 1938.

There were 32 finalists, as follows: Argentina, Austria, Belgium, Brazil, Bulgaria, Cameroon, Chile, Colombia, Croatia, Denmark, England, France, Germany, Holland, Iran, Italy, Jamaica, Japan, Mexico, Morocco, Nigeria, Norway, Paraguay, Romania, Saudi Arabia, Scotland, South Africa, South Korea, Spain, Tunisia, the United States and Yugoslavia.

Matches were played in 10 centres across the country. There were two stadia in Paris – the existing Parc des Princes and the new Stade de France at St Denis on the western edge of the city centre. Other venues were Bordeaux, Lens, Lyons, Marseilles, Montpellier, Nantes, Saint-Etienne and Toulouse.

The countries were divided into eight groups, each of four teams. When the draw was made, there were eight top seeds, eight second seeds, eight third seeds and eight fourth seeds.

The eight top seeds were Argentina, Brazil (the holders), France, Germany, Holland, Italy, Romania and Spain.

England had only a moderate build-up to the finals, losing to Chile and drawing with Saudi Arabia and Belgium. The only real source of encouragement was a win over Portugal.

In the run-up to the finals, Scotland drew three and lost two of their try-out games.

 **Facts** The 1998 World Cup

The match between France and Paraguay was the first in the history of the World Cup to be decided by the 'golden goal' method. Under this system, previously used in Euro '96, the team that wins is the one that scores first in extra time.

Germany left it very late against Mexico, after going behind in the 47th minute. Although they came through in the end, the Germans were widely thought to be struggling to paper the cracks in an old side – average age 31. Klinsmann gave everything, but the question remained: did he have enough left to get his side through another three high-pressure matches?

Holland almost lost to Yugoslavia, who were awarded a penalty but hit the crossbar with the kick. Edgar Davids' winner came in the last minute of normal time.

Croatia beat Romania thanks to Davor Suker, who remained calm when he had to retake his penalty kick because of encroachment in the area. He put the ball in the net both times.

The tie of the round was the match between Argentina and England. The South Americans went ahead through a penalty awarded against Seaman after six minutes, but England equalised four minutes later after Michael Owen was impeded in the Argentine area. Shearer scored from the resulting penalty.

England then took the lead with a goal from Owen, but Argentina made it 2-2 at half time when a cleverly worked free kick just outside the area was played through to Javier Zanetti.

The 1998 World Cup

Facts

After extra time produced no golden goal, the tie was decided on penalties. Argentina took the first and scored through Berti; Shearer made it 1-1, then Crespo's shot was saved by Seaman. Ince had the chance to make it 2-1 to England, but Roas saved his effort. Then Veron and Merson both scored to make it 2-2, and they were followed by Gallardo and Owen (3-3). Ayala made it 4-3 to Argentina and then David Batty's shot was saved by Roas. England were eliminated.

The quarter finals of the 1998 World Cup were between Holland and Argentina, Germany and Croatia, Italy and France and Brazil and Denmark.

Holland beat Argentina 2-1, with a goal by Patrick Kluivert after 12 minutes and a winner by Dennis Bergkamp from virtually the last kick of the game. In the meantime, the South Americans had equalised through Claudio Lopez.

Croatia beat a weary-looking Germany 3-0. Their goals were scored by Robert Jarni, Goran Vlaovic and Davor Suker. Germany had Christian Worns sent off.

Neither Italy nor France looked as if they would ever score, and they didn't. The tie was decided when Di Biagio missed in the penalty shoot-out.

Denmark took the lead against the favourites, Brazil, with a goal by Martin Jorgensen after two minutes. Brazil hit back through Bebeto and Rivaldo to take a half-time lead, but the Danes equalised after the break with a goal by Brian Laudrup. Brazil's winner was another goal for Rivaldo, whose speculative shot from outside the box evaded the dive of Peter Schmeichel.

 **Facts** The 1998 World Cup

In the second semi-final, France came from a goal down to beat Croatia 2-1. Davor Suker gave the Croats the lead straight after half time but Lilian Thuram equalised immediately and then scored the winner in the 70th minute. France had Laurent Blanc sent off for hitting Slaven Bilic. Television replays suggested that although the Frenchman raised his hand and did make contact with his opponent, Bilic seemed to have made the most of the moment, as if wishing to draw the referee's attention to it.

The 1998 World Cup Final between the holders Brazil and the hosts France was held at the Stade de France, St Denis, Paris on July 12, 1998 in front of 80,000 spectators.

Brazil: Taffarel, Cafu, Aldair, Junior Baiano, Roberto Carlos, Leonardo (sub: Denilson), Cesar Sampaio (sub: Edmundo), Dunga, Rivaldo, Ronaldo, Bebeto

France: Barthez, Thuram, Desailly, Leboeuf, Lizarazu, Karembeu (sub: Boghossian), Deschamps, Petit, Zidane, Djorkaeff (sub: Vieira), Guivarc'h (sub: Dugarry)

Ronaldo had been unsure of his place until the last minute because of illness. He is thought to have suffered a fit on the morning of the match. His performance was subdued to say the least, and the French won 3-0 with two goals by Zinedine Zidane and one in the last minute by Emmanuel Petit. Marcel Desailly was sent off for two bookable offences.

Leading scorer in the 1998 World Cup Finals was Davor Suker, with six goals for Croatia, who finished in third place.

Suker's closest challengers for the Golden Boot were Gabriel Batistuta of Argentina and Christian Vieri of Italy, who both finished the tournament with five goals. Ronaldo of Brazil, Marcelo Salas of Chile and Luis Hernandez of Mexico all scored four.

The 1998 World Cup

Facts

Scotland played in the opening match of the tournament against the holders, Brazil. The champions went ahead after four minutes through Cesar Sampaio, but Scotland got back on terms through a penalty by John Collins. The Scots were unlucky to lose through an own goal when an attempted clearance bounced in off Boyd.

England began their campaign with a 2-0 victory over Tunisia. Their first came from captain Alan Shearer after 42 minutes, the second from Paul Scholes in injury time.

Scotland drew their second game against Norway 1-1, a goal by Craig Burley cancelling out one by Tore Andre Flo immediately after the start of the second half.

England lost their second game to Romania, the top seeds in their group. Both Romanian goals came from players based in England – Viorel Moldovan of Coventry City scored the first, which was pulled back in the 83rd minute by substitute Michael Owen. Just as both sides seemed to have settled for a draw, Dan Petrescu of Chelsea stuck his foot between Graeme Le Saux and goalkeeper David Seaman to grab all three points.

 **Facts** The 1998 World Cup

At the start of the second half, David Beckham was sent off for retaliation after he had been fouled by Diego Simeone. The loss of a man greatly restricted England's capacity to attack, but they held out and seven minutes from time even had the ball in the Argentine net, but Sol Campbell's header was disallowed for a foul by Shearer on goalkeeper Carlos Roa.

In the first World Cup semi-final, Brazil beat Holland 4-2 on penalties after their match had ended 1-1 after extra time. Ronaldo had given Brazil the lead at the start of the second half, but Patrick Kluivert equalised three minutes from the end of normal time.

Holland, Hungary, Sweden, Spain and Italy all boycotted the first World Cup in 1930 because they were not installed as hosts.

The Dutch East Indies (now Indonesia) were the first Asian country to play in the Finals. They qualified for the 1938 tournament.

Haiti made their only appearance in the Finals when they beat Mexico in qualifying for the 1974 World Cup.

The Republic of Ireland have played nine games in the Finals and won only once. The single victory was against Italy in 1994 which they won 1-0.

HISTORY OF THE GAME

THE DAWN
OF TIME

The Dawn of Time

The first England versus Scotland match was played at The Oval, Kennington, London on March 5, 1870. The two teams drew 1-1.

The first FA Cup was won by The Wanderers, who beat The Royal Engineers 1-0 in the Final at the Kennington Oval on March 16, 1872.

The winning goal in the first FA Cup Final was scored by M.P. Betts.

The Cup-winning Wanderers captain, C.W. Alcock, was also Secretary of the Football Association.

The first FA Cup had 15 entrants.

 **Facts**

The Dawn of Time

The FA Cup itself was known throughout the game as The Little Tin Idol. It was 18 inches high, had two curved handles and was crowned with a figure of a footballer on the lid.

The Cup had been made by Martin, Hall & Co and cost £20.

Queen's Park of Glasgow – Scotland's first football club – took part in the first English FA Cup, and received byes to the semi-final.

In the semi-final, Queen's Park drew with The Wanderers but could not afford to stay in London for the replay, so had to scratch from the tournament.

The first Scotland versus England match was played at the West of Scotland Cricket Ground, Partick on November 30, 1872. The final score was 0-0.

The first official international between England and Scotland was played at The Oval, Kennington, London on March 8, 1873. The score was England 4 Scotland 2.

The Dawn of Time

The scorer of England's first ever international goal was Alexander Bonsor of Old Etonians and The Wanderers.

In March 1873, the Scots founded a Football Association and inaugurated their own FA Cup.

The first Scottish FA Cup trophy and badges cost £56.12s. 11d (about £56.64p).

In 1876, the Welsh FA was formed and Wales played their first international football match – they lost 4-0 to Scotland in Glasgow.

The first recorded match under electric lights was played on October 14, 1878, at Bramall Lane, Sheffield, between sides captained by the brothers J.C. and W.E. Clegg, both England internationals. 20,000 people are thought to have been present.

The first official football match in Northern Ireland was an exhibition game between the Scottish clubs Queen's Park and Caledonians on October 24, 1878.

Facts

The Dawn of Time

1878 was also the year in which referees used whistles for the first time.

FA Cup Finals of the 1870s

1872	The Wanderers	1	Royal Engineers	0
1873	The Wanderers	2	Oxford University	0
1874	Oxford University	2	Royal Engineers	0
1875	Royal Engineers	1	Old Etonians	1
	Replay			
	Royal Engineers	2	Old Etonians	0
1876	The Wanderers	1	Old Etonians	1
	Replay			
	The Wanderers	3	Old Etonians	0
1877	The Wanderers	2	Oxford University	1(aet)
1878	The Wanderers	3	Royal Engineers	1
1879	Old Etonians	1	Clapham Rovers	0

The Dawn of Time

Scottish FA Cup Finals of the 1870s

1874	Queen's Park	2	Clydesdale	0
1875	Queen's Park	3	Renton	0
1876	Queen's Park	1	Third Lanark	1
	Replay			
	Queen's Park	2	Third Lanark	0
1877	Vale of Leven	0	Rangers	0
	Replays			
	Vale of Leven	1	Rangers	1
	Vale of Leven	3	Rangers	2
1878	Vale of Leven	1	Third Lanark	0
1879	Vale of Leven	1	Rangers	1

(Vale of Leven then won the Cup by default when Rangers refused to take part in a replay because they had had a goal disallowed in the first match.)

In 1879, at the age of 17 years 245 days, James Prinsep of Clapham Rovers became the youngest man ever to appear in an FA Cup Final.

In 1883, the FA Cup went north for the first time, when Blackburn Olympic beat the Old Etonians 2-1 after extra time.

Blackburn Olympic retained the Cup the following year, 1884, but in 1885 the trophy was won by their neighbours, Blackburn Rovers, who beat Queen's Park 2-1 in the Final.

Blackburn Rovers then won the FA Cup three years running – they beat Queen's Park again 2-0 in the 1885 Final, then West Bromwich Albion 2-0 in a replay at the Racecourse Ground, Derby, after the first match at the Oval had been drawn 0-0.

The first Home International Championship was contested in 1884. Scotland won it with a clean sweep, beating Wales 4-1 in Glasgow, Ireland 5-0 in Belfast and England 1-0 at Cathkin Park, Glasgow.

 **Facts**   The Dawn of Time

The record score in any British first-class football match was Arbroath's 36-0 victory over Bon Accord in the Scottish FA Cup on September 5, 1885.

Arbroath winger John Petrie scored 13 goals in this match – a scoring record that still stands.

England's first professional footballer was James Forrest, who was paid to play against Scotland in 1885.

Scotland dominated the Home International Championship until 1886, when they shared the title with England.

In the first all-Midlands FA Cup Final in 1887, Aston Villa beat West Bromwich Albion 2-0 at Kennington Oval.

On their way to the trophy, Aston Villa had beaten Glasgow Rangers 3-1 in the semi-final.

In 1888, the winners of the English and Scottish FA Cups played each other for what was billed as 'The Championship of the World'. Renton beat West Bromwich Albion 2-1.

England won the Home International Championship outright for the first time in 1888, beating Ireland 5-1, Wales 5-1 and Scotland 5-0.

On April 17, 1888, the Football League was founded after a meeting at the Royal Hotel, Manchester. The mastermind – often known as The Father of League Football – was William McGregor, a director of Aston Villa.

The twelve founder members of the English Football League were Accrington, Aston Villa, Blackburn Rovers, Bolton Wanderers, Burnley, Derby County, Everton, Notts County, Preston North End, Stoke, West Bromwich Albion and Wolverhampton Wanderers.

The Dawn of Time

Facts

The first English League Champions were Preston North End, who went through the whole 1888-89 season undefeated. They also won the FA Cup in that year, thus completing the first ever double.

The First English Football League Final Table, Season 1888-89

		P	W	D	L	F	A	Pts
1	Preston North End	22	18	4	0	74	15	40
2	Aston Villa	22	12	5	5	61	43	29
3	Wolverhampton Wanderers	22	12	4	6	50	37	28
4	Blackburn Rovers	22	10	6	6	66	45	26
5	Bolton Wanderers	22	10	2	10	63	59	22
6	West Bromwich Albion	22	10	2	10	40	46	22
7	Accrington	22	6	8	8	48	48	20
8	Everton	22	9	2	11	35	46	20
9	Burnley	22	7	3	12	42	62	17
10	Derby County	22	7	2	13	41	61	16
11	Notts County	22	5	2	15	40	73	12
12	Stoke	22	4	4	14	26	51	12

Preston North End retained the Championship in 1889-90; the runners-up this time were Everton.

Blackburn Rovers beat The Wednesday 6-1 in the 1890 FA Cup Final and William Townley became the first man to score a hat-trick in this fixture.

In 1891-92, the First Division was enlarged to 14 clubs – the two new entrants were Darwen and Stoke.

 **Facts**   The Dawn of Time

FA Cup Finals of the 1880s

1880	Clapham Rovers	1	Oxford University	0
1881	Old Carthusians	3	Old Etonians	0
1882	Old Etonians	1	Blackburn Rovers	0
1883	Blackburn Olympic	2	Old Etonians	1 (aet)
1884	Blackburn Rovers	2	Queen's Park	1
1885	Blackburn Rovers	2	Queen's Park	0
1886	Blackburn Rovers	0	West Bromwich Albion	0
	Replay			
	Blackburn Rovers	2	West Bromwich Albion	0
1887	Aston Villa	2	West Bromwich Albion	0
1888	West Bromwich Albion	2	Preston North End	1
1889	Preston North End	3	Wolverhampton Wdrs	0

Scottish FA Cup Finals of the 1880s

1880	Queen's Park	3	Thornliebank	0
1881	Queen's Park	3	Dumbarton	0
1882	Queen's Park	4	Dumbarton	2
1883	Dumbarton	2	Vale of Leven	2
	Replay			
	Dumbarton	2	Vale of Leven	1
1884	Queen's Park beat Vale of Leven by default			
1885	Renton	0	Vale of Leven	0
	Replay			
	Renton	3	Vale of Leven	1
1886	Queen's Park	3	Renton	1
1887	Hibernian	2	Dumbarton	1
1888	Renton	6	Cambuslang	1
1889	Third Lanark	2	Celtic	1

The Dawn of Time

Facts

On March 15, 1890, England fielded two international sides on the same day – one beat Wales 3-1 at Wrexham, the other beat Ireland 9-1 in Belfast.

In 1890, the Scots followed the English lead and formed their own Football League. The eleven inaugural members were Abercorn, Celtic, Cowlair, Cambuslang, Dumbarton, Heart of Midlothian, Rangers, St Mirren, Renton, Third Lanark and Vale of Leven.

Renton were expelled from the Scottish League after only five matches, for professionalism.

At the end of the season in Spring 1891, there was a tie at the top between Dumbarton and Rangers. In an effort to break the deadlock, a play-off was arranged, but when this ended 2-2 it was decided to share the Championship – the only time this has ever happened.

There was not a single 0-0 draw throughout the whole of the first Scottish League season; 409 goals were scored in 90 matches, an average of 4.5 goals per game.

The First Scottish Football League Final Table, Season 1890-91

		P	W	D	L	F	A	Pts
1=	Dumbarton	18	13	3	2	61	21	29
1=	Rangers	18	13	3	2	58	25	29
3	Celtic	18	11	3	4	48	21	21
4	Cambuslang	18	8	4	6	47	42	20
5	Third Lanark	18	8	3	7	38	39	15
6	Heart of Midlothian	18	6	2	10	31	37	14
7	Abercorn	18	5	2	11	36	47	12
8	St Mirren	18	5	1	2	39	62	11
9	Vale of Leven	18	5	1	12	27	65	11
10	Cowlairs	18	3	4	11	24	50	6

Facts   The Dawn of Time

In 1891, the Scots expanded their First Division to 12 clubs. Cowlairs went out of the League after finishing last in 1891; the three newcomers were Clyde, Leith Athletic and a re-formed Renton.

In 1892, the English Second Division was inaugurated. At the end of the season, there were 'test matches' between the bottom three in Division One and the top three in Division Two to decide promotion and relegation.

The 12 founder members of the Second Division were Ardwick, Bootle, Burton Swifts, Burslem Port Vale, Crewe Alexandra, Darwen, Grimsby Town, Lincoln City, Northwich Victoria, Sheffield United, Small Heath and Walsall Town Swifts.

The English First Division was increased in size again, from 14 clubs to 16. The two new additions were Nottingham Forest and The Wednesday.

At the end of the 1892-93 season, Notts County and Accrington became the first clubs to be relegated from the English First Division.

The Dawn of Time

Facts

At the end of the 1892-93 season, Darwen and Sheffield United became the first clubs to be promoted from the English Second Division.

The top team in Division Two, Small Heath, lost their test match with Newton Heath, the third-from-bottom club in Division One, so neither of these clubs changed divisions the following season.

In 1893, the Scots again followed the English example by recognising professionalism and introducing their own Second Division. The ten clubs that played in it were Abercorn, Clyde, Cowlairs, Greenock Morton, Hibernian, Motherwell, Northern, Partick Thistle, Port Glasgow Athletic and Thistle.

At the end of the 1893-94 season, the English League was expanded from 28 clubs to 31, taking three more clubs into the Second Division.

The three new League members in 1894 were Bury, Leicester Fosse and Manchester City.

The British Ladies' Football Club was formed in 1895 and played its first match at Crouch End, London.

On the night of September 11, 1895, the FA Cup was stolen from the window of football outfitters William Shillcock in Newton Row, Birmingham while it was held by Aston Villa. It was never recovered.

The replacement FA Cup cost Villa £25, and the club were fined as much again by the FA for their negligence in allowing it to be stolen. For several years to come, the winners of the trophy were presented with a replica of the original until a newly designed Cup was specially commissioned in time for the 1911 Final.

 **Facts**   The Dawn of Time

English Football League Champions 1888-99

1888-89 Preston North End
1889-90 Preston North End
1890-91 Everton
1891-92 Sunderland
1892-93 Sunderland
1893-94 Aston Villa
1894-95 Sunderland
1895-96 Aston Villa
1896-97 Aston Villa
1897-98 Sheffield United
1898-99 Aston Villa

FA Cup Finals of the 1890s

1890	Blackburn Rovers	6	The Wednesday	1
1891	Blackburn Rovers	3	Notts County	1
1892	West Bromwich Albion	3	Aston Villa	0
1893	Wolverhampton Wdrs	1	Everton	0
1894	Notts County	4	Bolton Wanderers	1
1895	Aston Villa	1	West Bromwich Albion	0
1896	Sheffield Wednesday	2	Wolverhampton Wdrs	1
1897	Aston Villa	3	Everton	2
1898	Nottingham Forest	3	Derby County	1
1899	Sheffield United	4	Derby County	1

Scottish Football League Champions 1891-99

1890-91 Dumbarton and Rangers
1891-92 Dumbarton
1892-93 Celtic
1893-94 Celtic
1894-95 Heart of Midlothian
1895-96 Celtic
1896-97 Heart of Midlothian
1897-98 Celtic
1898-99 Rangers

The Dawn of Time

Scottish FA Cup Finals of the 1890s

1890	Queen's Park	1	Vale of Leven	1
	Replay			
	Queen's Park	2	Vale of Leven	1
1891	Heart of Midlothian	1	Dumbarton	0
1892	Celtic	5	Queen's Park	1
1893	Queen's Park	2	Celtic	1
1894	Rangers	3	Celtic	1
1895	St Bernard's	2	Renton	1
1896	Heart of Midlothian	3	Hibernian	1
1897	Rangers	5	Dumbarton	1
1898	Rangers	2	Kilmarnock	0
1899	Celtic	2	Rangers	0

In 1898-99, the English Football League was enlarged to 36 clubs by increasing both divisions to 18 clubs. The four new members were Barnsley, Burslem Port Vale, Glossop and New Brighton Tower.

THE EARLY 20TH CENTURY

The Early 20th Century

**The first League Champions of the 20th century were Aston Villa –
with 77 goals. They were the First Division's leading scorers for the
sixth season running.**

The first FA Cup winners of the 20th century were Bury – they won it
again in 1903, but had no other major honours before the millennium. The
attendance at the 1900 Cup Final was 68,945.

**The first Scottish League Champions of the 20th century were
Rangers.**

The first Scottish FA Cup winners of the 20th century were Celtic.

**The 1901 Cup Final between Tottenham Hotspur and Sheffield
United drew a record crowd of 114,815.**

The Sheffield United goalkeeper in the 1900 Final was Willie Foulke, who
weighed at least 20 stones throughout his career.

**There were numerous legends about Foulke. He was said to have
been able to carry a man under each arm and to punch the ball as
far as the halfway line. One match in which he played had to be
stopped when the crossbar snapped after he swung on it.**

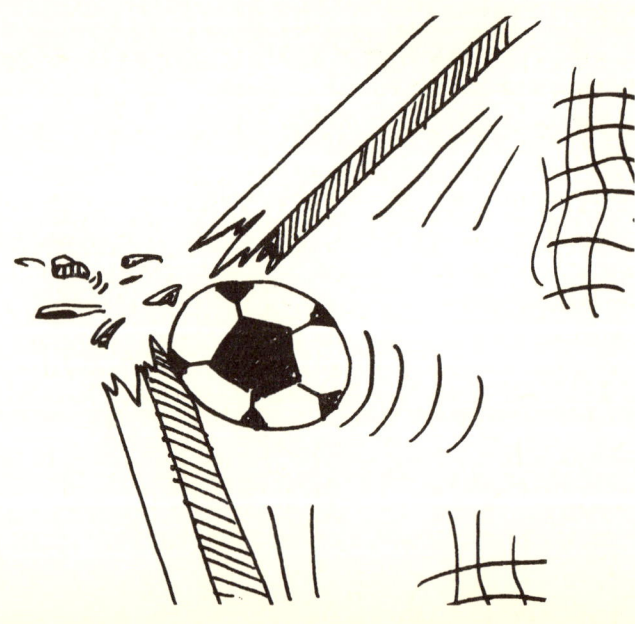

 **Facts**   The Early 20th Century

Of the bottom five clubs in the First Division at the end of the 1900-01 season, four – Sheffield United, Aston Villa, Preston North End and West Bromwich Albion – had won the Championship, the FA Cup or both.

In 1900-01, Linthous dropped out of the Scottish League but its total membership increased to 21 clubs with the addition of East Stirlingshire and St Bernard's.

Scotland beat England 4-1 in the 1900 Home International Championship match. Three of their goals were scored by R.S. McColl of Queen's Park, the last remaining Scottish amateur.

On February 23, 1901, Scotland notched up their highest score in an international, beating Ireland 11-0.

For the 1901-02 season, the Scottish League was expanded again, this time to 22 clubs, with the addition of Arthurlie.

On April 5, 1902, 26 people were killed and 500 were injured when a new stand collapsed at Ibrox Park, Glasgow, during the Scotland v England match.

The match was replayed at Villa Park, Birmingham. This was the first international in which all the players were professionals. The final score was England 2 Scotland 2.

In 1901-02, the maximum wage for professional footballers in England was £4 a week.

In 1901-02, goalscoring in the First Division reached a record low, averaging only 2.75 goals a game.

Pitch markings were changed for the 1902-03 season – henceforth, the goal area would be 20 yards wide and 6 yards deep; there would be a penalty area at 18 yards and a penalty spot 12 yards from the goal line.

The Early 20th Century

Facts

The 1902-03 Home International Championship was a three-way tie between England, Scotland and Ireland.

In 1903-04, the Scottish League grew again – this time to 26 clubs, with the addition of Albion Rovers and Ayr Parkhouse.

On May 21, 1904, the world governing body of football was formed at a meeting in Paris between representatives of the football associations of Belgium, Denmark, France, Holland, Spain, Sweden and Switzerland. It was called FIFA (Fédération Internationale de Football Association).

England became a member of FIFA in 1905 and thereafter rapidly took a leading role in its affairs.

The first international in South America, between Argentina and Uruguay for the Lipton Cup, ended in a draw.

In 1906, Daniel Burley Woolfall of the English FA was elected President of FIFA.

On December 5, 1904, Woolwich Arsenal beat a team of French internationals 26-1.

 **Facts**   The Early 20th Century

England international Alf Common became the first £1000 transfer when he moved from Sunderland to Middlesbrough.

In 1904, Sheffield FC – the oldest football club then in existence, founded in 1857 – won their first major honour, the FA Amateur Cup.

In 1904-05, Wales notched up their first international victory over Scotland at the 30th attempt, winning 3-1 at Wrexham.

In 1904-05, Rangers and Celtic finished level on points at the top of the Scottish First Division.

Celtic won the title in a play-off, but if either goal average or goal difference had been used, Rangers would have been Champions – they had scored 83 and conceded 28, which was superior by either method of reckoning to Celtic's 68 for and 31 against.

At the start of the 1905-06 season, the English Football League was enlarged to 40 clubs by increasing the two divisions to 20 clubs each. Because of the reorganisation, there was no relegation from Division One this year. The two clubs to benefit from this were Bury and Notts County, who finished in 17th and 18th place respectively in 1905.

Doncaster Rovers failed to gain re-election after finishing bottom of Division Two in 1904-05.

The five new clubs elected for 1905-06 were Chelsea, Hull City, Leeds City, Stockport County and Clapton Orient.

Also in 1905-06, the FA Cup was increased from five rounds to six.

Liverpool won the First Division in 1906, the first time a newly promoted club had gone on to take the title the following season.

The Early 20th Century

Facts

In 1905-06, the Scottish League was altered for the fifth time this century. The League was enlarged to 28 clubs – a 16-club First Division and a 12-club Second Division.

The two new clubs admitted to the Scottish Second Division were Cowdenbeath and Vale of Leven.

In 1906-07, the Scottish League was enlarged to 30 clubs – a First Division of 18 clubs and a Second Division of 12. The newcomers were Dumbarton and – back after a two-year absence – Ayr Parkhouse.

In 1907, Celtic became the first Scottish club to win the League and FA Cup double.

Wales won the 1907 Home International Championship – it was their first victory in this competition and the first time it had been won outright by anyone but England or Scotland.

Newcastle United dropped only one point at home in their Championship-winning 1906-07 season.

 **Facts**　　　　　The Early 20th Century

When Bristol City finished second in the First Division at the end of the 1906-07 season, this was the highest position ever achieved by a southern club.

A crowd of between 110,000 and 130,000 watched the 1-1 draw between Scotland and England on April 4, 1908.

Falkirk became the first club to score more than 100 goals in a League season – but their total of 103 was not enough to bring them the 1908 Championship, which went to Celtic.

In 1908, the first Charity Shield was played in England between League Champions Manchester United and Southern League winners Queen's Park Rangers.

The 1909 Scottish FA Cup was withheld after riots between groups of rival supporters during the final replay between Celtic and Rangers. The second match had finished 1-1 after a 2-2 draw in the first Final, and many fans were disgruntled because they suspected that the results had been rigged so that the two clubs might gain extra revenue.

On December 11, 1909, Vivian Woodward of Tottenham Hotspur became the first player to score a double hat-trick twice when he slotted six for England in an amateur international against Holland. His previous double hat-trick had been for England against France in 1906 – a match in which he had scored eight!

In 1911, a new FA Cup was commissioned at a cost of 50 guineas (£52.50).

The new trophy was made in Bradford and first presented to one of the local teams – Bradford City – when they won the Cup in 1911.

The Early 20th Century

Facts

The Final against Newcastle United featured twelve Scotsmen, eight of whom played for Bradford City.

The second FA Cup – a replica of the one that had been stolen in 1895 and never recovered – was presented to Lord Kinnaird to mark his 21st year as President of the FA.

In his playing career, Kinnaird (1847-1923) had played in nine FA Cup Finals and won five winners' medals with The Wanderers and The Old Etonians.

When the 1912 Cup Final became the third in a row to be drawn, the FA decided that, henceforth, there would be extra time in the first Final if it was needed.

After keeping an unaltered format since 1907, Scotland again increased the size of its League. Instead of 30 clubs, there would henceforth be 32, with a First Division of 18 and a Second Division of 14.

The two new clubs that came into the Scottish League as a result of this reorganisation were Dunfermline Athletic and St Johnstone.

In the 1912-13 season, every player who appeared for Morton in the Scottish First Division scored a goal for the club.

In 1913, England lost to Ireland for the first time, suffering a 2-1 defeat in Belfast. Three minutes before full-time, the crowd mistook a free kick for the final whistle and invaded the pitch. The match could not be restarted, but the result stood.

After this historic victory, Ireland went from strength to strength, and the following year (1914) won the Home International Championship outright for the first time.

 **Facts**

The Early 20th Century

The 1914 FA Cup Final between Burnley and Liverpool was the first to be watched by a reigning monarch, King George V.

The 1914 FA Cup Final was the last to be played at Crystal Palace – the following year, it was held at Old Trafford, then the Great War intervened. After the end of hostilities, the 1920, 1921 and 1922 Finals were held at Stamford Bridge. And then in 1923 the fixture moved to Wembley.

The Great War began in August 1914. By the next FA Cup Final on April 24, 1915, most of the spectators were in uniform.

The Khaki Cup Final – as the 1915 fixture became known – was a muted affair played at Old Trafford in front of 49,557 spectators.

The Cup was won by Sheffield United, who beat Chelsea 3-0 in the Final. The trophy was presented to the Blades' captain by Lord Derby, who took the opportunity to make a recruiting speech: 'It is now the duty of everyone to join with each other and play a sterner game for England'.

On Easter Monday 1915, in a First Division match at Middlesbrough, Oldham Athletic full-back Billy Cook refused to leave the field when ordered off by referee Mr H. Smith. So the referee himself went off, ending the game 30 minutes early.

The Early 20th Century

After an FA inquiry into this incident, Oldham were fined £350 and Cook was suspended for a year. But the result – a 4-1 Middlesbrough victory – was allowed to stand.

In the Scottish League Division Two, there was a tie at the top between Cowdenbeath, Leith Athletic and St Bernard's, necessitating a three-way play-off. Cowdenbeath won it – beating both the other teams – but none was promoted because only the Scottish First Division went on playing throughout the rest of the First World War.

The Football League and FA Cup programmes in England and Scotland continued after the outbreak of the First World War on August 4, 1914.

This was a matter of great controversy – the Church of England was particularly strong in its condemnation of those who watched football while others were serving their country.

 **Facts**   The Early 20th Century

Nevertheless, the decision had been taken in consultation with the War Office, who thought that maintaining a vestige of normality would be good for morale. Football clubs helped the recruitment drive – there was no conscription at first – and it is thought that eventually perhaps as many as half a million new soldiers were enlisted at football grounds.

At first, though, recruiting drives at football grounds were almost farcically unsuccessful. Only one person enlisted at a 1915 Arsenal game, while at a Nottingham Forest match there was no one at all ready to fight.

Yet although few spectators were keen to join up, many of those who earned their living from football were among the first to enlist. The game produced 100,000 recruits in the first four months of the War and FA statistics revealed that only 600 men who worked in football had not volunteered by August 1915.

The willingness of players to join up was used by the War Office in its recruitment drive. Outside Stamford Bridge, advertisement hoardings bore the legend: 'Do you want to be a Chelsea diehard? ... Follow the lead given by your favourite football players'.

Many professionals who enlisted went into the 17th Service Batallion of the Middlesex Regiment based at the Richmond Athletic Ground.

The Footballers' Batallion, as it became known, went into action in France in the summer of 1915. Their second-in-command, Major Frank Buckley, was wounded in the shoulder and lung in 1916. He was later manager of Wolverhampton Wanderers during the interwar years.

By the summer of 1915, gates had dwindled because so many men had gone to fight in France. It was decided to suspend the English League and carry on with regional leagues. Matches would be played only on Saturdays and holidays – there were to be no midweek games and no internationals.

The Early 20th Century

Facts

In Scotland, the FA Cup was suspended, but the First Division of the League continued throughout the War.

During the First World War, Scottish First Division players were not allowed to make their whole living from football and their earnings from the game were restricted to no more than £2 a week. The remainder of their income had to be from work that helped the war effort.

With no midweek matches, Scottish clubs sometimes had to play two matches a day. On April 15, 1915, Celtic beat Raith Rovers 6-0 in the afternoon. In the evening, they went to Motherwell – who had lost 3-0 to Ayr that afternoon – and won 3-1.

The First World War was a particularly successful period for Celtic, who went 62 matches without defeat from November 13, 1915 to April 21, 1917.

In 1918, Rangers broke Celtic's domination, winning the League Championship by a single point. Controversially, the Gers took full advantage of the temporary transfers that enabled footballing servicemen who found themselves in a new billet to play for the local side if picked. Their 1918 team had guest players from as far away as Sheffield.

In 1915 there was a match fixing scandal. A Football League committee of enquiry discovered that players in the Manchester United v Liverpool match at Easter had bet large sums on a 2-1 win for United at odds of 7-1. Four players from each side were suspended for life.

The players found guilty of match-fixing were Tom Fairfoul, Tommy Miller, Bob Purcell and Jackie Sheldon of Liverpool, Laurence Cook, Sandy Turnbull, Enoch West and Arthur Whalley of Manchester United.

 **Facts**   The Early 20th Century

Of the United players found guilty, only West had actually played in the fixed match. He was the only one of the eight who did not have his ban lifted at the end of the First World War.

In 1918 and 1919, the winners of the Lancashire regional league met the winners of the Midlands regional league in a play-off for the Championship Cup, the wartime equivalent of the League Championship.

In 1918, Midlands league winners Leeds City beat Lancashire league winners Stoke 2-1 on aggregate over the two-legged tie.

In the 1919 Championship Cup play-off – after the end of the War, but before normal fixtures could be resumed – Nottingham Forest (Midlands) beat Everton (Lancashire) 1-0 at Goodison Park after a goalless draw at the City Ground.

In the Nottingham Forest goal in that final was Sam Hardy, the England keeper who normally played for Aston Villa but who was permitted under wartime regulations to guest for a club closer to his billet.

Outstanding among the footballers honoured for their bravery in the First World War was Donald Bell, the Bradford full back, who won the Victoria Cross posthumously at the Battle of the Somme.

Steve Bloomer, the Derby and England forward, retired early in 1914 and was unlucky enough to take a coaching job in Berlin. Instead of taking up his post on arrival in the German capital, he was interned for the duration of the War.

The Early 20th Century

Facts

Title Winners of the First World War

London Combination
1915-16 Chelsea
1916-17 West Ham United
1917-18 Chelsea
1918-19 Brentford

Lancashire Regional Tournament
1915-16 Manchester City
1916-17 Liverpool
1917-18 Stoke
1918-19 Everton

Midland Regional Tournament
1915-16 Nottingham Forest
1916-17 Leeds City
1917-18 Leeds City
1918-19 Nottingham Forest

Wartime League Championship
1917-18 Leeds City
1918-19 Nottingham Forest

Scottish League Champions
1915-16 Celtic
1916-17 Celtic
1917-18 Rangers
1918-19 Celtic

BETWEEN
THE WARS

Between the Wars

The First World War ended on November 11, 1918, but it was not until the following season that football got back to normal and the League programme resumed.

The Home Nations – England, Ireland, Scotland and Wales – withdrew from FIFA because they refused to play against Germany. They remained outside the organisation until 1922.

For the 1919-20 season, the English Football League was increased from 40 to 44 clubs in two divisions of 22.

Glossop had dropped out of the League in 1915, while Leeds City were expelled from it in 1919 because of irregularities in payments to players during the First World War.

During the First World War, 35 guests had played for Leeds, including seven internationals. This was not a problem in itself, because it was permitted under wartime rules, but when the club refused to render accounts for the 1917-18 and 1918-19 seasons, the League threw them out.

In the aftermath of the Leeds scandal, four of its directors and two of its former managers were banned for life from involvement in football and were even forbidden to attend matches.

One of Leeds City's former managers was George Cripps; the other was Herbert Chapman.

Thus there were six vacancies in the new postwar English Second Division. These were taken up by Coventry City, Port Vale, Rotherham County, Stoke City, South Shields and West Ham United.

 **Facts** Between the Wars

COVENTRY CITY

Coventry City had been formed in 1883 by workers at a bicycle factory and originally played under the name Singer's FC.

Port Vale – who replaced Leeds City in mid-season and took their points – had been a League club before. Founded in 1876, from 1884 to 1911 they were known as Burslem Port Vale. They had been founder members of the Second Division in 1892 but failed to win re-election in 1896. Re-elected in 1898, they resigned from the League in 1907 because of financial difficulties.

Port Vale took their name from that of the house in Burslem, Stoke-on-Trent, where the founders first met.

Rotherham County grew out of a previous club called Thornhill United which had been founded in 1878. Neighbouring Rotherham Town had been a member of the League from 1893 to 1896, when they failed to win re-election. After joining the Second Division, Rotherham County amalgamated with Rotherham Town in 1925 to form Rotherham United.

Stoke were founder members of the League in 1888 but went bankrupt in 1908 and had to resign. They reformed as Stoke City in 1919 to fill one of the new vacancies.

Between the Wars

West Ham United started as Thames Ironworks FC, a club formed by workers at a shipyard owned by Arnold F. Hills. Renamed in 1900, the club won election to the Football League in 1919 under the management of Syd King.

The reorganisation of the League was not good news for everyone. Tottenham Hotspur were relegated to the Second Division. This might not have upset them, since they finished bottom of the First Division in 1915, had it not been for the fact that Arsenal took their place in Division One despite having finished only fifth in Division Two in 1915.

With 42 matches instead of 38, there were new records aplenty in the 1919-20 League season. West Bromwich Albion scored a record 104 goals in their Championship year, while Tottenham scored 102 goals to win the Second Division.

On March 15, 1920, at the age of 45 years 229 days, Billy Meredith of Manchester City became the oldest player to appear in an international match – for Wales against England.

 **Facts**   Between the Wars

For the 1919-20 season, the two divisions of the Scottish Football League were amalgamated into one division of 22 clubs.

Rangers won the Scottish Championship, with a record 71 points from their 42 matches. They scored 106 goals.

At the start of the 1920-21 season, there was another reorganisation of the English Football League. The total number of clubs was increased from 44 to 66 clubs by accepting the en bloc application of every member of the Southern League Division One.

All but one of the new clubs went into the newly formed Third Division. The exception was Cardiff City, who went straight into Division Two; to accommodate this, Grimsby Town, last season's bottom League club, were relegated to the Third.

Cardiff City went from strength to strength, winning promotion to the First Division in their first season in the League.

Lincoln City, who finished next to bottom of the Second Division in 1919-20, were not re-elected. Their place in Division Two was taken by Leeds United, a new club with the same ground and infrastructure as Leeds City.

The 21 Founder Members of the Third Division were as follows: Brentford, Brighton and Hove Albion, Bristol Rovers, Crystal Palace, Exeter City, Gillingham, Luton Town, Merthyr Town, Millwall Athletic, Newport County, Northampton Town, Norwich City, Plymouth Argyle, Portsmouth, Queen's Park Rangers, Reading, Southampton, Southend United, Swansea Town, Swindon Town and Watford.

Between the Wars

The new formation was immediately popular – Millwall's first gate was over 25,000, Portsmouth and Queen's Park Rangers had attendances of over 20,000.

At the other end of the scale, the Second Division match between Stockport County and Leicester City on May 7, 1921, was watched by fewer paying spectators than any other game in League history. Stockport were already doomed to relegation; their Edgeley Park ground was closed, so the match was played at Old Trafford, Manchester.

Only 13 people paid to watch the game, which was a 0-0 draw. Nevertheless, this statistic is not as impressive as it is sometimes made to sound – another 2000 fans stayed on after watching Manchester United earlier the same day.

Dumbarton goalkeeper James Williamson died on the night of November 12, 1921, from injuries sustained in a collision with a member of the opposition during his team's match with Rangers.

The 1921-22 season saw a further expansion of the English League from 66 clubs to 86. The 20 newcomers entered a new Third Division which was regionalised into Third Division (North) and Third Division (South).

The 20 clubs that joined the Football League in 1921 were as follows: Aberdare Athletic, Accrington Stanley, Ashington, Barrow, Charlton Athletic, Chesterfield, Crewe Alexandra, Darlington, Durham City, Halifax Town, Hartlepools United, Lincoln City, Nelson, Rochdale, Southport, Stalybridge Celtic, Tranmere Rovers, Walsall, Wigan Borough and Wrexham.

Lincoln City were making a return to League football after having failed to gain re-election in 1920.

 **Facts**   Between the Wars

Stockport County were relegated from Division Two at the end of the 1920-21 season but went straight back up again the following year as the first Champions of Division Three (North).

The inaugural winners of Division Three (South) were Southampton. They had come second in the year of the old Third Division but, because of the impending reorganisation, only champions Crystal Palace had been promoted.

In Scotland, the experiment with a single division was abandoned and the League reformed with 42 clubs – a top division of 22 and a second division of 20.

Because of this reorganisation, there was no relegation from the Scottish First Division at the end of the 1920-21 season, thus saving the bottom two clubs, Dumbarton and St Mirren, from the drop.

Some of the 20 clubs in the new Scottish Division Two had previously been members of the League before the disruptions caused by the First World War.

The full list of clubs in Scottish League Division Two (1921-22) was as follows: Alloa Athletic, Arbroath, Armadale, Bathgate, Bo'ness, Broxburn United, Clackmannan, Cowdenbeath, Dundee Hibernians, Dunfermline Athletic, East Fife, East Stirlingshire, Forfar Athletic, Johnstone, King's Park, Lochgelly United, St Bernard's, St Johnstone, Stenhousemuir and Vale of Leven.

At the end of the 1921-22 season, Alloa Athletic were promoted to the First Division as Champions of the Second.

However, during the course of the season the Scottish League had announced plans to alter its formation yet again – the two divisions were to be reduced to 20 teams each.

Between the Wars

This meant that three clubs – Dumbarton, Queen's Park and Clydebank – were relegated from the First Division in 1922.

The bottom two clubs in Division Two at the end of 1921-22 had to drop out of the League – the unlucky sides were Dundee Hibernians and Clackmannan.

On April 28, 1923, the English FA Cup Final was held for the first time at Wembley Stadium.

The finalists were Bolton Wanderers, who finished 13th in the First Division, and West Ham United, who were vying for promotion from Division Two.

Bolton won 2-0, but the day is best remembered for the near disaster in the crowd. The official attendance is given as 126,047, but many thousands of others scaled the walls and broke down flimsy barriers to watch the match.

Unofficially, there are thought to have been at least 200,000 and possibly a quarter of a million people in the stadium.

The masses flowed onto the pitch, making play impossible. They were eventually pushed back by the police, notably by PC George Scorey and his white horse, Billy.

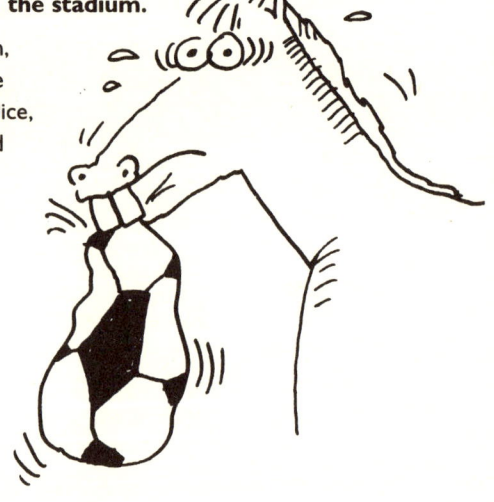

 **Facts**   **Between the Wars**

Constable Scorey later said: 'We arrived at kick-off time and were given orders to clear the pitch. Clear the pitch indeed! You couldn't see it'.

The match eventually got under way 45 minutes late. The crowd lined the edge of the playing area, making throw-ins and corners unusually hazardous – on several occasions, the ball stayed in play after bouncing off spectators on the line.

The Cup was presented to the winning captain by King George V.

This near disaster was an early warning of the need to control football crowds more closely. The FA acknowledged this by making all subsequent Finals strictly all ticket.

Two days after their Wembley disappointment, West Ham United had the consolation of winning promotion for the first time after only four years in the League.

Between the Wars

On Monday, April 30, West Ham went to Hillsborough and beat Sheffield Wednesday 2-0, a win which took them to the top of the Second Division, ahead of both Notts County and Leicester City on goal difference.

On May 5, the last Saturday of the 1922-23 season, West Ham's final game was at home to second-placed County. Leicester, meanwhile, were away to mid-table Bury.

Notts County beat West Ham 1-0 and went up as Second Division Champions, but the Hammers were still promoted as runners-up on goal difference because Bury beat Leicester.

The leading lights of West Ham's promotion campaign were centre forward Vic Watson, goalkeeper Ted Hufton and winger Jimmy Ruffell.

On January 30, 1923, Lord Kinnaird died. A Scottish international and the winner of five English FA Cup-winner's medals with Old Etonians, Kinnaird had been President of the FA for 33 years.

Since the end of the First World War, amateur football clubs had been increasing the frequency with which they used substitutes. This was frowned upon by the game's governing bodies.

In order to resist this trend and ensure that it did not spill over into the professional game, the International Board redrafted the rules specifically to emphasise that only 11 players were permitted in any game unless the match was a friendly and unless the use of substitutes had been agreed by the two captains in advance.

The growth of English football continued into the 1923-24 season. The League was enlarged again to 88 clubs by increasing the Third Division (North) from 20 to 22 clubs – this created four divisions, each of 22 teams.

 **Facts**

Between the Wars

At the end of 1922-23, both clubs relegated from Division Two went into the Third Division (North) – these were Rotherham County and Wolverhampton Wanderers.

One club – Nelson – was promoted to the Second Division from Division Three (North), which had previously been composed of 20 clubs.

One club – Bristol City – was promoted to the Second Division from Division Three (South).

This might have created a numerical imbalance, but the symmetry was maintained when Stalybridge Celtic dropped out of the Third Division (North) at the end of 1922-23 after only two seasons in the League.

There were consequently three vacancies in the League, which were filled by Bournemouth, Doncaster Rovers and New Brighton.

Bournemouth went into the Third Division (South), filling the vacancy created when Bristol City were promoted and no club was relegated to this division from Division Two.

Bournemouth were destined to remain in the Third Division (South) throughout its existence, until 1958.

Doncaster Rovers and New Brighton went into the Third Division (North). Their arrival, together with the fact that Rotherham County and Wolverhampton Wanderers were relegated from Division Two, maintained the total number of teams in Division Three (North) at 22, despite the demise of Stalybridge Celtic.

Doncaster Rovers had first joined the League as members of the Second Division in 1901. They lost their place in 1903, returned in 1904, then dropped out again in 1905. Their re-entry coincided with their move to a new, permanent home at Belle Vue.

Between the Wars

New Brighton lasted in the League until 1951, when they failed to gain re-election; their place was taken by Workington.

The English League Championship of 1923-24 was the closest ever, with Huddersfield Town beating Cardiff City into second place on goal average. (Goal average was calculated by dividing the number of goals scored by the number of goals conceded.)

At the end of the 1923-24 season, the top of the First Division table read as follows:

	P	W	D	L	F	A	Pts
Huddersfield Town	42	23	11	8	60	33	57
Cardiff City	42	22	13	7	61	34	57

This gave Huddersfield a goal average of 1.8181, which was 0.024 superior to that of Cardiff, who finished with a goal average of 1.7941.

 **Facts**   **Between the Wars**

At the age of 41 years and 8 months, Walter Hampson became the oldest player ever to appear in an FA Cup Final, helping Newcastle United to a 2-0 victory over Aston Villa.

Earlier in the season, Billy Meredith of Manchester City had become the oldest player to appear in any round of the FA Cup when he played against Newcastle United at the age of 49 years and 8 months.

The manager of Huddersfield Town was Herbert Chapman, the man who had been banned for life after the Leeds City debacle in 1919.

Between the Wars

Facts

In winning the 1924 Home International Championship, Wales defeated all three other nations in the same season for the first time. They beat Scotland 2-0 in Cardiff, England 2-1 at Blackburn, and Ireland 1-0 in Belfast.

In their one home match, both captains – Fred Keenor of Wales and Jimmy Blair of Scotland – played for the club at whose ground the game was played: Cardiff City.

In the same tournament, England played their first international match at Wembley – they drew 1-1 with Scotland.

At the start of the 1923-24 season, the Scottish League was expanded again. A 16-club Third Division was introduced, and there was to be a two-up, two-down system of promotion and relegation.

The 16 new clubs in Scottish League Division Three were as follows: Arthurlie, Beith, Brechin City, Clackmannan, Dumbarton Harp, Dykehead, East Stirlingshire, Galston, Helensburgh, Mid-Annandale, Montrose, Nithsdale Wanderers, Peebles Rovers, Queen of the South, Royal Albert and Solway Star.

One of the 16, Clackmannan, was making a return to the League after having been forced to drop out at the end of the 1921 season.

At the start of the 1924-25 season, the FA made two important changes to the rules of football. One concerned corners – before now, the ball was not in play until it had been touched by a player other than the one who took the corner kick. But henceforth it would be in play from the moment it left the corner semi-circle and, as a result, it was now for the first time legal to score direct from a corner.

The other change the FA made was to the offside rule (Law 6), which since 1866 had read as follows:

Facts

Between the Wars

'When a player plays the ball, any player of the same side who at such moment of playing is nearer to his opponents' goal line is out of play and may not touch the ball himself nor in any way interfere with an opponent, or with the play, until the ball has again been played, unless there are at such moment of playing at least three of his opponents nearer their own goal-line'.

The FA's alteration to this rule was simply: 'From the first sentence of Law 6 delete the word "three" and substitute the word "two"'.

The above 16 words changed football for ever. The effects were apparent immediately – in the last season under the old rule, 4700 goals had been scored in the English Football League; in the first season under the new rule, that total increased to 6373.

The first English League player to score directly from a corner was Billy Smith, for Huddersfield Town against Arsenal on October 11, 1924.

In 1925-26, so many clubs in the Scottish Third Division got into financial difficulties that the League was suspended before the completion of the programme. The bottom club, Galston, played only 15 of their 30 scheduled matches and dropped out of the League for ever only two years after having joined it.

After leading Huddersfield Town to two League Championships in 1924 and 1925, Herbert Chapman moved south to manage Arsenal. His legacy to the Yorkshire team was still powerful, however, and they won the League again in 1926 under the managership of Cecil Potter.

Just before he left Huddersfield, Chapman bought outside right Alex Jackson from Aberdeen for £2500. He scored 16 goals in his first season in England, and made many more for centre forward George Brown, who finished the season with 35, a club record.

Between the Wars

Facts

Chapman quickly laid the foundations of Arsenal's future greatness. He persuaded club chairman Sir Henry Norris to buy inside forward Charlie Buchan from Sunderland.

Although Norris baulked at the asking price for Buchan of £4000, the two clubs made a deal in which the player moved for £2000 plus £100 per goal.

In his first season with Arsenal, Buchan scored exactly 20 goals – 19 in the League and one in the FA Cup, so Sunderland eventually got the amount they had originally asked for.

Norris was a property developer who first became involved with Arsenal in 1910 when they had gone into liquidation. One of his earliest plans for the club was a proposed merger with Fulham. When this failed to happen, he was influential in the club's move from Woolwich to their present home in Islington.

In 1919, when the Football League was expanded, Sir Henry Norris used his money to secure the Arsenal a place in the First Division which strictly they should not have had because they had finished only fifth in the Second Division in 1915.

Sir Henry Norris moved out of football in 1925 after being found guilty of financial irregularities, including the unauthorised use of a chauffeur. His team, by contrast, have never since been out of the First Division or the Premiership – a record.

In 1926, Manchester City became the first club to reach the FA Cup Final and be relegated in the same season.

In 1927, the FA Cup left England for the only time in its history when the trophy was won by Cardiff City. They beat Herbert Chapman's Arsenal 1-0 in the Final.

 **Facts**   **Between the Wars**

The year was a Cup double for Cardiff, who also won the Welsh Cup for the fifth time in their history.

On January 22, 1927, the League match between Arsenal and Sheffield United became the first to be broadcast live on radio.

While the BBC commentator described the action, another voice in the background called out numbers which referred to squares in a diagram of a football pitch printed in that week's *Radio Times*. After a goal was scored, the ball would be returned to the centre circle: this was square No 1 on the diagram, and this popularised the expression 'Back to square one'.

In the Home International Championship, England won at Hampden Park for the first time since 1904. Both England's goals were scored by Everton centre forward William Ralph Dean.

Dean was born in Birkenhead in 1907 and joined local club Tranmere Rovers in 1924. He moved to Everton in 1925, but his career was threatened when he fractured his skull in a motorbike accident.

Dean was almost universally known as Dixie because of his dark complexion (Dixieland – the American Deep South – was famous for its black slaves). The player himself hated the name.

In 1927-28, Dean scored 60 goals in 39 games for Everton in their Championship-winning season, a First Division record that has never been beaten.

One of the all-time greats, Dean scored 18 goals in only 16 appearances for England. In his League career, he scored 379 goals in 437 games.

As the table overleaf shows, Dean is the only England international ever to have scored more than a goal a game.

Between the Wars

Facts

England's Most Prolific Scorers

	Caps	Goals	Ratio
Dixie Dean	16	18	1.12
Tommy Lawton	23	22	0.96
Stan Mortensen	25	23	0.92
Nat Lofthouse	33	30	0.91
Jimmy Greaves	57	44	0.77
Gary Lineker	80	48	0.60
Geoff Hurst	49	24	0.49
Alan Shearer	38	18	0.47
Bobby Charlton	106	49	0.46
David Platt	62	27	0.43
Tom Finney	76	30	0.39

William Ralph Dean died in 1980 at Goodison Park after watching Everton play Liverpool.

On September 14, 1928, Jimmy McGrory set a Scottish First Division individual scoring record when he netted eight goals in Celtic's 9-0 victory over Dunfermline Athletic.

In 1927-28, Jim Smith of Ayr United in the Scottish Second Division set a British record of 66 goals in a season. This magnificent tally was run up in 38 matches.

Bathgate dropped out of the Scottish Second Division during the 1928-29 season and were not replaced, thus reducing the Scottish League from 40 clubs to 39.

Arthurlie, another Scottish Second Division club, resigned from the League with four matches unplayed. These were against Bo'ness, East Fife, Forfar Athletic and Stenhousemuir.

 **Facts** Between the Wars

Despite these troubles in the lower reaches of the League, top-grade Scottish football had never been healthier on the field. In March, the national side came to Wembley and beat England 5-1. Three of their goals were scored by Alex Jackson of Huddersfield Town. At 5 feet 7 inches in height, Jackson was the tallest of a Scottish forward line that also featured 'The Wee Blue Devil', Rangers' Alan Morton.

When Arsenal's Charlie Buchan retired at the end of the 1927-28 season, manager Herbert Chapman moved swiftly and replaced him with David Jack, an inside right whom he bought from Bolton Wanderers for a then British record transfer fee of £10,890.

On August 25, 1928, Arsenal and Chelsea became the first League clubs to wear numbered shirts.

On April 6, 1929, Jock Buchanan of Rangers became the first player to be sent off in a Cup Final as the Gers went down 2-0 to Kilmarnock.

On May 15, England suffered their first ever defeat on foreign soil, losing 4-3 to Spain in Madrid.

Bradford City won Division Three (North), scoring 128 goals in the process, a League record.

The Scottish League was reorganised again, for the 16th time since 1900, this time into two Divisions of 20 clubs each. As there had previously been 19 in the Second Division and Bathgate had resigned during the previous season, this created two vacancies. These were filled by Brechin City and Montrose.

Brechin City had been formed in 1906 through the amalgamation of the Angus clubs Hearts and Harp. Despite the new team's grand name, the town in which it played was – and remains – the smallest place in the British Isles with its own League football team.

Between the Wars

The British Isles were not represented at the inaugural World Cup because of a dispute over payments to amateur players to compensate them for the regular earnings they would have lost by playing football for their countries. FIFA demanded that players be paid for what was known as broken time. The home countries claimed that to make such payments would damage the game and in 1928 all four of them withdrew from both FIFA and from the Olympic football competition.

The first World Cup was staged in Uruguay in 1930. Thirteen nations took part: Argentina, Belgium, Bolivia, Brazil, Chile, France, Mexico, Paraguay, Peru, Romania, Uruguay, the USA and Yugoslavia.

Montrose, the other newcomers, were founded in 1879 and later merged with Montrose United. Nicknamed The Gable Endies, Montrose play their home matches at a ground called Links Park.

POSTWAR FOOTBALL

Postwar Football

Facts

The Second World War ended in August 1945. Although the Football League was not ready to restart in full until the 1946-47 season, the FA recommenced the Cup for 1945-46 on a two-leg, home-and-away basis.

The 1946 Cup campaign was marred by the Burnden Park disaster on March 9, when 33 people were crushed to death and more than 500 injured at Bolton Wanderers' sixth round match with Stoke City. The ground was full to its 65,000 capacity, but more than 20,000 other people were milling around outside. Many had turned up in the hope of catching a glimpse of Stoke star Stanley Matthews. They forced their way into the stadium shortly before kick-off, and the weight of the extra people caused a crash barrier to collapse.

In the aftermath of the tragedy, the Moelwyn Hughes Report recommended limitations on the size of crowds and the licensing of football grounds.

The FA Cup semi-final replay at Maine Road, Manchester, between Derby County and Birmingham City was watched by a crowd of 80,407, which remains the record attendance for a British midweek match at any venue other than Wembley.

This match was held in the afternoon, and the huge crowd it attracted alarmed the government who were concerned about the popularity of football leading to absenteeism from work. They quickly passed legislation to ensure that henceforth matches on working days should be evening kick-offs only.

After six years of War, many people were keen to make the best use of their leisure time and football became more popular than ever before. The greatly increased sums that League clubs were taking on the turnstiles did not, however, lead to an increase in the players' wages. This caused discontent and threats of strikes unless pay was increased from its pre-War ceiling of £8 a week. The threat of industrial action got a result of sorts – the players won an increase to £9 a week.

 **Facts**

Postwar Football

Bolton Wanderers eventually reached the semi-final of the 1946 FA Cup competition, in which they lost 2-0 to Charlton Athletic. The other semi-final was won by Derby County, who beat Birmingham City 5-1 on aggregate.

The 1946 FA Cup Final was held on April 27 at its now traditional Wembley venue. Derby County were favourites, not least because they had been greatly strengthened by the recent purchase of Raich Carter from Sunderland and Peter Doherty from Manchester City. Although they won – handsomely, in the end – they needed extra time and an own goal from Charlton's Herbert Turner to set them on their way.

A minute later, Turner equalised with a deflected goal for Charlton, thus becoming the first man to score for both teams in a Wembley Cup Final.

During the summer, Dynamo Moscow toured Britain. The Russians led a cloistered existence while they were abroad, eating all their meals at the Soviet Embassy in London and insisting that at least one of their matches be refereed by a Russian.

At the start of their first match, against Chelsea at Stamford Bridge, they presented their opponents with bunches of flowers. Then they drew 3-3 with the Londoners in front of 82,000 people.

In their next match, Dynamo Moscow beat Cardiff City 10-1, then returned to the capital for a game against Arsenal, who fielded Stanley Matthews and Stan Mortensen as guests. The match was played at White Hart Lane because Highbury was being rebuilt. In thick fog, the Russians won 4-3.

In their next game, the Russians drew 2-2 with Rangers. They were then slated to play an FA XI at Villa Park but flew home without notice before the kick off.

Postwar Football

Jack Stamps might have won the Cup for Derby in normal time, but his goal-bound effort was thwarted when the ball burst after he had kicked it and it was gathered easily by Charlton keeper Sam Bartram.

In extra time, Derby pulled away, with a goal from Doherty and two from Stamps – final score Derby County 4 Charlton Athletic 1.

The 1946 FA Cup was Derby County's first major honour since joining the Football League in 1888.

In Scotland, a new competition was launched in the 1945-46 season to herald the postwar era. However, the League Cup failed at first to attract a great deal of public interest.

The inaugural Scottish League Cup was won by Aberdeen, who beat Rangers 3-2 in the Final at Hampden. Aberdeen also won the FA Cup in the same year, thus becoming the first British club to do the so-called 'new double'.

At the start of the 1946-47 season, the Scottish League was re-formed again, now with 30 teams divided into Division 'A' of 16 and Division 'B' of 14. This was eight fewer teams than had competed in the Scottish League in 1939 – the clubs that had dropped out in the meantime were Brechin City, East Stirlingshire, Edinburgh City, Forfar Athletic, King's Park, Leith Athletic, Montrose and St Bernard's.

The first English Football League Champions of the postwar era were Liverpool – the 1947 title was the fifth in their history.

 **Facts**   **Postwar Football**

On October 3, 1946, Len Shackleton scored six goals on his debut for Second Division Newcastle United after his £13,000 transfer from Bradford Park Avenue. Newcastle went on to beat Newport County 13-0, despite missing a penalty in the second minute.

Newport County eventually conceded a total of 133 goals in the 42-match season and were relegated to the Third Division (South).

Charlton Athletic put last year's disappointment behind them by beating Burnley 1-0 in the 1947 FA Cup Final.

The winning goal was scored in extra time by Chris Duffy. The other incident of note in the match was that – for the second year running – the ball burst.

Doncaster Rovers had a record-breaking season as they won the Third Division (North) – the most wins (33), the most away wins (18), the most away points (37) and the highest points total (72) while there were two points for a win. They also had the League's leading scorer – Clarrie Jordan, with 42 goals in the season.

In 1946, the FAs of England, Northern Ireland, Scotland and Wales finally rejoined FIFA, from which they had withdrawn in 1928 because of a dispute over broken time. To celebrate their re-entry, the Home Nations played a Rest of Europe XI in an exhibition match in front of a crowd of 135,000 at Hampden Park, Glasgow.

Great Britain won the match 6-1, with three goals from Wilf Mannion, two from Tommy Lawton and one from Billy Steel.

The only player in the Rest of Europe XI with English as his native language was Johnny Carey of Manchester United and Eire.

Postwar Football

England centre forward Tommy Lawton moved from Everton to Chelsea after the War but never settled at the London club because of a contractual dispute. In 1947, he was sensationally transferred to Third Division Notts County for a record fee of £20,000 plus wing half Bill Dickson.

At the start of the 1947-48 season, the Scottish League was increased from 30 clubs to 32. The two teams added to Division 'B' were Leith Athletic – returning after a season's absence – and newcomers Stirling Albion.

Stirling Albion were founded in 1945 after the demise of King's Park, another club from the same town. King's Park had dropped out of the Scottish League in 1939; thereafter, they had been plagued by accusations of financial mismanagement and had their ground at Forthbank Park destroyed by German bombs during the War. Stirling Albion had a new ground at Annfield Park.

On January 17, 1948, a record First Division crowd of 83,260 watched Manchester United draw 1-1 with Arsenal. The match was played at United's temporary home, Maine Road.

Old Trafford had suffered greater bomb damage in the War than any other Football League ground – the Main Stand and some of the terraces had been destroyed in 1941 by two German bombs and the pitch itself had been scorched by the resulting inferno. The refurbished stadium did not open again until 1949.

On March 27, 1948, a crowd of 143,570 attended the Scottish FA Cup semi-final between Rangers and Hibernian at Hampden Park, Glasgow – this is a British attendance record for a match other than a cup final.

 **Facts**

Postwar Football

Arsenal won the 1948 Championship, leading the table from start to finish. They conceded only 32 goals (a First Division record) and more than 2,000,000 watched their games. This was their sixth title, bringing them level with Aston Villa and Sunderland.

The 1948 FA Cup was won by Manchester United, who beat Blackpool 4-2 in a classic Wembley Final.

Blackpool's Stan Mortensen scored in every round of the 1947-48 FA Cup, a total of 10 goals.

On May 4, 1949, a plane carrying the Torino team back from a testimonial game in Portugal against Benfica hit the Basilica of Superga, a village outside Turin. Among the 31 people killed in the crash were 18 footballers, including the entire Torino first team who made up most of the Italian national side.

Torino had been the dominant club in Italy throughout the 1940s, with five successive Championships and victory in the 1943 Italian Cup. In 1948, they had beaten Alessandria 10-0, the highest margin of victory in the history of Serie A.

The victims included Leslie Lievesely, their English manager, captain Valentino Mazzola and Ezio Loik.

After the crash, Torino fielded their youth team in the remaining four matches of the season and, as a mark of respect, their opponents fielded their youth teams against them. Torino won all these games and, with them, the Italian Championship.

Postwar Football

In 1948-49, the English League Championship was won for the first time by Portsmouth. Although they had not a single international player, Pompey were a formidable side with an unbeaten home record – in the 1948-49 season, they won 18 and drew three of their 21 matches at Fratton Park.

Portsmouth also had a good Cup run, but lost in the semi-final to unfancied Leicester City of the Second Division.

The 1948 FA Cup went to Wolverhampton Wanderers. They won the Final 3-1 against a Leicester side suffering from the absence through illness of their promising inside right Don Revie.

Wolverhampton Wanderers captain Billy Wright received the FA Cup from Princess Elizabeth.

 **Facts**   **Postwar Football**

The architect of the great Wolves sides of the period was their former centre half Stan Cullis, who had taken over as secretary manager in 1948 from Ted Vizard. The 1949 FA Cup was the start of the most successful period in the club's history, other highlights of which included three League Championships in 1954, 1958 and 1959, and a second FA Cup in 1960.

In 1948-49, Rangers became the first Scottish club to do the domestic treble of League Championship, FA Cup and League Cup.

On March 8, 1950, John Charles of Leeds United became Wales' youngest international when he played for them against Northern Ireland at Wrexham at the age of 18 years 71 days.

Portsmouth retained the League title in 1950, but only just. In 1949, they had romped home, five points ahead of runners-up Manchester United. This year, they needed to beat Aston Villa on the last day of the season to make sure. They won 5-1, making Wolverhampton Wanderers only the second team in League history to be denied the title by goal difference (1.95 against 1.55). The other was Cardiff City, who had been edged out by Huddersfield Town in 1924.

Postwar Football

Facts

1949-50 Top of the First Division Final Table

	P	W	D	L	F	A	Pts
Portsmouth	42	22	9	11	74	38	53
Wolverhampton Wanderers	42	20	13	9	76	49	53

Arsenal won the FA Cup without leaving London – even their semi-final was played at White Hart Lane because their opponents were fellow Londoners Chelsea.

Losing finalists Liverpool also had a local derby in the semi-finals, beating Everton 2-0.

Arsenal won the FA Cup Final 2-0, both goals being scored by Reg Lewis.

In Scotland, Rangers did the double and completed their second hat-trick of FA Cup wins. The only shadow over their season was defeat in the semi-finals of the League Cup by East Fife, the eventual winners of the trophy.

On September 21, 1949, the Republic of Ireland played their first international on British soil, beating England 2-0 at Goodison Park. They were captained by Johnny Carey of Manchester United, and their goals were scored by Con Martin of Leeds United from a penalty and Peter Farrell of Everton, who was playing for the visiting team on his home ground.

 **Facts**   Postwar Football

After a 12-year gap because of the Second World War, the fourth World
Cup was staged in Brazil in June and July 1950. Twelve nations took part –
Bolivia, Brazil, Chile, England, Italy, Mexico, Paraguay, Spain, Sweden,
Switzerland, Uruguay, the USA and Yugoslavia.

**Scotland could have gone to the 1950 World Cup Finals, too, but
declined to take part after losing to England in the Home
International in Glasgow. FIFA had promised the Home Nations
two places in the finals, but the Scottish FA announced that they
would go only as British Champions. They needed just a draw to
win the tournament, but lost 1-0 to England, whose goal was
scored by Roy Bentley of Chelsea.**

After the match, England captain Billy Wright and Scotland captain
George Young pleaded with the Scottish FA to reverse their decision, but
to no avail.

**West Germany were ineligible for the 1950 World Cup because
they were not yet members of FIFA.**

Scotland's place in the 1950 World Cup Finals was offered to Portugal, but
they turned it down.

**Turkey qualified for the 1950 World Cup Finals but then withdrew
– their place was offered to France, who accepted and then
changed their minds when they learned the proposed itinerary.**

India also withdrew from the 1950 World Cup Finals because they refused
to wear boots.

**Because of these withdrawals, the four South American qualifiers –
Bolivia, Brazil, Chile and Uruguay – made it through to the finals
without playing a match.**

Postwar Football

It had originally been thought that the finalists would be divided into four groups of four, but it was so late in the day when it became apparent that only 13 countries would be taking part that other arrangements could not be made – this created a lop-sided tournament with two groups of four, one group of three and one group of only two.

The finals began satisfactorily for England, who beat Chile 2-0 in their opening match with goals by Stan Mortensen and Wilf Mannion. There was little warning of the disaster to come.

The next match was one of the great humiliations in England's footballing history – they lost 1-0 to the USA. The winning goal was scored by Haitian-born Larry Gaetjens. Then they lost 1-0 to Spain and failed to progress beyond the group stage.

Instead of a dramatic knockout, the later stages of the 1950 World Cup were a pool of four countries – Brazil, Spain, Sweden and Uruguay. Brazil and Uruguay beat Sweden and Spain and then faced each other in the deciding match – effectively the Final. This was played at the Maracana Stadium, Rio de Janeiro, on July 16, 1950, in front of the largest crowd in football history – 173,830 people paid, but history books record a total attendance of 199,854.

1950 World Cup 'Final'

Brazil	1	Uruguay	2
Friaca		*Schiaffino, Ghiggia*	

BRAZIL: Barbosa, Augusto, Juvenal, Bauer, Danilo, Bogode, Friaca, Zizinho, Ademir, Jair, Chico
URUGUAY: Maspoli, Gonzales, Tejera, Gambetta, Varela, Andrade, Ghiggia, Perez, Miguez, Schiaffino, Moran.

 **Facts**   **Postwar Football**

**At the end of the match, the football World Cup – which had
newly been named The Jules Rimet Trophy in honour of the French
President of FIFA – was awarded to Obdullo Varela, the captain of
champions Uruguay.**

For the 1950-51 season, the English League was enlarged to 92 clubs by
increasing both the Third Division (North) and the Third Division (South)
from 22 to 24 clubs.

**The four new clubs thus admitted to the League for the first time
were Scunthorpe United and Shrewsbury Town to the Third
Division (North) and Colchester United and Gillingham to the
Third Division (South).**

Scunthorpe United had been founded in 1899. After entering the League,
they won the Third Division Championship in 1958. Their best season in the
Second Division was 1961-62, when they finished fourth.

**Shrewsbury Town had been founded in 1886 and had twice won
the Welsh Cup (1891 and 1938). After election to the English
League, they went on to win the Third Division Championship in
1979 and 1994, and have since added a further four Welsh Cup
victories – 1977, 1979, 1984 and 1985. In the FA Cup, they reached
the sixth round in 1979 and 1982.**

Colchester United were founded in 1937 as successors to amateur
Colchester Town. They lost their League status in 1990, after finishing
bottom of the Fourth Division, but returned in 1992 after winning the GM
Vauxhall Conference. The greatest moment in the club's history is probably
their victory over Leeds United in the fifth round of the FA Cup in 1971.
Colchester won 3-2, and had been 3-0 ahead. Seven members of the team
that achieved this great result were over 30 years of age, and it was thus
that they acquired the nickname 'Grandad's Army'. In the Football League,
Colchester United's best position was third in the Third Division (South)
in 1956-57.

Postwar Football

Facts

Gillingham were founded in 1893 in the wake of the success of another local club, the Royal Engineers. They started life as Excelsior, but in 1894 turned professional and changed their name to New Brompton. They took their present name in 1913. They first joined the Third Division in 1920, but dropped out in 1938 before returning in 1950. Their major League honour has been the Fourth Division Championship in 1964 – their run of 52 home matches without defeat was a record which was not broken until 1981, when Liverpool completed a run of 85 home games without defeat. Gillingham's best FA Cup performance came in 1970, when they reached the fifth round.

On November 15, 1950, Leslie Compton of Arsenal became the oldest British player in history to make his international debut when he played for England against Wales at the age of 38 years 2 months.

On December 13, 1950, Scotland lost for the first time at home to foreign opposition when they went down 1-0 to Austria.

On May 27, 1950, Billy Steel of Derby County became the first Scot to be sent off in an international. Scotland lost 4-0 to Austria in Vienna.

A father and son – Alec (39) and David Herd (17) – played in the same Stockport County team as they beat Hartlepool 2-0 on the last day of the 1950-51 season.

Tottenham Hotspur won the League Championship for the first time in the season after they were promoted from Division Two. Among the stars of their team were two great managers of the future – Alf Ramsey at right back and Bill Nicholson at right half.

 **Facts**   Postwar Football

Newcastle United won the FA Cup, beating Blackpool 2-0 in the Final. Both goals were scored by Jackie Milburn, and the match is often known simply as 'Milburn's Final'. Many commentators believed that the Seasiders lost this match because they were over-reliant on Stan Mortensen, who was the First Division's leading scorer with 30 goals. Other Blackpool stars of the period were Footballer of the Year Harry Johnson and the incomparable Stanley Matthews on the wing.

George Robledo, the maker of Milburn's first goal, had come to England as a refugee following the revolution in his native Chile. He made his name with Barnsley just after the Second World War and then Newcastle bought him and his brother Ted for £26,500. In his career at St James' Park, George scored 91 goals in 164 matches. When they retired, the pair returned to South America.

On September 19, 1951, Arsenal beat Hapoel Tel Aviv (Israel) 6-1 in the first official match under floodlighting since 1878. Floodlights had been built into the West Stand at Highbury in the 1930s on the orders of their great manager Herbert Chapman, but clubs had been banned from using them by the FA, which feared too much money might be spent.

Newcastle United won the FA Cup again in 1952, thus becoming the first club to retain the trophy in the 20th century.

The last club to win the FA Cup for two years in succession had been Blackburn Rovers (1890 and 1891).

Newcastle beat Arsenal 1-0 in the 1952 Final – the winning goal was scored by George Robledo.

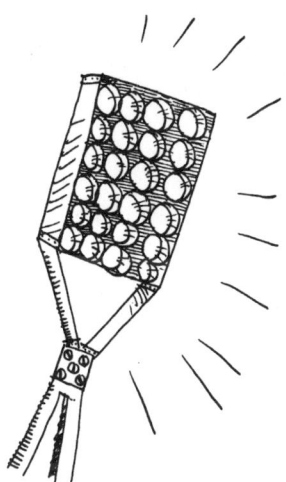

Postwar Football

George Robledo was also the First Division's leading scorer, with 33 goals in the 1951-52 season.

Arsenal were desperately unfortunate in this match – Ray Daniel played with a plaster cast on his broken wrist, Doug Lishman had a septic cut and Jimmy Logie an internal haemorrhage. During the game, Walley Barnes had to go off with a knee injury after half an hour, reducing the Londoners to 10 men.

Manchester United won the 1952 Championship after finishing second in four seasons out of the five since the end of the Second World War. It was the third League title in their history, but their first since 1911.

England and Austria drew 2-2 at Wembley on November 28, 1951. The visitors scored first through Melchior, who had been set up by Ernst Ocwirk, their great ball-playing centre half who was nicknamed 'Clockwork' by the British press. England equalised through a penalty by Alf Ramsey and took the lead seven minutes from time through Nat Lofthouse. Two minutes later, however, Stojaspal brought the Austrians back level with another penalty for handball.

 Facts

Postwar Football

On May 25, 1952, England beat Austria 3-2, thanks mainly to Nat Lofthouse, the Bolton Wanderers centre forward. He scored the first goal after 20 minutes, but Huber equalised almost immediately from a penalty after Froggatt had fouled Dienst. England regained their lead through Sewell of Sheffield Wednesday, then Dienst levelled again just before half time. Lofthouse scored the winner at the end of a 50-yard run, then went off injured but returned to help England hang on to their lead. Henceforth, Lofthouse was always popularly known as The Lion of Vienna.

The 1953 English Champions were Arsenal, winning their seventh League title – a record at the time. The race was very tight, and the Gunners only pipped Preston North End on the very last day of the season, when they beat Burnley 3-2 at home.

1952-53 Top of the First Division Final Table

	P	W	D	L	F	A	Pts
Arsenal	42	21	12	9	97	64	54
Preston North End	42	21	12	9	85	60	54

Arsenal and Preston North End were separated only by goal average – 1.51 against 1.41.

On September 24, 1952, Nat Lofthouse scored six goals for the Football League against the League of Ireland at Molineux – a record for this fixture.

Postwar Football

On Boxing Day, 1952, Sheffield Wednesday lost 5-4 at home to West Bromwich Albion and three of their players scored own goals. The unlucky trio were Vince Kenny, Norman Curtis and Eddie Gannon.

Sheffield Wednesday centre forward Derek Dooley broke a leg while challenging the Preston North End goalkeeper in a game on St Valentine's Day, 1953. The fracture turned gangrenous and had to be amputated. Dooley had scored 16 goals in 29 matches that season.

In the Scottish FA Cup on February 28, 1953, Celtic's Charlie Tully put the ball into the net direct from a corner against Falkirk. When the referee disallowed the goal because there had been spectators on the pitch, Tully put the ball in almost exactly the same spot – this time, the goal stood.

The great highlight of the 1952-53 season was the FA Cup Final between Blackpool and Bolton Wanderers. In the year of the accession of Queen Elizabeth II, it would probably be remembered as the Coronation Cup Final, but it is known as the Matthews Final because of the extraordinary performance of – and the nation's sentimental attachment to – one great man: Stanley Matthews.

Stanley Matthews had twice finished on the losing side in classic Cup Finals – in 1948, when Manchester United won and 1951, the year of Jackie Milburn.

Facts

Postwar Football

Bolton went 3-1 up after 55 minutes and it looked as if history was about to repeat itself. At the age of 38, it was almost certainly Matthews' last appearance at Wembley. But after 68 minutes Stan Mortensen scored his own and Blackpool's second as Matthews began to show the world why he was called the Wizard of Dribble.

Bolton held on until the last minute of normal time, when Mortensen became the only man to score a hat trick in the Cup Final, equalising from a free kick just outside the area.

In extra time, Matthews went on another run and set up the winner for Perry, who became the only South African to score in the English FA Cup Final. Final score: Blackpool 4 Bolton Wanderers 3.

Postwar Football

Facts

Stanley Matthews played until 1965, retiring at the age of 50. He played 54 times for England. He was knighted in 1965.

Rangers did the double in Scotland, but it was a close run thing in both competitions. In the FA Cup, they needed a replay to overcome Aberdeen. Three days after securing the Cup, they beat Dundee 3-1 in their penultimate League match – this left them needing at least a draw in their last game at Queen of the South. The Dumfries team led for much of the game, but thanks to a 75th minute equaliser by Willie Waddell, they finished level on points with Hibernian but took the title because of a greatly superior goal average – 2.05 against 1.82. (If the Championship had been decided on goal difference, the Edinburgh team would have won it.)

1953-54 Top of the Scottish Division 'A' Final Table

	P	W	D	L	F	A	Pts
Rangers	30	18	7	5	80	39	43
Hibernian	30	19	5	6	93	51	43

Since Willie Struth took over as manager in 1920, Rangers had won 18 Championships, 10 FA Cups and three League Cups.

In 1953-54, a new force emerged in English football as Wolverhampton Wanderers won the Championship for the first time in their history. Founder members of the Football League and twice winners of the FA Cup in 1893 and 1908, their history had been otherwise unremarkable. The arrival of Stan Cullis as manager in 1948 and the development of the new so-called 'kick and rush' style led Wolves to the pinnacle of achievement. They were English champions again in 1958 and 1959.

THE SIXTIES

The Sixties

Facts

The Sixties began with the launch of a new competition in England – the League Cup. Originally, both the semi-finals and the Final of this competition were on a two-legged basis.

The League Cup took a long time to establish itself, and in the first year five leading clubs – Arsenal, Sheffield Wednesday, Tottenham Hotspur, West Bromwich Albion and Wolverhampton Wanderers – all turned down invitations to take part.

The first winners of the League Cup were Aston Villa, who beat Second Division Rotherham United 3-2 on aggregate in the Final.

Tottenham Hotspur became the first team in the 20th century to win the League and FA Cup double. The feat had previously been achieved only twice – by Preston North End in 1889 and Aston Villa in 1897 – and the consensus had long been that the feat could never be repeated because of the higher level of competition and the greater number of fixtures – in 1897, there had been only 16 teams in the First Division; now there were 22.

But Spurs announced their intention of confounding the sceptics by kicking off the with 11 straight wins in the League. By the end of the season, they had scored 115 goals – the highest total since since Arsenal scored the same number in 1934-35 – and clocked up more wins (31) and more away wins (16) than any other team in First Division history. Spurs also equalled Arsenal's 1931 record number of points (66) under the two-points-for-a-win system.

 **Facts**   The Sixties

In the modern age of huge squads, it is remarkable to note how few players Tottenham called on throughout their greatest season. The 12 main contributors to their great triumphs were Bill Brown, Peter Baker, Ron Henry, Danny Blanchflower, Morris Norman, Dave Mackay, Cliff Jones, John White, Bobby Smith, Les Allen, Terry Dyson and Terry Medwin.

Spurs' leading scorers in their double year were Bobby Smith, with 28, and Les Allen with 23.

The First Division's leading scorer was Jimmy Greaves, with 41 goals for 12th-placed Chelsea. At 21, Greaves also became the youngest player to score 100 goals in English League football.

In the FA Cup Final, Spurs' opponents, Leicester City, were reduced to 10 men when their right back Len Chalmers had to go off injured after only 18 minutes. The rest of the team hung on grimly, however – outstanding in goal was a young keeper called Gordon Banks. The deadlock was not broken until midway through the second half when Bobby Smith scored for Spurs. Their second goal was scored by Terry Dyson.

After 12 previous unsuccessful applications, Peterborough United were finally elected to the Football League as replacements for Gateshead. They then won the Fourth Division at a canter, scoring 134 goals – a League record. An amazing 52 of them were scored by centre forward Terry Bly.

A threatened strike by members of the Professional Footballers' Association was called off at the last minute in January 1961 when the Football League abolished the £20-a-week maximum wage and agreed to scrap the standard contract which bound players to a club for life.

The Sixties

Facts

The PFA's spokesman and one of the main agitators for fairer terms of employment was Jimmy Hill, then an inside forward at Fulham, who later became chairman of Coventry City and afterwards took over his former club. Today, Hill is best known as a football pundit on BBC Television.

The agreement reached between the League and the PFA also headed off the threat of litigation by George Eastham, now of Arsenal, against his former club, Newcastle United, which he accused of restraint of trade when they refused to sell him. This case eventually dragged on until July 4, 1963.

After the abolition of the maximum wage, footballers' pay rose rapidly. The same season, Johnny Haynes of Fulham and England became the country's first £100-a-week player.

 **Facts**   The Sixties

Other players had moved to Italy in search of better wages. Among the most prominent were Joe Baker, who moved from Hibernian to Torino for £73,000; Denis Law, who had gone from Manchester City to Torino for £100,000; and Jimmy Greaves, sold by Chelsea to AC Milan for £80,000.

England won the 1961 Home International Championship with a hundred per cent record, beating Northern Ireland 5-2, Wales 5-1 and then Scotland 9-3 at Wembley on April 15. England's goals in this match were scored by Jimmy Greaves (3), Johnny Haynes (2), Bobby Smith (2), Bobby Robson of West Bromwich Albion and Bryan Douglas of Blackburn Rovers.

In Scotland, Rangers took the League and the League Cup, while Dunfermline Athletic won the FA Cup for the first time.

In the European Cup, Real Madrid finally lost a match after winning the trophy every year since the competition started in 1956. They were knocked put in the first round of the 1960-61 competition by fierce national rivals Barcelona.

Barcelona themselves were eventually beaten in the Final, 3-2 by Benfica, the Champions of Portugal.

English Champions Burnley reached the third round of the European Cup, where they took a 3-1 lead against Hamburg in the home leg at Turf Moor but lost the return in Germany 4-1.

The new competition in Europe was the Cup Winners' Cup. Britain's representatives met in the semi-final, where Rangers beat Wolverhampton Wanderers.

Rangers thus became the first British club to play in a major European final. In the only Cup Winners' Cup Final to be played over two legs, Rangers lost 4-1 on aggregate to Fiorentina of Italy.

The Sixties

Facts

Rangers had been greatly strengthened by the purchase from Raith Rovers in 1960 of Jim Baxter, who went on to play 34 times for Scotland.

In the third year of the Inter-Cities Fairs Cup, Birmingham City lost for the second time in the Final, beaten 4-2 on aggregate by Roma.

The 1961 Second Division Championship was won by Ipswich Town, managed by Alf Ramsey. Ramsey had taken over from Scott Duncan in 1955 and guided Ipswich to the Third Division (South) Championship in 1957.

In 1961-62, newly-promoted Ipswich Town won the League Championship in their first ever season in the First Division.

Their leading scorer – and the First Division's – was Ray Crawford, with 33 goals. Ted Phillips chipped in with another 28.

Ray Crawford played twice for England that season, against Northern Ireland and Austria.

Burnley were runners-up in both the League and the FA Cup, losing 3-1 in the Final to the holders, Tottenham Hotspur.

Burnley's leading players were Jimmy Adamson – voted Footballer of the Year 1962 – and Northern Ireland international inside forward Jimmy McIlroy, who had come second in the same Football Writers' poll.

Spurs were bolstered by the signing of Jimmy Greaves from AC Milan, after the former Chelsea forward had spent only a year in Italy. The fee was set at £99,999 because Spurs' manager Bill Nicholson did not want to saddle the player with the tag of 'the world's first £100,000 player'. Greaves started to repay the investment – a British transfer record – with a goal in the FA Cup Final.

 **Facts** The Sixties

Burnley's equaliser in this match – scored by Jimmy Robson – was the 100th goal in a Wembley Cup Final.

Spurs won the 1962 FA Cup Final 3-1. Bobby Smith scored their second and Danny Blanchflower clinched it with a late penalty.

Brian Clough – who had scored 197 goals in his 213 League games for Middlesbrough – moved to Sunderland for £45,000. He scored 29 goals in 34 matches for his new club, who missed promotion from the Second Division by a single point.

At the age of 46, Stanley Matthews left First Division Blackpool and went back to Second Division Stoke City for £2500. The local hero's return to the Potteries trebled home gate receipts.

On November 1, the Italian League beat the Scottish League 2-0 at Hampden Park. Outstanding for the visitors were a Welshman, an Englishman and a Scotsman – John Charles, Gerry Hitchens and Denis Law.

In the second League Cup Final, Second Division Norwich City beat Fourth Division Rochdale 4-0 on aggregate over two legs.

The 1962 Second Division Championship was won by Liverpool, who returned to the top flight for the first time since 1954.

Also promoted at the end of 1961-62 were Leyton Orient, for whom the following season would be their first taste of First Division football.

On March 6, 1962, financially beleaguered Accrington Stanley resigned from the Football League with debts of £60,000 and insufficient assets to continue trading. Their results to date that season were expunged from the Fourth Division record and their place in the League was taken the following season by Oxford United.

The Sixties

 **Facts**

Accrington Stanley's record at the time of their demise was as follows:

P	W	D	L	F	A	Pts
33	5	8	20	19	60	18

Accrington were founder members of the League, but they had had a chequered history. They had resigned from the League once before, in 1893, in the wake of accusations that they had paid one of their players. In 1896, they disbanded altogether. They pulled themselves together in the early years of the 20th century, however, and regained League status in 1921. Between the Wars, they regularly attracted crowds of about 20,000 and, in 1955, became one of the first clubs to have a match televised. Also in the 1950s, Accrington Stanley became the first English League club to field a side composed entirely of Scots.

Accrington Stanley's last ever match in the Football League was at Crewe Alexandra, where they lost 4-0.

Peel Park – Accrington Stanley's ground from 1919-1962 – is no more. In 1968, a new Accrington Stanley was founded – their home ground is at Livingstone Road and they play in the Northern Premier League.

In the Fourth Division, Wrexham (who won promotion this year) beat Hartlepools United (who had to apply for re-election) 10-1. Three of the Welsh side's players scored hat-tricks – Ron Barnes, Roy Ambler and Wyn Davies.

Reigning English Champions Tottenham Hotspur reached the semi-final of the 1962 European Cup, going down heroically to the Cup holders Benfica, 4-3 on aggregate.

Benfica went on to retain the European Cup, beating Real Madrid 5-3 in the 1962 Final. Hungarian star Ferenc Puskas scored a first-half hat-trick for the Spaniards, but the Portuguese Champions hit back with two goals from their emerging star, 20-year-old Eusebio.

 **Facts**   **The Sixties**

The 1962 European Cup Winners' Cup Final was held in Glasgow – Atletico Madrid drew 1-1 with Fiorentina. The replay in Stuttgart was won by the Spaniards 3-0.

The 1962 Final of the Inter-Cities Fairs Cup was an all-Spanish affair in which Valencia beat Barcelona 7-3 on aggregate.

Dundee won the Scottish League Championship for the first – and, to date, the only – time in their history. Their team included forward Alan Gilzean and defender Ian Ure, two players destined to go on to greater fame south of the border.

Gilzean was the season's leading scorer in the Scottish First Division, with 24 goals.

Rangers did a Cup double. Their 2-0 FA Cup Final victory over St Mirren was the 16th time they had won the trophy. The League Cup Final went to a replay when they drew 1-1 with Heart of Midlothian. But Rangers won the replay 3-1 to take the new Cup for the fourth time in its history.

Scotland recovered well from the fiasco of the previous year and won the Home International Championship handsomely with maximum points, beating Northern Ireland 6-1, Wales 2-0 and England 2-0. This was England's first defeat at Hampden Park for 25 years.

The 1962 World Cup Finals were held in Chile, a country that had not recovered after having been severely damaged by a series of devastating earthquakes in 1960. In fact, Chile was preferred to the other main candidates, Argentina, not despite the natural disasters that had befallen it, but because of them. As Chilean FA President Carlos Dittborn put it: 'We have nothing – that is why we must have the World Cup'.

The Sixties

Facts

Sixteen countries took part in the 1962 World Cup Finals: Argentina, Brazil, Bulgaria, Chile, Colombia, Czechoslovakia, England, Hungary, Italy, Mexico, Spain, Switzerland, Uruguay, the USSR, West Germany and Yugoslavia.

The 1962 tournament is remembered for all the wrong reasons – four players were sent off and four more broke limbs in the first eight matches.

The World Cup organising committee called the 16 national managers together and warned them not to let things degenerate. But the next group stage match – between Chile and Italy – was already charged with enormous ill-feeling, not least because of disparaging remarks made about conditions in the host country by Italian pressmen.

The match had only just begun when Chilean players began spitting at their Italian opponents. Chile's Leonel Sanchez punched Italy's Humberto Maschio and broke his nose, an assault seen clearly by most people in the stadium and millions on television, but missed by the linesman who was standing right next to the incident.

 **Facts**   The Sixties

Just before half time, Mario David of Italy was sent off by English referee Ken Aston for trying to kick Sanchez. This reduced Italy to nine men, and they duly lost the match 2-0. The game is often known as The Battle of Santiago.

The eight teams to qualify for the 1962 World Cup quarter finals were Brazil, Chile, Czechoslovakia, England, Hungary, Uruguay, West Germany and Yugoslavia.

England lost 3-1 to Brazil. The scorers were Garrincha (2) and Vava for Brazil, Gerry Hitchens for England.

In the semi-finals, Brazil beat Chile 4-2 in front of the biggest crowd of the tournament – 76,594 – while Czechoslovakia beat Yugoslavia 3-1 in front of the smallest – 6000.

The star of Brazil's defeat of the host country was again Garrincha, who made one of Vava's two goals and scored twice himself before being sent off for retaliation against kicking, spitting and virtually incessant verbal abuse.

Despite his dismissal, however, FIFA ruled that Garrincha would be permitted to play in the Final, which was held in the National Stadium, Santiago, on June 17, 1962 in front of a crowd of 68,679.

BRAZIL: **Gylmar, D. Santos, N. Santos, Zito, Mauro, Zozimo, Garrincha, Didi, Vava, Amarildo, Zagalo**

CZECHOSLOVAKIA: **Schroif, Tichy, Novak, Pluskal, Popluhar, Masopust, Pospichal, Scherer, Kadraba, Kvasnak, Jelinek**

Czechoslovakia went ahead with a goal by left half Masopust; Amarildo equalised for Brazil, then went ahead in the second half through Zito. In the 77th minute, Vava scored the killer goal after the Czech keeper had dropped an innocuous lob from D. Santos.

The Sixties

Facts

There were six leading scorers in the 1962 World Cup Finals, each with four goals – Albert (Hungary), Garrincha (Brazil), Ivanov (USSR), Jerkovic (Yugoslavia), Sanchez (Chile) and Vava (Brazil).

This was Brazil's second World Cup triumph, putting them level with Italy and Uruguay on number of trophies won.

At the end of the 1962 World Cup, England manager Walter Winterbottom announced his retirement. He was replaced on May 1, 1963, by the first ever full time manager – Alf Ramsey, who had led Ipswich to the League Championship earlier that year.

During the close season, Denis Law returned to England from Italy, purchased by Manchester United from Torino for £115,000.

Torino also sold Joe Baker, their acquisition from Hibernian, to Arsenal for £70,000.

On August 23, 1962, Fulham's England international Johnny Haynes suffered a serious knee injury in a car accident which caused him to miss the greater part of the following season and brought an end to his England career. Haynes played 56 times for his country between 1955 and 1962 and had been captain since 1960.

Everton won the 1962-63 Championship – their sixth league title altogether, but their first since 1939 – under the management of Harry Catterick.

Everton's leading scorers were captain Roy Vernon, with 24 goals, and centre forward Alex Young, with 22.

Their other outstanding player was Brian Labone. This strong and skilful centre half went on to play 26 times for England between 1963 and 1970, and would almost certainly have won many more caps had he not had Jack Charlton to compete with for his international place.

 **Facts**   The Sixties

Everton made two big signings in the early months of 1963 – right winger Alex Scott for £40,000 from Rangers and left half Tony Kay for £60,000 from Sheffield Wednesday. On June 5, Kay won his first England cap in their 8-1 defeat of Switzerland in Basel – he had the world at his feet, but two years later he was in jail.

The First Division's leading scorer was again Jimmy Greaves, who scored 37 goals for second-placed Tottenham Hotspur.

The winter of 1962-63 caused the worst disruption ever to the British football programme. Between December 22 and March 16, there was not one Saturday on which it was possible to play the complete programme of fixtures. On FA Cup third round day, only three of the scheduled 32 fixtures were played, and 14 of them were subsequently postponed at least 10 times. This led to an immense log-jam of fixtures – the third round was not completed until March 11.

Bolton Wanderers went the longest period without a match in the history of the English Football League – 70 days from December 8, 1962 to February 16, 1963.

It was during this big freeze that the pools companies first used the pools panel to predict results.

Tottenham Hotspur became the first British club to win a major European trophy when they beat Atletico Madrid 5-1 in the Cup Winners' Cup Final in Rotterdam. Their scorers on that great night were Jimmy Greaves (2), John White and Terry Dyson (2).

For his first match in charge of England – against France in the away leg of the European Nations' Cup first round – Alf Ramsey brought in only one new face, Ron Henry of Tottenham Hotspur. England lost 5-2 in Paris on February 27.

The Sixties

Facts

Manchester United won the FA Cup, beating Leicester City 3-1 in the Final with a goal from Denis Law and two from Alex Herd. This was Leicester City's third disappointment in the FA Cup at Wembley.

Stoke City were Champions of Division Two. Their inspiration throughout the season was Stanley Matthews, still the Wizard of Dribble despite his 48 years.

Birmingham City won the League Cup, beating Aston Villa 3-1 on aggregate in the Final. To date, this is the only major trophy in their history.

In Scotland, Rangers did the double. They finished nine points ahead of second-placed Kilmarnock in the League and beat Celtic 3-0 in the replayed FA Cup Final after the first match had been drawn 1-1.

Rangers' – and Scotland's – leading scorer was Jimmy Millar, with 27 goals.

The Scottish League Cup was won by Heart of Midlothian, who beat Kilmarnock 1-0 in the Final.

AC Milan won the 1963 European Cup, beating the holders, Benfica, 2-1 in the Final at Wembley.

AC Milan then went on to make a bid for the World Club Championship against the holders, Santos of Brazil, whose star player was the great Pele. Both legs were won 4-2 by the home team. This necessitated a play-off, which the Brazilians won 1-0.

Valencia became the second club to retain the Inter-Cities Fairs Cup, beating Dynamo Zagreb 4-1 on aggregate in the Final.

The Sixties

On July 4, 1963, in the High Court of England, sitting in judgment in the case of George Eastham v Newcastle United, Mr Justice Wilberforce ruled that Football League regulations concerning the retention and transfer of professional footballers were 'in unreasonable restraint of trade'.

1963-64 was the hundredth anniversary of the founding of the Football Association. To mark the centenary, an exhibition match was held at Wembley in which England defeated a Rest of the World XI featuring Eusebio, Denis Law, Ferenc Puskas, Alfredo di Stefano and Lev Yashin.

The celebrations were overshadowed by allegations in the Sunday newspaper, *The People*, that three Sheffield Wednesday players – Tony Kay, David 'Bronco' Layne and Peter Swan – had conspired to fix the result of their game at Ipswich Town in December 1962. The case eventually came to trial in January 1965.

Liverpool won the 1964 Championship, two years after being promoted from Division Two. This was their sixth League title and their first under the management of Bill Shankly.

Bill Shankly was born in 1919. His playing career started at Carlisle United and he then moved to Preston North End, where he won an FA Cup winner's medal in 1938, the same year as that in which he won all his five caps for Scotland.

The Sixties

Facts

Shankly became manager of his old club, Carlisle United, in 1949. He then had spells at Grimsby Town (1951-53), Workington (1953-56) and Huddersfield Town (1956-59) before taking over from Phil Taylor at Liverpool in 1959.

When Shankly arrived at Anfield, Liverpool were a Second Division club, having been relegated in 1954. The new manager built a new-style team around the nucleus of three outstanding players – Roger Hunt, Ian St John and Ron Yeats.

Roger Hunt was a goalscorer, with 245 goals in 401 professional matches. He was especially prolific in Liverpool's promotion year (1961-62), when he scored 42 goals in the season. He went on to win 34 England caps and a World Cup winner's medal.

Ian St John was a centre forward bought by Shankly for £37,500 from Motherwell in 1961. Highlights of his distinguished playing career included the winning goal for Liverpool in the 1965 FA Cup Final and 21 caps for Scotland. He is now a television soccer pundit.

Defender Ron Yeats was bought by Liverpool for £22,000 from Dundee United in 1961. Shankly was especially proud of this purchase, reportedly introducing him to the press with the words: 'He's a colossus – come outside and I'll give you a walk round him'. Yeats played twice for Scotland in 1965-66.

 **Facts** **The Sixties**

With 35 goals in the season for fourth-placed Tottenham Hotspur, Jimmy Greaves was the First Division's leading scorer for the fourth year out of five.

West Ham United won the FA Cup for the first time in their history, beating Preston North End 3-2 in a thrilling Final at Wembley. The London club were twice behind to goals by Holden and Dawson but they came back through John Sissons and Geoff Hurst and eventually won with a headed goal by Ron Boyce in injury time.

Sissons was only 18 at the time, but even younger was Howard Kendall of Preston who – at 17 years 345 days – became the youngest FA Cup finalist this century (in fact, since 1879).

The Hammers' Final victory came shortly after they had suffered their record defeat – 8-2 at home to Blackburn Rovers.

Leicester City won their first major honour, beating Stoke City 4-3 on aggregate in the League Cup Final.

In only their second season in the Football League, Oxford United became the first Fourth Division club to reach the sixth round of the FA Cup.

On November 20, 1963, England v Northern Ireland was the first match at Wembley to be played under floodlights. Although England won the game 8-3, the Home International title ended up as a three-way tie between both these countries and Scotland.

On April 25, 1964, Jim Fryatt of Bradford Park Avenue scored the fastest goal on record after only four seconds of the game against Tranmere Rovers.

The Sixties

 Facts

In Scotland, Rangers won the League, the FA Cup and the League Cup. Already the only club to have done the treble (in 1949), Rangers had now done it twice.

Kilmarnock were runners-up in the Scottish First Division for the second year running.

The European Cup stayed in Milan, but moved across town from AC to Inter, who beat Real Madrid 3-1 in the Final in Vienna.

The 1964 Cup-Winners' Cup Final went to a replay for the second time in its four-year history. Sporting Lisbon and MTK Budapest drew 3-3 after extra time in the first match in Brussels, so they reconvened in Antwerp, where the Portuguese side won 1-0.

The Inter-Cities Fairs Cup stayed in Spain, but moved from Valencia to Zaragoza, who beat the holders 2-1 in the Final in Barcelona. In a departure from established tradition, this Final was a one-off match.

On May 24, 1964, more than 318 people were killed and 500 seriously injured in Lima when riots broke out after Peru had an equalising goal disallowed in their Olympic qualifying match against Argentina. Police responded to the initial disturbance by firing into the air above the heads of the spectators, who panicked and caused a stampede.

Stanley Matthews was knighted in the Queen's 1965 New Year's list, the first footballer to be so honoured. Sir Stanley retired on February 6, five days after his 50th birthday. He went out on a winning note – in his final League match, Stoke City beat Fulham 3-1.

 **Facts**   The Sixties

Manchester United won the 1965 League Championship on goal average from Leeds United.

1964-65 Top of The First Division Final table

	P	W	D	L	F	A	Pts
Manchester United	42	26	9	7	89	39	61
Leeds United	42	26	9	7	83	39	61

Manchester United's goal average was 2.28; Leeds' was 2.12.

Leeds were also runners-up in the FA Cup, losing 2-1 to Liverpool after extra time in the Final. This was Liverpool's first FA Cup triumph.

The 1964 Final was goalless at full time. Liverpool then scored through Roger Hunt, but Billy Bremner equalised for Leeds. Then, with nine minutes left, Ian St John headed the Liverpool winner.

Following the match-fixing allegations made in *The People* newspaper the previous year, on January 26, 1965, at Nottingham Assizes, 10 professional footballers were sent to prison for periods of between four years and four months.

In April, all 10 men were banned from football for life by the FA.

The most prominent of those convicted were Dick Beattie, Jimmy Gauld, Tony Kay and Peter Swan.

Dick Beattie was a former Celtic and Scotland Under-23 goalkeeper who later played for Portsmouth and Peterborough United.

Jimmy Gauld played inside forward for Charlton Athletic, Everton, Plymouth Argyle, Swindon Town and Mansfield Town. It was he who had 'come clean' to the Sunday newspapers the previous April for £7000. He was sentenced to four years' imprisonment and ordered to pay £5000 costs.

The Sixties

Facts

Tony Kay and Peter Swan were England internationals. Their account of what had happened sounded more like naivete than conspiracy – they had simply put a small bet on Ipswich Town, to win at home against their own club, Sheffield Wednesday. They had in no way sought to throw the game – it was just that their opponents were the reigning League Champions and might have been expected to win an end-of-season game against visitors with little to play for.

At the end of the 1964-65 season, Jimmy Dickinson retired after playing 764 games at wing half for Portsmouth – his only club – in a career that began in 1946. He won two Championship medals, in 1949 and 1950, and played 48 times for England. Dickinson died in 1982 at the age of 57.

On July 21, 1965, John White, the Tottenham Hotspur inside forward, was killed at the age of 27 when he was struck by lightning while playing golf in Enfield, Middlesex. White was a member of the great Spurs double-winning side of 1961 and played 22 times for Scotland.

Arthur Rowley retired at the end of the season as player-manager of Shrewsbury Town. Rowley was the most prolific League scorer of all time, with 434 goals in a 619-match career. He scored four goals in 24 games for West Bromwich Albion, 27 goals in 56 games for Fulham, 251 goals in 303 games for Leicester City and 152 goals in 236 games for Shrewsbury Town.

1964 FA Cup winners West Ham United returned to Wembley a year later to beat Munich 1860 in the Final of the European Cup Winners' Cup. Both goals in their 2-0 victory were scored by newcomer Alan Sealey. This was the second time an English club had claimed a major European trophy.

 **Facts**

The Sixties

In the 1965 League Cup Final, Chelsea beat the holders, Leicester City, 3-2 on aggregate.

Jimmy Greaves was yet again the First Division's leading scorer, but this time he shared the accolade with Andy McEvoy of Blackburn Rovers, both players finishing with 29 goals.

In Scotland, it was third time lucky for Kilmarnock. After finishing in second place in 1962 and 1963, they finally took their first title by a whisker from Heart of Midlothian.

Scottish First Division 1964-65 Top of the Final Table

	P	W	D	L	F	A	Pts
Kilmarnock	34	22	6	6	62	33	50
Heart of Midlothian	34	22	6	6	90	49	50

The margin of Kilmarnock's dramatic last-day victory was one of the narrowest ever recorded: they needed to win their final game of the season by two clear goals away to Hearts themselves. And that is exactly what they did, edging out the Edinburgh club on goal average – 1.88 to 1.84 – a difference of 0.04.

The leading scorer in the Scottish First Division was Jim Forrest, with 30 goals for fifth-placed Rangers.

Celtic won the Scottish FA Cup, beating Dunfermline Athletic 3-2 in the Final.

Rangers won the Scottish League Cup, beating Celtic 2-1 in the Final.

Internazionale retained the European Cup, beating Benfica 1-0 in the Final in their home city, Milan.

The Sixties

Facts

For the second and last time to date, the Final of the Inter Cities Fairs Cup was played as a one-off, rather than over two legs, home and away. In it, Ferencvaros of Hungary beat Juventus of Italy 1-0 in the latter's home city, Turin.

In a change to the rules at the start of 1965-66, every League club was henceforth to be allowed one substitute, who could come on for an injured player. On the first day of the new season, Keith Peacock of Charlton Athletic became the first player to come on in this role.

Liverpool won the 1966 League Championship – their second title in three years and the seventh in their history, the same number as Arsenal.

The First Division's leading scorer was Liverpool's Roger Hunt, with 30 in the season.

On December 4, 1965, at Burnley, Frank Saul became the first Tottenham Hotspur player to be sent off in a League match since October 27, 1928.

Everton won the FA Cup for the third time, beating Sheffield Wednesday 3-2 in the 1966 Final. Wednesday went two up through Jim McCalliog and Dave Ford, but Everton hit back with two goals from 21-year-old Mike Trebilcock. Derek Temple scored the winner.

West Bromwich Albion won the 1966 League Cup, beating West Ham United 5-3 on aggregate in the Final.

Facts   **The Sixties**

On 20 March, 1966, the World Cup was stolen from a glass-fronted cabinet in Central Hall, Westminster, London, where it was being displayed in advance of the summer's finals in England. Shortly after the theft, the lid of the Jules Rimet trophy was sent to FA headquarters with a ransom demand. At the subsequent 'drop' a 47-year-old dock labourer was arrested, but the police failed to recapture the Cup itself. Then, a week after the robbery, David Corbett was walking his dog, Pickles, in Beulah Hill, Norwood, South London, when the black-and-white mongrel stopped to dig up a paper parcel that had been hidden under a bush. When the package was opened, it was found to contain the World Cup.

The Scottish Championship went back into the hands of the Old Firm, with Celtic winning their 21st League title.

Celtic also won the Scottish League Cup, beating Rangers 2-1 in the Final. Rangers' consolation was the FA Cup, which they won with a 1-0 win over Celtic in the Final replay after the first match had ended goalless.

The Sixties

Facts

Joint leading scorers in the Scottish First Division were Joe McBride of Celtic and Alex Ferguson of Dunfermline Athletic, both with 31 goals. (This Alex Ferguson is not the future manager of Aberdeen and Manchester United.)

After a six-year gap, Real Madrid recaptured the European Cup, beating Partizan Belgrade 2-1 in the Final in Brussels.

Borussia Dortmund won the Cup Winners' Cup, beating Liverpool 2-1 in the Final in Glasgow.

The Inter-Cities Fairs Cup stayed in Spain in 1966, as Barcelona beat Real Zaragoza 4-3 on aggregate in the Final.

The early rounds of the Inter-Cities Fairs Cup were overshadowed by foul play and controversy. In the first leg of the first round tie between Chelsea and Roma, Eddie McCreadie was sent off for retaliation. In the second leg, the English players were pelted with missiles outside the stadium.

Even worse, in the first round match between Leeds United and Torino, Bobby Collins had his thigh broken when tackled crudely by Poletti.

When Leeds United met Valencia in the third round, police were called onto the pitch to deal with fighting between the players, who were taken off by the referee for a 10-minute cooling-off period.

The 1966 World Cup Finals were held in England. The main stadium was, of course, Wembley; other matches were held at Ayresome Park (Middlesbrough's ground), Goodison Park (Everton) and Hillsborough (Sheffield Wednesday).

The 16 countries that took part were as follows: Argentina, Brazil, Bulgaria, Chile, England, France, Hungary, Italy, Mexico, North Korea, Portugal, Spain, Switzerland, Uruguay, the USSR and West Germany.

Facts

The Sixties

The opening match of the tournament on July 11 between the hosts, England, and Uruguay, was a goalless draw.

The first goal of the tournament was scored by Pele in the group match between Brazil and Bulgaria. He played little further part in the World Cup, however – he was treated so roughly by the Bulgarian defence that he was not fit for the next game against Hungary. Brazil lost this match 3-1, their first defeat in the World Cup since the so-called Battle of Berne against Hungary in 1954.

Pele returned for the final group match against Portugal. Brazil needed to win to remain in the competition, but Eusebio played brilliantly and the Portuguese defence chopped Pele at every opportunity. Result: Portugal 3 Brazil 1, and the holders were out.

England's first goal of the tournament was scored by Bobby Charlton in their second group match, a 2-0 victory over Mexico.

During England's third group match – a 2-0 victory over France – Manchester United half back Nobby Stiles committed an ugly-looking challenge which, despite not being considered a foul by the match referee, moved the FA council to request the withdrawal of the player from the following match. Manager Alf Ramsey replied that he would pick the team he wanted or resign at once. Stiles kept his place in the side.

The Sixties

 Facts

The surprise package of the 1966 World Cup Finals group stages were North Korea, who eliminated Italy with a 1-0 victory at Ayresome Park. The winning goal was scored by Pak Doo Ik.

The eight teams in the 1966 World Cup quarter final line-up were Argentina, England, Hungary, North Korea, Portugal, Uruguay, the USSR and West Germany.

In their quarter final match, North Korea went 3-0 up against Portugal before four goals from Eusebio – two of them penalties – enabled the European nation to come through 5-3.

Meanwhile, the workmanlike USSR edged past Hungary 2-1.

In England's quarter final match against Argentina, the visiting captain, Antonio Rattin, became the first player to be sent off in a World Cup Finals tournament. He carried on arguing for eight minutes after the referee had pointed to the tunnel. England won the match 1-0, thanks to a Hurst header after 77 minutes.

West Germany won their quarter final 4-0 against Uruguay, who had two men sent off.

Both England's goals in their 2-1 semi-final victory over Portugal were scored by Bobby Charlton.

In the other semi-final, West Germany defeated the USSR 2-1.

The 1966 World Cup Final was held at Wembley on July 30, 1966 in front of a crowd of 93,000.

ENGLAND: Banks, Cohen, Wilson, Stiles, J. Charlton, Moore, Ball, Hurst, Hunt, R. Charlton, Peters

WEST GERMANY: Tilkowski, Hottges, Schnellinger, Beckenbauer, Schulz, Weber, Held, Haller, Seeler, Overath, Emmerich

 **Facts**

West Germany opened the scoring after 13 minutes through Haller, but Hurst equalised on 19 minutes with a header from Moore's free kick. After 78 minutes, England went took the lead through Peters. The Cup looked like England's, but Weber equalised in the dying seconds of normal time.

In extra time, Ball pulled the ball back to the edge of the six-yard box, where Hurst kicked the ball past the West German keeper and onto the crossbar. Almost everyone has an opinion about what happened next, but no one is sure whether the ball then crossed the line or bounced slightly in front of it. Nevertheless, there were only two people in the world whose opinions on the subject mattered – the Russian linesman, Tofik Bakhramov, and the Swiss referee Gottfried Dienst. The former gave a goal and the latter upheld his decision – 3-2 to England.

In the last minute of extra time, Moore sent a long clearance through to Hurst, who ran alone from the half way line to score a conclusive final goal moments before the final whistle.

The Sixties

Facts

Leading scorer in the 1966 World Cup Finals was Eusebio, with nine goals for Portugal.

In 1966-67, Manchester United won the League Championship for the seventh time in their history, thus equalling the record jointly held at the time by Arsenal and Liverpool.

The First Division's leading scorer was Ron Davies, with 37 goals for 19th-placed Southampton.

The first all-London FA Cup Final was between Tottenham Hotspur and Chelsea. Spurs won 2-1, with goals from Jimmy Robertson and Frank Saul. Chelsea replied through Bobby Tambling four minutes from the end.

It was Spurs' third FA Cup of the 1960s. None of the 1961 double-winning side remained, and there were only two players from their previous Cup victory in 1962 – Jimmy Greaves and Dave Mackay.

The format of the League Cup Final was changed from a two-legged, home and away affair to a one-off showcase match at Wembley.

On March 4, 1967, a crowd of 97,952 saw Third Division Queen's Park Rangers win the League Cup at Wembley by coming back from two goals down to beat First Division West Bromwich Albion 3-2.

Both West Brom's goals were scored in the first half by ex-QPR winger Clive Clark. Then, after 63 minutes, Roger Morgan put Rangers back into contention and after 75 minutes the Londoners equalised through a solo effort by the mercurial Rodney Marsh. The winner – scored by Mark Lazarus – was controversial because the chance came after QPR centre half Ron Hunt had bundled into West Brom keeper Dick Sheppard.

Despite their League Cup triumph, QPR were not allowed to enter the Inter Cities Fairs Cup because the European competition was open only to members of the First Division.

 **Facts**   **The Sixties**

In the first ever six-figure transfer between British clubs, World Cup winner Alan Ball was transferred from Blackpool to Everton for £110,000.

World Cup winning manager Alf Ramsey was knighted in the 1967 New Year's Honours List.

In addition to winning the 1967 Home International Championship, on April 15, Scotland had the extra thrill of becoming the first team to beat the new world champions England, winning 3-2 at Wembley.

In 1967, the club side that stood head and shoulders above everyone else in the northern hemisphere was Celtic, who made a clean sweep of the European Cup, the Scottish League Championship, the Scottish FA Cup, the Scottish League Cup and the Glasgow Cup.

Celtic became the first British team to win the European Cup, with a 2-1 victory over Inter Milan in the Final in Lisbon.

Inter Milan went a goal up after eight minutes from a Mazzola penalty. Thereafter they sat back and soaked up everything the Scots could throw at them.

Inter Milan were the world's leading exponents of a defensive formation known as *catenaccio* (the Italian for 'door bolt').

The rest of the match was wave after wave of Celtic pressure which was all absorbed by the Inter defence until their attacking left back Tommy Gemmell hit the equaliser from 25 yards out after 63 minutes.

Eight minutes from time, Gemmell again advanced down the left, pushed the ball inside to Bobby Murdoch who drove the ball into the area where Steve Chalmers deflected it into the Italian goal for the winner.

The Sixties

Club chairman Robert Kelly acclaimed the European Cup winners as the greatest Celtic team of all time. They are popularly known as The Lions of Lisbon.

Bobby Murdoch's 1967 European Cup Final winner was Celtic's 200th goal of the season.

Of Celtic's other goals, 111 had come in the Scottish League, which they won finishing three points ahead of second-placed Rangers. Twenty-one of these goals were scored by Scotland's leading marksman, Steve Chalmers.

Scottish Footballer of the Year was Ronnie Simpson, the veteran Celtic goalkeeper.

Rangers were also runners-up to Celtic in the Scottish League Cup Final. The two sides were separated on this occasion by a single goal from Bobby Lennox.

In the Scottish FA Cup, Celtic beat Aberdeen 2-0 in the Final, with two goals from Wallace.

In one of the greatest upsets in Cup history, Rangers had been knocked out of the Scottish FA Cup in the first round by Berwick Rangers. Berwick's goal was scored by Sammy Reid after 32 minutes – thereafter, the Glasgow Rangers were held at bay by Berwick's goalkeeper-manager Jock Wallace.

Although Rangers reached the Final of the Cup Winners' Cup, they lost 1-0 in extra time to Bayern Munich.

In the Final of the Inter Cities Fairs Cup, Dynamo Zagreb beat Leeds United 2-0 on aggregate over two legs.

A new rule was introduced at the start of the 1967-68 season – goalkeepers were restricted to four steps before they had to release the ball.

 **Facts**   **The Sixties**

The season began spectacularly on August 12, when Tottenham Hotspur goalkeeper Pat Jennings scored in the Charity Shield against Manchester United with a punt that bounced on the edge of the opposition penalty area and over the head of United keeper Alex Stepney. The match ended 3-3.

The existing British transfer record – Alan Ball's £110,000 move from Blackpool to Everton the previous year – was broken twice this season. First in January, when Martin Chivers went from Southampton to Tottenham Hotspur for £125,000, and again in June, when Leicester City bough Allan Clarke from Fulham for £150,000.

The League Championship stayed in Manchester, but moved across town from United to City. This was City's second title – they had previously won it in 1937.

Much of the credit for Manchester City's achievement went to manager Joe Mercer, the former Everton, Arsenal and England player who had been lured out of retirement to take the helm at Maine Road in 1965, when the club languished in the wrong half of Division Two.

Within a week of taking over, Mercer signed as coach and assistant manager the former Charlton and West Ham player Malcolm Allison. Under the pair of them City won promotion back to the First Division in 1966.

Among the great Mercer-Allison signings were Colin Bell from Bury for £45,000, Francis Lee from Bolton Wanderers for £60,000 and Mike Summerbee from Swindon Town for £35,000.

Tony Book, the Championship-winning Manchester City captain and right back, had been signed at the age of 29 for £13,500 from Plymouth Argyle.

The joint top scorers in the First Division were George Best of Manchester United and Ron Davies of Southampton, both with 28 goals.

The Sixties

Facts

Fulham finished bottom of the First Division and were relegated. Since winning promotion in 1959, they had become the League's perennial escapologists – they never finished higher than 10th in the First Division, and were 20th – one place above the drop – three times, in 1962, 1965 and 1966.

Peterborough United were relegated from the Third Division after having had 19 points deducted for offering illegal bonuses to their players.

West Bromwich Albion won their fifth FA Cup on their record-breaking 10th appearance in the Final, beating Everton 1-0 after extra time through a goal by Jeff Astle, who had scored in every round of that season's competition.

Leeds United won the 1968 League Cup, beating Arsenal 1-0 in the Final at Wembley.

In Scotland, Celtic retained the Championship – indeed, they lost only once in the League all season, a 1-0 defeat by Rangers.

Celtic also kept the League Cup, beating Dundee 5-3 in the Final.

The Scottish FA Cup went to Dunfermline Athletic for the second time in their history. They beat Heart of Midlothian 3-1 in the Final.

At the start of the 1967-68 season, the Scottish League was enlarged from 37 to 38 clubs by the admission of Clydebank.

On entry into the Scottish Second Division, Clydebank took the unusual decision not to have a manager, making do with a coach.

THE SEVENTIES

The Seventies

In 1971, Arsenal became only the second club this century – after fierce local rivals Tottenham Hotspur – to win the League and FA Cup double.

Arsenal's manager was Bertie Mee, their captain Frank McLintock.

Runners-up were Leeds United – their 64 points in the season was the highest number of points that had ever failed to secure the Championship.

Fifth-placed Liverpool conceded only 24 goals in the 1970-71 season – an all-time low.

The First Division's leading scorer was Tony Brown, with 28 goals for 17th-placed West Bromwich Albion.

In the FA Cup Final, Arsenal beat Liverpool 2-1 after extra time. Liverpool went ahead with a goal from Steve Heighway, and then Eddie Kelly became the first substitute ever to score in an FA Cup Final. The winner came eight minutes from time – scorer Charlie George.

Among the giant-killers in this season's FA Cup were Barnet – then a non-League club – who beat Fourth Division Newport County 6-1.

 **Facts**   **The Seventies**

Tottenham Hotspur won the League Cup. They beat Aston Villa 2-0 in the Final, both their goals being scored by Martin Chivers, their record signing from Southampton in 1968.

The season was a disaster for the 'Bs' of Lancashire – Burnley and Blackpool were relegated from the First Division, Blackpool after only a year back in it; Blackburn Rovers and Bolton Wanderers – founder members of the League – were relegated to the Third Division for the first time in their histories.

North of the border, Celtic did the League and FA Cup double for the third time in five seasons. Their – and Scotland's – leading scorer was Harry Hood, with 22 goals in the season.

Rangers prevented Celtic from doing the treble by beating them 1-0 in the Final of the Scottish League Cup. It was five years since Rangers had won a trophy – their last success had been in the 1966 FA Cup Final. This was the longest barren period in their history.

This season, the Scottish League introduced goal difference instead of goal average as a means of separating teams level on points.

Ajax of Amsterdam won the European Cup for the first time, beating Greek League Champions Panathinaikos 2-0 in the Final at Wembley.

Chelsea won the Cup Winners' Cup, beating Real Madrid 2-1 after extra time in the Final replay after the first match had been drawn 1-1. Peter Osgood scored in both games; Chelsea's other goal came from John Dempsey. Both games were played in Athens.

In the semi-final of the Cup Winners' Cup, Chelsea had eliminated the holders, Manchester City, 1-0 on aggregate.

The Seventies

Leeds United finally won a trophy – the Inter-Cities Fairs Cup for the second time. They drew with Juventus 3-3 in the Final, but took the Cup on away goals after their 2-2 draw in the first leg in Turin.

This was the last season of the Inter-Cities Fairs Cup. The following year it was replaced by the UEFA Cup. It was also the fourth year running that it had been won by an English club.

The 1972 English First Division Championship was won by Derby County, the first League title in their history.

Derby had finished the 1966-67 season in 17th place in Division Two. But then Brian Clough and Peter Taylor took over the management of the club and the upturn in their fortunes began. They won the Second Division Championship in 1969, then came fourth in the First Division in 1970 and ninth in 1971.

The First Division's leading scorer was Francis Lee of Manchester City. Of his 33 League goals, 13 were penalties – an all-time record. Many of these spot kicks were the result of fouls on the player himself – this gave rise to his Oriental-sounding nickname Lee Won Pen.

 **Facts**
                                    The Seventies

Leeds United won the 100th FA Cup, beating the holders, Arsenal, 1-0 in the Final with a goal from Allan Clarke.

Arsenal reached Wembley the hard way – for the second season running, they did not have a single home draw in the competition.

FA Cup giantkillers of the season were Hereford United – then still a non-League club – who drew 2-2 with First Division Newcastle United at St James' Park and then beat them 2-1 at Edgar Street with goals from Ronnie Radford and Ricky George.

Leeds were again runners-up in the First Division. This was despite having been ordered to play their first four home matches away from Elland Road – a punishment for a pitch invasion in April.

This was the year in which Leeds almost bought Asa Hartford from West Bromwich Albion, but pulled out of the deal after a medical examination revealed that the player had a hole in his heart. Despite this condition, Hartford went on to play with great distinction for several clubs, including Manchester City – where he won two League Cup winner's medals – and 50 times for Scotland.

Stoke City won the League Cup – the first trophy in their history – beating Chelsea 2-1 in the Final at Wembley. Their goals were scored by Terry Conroy and veteran George Eastham, aged 35. Chelsea's goal was scored by Peter Osgood.

The great match of the season's League Cup was Stoke's epic semi-final against West Ham United. Stoke lost the first leg 2-1 but levelled the tie at Upton Park. Then, with three minutes of extra time remaining, Stoke's England keeper Gordon Banks saved a penalty from Geoff Hurst.

The Seventies

Facts

The first West Ham v Stoke play-off, at Hillsborough, ended goalless, so a second replay was held at Old Trafford. West Ham's keeper Bobby Ferguson was hurt in this match and had to leave the field. His place in goal was taken by captain Bobby Moore, who saved a penalty, but Mike Bernard scored from the rebound.

West Ham plugged on with 10 men – they expected Ferguson to return – and took the lead with goals by Billy Bonds and Trevor Brooking. But Stoke equalised through Peter Dobing and scored the winner shortly after half time through Terry Conroy.

In Scotland, Celtic again did the double. They won the League Championship by 10 points from second-placed Aberdeen and beat Hibernian 6-1 in the Final of the FA Cup.

Surprisingly, however, Celtic were beaten 4-1 in the League Cup Final by unfancied Partick Thistle. This was only Thistle's second trophy – their previous triumph had been in the 1921 FA Cup.

Partick Thistle's goals came in the first 37 minutes through Alex Rae, Bobby Lawrie, Denis McQuade and Jimmy Bone. Celtic's reply was scored by Kenny Dalglish.

Ajax Amsterdam retained the European Cup, beating Inter Milan 2-0 in the Final in Rotterdam. Star of the match was European Footballer of the Year Johan Cruyff.

Rangers won the Cup Winners' Cup, for which they had only qualified as losing FA Cup finalists because Celtic did the double and went into the European Cup. They beat Moscow Dynamo 3-2 in the Final in Barcelona, with one goal from Colin Stein and two from Willie Johnston.

Rangers never defended their trophy. The match was marred by pitch invasions by their fans, and as a result the club was banned from European competition for a year.

 **Facts**

The Seventies

The first UEFA Cup Final was an all-England affair, Tottenham Hotspur beating Wolverhampton Wanderers 3-2 on aggregate. They won the first leg at Molineux 2-1, with two goals by Martin Chivers. Wolves' scorer was Jim McCalliog. At White Hart Lane, Alan Mullery increased the London club's lead, but David Wagstaffe equalised for Wolves. Spurs thus became the first English club to win two different European trophies – they had lifted the Cup Winners' Cup in 1963.

In the European Championship, England were eliminated by West Germany after losing 3-1 at Wembley. The German star was Gunter Netzer, who scored from a penalty and set up two goals for Gerd Muller. In the second leg, although England brought in Norman Hunter to neutralise Netzer, they could only draw 0-0 and were knocked out.

The semi-finals and Final of the 1972 European Championship were held in Belgium. West Germany beat the hosts 2-1, while in the other match the USSR beat Hungary 1-0.

The Final was held in Brussels on June 18, 1972. West Germany beat the USSR 3-0 with another two goals from Muller and one from Wimmer.

In 1973, Liverpool won the League Championship for a record eighth time.

The First Division's leading scorer was Bryan 'Pop' Robson, with 28 goals for West Ham United.

The Champions of all four Divisions of the Football League came from Lancashire – Liverpool won the First Division, Burnley the Second, Bolton Wanderers the Third and Southport the Fourth.

The Seventies

Facts

Sunderland became the first Second Division side to win the FA Cup since West Bromwich Albion in 1931 when they beat Leeds United 1-0 in the Final at Wembley with a goal from Ian Porterfield. Thereafter, Jim Montgomery held Leeds at bay almost singlehandedly with a magnificent display in goal.

Tottenham Hotspur won the League Cup, beating Norwich City 1-0 in the Final. Spurs' winner was scored by Ralph Coates.

In May 1973, Derby County bought Leicester City full back David Nish for £225,000, a British record transfer fee.

Huddersfield Town – three times League Champions – were relegated to the Third Division for the first time in their history.

In Scotland, Celtic won the League Championship and finished runners-up in both the Cups.

Rangers took the Scottish FA Cup in their centenary year, beating Celtic 3-2 in the Final with goals from Parlane, Conn and Forsyth. Celtic opened the scoring through Dalglish, and later brought the game back to 2-2 with a penalty scored by Scottish Footballer of the Year George Connelly.

Hibernian won the Scottish League Cup, beating Celtic 2-1 in the Final.

Ajax of Amsterdam won the European Cup for the third year in succession, beating Juventus 1-0 in the Final in Belgrade.

AC Milan won the Cup Winners' Cup, beating Leeds United 1-0 in the Final in Salonika. Yet again, Leeds finished empty-handed a season that had promised so much – they had nearly won the League, but finished third, lost in the FA Cup Final to unfancied opposition, and now this defeat by an Italian team they outplayed for much of the match.

 **Facts**   The Seventies

Liverpool won the 1973 UEFA Cup, beating Borussia Moenchengladbach 3-2 on aggregate in the Final.

Leeds United won the League Championship in 1974 for the second time in their history. At the start of the season, they went 23 matches without defeat – a record.

Promotion and relegation changed from two- to three-up and down between the First and Second and the Second and Third Divisions. The first club to be relegated from the First Division after finishing 20th out of 22 was Southampton.

The First Division's leading scorer was Mike Channon, with 21 goals for relegated Southampton.

Manchester United finished 21st (next to last) and were relegated – they had been in the First Division since 1938. Their final match was at home to local rivals Manchester City – they lost 1-0, and the goal was scored by ex-United hero Denis Law. Shortly afterwards, a massive pitch invasion led the referee to abandon the match on the advice of police, but the result stood.

In his first season as a manager, England World Cup hero Jack Charlton guided Middlesbrough to the Second Division Championship, thus getting them back into the top flight for the first time since 1954.

On September 22, 1973, three Notts County players missed the same penalty in their Second Division match against Portsmouth at Fratton Park.

The Eagles of Crystal Palace went into a free fall, as they were relegated from the First to the Third Division of the League in successive seasons.

The Seventies

Facts

Fourth Division Exeter City unilaterally cancelled their League match against Scunthorpe United because they had nine players unfit. In doing this, they risked expulsion from the League, but escaped with a fine of £5000 and two points (the League awarded the game to Scunthorpe).

League runners-up Liverpool won the FA Cup, beating Newcastle United 3-0 in the Final. Their goals were scored by Kevin Keegan (2) and Steve Heighway.

At 11 o'clock on the morning of January 6, 1974, professional football was played on Sunday in England for the first time – Cambridge United drew 2-2 with Oldham Athletic in the third round of the FA Cup.

Wolverhampton Wanderers won the League Cup Final, beating Manchester City 2-1 in the Final.

Plymouth Argyle of the Third Division reached the League Cup semi-finals. En route, they beat three First Division clubs away – Burnley, Queen's Park Rangers and Birmingham City – before losing 3-1 on aggregate to Manchester City, the eventual runners-up.

Celtic won the Scottish Championship for the ninth year in a row. They also did the double, beating Dundee United 3-0 in the Final of the Scottish FA Cup.

Celtic's – and the Scottish First Division's – leading scorer was Dixie Deans, with 24 goals.

Dundee won the Scottish League Cup was won by Dundee, who beat Celtic 1-0 in the Final.

In the first European Cup Final to require a replay, Bayern Munich eventually beat Atletico Madrid 4-1 after the first match had been drawn 1-1. Both games were played in Brussels.

 **Facts**   **The Seventies**

Feyenoord of Rotterdam made it a double Dutch Cup celebration when they beat Tottenham Hotspur 4-2 on aggregate in the Final of the UEFA Cup. The second leg was marred by Spurs fans who rioted in the stadium and had to be dispersed by Dutch police.

FC Magdeburg of East Germany won the Cup Winners' Cup, beating AC Milan 2-0 in the Final in Rotterdam.

On September 26, 1973, Trevor Hockey of Aston Villa became the first Welsh player to be sent off in an international during his country's 3-0 defeat by Poland in Katowice in the World Cup qualifying match.

England were knocked out of the World Cup when they finished behind Poland in their qualifying group. The killer blow came when the Poles came to Wembley and went ahead through Domarski who shot under Peter Shilton's body after 58 minutes. The rest of the match was sustained England pressure, and although they salvaged a draw with a penalty from Allan Clarke, the home team were denied the win they needed by Polish keeper Jan Tomaszewski, memorably – but inaccurately – described by Brian Clough on television as 'a clown'.

In the aftermath of England's failure to reach the World Cup Finals, the FA sacked Sir Alf Ramsey. Of their 113 matches under Ramsey, England had won 69 and drawn 27 and one of these victories had been their greatest triumph – the 1966 World Cup Final. There was widespread distaste that, given his distinguished record, Sir Alf had not been given the opportunity to resign.

Sir Alf Ramsey was replaced by Joe Mercer, who took over as England caretaker-manager while a long-term successor was sought.

Three days before the opening ceremony of the 1974 World Cup Finals, Brazilian Joao Havelange replaced Sir Stanley Rous as President of FIFA.

The Seventies

The 1974 World Cup Finals were held in West Germany. The 16 qualifying nations were Argentina, Australia, Brazil, Bulgaria, Chile, East Germany, Haiti, Holland, Italy, Poland, Scotland, Sweden, Uruguay, West Germany, Yugoslavia and Zaire.

In a departure from the practice in previous tournaments, goal difference was brought in for the first time to separate teams equal on points in the qualifying groups.

In another change to previous formats, the top two teams in each of the four qualifying groups were to progress into two more groups of four – the winners of these two groups would contest the Final, which would thus become the only true knockout match in the entire tournament.

Scotland went out in the group stage, but only because they scored one goal fewer than Brazil against Zaire. Quite how close they came to reaching the second stage may be seen from the Group Two Final Table:

	P	W	D	L	F	A	Pts
Yugoslavia	3	1	2	0	10	1	4
Brazil	3	1	2	0	3	0	4
Scotland	3	1	2	0	3	1	4
Zaire	3	0	0	3	0	14	0

The shock of round one was the 1-0 defeat of hosts and favourites West Germany by their neighbours East Germany.

Poland – who had been regarded as no-hopers, even after they had qualified at England's expense – won Group Four at a canter, with maximum points against Argentina, Italy and Haiti. They eventually finished third in the tournament and had the two leading scorers – Grzegorz Lato with seven goals and Andrzej Szarmach with five.

 **Facts**

The Seventies

In the second round, Group A contained Argentina, Brazil, East Germany and Holland; in Group B were Poland, Sweden, West Germany and Yugoslavia.

The winners of these groups were West Germany and Holland, each with hundred per cent records.

The 1974 World Cup Final was played at the Olympic Stadium, Munich, on July 7, 1974, before a crowd of 77,833.

West Germany: Maier, Vogts, Schwarzenbeck, Beckenbauer, Breitner, Hoeness, Bonhof, Overath, Grabowski, Muller, Holzenbein

Holland: Jongbloed, Suurbier, Rijsbergen (sub: De Jong), Haan, Krol, Jansen, Neeskens, Van Hanegem, Rep, Cruyff, Rensenbrink (sub: R. Van Der Kerkhof)

Holland scored before a German had touched the ball when Uli Hoeness fouled Johann Cruyff inside the penalty area and Johan Neeskens scored from the spot.

This was the first penalty in a World Cup Final. The referee who awarded it was Englishman Jack Taylor.

The second penalty In a World Cup Final came less than 25 minutes later. This time, it went to West Germany after Holzenbein had been fouled in the box. Paul Breitner took the spot kick and made the score 1-1.

Two minutes before half-time, Bonhof fed Gerd Muller in the area – he swivelled and scored what turned out to be the World Cup-winning goal for West Germany.

The Seventies

Facts

The 1974-75 season began with the unprecedented spectacle of a double sending-off in the Charity Shield match between last year's Champions Leeds United and the FA Cup winners Liverpool. The two to get their marching orders for fighting were no less than the international stars Billy Bremner and Kevin Keegan – the first Britons ever to be sent off at Wembley. They were later fined £500 each and banned for what turned out to be 11 matches.

Derby County won the League Championship for the second time in four years, this time under the management of Dave Mackay.

Brian Clough and Peter Taylor had quit Derby after the former had refused to accept an ultimatum from the club that he stop writing for the newspapers and appearing on television. Derby chairman Sam Longston was particularly concerned about Clough's accusation that some of his own players were giving less than one hundred per cent.

The First Division's leading scorer in 1974-75 was Malcolm Macdonald, with 21 goals for Newcastle United.

Malcolm Macdonald also became the only player to score five goals in a Wembley international when England beat Cyprus 5-0 in the European Championships.

Manchester United came straight back up, winning the Second Division Championship at their first attempt.

West Ham United won the FA Cup in 1975, beating Fulham 2-0 in the Final. Both their Wembley goals were scored by Alan Taylor.

 **Facts** The Seventies

Taylor – purchased from Rochdale shortly before Christmas – had also scored two goals for West Ham in the sixth round versus Arsenal and in the semi-final replay versus Ipswich Town.

Playing for Fulham in that Final was West Ham's former captain and greatest legend – Bobby Moore.

The 1975 League Cup was won by Aston Villa, who beat Norwich City 1-0 in the Final. This was Norwich's second defeat at Wembley in this competition – they had been beaten by Spurs in the 1973 Final.

For Villa manager Ron Saunders, it was third time lucky – this was his third consecutive match in charge of a League Cup finalist, but on the two previous occasions he had seen his team lose – with Manchester City in 1974 and the year before with Norwich.

In Scotland, Celtic's great run of victories came to an end after nine League titles in a row – Rangers won their first title since 1964.

The joint leading scorers in the Scottish First Division were Andy Gray of Dundee United and Willie Pettigrew of Motherwell, each with 20 goals.

Celtic won the 1975 Scottish FA Cup, beating Airdrieonians 3-1 in the Final, which was European Cup-winning captain Billy McNeill's swansong for the club as a player.

The League Cup also went to Celtic, who beat Hibernian 6-3 in the Final.

The Seventies

Facts

Bayern Munich won the European Cup for the second year running, beating Leeds United 2-0 in the Final in Paris. The English Champions were incredibly unlucky in this match – they had two legitimate-looking penalty appeals against Beckenbauer turned down by French referee Kitabdjian, and a second-half goal by Peter Lorimer disallowed for offside. The Leeds fans rioted. There have since been strong and persistent rumours that the result was somehow fixed.

In an all-Eastern European Final, Dynamo Kiev of the USSR beat Ferencvaros of Hungary 2-0 to win the Cup Winners' Cup.

Borussia Moenchengladbach (West Germany) won the UEFA Cup, beating Twente Enschede (Holland) 5-1 on aggregate in the Final.

On July 4, 1974, the FA announced the appointment of Leeds United boss Don Revie as Sir Alf Ramsey's permanent successor as England manager.

Revie was succeeded at Leeds by Brian Clough, the man who had taken Derby County to their first League title and then taken over at Brighton and Hove Albion. He lasted only 43 days in the post, unable to make an impact on the well-established cliques among the senior players in the Leeds dressing room.

During the 1974-75 season, three England international players went absent without leave – Kevin Keegan, Stan Bowles and Kevin Beattie.

After 15 years in charge at Anfield, Bill Shankly announced that he was stepping down as manager of Liverpool. Under him, Liverpool won the Second Division in 1962, the League Championship in 1964, 1966 and 1973, the FA Cup in 1965 and 1974, and the UEFA Cup in 1973.

 **Facts**   **The Seventies**

Bill Nicholson, for 38 years a Tottenham Hotspur employee and their manager since 1958, also announced his retirement. He gave as his reason the unreasonable demands and expectations of modern players. Under Nicholson, Spurs had won the double in 1961, two more FA Cups in 1962 and 1967, the Cup Winners' Cup in 1963 and the UEFA Cup in 1972.

In 1975-76, Liverpool won the League Championship for a record ninth time and the first time under Bob Paisley in his first season as manager in succession to Bill Shankly. They pipped Queen's Park Rangers to the title by a single point.

The First Division's leading scorer in 1975-76 was Ted MacDougall, with 23 goals for 16th-placed Norwich City.

Second Division Southampton won the 1976 FA Cup – the first major honour in their history – beating the favourites Manchester United 1-0 in the Final. The winning goal was scored by Bobby Stokes.

Manchester City won the League Cup for the second time, beating Newcastle United 2-1 in the Final. Peter Barnes and Denis Tueart scored for the winners; Alan Gowling replied for the Magpies.

In Scotland, the League was reorganised yet again. The two old Divisions – the First of 18 clubs the Second of 20 – were changed into a Premier League of 10 clubs and a First and Second Division, each of 14 clubs.

Rangers did the treble, winning the League, the Cup and the League Cup. They retained the Championship and thus became the first winners of the new Premier League. They beat Heart of Midlothian 3-1 in the FA Cup Final and Celtic 1-0 in the League Cup Final.

The leading scorer in the Scottish Premier Division was Kenny Dalglish, with 24 goals for Celtic.

The Seventies

Facts

Bayern Munich won the European Cup for the third time running, beating St Etienne of France 1-0 in the Final.

Anderlecht of Belgium won the Cup Winners' Cup, beating West Ham United 4-2 in the Final in Brussels.

West Ham United came close to repeating their 1965 Cup Winners' Cup triumph. They went ahead with a goal from Pat Holland and were on top until Frank Lampard injured himself while trying to pass back to keeper Mervyn Day – the ball fell short and Dutch international Robbie Rensenbrink scored easily. In the second half, Anderlecht took the lead with a goal from François Van Der Elst, but West Ham got back on level terms with a goal from 'Pop' Robson. But after that, Anderlecht took charge – Holland brought down Rensenbrink, who scored from the penalty spot, and then Van der Elst broke through on his own, rounded the West Ham right back and keeper and scored a brilliant individual clinching goal.

League Champions Liverpool did a unique double by also winning the UEFA Cup, beating FC Bruges of Belgium 4-3 on aggregate in the Final. This was Liverpool's second UEFA Cup in four years.

The semi-finals and Final of the 1976 European Championship were held in Yugoslavia. In the semi-finals, Czechoslovakia beat Holland 3-1 and West Germany beat Yugoslavia 4-2.

The Final between Czechoslovakia and West Germany, the holders and World Champions, was played in Belgrade on June 20, 1976, in front of 45,000 spectators. The Czechs went two up with goals from Svehlik and Dobias; the Germans pulled one back through Dieter Muller and equalised through Holzenbein in the dying seconds of normal time. The score remained unchanged at the end of extra time and the Championship had to be decided on a penalty shoot-out, which the Czechs won 5-3.

 **Facts**

At the start of the 1976-77 season, the English Football League abolished goal average – from now on, teams equal on points would be separated by goal difference (the number of goals they had conceded subtracted from the number of goals they had scored).

1976-77 was the first League season in which yellow and red cards replaced (respectively) the notebook and the finger pointed towards the tunnel.

Liverpool retained the League Championship, a point ahead of Manchester City in second place.

Joint leading scorers with 25 in the First Division were Malcolm Macdonald, formerly of Newcastle United but now of eighth-placed Arsenal, and Andy Gray of fourth-placed Aston Villa.

Manchester United won the FA Cup, beating Liverpool 2-1 in the Final. Stuart Pearson scored the first, Jimmy Case equalised for Liverpool and then Jimmy Greenhoff scored the winner with a fluke as he tried to get out of the way of a shot from Lou Macari.

Aston Villa won the League Cup after a marathon Final against Everton. The first match finished 0-0, the replay was 1-1 after extra time. The second replay went to extra time before Villa clinched it 3-2, with two goals from Brian Little and another by Chris Nicholl. Everton's replies came from Bob Latchford and Mick Lyons.

Terry Paine of Southampton retired at the end of the season after 824 League appearances – a record.

Bobby Moore – now of Fulham, but famously of West Ham and England – retired at the end of his 1000th first class match on May 14 at Blackburn.

The Seventies

Facts

After finishing bottom of the Fourth Division for the second year running – and next to bottom in both previous seasons – Workington failed to win re-election. Their place in the Football League was taken by Wimbledon.

In Scotland, Celtic did the double. They won the Premier Division by nine points from second-placed Rangers and beat the same club 1-0 in the Final of the FA Cup.

Celtic's dreams of another treble were shattered by a 2-1 defeat by Aberdeen in the Final of the League Cup.

Liverpool more than made up for their FA Cup Final disappointment by beating Borussia Moenchengladbach 3-1 in the European Cup Final in Rome. Their goals were scored by Terry McDermott, Tommy Smith and Phil Neal (penalty). The German team's replay was scored by Danish international Allan Simonsen.

SV Hamburg won the Cup Winners' Cup, beating the holders Anderlecht 2-0 in the Final in Amsterdam.

Hamburg captured another prize at the end of the season – they bought Kevin Keegan from Liverpool for £500,000.

Juventus won the UEFA Cup on away goals after drawing 2-2 on aggregate in the Final with Athletic Bilbao.

Scotland won the Home International Championship and Wales won at Wembley for the first time in their history.

 **Facts**   The Seventies

After three years in which the national team won only 14 times in 29 internationals, Don Revie resigned as England manager on July 12, 1977, and took a £60,000-a-year job as coach to the United Arab Emirates.

In July 1977, former West Ham manager Ron Greenwood took over from Revie as England manager. The appointment was temporary at first, but was soon extended to the end of the 1980 European Championship.

In his first match in charge – a 0-0 draw against Switzerland at Wembley on September 7 – Greenwood picked six Liverpool players plus a seventh – Kevin Keegan – who had been at the club until the end of last season. This was the highest number of players from a single club to represent England since seven Arsenal players took the field against Italy on November 14, 1934 – the notorious match that became known as The Battle of Highbury.

Shortly after selling Kevin Keegan to Hamburg, on August 10, 1977, Liverpool spent £400,000 on a replacement – 27-year-old Kenny Dalglish of Celtic.

Tommy Docherty was sacked as manager of Manchester United only six weeks after leading them to victory in the FA Cup Final because of tabloid revelations about his love affair with the wife of Laurie Brown, the Old Trafford club's physiotherapist .

Scotland qualified for the World Cup Finals in Argentina with a 2-0 victory over Wales in a play-off at neutral Anfield. The first goal was scored by Don Masson from a penalty which television replays showed should not have been awarded – the handler was not a Welshman but Scotland's Joe Jordan. The clincher was scored after 87 minutes by Kenny Dalglish with a header.

Liverpool were denied a third consecutive League title by Nottingham Forest, who won the Championship in their first season back in the First Division.

The Seventies

Facts

Among Forest's stars were goalkeeper Peter Shilton – the club's record £250,000 buy from Stoke City – and defender Kenny Burns, a player with a reputation as a wild man whom manager Brian Clough bought from Birmingham City for £150,000 and promptly made club captain. At the end of the season, Shilton was voted the PFA Player of the year; Burns won the Football Writers' award.

Having won the League with Derby County in 1972, Brian Clough now became only the second manager to lead two different clubs to the English Championship – the other was Herbert Chapman, who won it with Huddersfield Town and Arsenal in the 1930s.

Leading scorer in the First Division was Bob Latchford, with 30 goals for third-placed Everton.

On February 9, 1978, Manchester United bought Scottish international defender Gordon McQueen from Leeds United for a British record fee of £495,000.

Nottingham Forest did the so-called 'New Double' by winning the League Cup as well as the League. They drew 0-0 with Liverpool after extra time in the Wembley Final and then scraped home 1-0 in the replay at Old Trafford with a penalty by John Robertson.

In both the Final matches, Forest's goalkeeper was Chris Woods, who played because first choice Peter Shilton was Cup-tied.

Ipswich Town won the 1978 FA Cup, beating Arsenal 1-0 in the Final with a goal by Roger Osborne.

In Scotland, Rangers did the treble for the second time in three seasons. They won the League by two points from runners-up Aberdeen, beat them again in the FA Cup Final, by two goals to one, and beat Celtic 2-1 after extra time in the League Cup Final.

 **Facts**   The Seventies

Rangers' – and the Scottish First Division's – leading scorer was Derek Johnstone, with 25 goals.

Liverpool retained the European Cup, beating FC Bruges in the Final at Wembley. The only goal of the game was scored in the 66th minute by Kenny Dalglish.

Anderlecht made it two Cup Winners' Cups in three years, beating Austria/WAC 4-0 in the Final in Paris.

PSV Eindhoven of Holland won the UEFA Cup, beating Bastia of France 3-0 on aggregate in the Final.

The 1978 World Cup Finals were held in Argentina. The 16 qualifying nations were Argentina, Austria, Brazil, France, Holland, Hungary, Iran, Italy, Mexico, Peru, Poland, Scotland, Spain, Sweden, Tunisia and West Germany.

Scotland – Britain's only representatives in Argentina – had been enormously hyped in the build-up to the finals, especially by their manager, Ally MacLeod. This made their performance all the more of a let-down – they lost their opening group match 3-1 to Peru and then almost guaranteed elimination by managing only a 1-1 draw with widely unfancied Iran. In between these matches, Willie Johnston failed a drugs test and was sent home in disgrace.

The Seventies

Facts

The Scots almost retrieved the situation with a 3-1 victory in their final group match against Holland. This was a magnificent performance, which owed much to Graeme Souness and Archie Gemmill, but it was too little, too late.

The eight nations who went through to the second round of the finals were Argentina, Austria, Brazil, Holland, Italy, Peru, Poland and West Germany.

Holland won Group A, beating Austria and Italy and drawing with West Germany, the holders.

Argentina won Group B, with victories over Poland and Peru and a draw with Brazil.

The 1978 World Cup Final was held in the River Plate Stadium, Buenos Aires on June 25, 1978 in front of a crowd of 77,260.

Argentina: Fillol, Olguin, Galvan, Passarella, Tarantini, Ardiles (sub: Larrosa), Gallego, Kempes, Bertoni, Luque, Ortiz (sub: Houseman)

Holland: Jongbloed, Poortvliet, Krol, Brandts, Jansen (sub: Suurbier), Neeskens, Haan, W. Van Der Kerkhof, R. Van Der Kerkhof, Rep (Sub: Nanninga), Rensenbrink

Mario Kempes, the tournament's leading scorer, put Argentina ahead after 38 minutes, but Holland equalised after 82 minutes through a header from Dirk Manninga, who had come on as substitute for Johnny Rep. Argentina pulled away in extra time, with another goal from Kempes and a clincher from Ricardo Bertoni after 115 minutes.

Just over a fortnight after winning the 1978 World Cup, two of Argentina's squad were signed by Tottenham Hotspur. Osvaldo Ardiles and Riccardo Villa came from Huracan and Racing Club respectively for a combined total of £750,000. The deal was brokered on Spurs' behalf by Sheffield United manager Harry Haslam.

 **Facts** The Seventies

Liverpool regained the League Championship, eight points ahead of last year's title-winners Nottingham Forest in second place. Their points total – 68- was a new record for the 22-club First Division under two points for a win. They also conceded only 16 goals in the season – an all-time low.

When Forest lost 2-0 at Liverpool on December 9, 1978, it was their first League defeat in 42 matches over one year and 13 days – the longest unbeaten run in the history of the Football League.

The First Division's leading scorer in 1978-79 was Frank Worthington of 17th-placed Bolton Wanderers.

Nottingham Forest had the consolation of retaining the League Cup, beating Southampton 3-2 in the 1979 Final. Forest's Wembley goals came from Garry Birtles (2) and Tony Woodcock; Southampton replied through David Peach and Nick Holmes.

Arsenal won the 1979 FA Cup, beating Manchester United 3-2 in one of the most exciting Finals for years. They went ahead in the first half with a goal by Brian Talbot, but then United scored twice in two minutes through Gordon McQueen and Sammy McIlroy. With a minute to go, Frank Stapleton levelled the scores again. Then, just as the crowd was preparing for extra time, Liam Brady broke down the left for Arsenal, then passed to Graham Rix who centred for Alan Sunderland to score the winner.

In Scotland, Celtic won the League Championship, finishing three points ahead of Rangers in second place.

Rangers did a Cup double. They won the Scottish FA Cup – beating Hibernian 3-2 in a second Final replay after the first two matches had ended goalless – and the League Cup with a 2-1 victory in the Final over Aberdeen.

The Seventies

Facts

The Scots almost retrieved the situation with a 3-1 victory in their final group match against Holland. This was a magnificent performance, which owed much to Graeme Souness and Archie Gemmill, but it was too little, too late.

The eight nations who went through to the second round of the finals were Argentina, Austria, Brazil, Holland, Italy, Peru, Poland and West Germany.

Holland won Group A, beating Austria and Italy and drawing with West Germany, the holders.

Argentina won Group B, with victories over Poland and Peru and a draw with Brazil.

The 1978 World Cup Final was held in the River Plate Stadium, Buenos Aires on June 25, 1978 in front of a crowd of 77,260.

ARGENTINA: Fillol, Olguin, Galvan, Passarella, Tarantini, Ardiles (sub: Larrosa), Gallego, Kempes, Bertoni, Luque, Ortiz (sub: Houseman)

HOLLAND: Jongbloed, Poortvliet, Krol, Brandts, Jansen (sub: Suurbier), Neeskens, Haan, W. Van Der Kerkhof, R. Van Der Kerkhof, Rep (Sub: Nanninga), Rensenbrink

Mario Kempes, the tournament's leading scorer, put Argentina ahead after 38 minutes, but Holland equalised after 82 minutes through a header from Dirk Manninga, who had come on as substitute for Johnny Rep. Argentina pulled away in extra time, with another goal from Kempes and a clincher from Ricardo Bertoni after 115 minutes.

Just over a fortnight after winning the 1978 World Cup, two of Argentina's squad were signed by Tottenham Hotspur. Osvaldo Ardiles and Riccardo Villa came from Huracan and Racing Club respectively for a combined total of £750,000. The deal was brokered on Spurs' behalf by Sheffield United manager Harry Haslam.

THE EIGHTIES

The Eighties

In 1980-81, the FA stopped the red and yellow card system that had been introduced in 1976.

In 1981, Aston Villa won the League Championship for the seventh time in their history but the first time since 1910. They used only 14 players throughout the 42-match season.

With 20 goals apiece, joint leading scorers in the First Division were Steve Archibald of Tottenham Hotspur and Peter Withe of Aston Villa.

When they lost 2-1 at home to Leicester City on January 31, 1981, Liverpool suffered their first defeat at Anfield for three years and 10 days (85 matches in all competitions).

Tottenham Hotspur won the FA Cup for the sixth time in their history, beating Manchester City 3-2 in a replay after the first match – the 100th FA Cup Final – had finished 1-1 after extra time. In the first Final, City's Tommy Hutchison had scored for both sides – but not, as he has since been quick to point out to anyone who uses the wrong phrase, at both ends – his goal for City came in the first half and his own goal was scored in the second.

The hero of the replay – again held at Wembley – was Argentine Ricardo Villa, who had been substituted in the first match. He scored twice for Spurs, the second time after a fantastic dribble through a crowded City penalty area. Spurs' other goal was scored by Garth Crooks; City's goals came from Steve Mackenzie and a Kevin Reeves penalty.

Liverpool won the League Cup – the only domestic trophy that had previously eluded them – beating Second Division West Ham United 2-1 in a replay at Villa Park after the Wembley Final had ended 1-1 after extra time.

 **Facts**   **The Eighties**

Liverpool regained the European Cup in 1981 after a two-year gap, beating Real Madrid in the Final in Paris with a goal by Alan Kennedy. This was Liverpool's third triumph in the competition and the fifth time running that the Cup had been won by an English club. One of the stars of the Real Madrid team was England international Laurie Cunningham.

Dynamo Tbilisi of the USSR won the Cup Winners' Cup, beating Carl Zeiss Jena of East Germany 2-1 in the Final in Dusseldorf.

In the second round of the Cup Winners' Cup, West Ham United had been forced to play the second leg of their match against Castilla of Spain behind closed doors after crowd trouble during the first match in Madrid.

Ipswich Town won the UEFA Cup, beating AZ 67 Alkmaar of Holland 5-4 on aggregate in the Final.

John Trollope of Swindon Town retired in November shortly after setting a new record for the number of League appearances for a single club – 770 since 1960. The previous record-holder had been Jimmy Dickinson, who played 764 games for Portsmouth between 1946 and 1965.

Celtic won the Scottish Premier Division – their 32nd League Championship. Their forward Frank McGarvey was the leading scorer, with 23 goals.

Rangers won the FA Cup, beating Dundee United 4-1 in a Final replay after the first match had ended goalless.

Dundee United retained the League Cup, beating Dundee 3-0 in the Final.

At the start of the 1981-82 season, the English Football League instituted three points for a win.

The Eighties

Facts

Second Division Queen's Park Rangers became the first English League club to install a plastic pitch. The material used was marketed under the name Omniturf.

The English transfer market boomed – enormous fees were paid for Justin Fashanu, who moved from Norwich City to Nottingham Forest for £1 million, Trevor Francis (£1.2 million from Nottingham Forest to Manchester City) and Frank Stapleton (Arsenal to Manchester United for £1.1 million). The biggest of the lot, however, was Bryan Robson, whose £1.7 million move from West Bromwich Albion to Manchester United was a new British record.

Liverpool won the League Championship for a record 13th time – their fifth title in seven seasons.

Liverpool also retained the League Cup (now renamed the Milk Cup), beating Tottenham Hotspur 3-1 after extra time in the 1982 Final. Their goals came from Ronnie Whelan (2) and Ian Rush; Spurs' reply came from Steve Archibald.

The First Division's leading scorer was Liverpool old boy Kevin Keegan, with 26 goals for his new club, Southampton.

Tottenham Hotspur retained the FA Cup, beating Second Division Queen's Park Rangers 1-0 in the Final replay after the first match had been drawn 1-1. Both Spurs' goals were scored by Glenn Hoddle, the second from the penalty spot.

Aston Villa won the 1982 European Cup, making it six in a row for English teams in this competition. They beat Bayern Munich in the Final in Rotterdam with a goal by Peter Withe.

Villa's victory came less than four months after Tony Barton had taken over as manager from Ron Saunders.

 **Facts**　　　　　　　　　　　　**The Eighties**

First-choice Villa keeper Jimmy Rimmer had to leave the field after only nine minutes of the Final because of a neck injury sustained during the pre-match warm-up. His place in goal was taken by Nigel Spink, playing in only his second game for the first team.

Barcelona won the Cup Winners' Cup in their own stadium, where they beat Standard Liege 2-1 in the Final.

IFK Gothenburg won the UEFA Cup, beating SV Hamburg 4-0 on aggregate in the Final.

In Scotland, Celtic won the League Championship. Their striker George McCluskey was the Premier Division's leading scorer, with 21 goals.

Aberdeen won the FA Cup, beating Rangers 4-1 in the Final after extra time.

Rangers won the League Cup, beating Dundee United 2-1 in the Final.

The 1982 World Cup Finals were held in Spain. The tournament was now expanded to include 24 countries for the first time. The competing nations were Algeria, Argentina, Austria, Belgium, Brazil, Cameroon, Chile, Czechoslovakia, El Salvador, England, France, Honduras, Hungary, Italy, Kuwait, New Zealand, Northern Ireland, Peru, Poland, Scotland, Spain, the USSR, West Germany and Yugoslavia.

The surprise package in the first round of group matches was Cameroon, playing in their first finals. They were unbeaten against Italy, Peru and Poland and went out of the competition only because they had scored fewer goals than the Italians. Their stars were captain and keeper Thomas N'Kono and striker Roger Milla.

England had a hundred per cent record in the first round, beating France 3-1, Czechoslovakia 2-0 and Kuwait 1-0.

The Eighties

Facts

Scotland began the tournament by taking the lead against Brazil, but eventually lost 4-1. They then drew 2-2 with the USSR and, although they scored five goals against New Zealand, they carelessly conceded two – because of this they went out of the competition when a clean sheet would have seen them through to the second round.

Northern Ireland topped their group after drawing 0-0 with Yugoslavia and 1-1 with Honduras and then beating the hosts, Sapin, 1-0 with a goal by Gerry Armstrong.

The 12 countries that went forward to the second round of group matches were Argentina, Austria, Belgium, Brazil, England, France, Italy, Northern Ireland, Poland, Spain, the USSR and West Germany.

Most of the games between the three countries in each of the four groups were marred by defensive-mindedness. England drew their matches against Spain and West Germany and thus went out of the competition without having lost a match.

Northern Ireland drew with Austria but were soundly beaten 4-1 by France.

The four group winners – France, Italy, Poland and West Germany – went forward to the semi-finals, the first knockout matches of the 1982 tournament.

Italy beat Poland 2-0 and then France and West Germany drew 3-3 after extra time before the Germans won 5-4 on penalties.

 **Facts** The Eighties

The 1982 World Cup Final between Italy and West Germany was held in the Santiago Bernabeu Stadium, Madrid, on July 11 in front of 90,000 spectators.

ITALY: Zoff, Gentile, Collovati, Scirea, Cabrini, Conti, Oriali, Bergomi, Tardelli, Rossi, Graziani (subs: Altobelli, then Causio)

WEST GERMANY: Schumacher, Kaltz, K-H. Forster, Stielike, B. Forster, Briegel, Breitner, Dremmler (sub: Hrubesch), Littbarski, Fischer, Rummenigge (sub: Muller)

The main talking-point in the first half of the World Cup Final was a penalty miss by Cabrini. Italy eventually took the lead after 57 minutes with a goal by Paolo Rossi and then Marco Tardelli and Alessandro Altobelli made the Cup safe for Italy before West Germany's Paul Breitner became the first man to score in two World Cup Finals.

Paolo Rossi was the leading scorer in the 1982 World Cup Finals, with six goals for Italy.

Shortly before the 1982 World Cup Final, the FA announced that the new England manager in succession to Ron Greenwood would be Bobby Robson of Ipswich Town.

In 1983, Liverpool won the Championship for the second year in succession and the sixth time in eight years. It was the 14th title in their history.

Runners-up were Watford, their highest ever League position in the year after they won promotion. Their leading scorer – and the First Division's – was Luther Blissett, with 27 goals.

Manchester United won the FA Cup in 1983 for the fifth time in their history, beating Brighton and Hove Albion 4-0 in the Final replay, with goals from Bryan Robson (2), Norman Whiteside and Arnold Muhren (penalty).

The Eighties

Facts

The first FA Cup Final had been drawn 2-2 – Frank Stapleton and Ray Wilkins scored for United, Gordon Smith and Gary Stevens for Brighton.

Brighton were also relegated in 1983, after three years in the First Division.

Liverpool retained the League (Milk) Cup, beating Manchester United 2-1 in the 1983 Final. United took the lead after 12 minutes with a goal by Norman Whiteside, but Liverpool fought back, drawing level with a goal by Alan Kennedy. Ronnie Whelan scored the winning goal in extra time.

On his 12th and final visit to Wembley, Bob Paisley became the first manager to lead his team up and collect a major trophy.

In Scotland, Dundee United won the League for the first time in their history under the management of Jim McLean.

Leading scorer was Charlie Nicholas, with 29 goals for second-placed Celtic.

Aberdeen became the first Scottish club this century other than Celtic and Rangers to retain the FA Cup, beating Rangers 1-0 after extra time in the Final. They then proceeded to do a Cup double, beating Real Madrid 2-1 in the Final of the Cup Winners' Cup in Gothenburg, Sweden.

Celtic won the League Cup, beating Rangers 2-1 in the Final.

SV Hamburg won the European Cup, beating Juventus 1-0 in the Final in Athens.

Anderlecht won the 1983 UEFA Cup, beating Benfica 2-1 on aggregate in the Final over two legs.

 **Facts** The Eighties

In 1983-84, for the first time in its history, the English First Division had a commercial sponsor – the Japanese-based camera-makers Canon.

Liverpool – now under the management of Joe Fagan – won the League Championship for the 15th time. This was one of three major trophies lifted by Liverpool this season. They also retained the Milk Cup, beating Everton 1-0 in the Final replay after the first match had been drawn 0-0. Then they won the European Cup for the fourth time, beating AS Roma 4-2 on penalties after the match had ended 1-1.

Liverpool's – and the First Division's, and Europe's leading scorer – was Ian Rush, with 32 goals.

Everton won the FA Cup, beating Watford 2-0 in the Final with goals by Graeme Sharp and Andy Gray.

The season's great giantkillers were both from the Third Division – Plymouth Argyle reached the semi-final of the FA Cup and Walsall reached the same stage of the Milk Cup.

In Scotland, Aberdeen did the double. They won the League Championship for the third time in their history – their previous victories had been in 1955 and 1980. They also became the first club other than Rangers to win the FA Cup three years running, beating Celtic 2-1 in the 1984 Final. Like their two previous Cup wins, this one was achieved after extra time.

Rangers won the League Cup, beating Celtic 3-2 after extra time in the Final.

Juventus won the 1984 Cup Winners' Cup Final, beating FC Porto 2-1 in the Final in Basle.

Tottenham Hotspur won the UEFA Cup 5-4 in a penalty shoot-out at White Hart Lane after each leg had been drawn 1-1.

The Eighties

Northern Ireland won the last Home International Championship on goal difference after all four countries finished with three points. The competition was not held again after England and Scotland withdrew because of fears for their safety in Belfast.

The finals of the 1984 European Championship were held in France. The eight qualifying nations were Belgium, Denmark, France, Portugal, Romania, Spain, West Germany and Yugoslavia.

France beat Portugal 3-2 in one semi-final; the other, between Denmark and Spain, finished 1-1 after extra time but Spain won the penalty shoot-out 5-4.

The European Championship Final was held at the Parc des Princes, Paris on June 27, 1984, in front of 80,000 spectators. France, the hosts, won the competition for the first time, beating Spain 2-0 with goals by Platini and Bellone.

The 1984-85 season was overshadowed by two great tragedies – the Bradford fire and the Heysel Stadium disaster.

On May 11, 1985, 56 people were burned to death, 70 more detained in hospital with severe burns, and a further 211 supporters and police injured when a timber stand caught fire at Bradford City's Valley Parade ground during an end-of-season match against Lincoln City. The game was fairly well attended, because Bradford had just ensured promotion from the old English Third Division, and many fans had come to celebrate.

The fire began amid rubbish which had accumulated beneath the stand over a long period and had never been swept up. Turnstiles had been locked to prevent latecomers getting in without paying. To make matters worse, there were no fire extinguishers in this part of the ground: they had been removed and stored in a room in the clubhouse because during previous games they been set off and used as missiles by unruly fans.

 **Facts** The Eighties

The Heysel Stadium disaster took place on May 29, 1985 just before the kick-off in the European Cup Final between Juventus and Liverpool in Brussels, Belgium. Thirty-nine people – most of them Italians – were killed and 454 others injured, many seriously, when groups of rival supporters charged each other through Block Z, which had been reserved for neutral spectators. Contributory factors included the easy availability of alcohol, poor segregation and inadequate safety barriers.

The League Championship moved across Stanley Park from Anfield to Goodison Park. It was the eighth title in Everton's history.

Everton also won the 1985 Cup Winners' Cup, beating Rapid Vienna 3-1 in the Final in Rotterdam.

With 24 goals apiece, the joint leading scorers in the First Division were Kerry Dixon of sixth-placed Chelsea and Gary Lineker of 15th-placed Leicester City.

Manchester United prevented a Goodison double by beating Everton 1-0 in the FA Cup Final. The winning goal was scored by Norman Whiteside.

Kevin Moran of Manchester United became the first player ever to be sent off in an FA Cup Final when he was dismissed by referee Peter Willis for a foul on Peter Reid.

Norwich City won the 1985 League Cup, beating Sunderland 1-0 in the Final. Both clubs were relegated from Division One at the end of the season.

Aberdeen retained the Scottish League Championship, finishing on 59 points, seven ahead of runners-up Celtic. Their leading scorer – and Scotland's – was Frank McDougall, with 24 goals.

The Eighties

Rangers won the 1985 League Cup – now renamed the Skol Cup – with a 1-0 Final victory over Dundee United.

Dundee United were again unlucky in the FA Cup, losing 2-1 in the Final to Celtic.

Real Madrid won the 1985 UEFA Cup, beating Videoton of Hungary 3-1 on aggregate in the Final.

Queen's Park Rangers – who qualified for the UEFA Cup by finishing fifth in 1984 – had to play their home matches in the competition at Highbury because UEFA refused to allow them to play on the synthetic pitch they had installed in 1981.

In the UEFA Cup second round, first leg, Queen's Park Rangers beat Partizan Belgrade 6-2 but lost the return 4-0 and went out of the competition.

In spite of the Heysel Stadium disaster, the European Cup Final went ahead as scheduled, kicking off 85 minutes late. Juventus won 1-0, the winning goal coming from a penalty by Michel Platini.

In the aftermath of Heysel, all English clubs were banned from European competitions. None was allowed back until 1990; Liverpool were readmitted in 1991. Joe Fagan stepped down and handed over to Kenny Dalglish, who became Liverpool's first player-manager.

In 1985-86, Liverpool won the double. Their League Championship was their eighth in 11 seasons and the 16th in their history. They finished two points ahead of last year's Champions, Everton, who came second.

Liverpool also beat Everton in the FA Cup Final. The score in the first ever Merseyside Cup Final was 3-1 – Liverpool's goals came from Ian Rush (2) and Craig Johnston.

 **Facts**   The Eighties

Everton's goal in the 1986 FA Cup Final was scored by Footballer of the Year Gary Lineker. Lineker was also the First Division's leading scorer, with 30 goals.

A year after winning the Second Division Championship, Oxford United won the League (Milk) Cup, beating Queen's Park Rangers 3-0 in the Final with goals by Trevor Hebberd, Ray Houghton and Jeremy Charles.

On their way to the Third Division Championship, Reading created a new League record by winning their first 13 games of the season.

In Scotland, Celtic won the League Championship for the 34th time, finishing ahead of second-placed Heart of Midlothian on goal difference.

Scottish Premier Division 1985-86 Top of Table

	P	W	D	L	F	A	Pts
Celtic	36	20	10	6	67	38	50
Heart of Midlothian	36	20	10	6	59	33	50

Fifth-placed Rangers announced the appointment of Graeme Souness as player-manager in succession to Jock Wallace. The former Middlesbrough, Liverpool and Sampdoria midfielder had played 54 times for Scotland.

Aberdeen did a domestic double, winning both the FA Cup and the League Cup. They beat Heart of Midlothian 3-0 in the FA Cup Final, with two goals from John Hewitt and one from John Stark. In the League Cup Final, they beat Hibernian by the same score, two of their goals this time coming from Eric Black and another from John Stark.

Steua Bucharest of Romania won the European Cup, beating Barcelona 2-0 on penalties after the Final in Seville had finished 0-0 after extra time.

The Eighties

Facts

Dynamo Kiev won the Cup Winners' Cup, beating Atletico Madrid 3-0 in the Final in Lyon.

Real Madrid won the UEFA Cup, beating Cologne 5-3 on aggregate in the Final.

The 1986 World Cup was held in Mexico, which thus became the first country to stage the tournament twice. It had originally been awarded to Colombia, but it was subsequently decided that the country was too politically and socially unstable, and that the personal safety of those attending could not be guaranteed.

The 24 nations that reached this stage of the competition were Algeria, Argentina, Belgium, Brazil, Bulgaria, Canada, Denmark, England, France, Hungary, Iraq, Italy, Mexico, Morocco, Northern Ireland, Paraguay, Poland, Portugal, Scotland, South Korea, Spain, Uruguay, the USSR and West Germany.

England lost their opening match 1-0 to Portugal, then drew 0-0 with Morocco in a match in which Ray Wilkins was sent off for throwing the ball at the referee.

England came good in their final group match. Captain Bryan Robson's shoulder injury forced manager Bobby Robson to rejig his team's formation – Peter Beardsley replaced Mark Hateley up front; Gary Lineker responded by scoring all the goals in their 3-0 victory over Poland.

Scotland lost their first two matches – 1-0 to Denmark and 2-1 to West Germany. After less than a minute of their final game, Jose Batista of their opponents Uruguay was sent off. But the Scots could not capitalise on their numerical advantage – a 0-0 draw was not enough to keep them in the World Cup.

 **Facts**

The Eighties

Northern Ireland found themselves in what was probably the toughest group of the finals. They drew their opening game against Algeria but lost 2-1 to Spain and 3-0 to Brazil.

FIFA again altered the format of the World Cup Finals. Although commencing the knockout stage in the second round was preferable to the stultifying groups of three there had been in Spain in 1982, the problem was how to reduce 24 finalists to 16. The solution – taking the top two in each group of four and adding the four best-place third teams – was unsatisfactory.

Belgium and Poland clearly deserved to go through to the next stage of the competition, finishing third in their groups with three points each. But although both Bulgaria and Portugal finished with two points and a goal difference of minus two, only Bulgaria went through. Uruguay took the 16th second round berth simply because they had finished third in their group – the fact that they had two points and a goal difference of minus five – inferior to Portugal's record – was discounted, and it was the Portuguese who went home.

In the second round of the 1986 World Cup Finals, England beat Paraguay 3-0 (two more for Lineker) and Argentina beat Uruguay 1-0. The two victorious nations then met each other in one of the greatest – and most controversial – matches in the history of the World Cup.

Argentina's opening goal in the quarter-final was scored by Diego Maradona with his hand. This was clearly visible on television, but the linesman's view was obstructed by Peter Shilton, whose outstretched arm fortuitously eclipsed that of the Argentine striker – from behind the England keeper, Maradona appeared to have won the ball fairly with his head. Maradona then clinched it for Argentina with a run from his own half which cut through the heart of the by no means absent England defence – this was undeniably a good goal in both senses. England rallied and pulled a goal back through Gary Lineker, who later had a chance to bring the scores back level. But Argentina won 2-1.

The Eighties

Facts

Afterwards, Maradona said his first goal was 'A little bit the head of Maradona, a little bit the hand of God' – the irony of which has never been much appreciated in England.

Brazil were widely fancied to repeat their 1970 success in the previous Mexico World Cup, but they went out on penalties in the quarter-final to France.

West Germany progressed quietly to the semi-finals, beating Morocco 1-0 and Mexico 4-1 on penalties after their quarter-final finished goalless after extra time.

Belgium progressed by beating the USSR 4-3 and then Spain 5-4 on penalties in the quarter-final after the match had been drawn 1-1.

In the semi-finals, Argentina beat Belgium 2-0 and West Germany beat France 2-0.

The 1986 World Cup Final was held in the Aztec Stadium, Mexico City on June 29, 1986 in front of a crowd of 114,590.

ARGENTINA: Pumpido, Cuciuffo, Brown, Ruggeri, Olarticoechea, Giusti, Batista, Burruchaga (sub: Trubbiani), Enrique, Maradona, Valdano

WEST GERMANY: Schumacher, Berthold, Briegel, Jakobs, Forster, Eder, Brehme, Matthaus, Allofs (sub: Voller), Magath (sub: Hoeness), Rummenigge

Argentina went two up with a first half goal by José Luis Brown and another after 56 minutes by Jorge Valdano. But the Germans clawed their way back to 2-2, with goals by Karl-Heinz Rummenigge and substitute Rudi Voller. Then, six minutes from time, Maradona released Jorge Burruchaga who raced away to leave the final score Argentina 3 West Germany 2.

 **Facts**   The Eighties

The leading scorer in the 1986 World Cup Finals was England's Gary Lineker, with six goals. Three players scored five – Emilio Butragueno (Spain), Diego Maradona (Argentina) and Careca (Brazil).

During the close season, Everton sold England striker Gary Lineker to Barcelona for £4,262,000. The Spanish club was managed by Terry Venables.

In 1987, Everton won the League Championship for the ninth time.

The leading scorer in the First Division was Clive Allen, with 33 goals in the season for third-placed Tottenham Hotspur.

Coventry City won the 1987 FA Cup, their first major honour since they entered the Football League in 1919. They beat Tottenham Hotspur 3-2 after extra time in the Final, with goals by Dave Bennett and Keith Houchen and an own goal by Spurs' Gary Mabbutt. Mabbutt also played a major part in his own side's second goal, when his shot was deflected in off Coventry defender Brian Kilcline. Spurs had opened the scoring through Clive Allen but had been pulled back to 1-1.

The Littlewoods Cup (as the League Cup was now named, after its new sponsor) was won by Arsenal, who beat Liverpool 2-1 in the Final. Both Gunners Wembley goals were scored by Charlie Nicholas. This was the first match in which Ian Rush had scored for Liverpool and finished on the losing side.

After five years at Old Trafford, Ron Atkinson was sacked as manager of Manchester United on November sixth despite having led the club to two FA Cup triumphs and never finishing lower than fourth in the League. His successor was Aberdeen's title-winning manager Alex Ferguson.

Fulham and Queen's Park Rangers announced plans to merge, but the scheme was rejected by the Football League.

The Eighties

At the end of the season, the English First Division was reduced from 22 to 21 clubs and the Second Division increased from 22 to 23.

The final promotion and relegation places in England were decided for the first time by play-offs. Under the new system, the three teams just below the automatic promotion places played off against each other and against the club that finished just above the automatic relegation positions in the division above.

There was also to be automatic relegation to the Conference for the team finishing bottom of the Fourth Division. The first team to suffer this fate were Lincoln City.

The Scottish Premier Division was increased from 10 clubs to 12 and the First Division reduced from 14 clubs to 12.

Rangers won the Scottish League Championship. This was Graeme Souness's first season as player-manager. He was sent off on his debut, leaving the field at the same time as the victim of his tackle, George McCluskey of Hibernian, was carried off. Rangers lost the match 2-1.

Rangers also won the 1987 League Cup, beating Celtic 2-1 in the Final. This was Souness's first trophy with his new club, but the sweetness of victory was soured by a nasty match in which nine players were booked and Celtic's Mo Johnston was sent off.

Rangers were knocked out of the UEFA Cup in the second round by Borussia Moenchengladbach. Two Rangers players were sent off during the second leg in Germany.

 **Facts**

The Eighties

Leading scorer in the Scottish First Division was Brain McClair, with 35 goals for second-placed Celtic.

St Mirren won the Scottish FA Cup for the third time in their history, beating Dundee United 1-0 after extra time in the Final.

Porto won the 1987 European Cup, beating Bayern 1987 Munich 2-1 in the Final in Vienna.

Ajax won the Cup Winners' Cup, beating Lokomotiv Leipzig 1-0 in the Final in Athens.

IFK Gothenburg won the UEFA Cup, beating Dundee United 2-1 on aggregate in the Final. Dundee's disappointment came only four days after their defeat in the Scottish FA Cup Final.

In 1987-88, for the first time, the Football League permitted two substitutes per team per match.

Liverpool won the 1988 Championship in the Football League's centenary year. Manchester United were runners-up.

With 26 goals for the Champions, the First Division's leading scorer was John Aldridge.

After only 11 years in the Football League, Wimbledon won the FA Cup, beating Liverpool 1-0 in the 1988 Final. Lawrie Sanchez scored the winner in the first half and after 61 minutes Dons' keeper Dave Beasant saved a penalty from John Aldridge.

Luton Town won the Littlewoods Cup (formerly the League Cup), beating Arsenal 3-2 in the Final. Much of the credit for capturing their first major trophy went to two-goal Brian Stein.

The Eighties

Facts

On October 23, 1987, David Pleat resigned as manager of Tottenham Hotspur after tabloid press allegations about his private life.

On April 9, 1988, at the age of 17 years 240 days, Alan Shearer became the youngest player ever to score a hat-trick in the First Division in Southampton's 4-2 defeat of Arsenal.

On April 14, 1988, Chris Kamara of Swindon Town appeared in court where he was fined £1200 and ordered to pay £250 compensation for causing grievous bodily harm on the field of play to Shrewsbury Town striker Jim Melrose.

Chelsea became the first – and as it turned out, the only – team ever to be relegated from the First Division after a play-off. They lost their top-flight status after finishing 18th and then losing to Middlesbrough, who came third in the Second Division.

In Scotland, Celtic did the double, winning the League Championship for the 35th time and the FA Cup for the 28th time.

The leading scorer in the Scottish Premier Division was Tommy Coyne, with 33 goals for seventh-placed Dundee.

The Scottish League Cup went to Rangers, who beat Aberdeen 5-3 on penalties in the Final after the match ended 3-3 after extra time. This was the first time a major British trophy had been decided by a shoot-out.

 **Facts**   The Eighties

Less than a week before this Final, Rangers' player-manager Graeme Souness had been suspended for five matches after his third sending-off in 14 months for fouling Billy Stark of Celtic.

There was more trouble for Rangers in April 1988, when Glasgow Sheriff Court fined England internationals Terry Butcher and Chris Woods for disorderly conduct and a breach of the peace on the field of play. The incident had occurred during an Old Firm match the previous October. Frank McAvennie, the only Celtic player charged, was acquitted. The case against another Rangers and England player, Graham Roberts, was not proven.

The Finals of all three major European Cup competitions in 1988 were decided on penalties.

PSV Eindhoven of Holland won the European Cup, beating Benfica 6-5 on penalties after the Final in Stuttgart had been drawn 0-0.

Mechelen of Belgium won the Cup Winners' Cup in their first ever season in European competition. They beat Ajax 1-0 in the Final in Strasbourg.

Bayer Leverkusen of West Germany won the UEFA Cup, beating Espanol of Spain 3-2 on penalties in front of their home crowd after the scores had finished 3-3 on aggregate over two legs.

The finals of the 1988 European Championship were held in West Germany. The eight qualifying nations were Denmark, England, Holland, Italy, the Republic of Ireland, Spain, the USSR and West Germany.

The Republic of Ireland and England were quickly eliminated after finishing third and fourth respectively in the group that also contained the USSR and Holland.

In the semi-finals, Holland beat the hosts, West Germany 2-1 and the USSR beat Italy 2-0.

The Eighties

Facts

The 1988 European Championship Final between Holland and the USSR was held in the Olympic Stadium, Munich on June 25 in front of 72,308 spectators.

The Dutch won their first major international trophy 2-0 thanks to goals by Marco Van Basten and Ruud Gullit and a penalty save by Hans Van Breukelen.

1989 was the year of the Hillsborough disaster, the worst tragedy in the history of British football. On April 15, 95 spectators were crushed to death and 170 injured shortly before the start of the FA Cup semi-final between Liverpool and Nottingham Forest. The Leppings Lane enclosure became swamped with Liverpool supporters who kept coming in, pressing those at the front up against the fencing which had been erected around the perimeter to prevent pitch invasions. The match kicked off on time and was six minutes old before the authorities realised that the activity behind the goal was not routine unrest but the unfolding of a major disaster.

Arsenal won the League Championship for the first time in 18 years. In the final game of the season, they went to Anfield needing to win by two goals – anything less, and the title would go to Liverpool. And that is exactly what they did, with goals by Alan Smith and Michael Thomas.

 **Facts** The Eighties

League Division One 1988-89 – Top of Final Table

	P	W	D	L	F	A	Pts
Arsenal	38	22	10	6	73	36	76
Liverpool	38	22	10	6	65	28	76

Alan Smith was the First Division's leading scorer, with 23 goals in the season.

In the aftermath of Hillsborough, there were calls for the FA Cup to be held over for a year as a mark of respect to the victims of the tragedy. But eventually the Liverpool v Nottingham Forest semi-final was replayed and won 3-1 by Liverpool, who went on to win the trophy with a 3-2 extra time Final victory over Everton. John Aldridge and Ian Rush (2) scored for Liverpool; both Everton's goals came from substitute Stuart McCall.

Nottingham Forest won the Littlewoods (League) Cup, beating Luton Town 3-1 in the Final with two goals from Nigel Clough (one of them a penalty) and one from Neil Webb. Ray Harford scored for Luton.

After the crowd trouble that had marred the previous season's First/Second Division play-off between Chelsea and Middlesbrough, the format of these games was altered. From now on, only the teams seeking promotion would be involved.

In May, 1989, former Leeds United and England manager Don Revie died after a long battle against motor neurone disease.

On June 7, 1989, Peter Shilton became England's most capped player when he made his 109th appearance against Denmark. The previous record holder, with 108 caps, had been Bobby Moore.

On June 20, Gary Lineker returned to England from Barcelona – where he had moved after the 1986 World Cup Finals – when he signed for Tottenham Hotspur.

The Eighties

Facts

The Scottish League was restructured again – the Premier Division reverted to 10 clubs and the First Division to 14.

Rangers won the Scottish League Championship and began their sequence of nine titles in a row which equalled Celtic's record achievement of 1966-74. They also took the League Cup, beating Aberdeen 3-2 in the Final.

Joint leading scorers in the Scottish Premier Division were Charlie Nicholas of Aberdeen and Mark McGhee of Celtic, each with 16 goals.

Celtic won the Scottish FA Cup, beating Rangers 1-0 in the Final.

AC Milan won the 1989 European Cup, beating Steua Bucharest 4-0 in the Final in Barcelona.

Barcelona won the Cup Winners' Cup, beating Sampdoria 2-0 in the Final in Berne.

Napoli of Italy beat Stuttgart of West Germany 5-4 on aggregate in the Final of the UEFA Cup.

Lord Justice Peter Taylor's Report on the 1989 Hillsborough disaster was published on January 29, 1990. His findings were severely critical of the squalid condition of many grounds and led directly to the introduction of all-seater stadiums.

In 1990, Liverpool won the League Championship for the 18th time.

The First Division's leading scorer was Gary Lineker, with 24 goals for his new club, Tottenham Hotspur.

Manchester United won the FA Cup for the seventh time, beating Crystal Palace 1-0 in the 1990 Final replay after the first match had been drawn 3-3.

THE NINETIES

The Nineties

Facts

The 1990-91 season was the first in which English clubs other than Liverpool were allowed back into Europe after the ban that had been imposed on them in the wake of the Heysel tragedy on May 29, 1985.

Thus the season started with a note of optimism. The total attendance at League matches on the first day of the season was the highest since the start of 1981-82.

At half time in Everton's first game of the season, goalkeeper Neville Southall refused to go back to the dressing room to discuss tactics. He was fined a week's wages by manager Howard Kendall.

On September 8, York City forward David Longhurst collapsed and died from a heart attack during the match against Lincoln City.

Peter Taylor – Brian Clough's managerial assistant in the great days at Derby County – died on October 5 after a long illness at the age of 62.

Arsenal won their 10th League Championship. Their leading scorer – and the First Division's – was Alan Smith, with 23 goals.

Arsenal won the title despite having had two points deducted from their total after a players' brawl during a League game at Old Trafford. Manchester United were docked one point for their involvement in the same incident. Both clubs were fined £50,000.

Liverpool led the table for much of the season, but were stunned by the resignation of manager Kenny Dalglish on February 22, 1991 after 14 years at the club.

Dalglish announced his decision just after Liverpool had drawn 4-4 with local rivals Everton.

 **Facts**

The Nineties

The reasons for Dalglish's departure were not made entirely clear, but he was thought to have become sick of the stress of such a high-profile job. However, there must have been some compensations to being a successful manager of England's most successful club. Leeds United manager Howard Wilkinson expressed the thoughts of many when he said: 'If he has resigned because of pressures, the rest of us have no chance'.

Over the next seven weeks, Liverpool lost the League leadership and saw Arsenal move five points ahead of them at the top of the table. On April 16, the Anfield board announced that Dalglish's successor would be Graeme Souness, their former player who was currently manager of Rangers.

Another famous figure who seemed to have grown tired of the game was rock star Elton John, who in August sold his stake in Watford to Jack Petchey for £6 million.

Former Liverpool and Wales forward John Toshack was sacked as manager of Real Madrid despite the club having suffered only eight defeats during his 64 matches in charge.

During the 1990-91 season, Atletico Madrid goalkeeper Abel Resino went more than 14 matches (1275 minutes) without conceding a goal – a new world record.

On January 1, 1991, Paul Gascoigne became the first player to be sent off on live British television when he got his marching orders for dissent during Tottenham Hotspur's League game against Manchester United.

In recognition of the fact that he had never been booked or sent off in his career, FIFA awarded Gary Lineker their Fair Play prize, worth £20,000.

UEFA announced that, from the start of the 1991-92 season, clubs would be allowed to field up to five foreign players in domestic League games.

The Nineties

Tottenham Hotspur won the FA Cup, beating Nottingham Forest 2-1 after extra time in the 1991 Final. This was the match in which Paul Gascoigne was stretchered off after a quarter of an hour with a serious knee injury after launching a high, illegal tackle on Forest's Garry Parker. Stuart Pearce scored from the resulting free kick, but Spurs equalised through Paul Stewart. The Londoners should have gone ahead when they were awarded a penalty, but Mark Crossley saved Gary Lineker's spot kick. The winner eventually came from a headed own goal by Forest's Des Walker.

The semi-final between Tottenham and Arsenal had been played at Wembley – the first time an FA Cup tie other than the Final had been held at the stadium. Spurs won 3-1 with one goal from Gascoigne and two from Lineker. Arsenal's goal was scored by Alan Smith.

The injured Gascoigne spent the next year in limbo, uncertain of whether he would remain at Spurs or if he would even play again. At the end of the following season, however, he eventually completed his expected £8.5 million transfer to Lazio of Italy.

Sheffield Wednesday won the 1991 League Cup, which had now been renamed the Rumbelows Cup after its new sponsor. They beat Manchester United 1-0 in the Final with a goal by John Sheridan. The victory was particularly sweet for Wednesday manager Ron Atkinson, who had been sacked by United in 1986.

Wednesday also won promotion back from the Second Division, to which they had been relegated at the end of 1989-90.

Torquay United became the first team to win promotion on penalties. Their play-off final against Blackpool ended 2-2 after extra time and the Devon club won the shoot-out 5-4.

Despite losing their manager, Graeme Souness, to Liverpool, Rangers won the Scottish Championship for the third year running. They also won the League Cup, beating Celtic 2-1 after extra time in the Final.

 **Facts**   **The Nineties**

The leading scorer in the Scottish Premier Division was Tommy Coyne, with 18 goals for third-placed Celtic.

Red Star Belgrade won the European Cup, beating Marseille 5-3 on penalties after the Final in Bari, Italy, had finished goalless at the end of extra time.

Manchester United won the 1991 Cup Winners' Cup, beating Barcelona 2-1 in the Final in Rotterdam. Both United's goals were scored by Mark Hughes, who had returned to Old Trafford in 1988 after spending the least successful period of his career with the Spanish club. Barcelona's goal was scored by Dutch international Ronald Koeman.

Manchester United manager Alex Ferguson thus became the second man after Johann Cruyff to manage two Cup Winners' Cup-winning sides, having previously lifted the trophy with Aberdeen.

In another all-Italian UEFA Cup Final, Inter Milan beat Roma 2-1 on aggregate.

Leeds United won the First Division Championship in 1992, the last year before it became the Premiership. This was the third title in their history.

The leading scorer in the First Division was Ian Wright, with 29 goals in the season. Five of them were scored for Crystal Palace; the other 24 came after his mid-season transfer to Arsenal.

Liverpool won the FA Cup for the fifth time, beating Second Division 2-0 in the Final with goals by Michael Thomas and Ian Rush.

In a departure from tradition, this year's FA Cup runners-up went up the steps first. But, owing to a mix-up, Sunderland were mistakenly given the winners' medals.

Cup-winning manager Graeme Souness was just recovering from major heart surgery.

The Nineties

One of the results of the Taylor Report on the Hillsborough disaster was that there could no longer be an infinite number of Cup replays, partly because of the difficulty of organising security and policing at the grounds. Henceforth, if two clubs were still level after extra time in the first replay, ties would be decided by a penalty shoot-out. Manchester United became the first First Division club to go out of the FA Cup on penalties when they lost in the fourth round in 1992 to Southampton.

Manchester United won the League Cup in its second and last year under the aegis of Rumbelows. They beat Nottingham Forest 1-0 in the Final with a goal by Brian McClair.

On February 5, 1992, Newcastle United, languishing near the bottom of the Second Division, sacked manager Ossie Ardiles and appointed Kevin Keegan to replace him.

Seven months after leaving Liverpool, Kenny Dalglish took over as manager of Blackburn Rovers. Under his guidance, Rovers returned to the top flight of English football after a 26-year absence when they beat Leicester City in the Second Division play-off final at Wembley.

In Scotland, Rangers did the double. They won their fourth consecutive Scottish League title and beat Airdrieonians 2-1 in the Final of the FA Cup.

The Premier Division's leading scorer was Ally McCoist, with 34 goals for Rangers.

Hibernian won the League Cup, beating Dunfermline Athletic 2-0 in the Final.

Barcelona won the European Cup, beating Sampdoria 1-0 after extra time in the 1992 Final at Wembley.

 **Facts**   **The Nineties**

Werder Bremen won the Cup Winners' Cup, beating Monaco 2-0 in the Final in Lisbon.

Ajax Amsterdam won the UEFA Cup, beating Torino on away goals after the Final had finished 2-2 on aggregate.

The 1992 European Championships were held in Sweden. The eight competing nations were the CIS (a team representing the new republics of the former USSR), Denmark, England, France, Germany (the old East and West Germany had now been reunified), Holland, Scotland and Sweden.

Denmark appeared in the finals despite having failed to qualify when Yugoslavia were expelled from the tournament because of civil war in the disintegrating federation.

England performed disappointingly, drawing 0-0 with Denmark and France and losing 2-1 to Sweden in the group stage.

In the closing stages of the match against Sweden, England manager Graham Taylor controversially substituted Gary Lineker when the striker needed just one more goal to equal Bobby Charlton's England record of 49. This turned out to be Lineker's last international appearance.

Scotland also went out in the group stage – although they beat the CIS 2-0, they lost 1-0 to Holland and 2-0 to Germany.

In the semi-finals, Germany beat the hosts, Sweden, 3-2. Denmark drew 2-2 with Holland after extra time but went through 5-4 on penalties.

The 1992 European Championship Final was held on June 26, 1992 in Gothenburg in front of a crowd of 37,800. Rank outsiders Denmark beat red-hot favourites Germany 2-0, with goals by John Jensen and Kim Vilfort.

The Nineties

Facts

In 1992-93, the Football League disbanded after 104 years and re-formed as the FA Premier League, the first main commercial sponsor of which was Barclays Bank. The Premier League will carry on with 22 clubs for this season, and then reduce its size to 20 by the end of 1994-95. The old Second Division would henceforth be known as the First Division and there would be three-up, three-down between it and the Premiership.

The first FA Premier League Champions were Manchester United.

Alex Ferguson thus became only the third British manager to win a League title with two different clubs – the other two were Herbert Chapman (Huddersfield Town and Arsenal) and Brian Clough (Derby County and Nottingham Forest).

One of the main contributory factors to United's success was their capture of Eric Cantona, who they bought for about £1.5 million on November 26 after the French striker had fallen out with his previous boss, Howard Wilkinson of Leeds United.

Teddy Sheringham was the Premiership's leading scorer, with 22 goals (one for Nottingham Forest, 21 for Tottenham Hotspur).

Facts   The Nineties

Arsenal did a Cup double, beating Sheffield Wednesday 2-1 in both Finals. They won the FA Cup, beating the Owls 2-1 in a replay after the first match had finished 1-1 after extra time. Ian Wright scored for Arsenal in both games.

In the Final of the League Cup (which was now known as the Coca-Cola Cup), the Arsenal scorers were Paul Merson and Steve Morrow. Morrow then broke his arm when he fell off Tony Adams during celebrations after the final whistle.

The FA Cup semi-finals were both local derbies – Sheffield Wednesday v Sheffield United and Arsenal v Tottenham Hotspur – and were both played at Wembley.

WEMBLEY

On February 24, 1993, England's World Cup-winning captain, Bobby Moore, died of cancer at the age of 51.

On May 1, 1993, Brian Clough retired after 18 years as manager of Nottingham Forest. Under him, Forest had won the League Championship in 1978, the European Cup in 1979 and 1980 and the League Cup in 1978, 1979, 1989 and 1990. The only trophy to have eluded Clough throughout his career was the FA Cup.

On May 14, 1993, Terry Venables was sacked as chief executive of Tottenham Hotspur by the club chairman, Alan Sugar.

The Nineties

Kevin Keegan guided Newcastle United to the Championship of the First Division (the old League Division Two).

Maidstone United of Division Three were declared bankrupt and went out of the Football League.

In Scotland, Rangers did the treble. They won their fifth consecutive League title and for the second year running their leading scorer was Ally McCoist, again with 34 goals.

Rangers also won the FA Cup and the League Cup, beating Aberdeen 2-1 in both Finals (the League Cup after extra time).

Olympique Marseille won the 1993 European Cup Final, beating AC Milan 1-0 in Munich, but they were stripped of the title the following year when it emerged that they had fixed a French league fixture against Valenciennes. Their chairman, Bernard Tapie, was charged with corruption and suborning witnesses and ordered to give up ownership of the club. He was subsequently sentenced to two years' imprisonment. The team was relegated to the Second Division.

Parma won the European Cup Winners' Cup, beating Royal Antwerp 3-1 in the Final at Wembley.

Juventus won the UEFA Cup, beating Borussia Dortmund 6-1 on aggregate in the Final.

In 1994, Manchester United did the double. They won the FA Premiership again and beat Chelsea 4-0 in the FA Cup Final thanks to two penalties by Eric Cantona and two goals by Mark Hughes and Brian McClair.

The leading scorer in the Premier League was Andy Cole, with 34 goals for newly-promoted Newcastle United, who finished third.

 **Facts**   The Nineties

United nearly did an unprecedented treble, but lost 3-1 to Aston Villa in the Final of the League (Coca-Cola) Cup. Villa's goals in this match were scored by Dalian Atkinson and Dean Saunders (two – one penalty). United's scorer was Mark Hughes.

On January 20, 1994, Sir Matt Busby, president of Manchester United, died at the age of 84.

Graeme Souness resigned as Liverpool manager after his team was knocked out of the FA Cup by First Division Bristol City. He was succeeded by Roy Evans.

The penalties imposed on Tottenham Hotspur for illegal loans to players in the 1980s were unprecedented in their severity – they were fined £1.5 million, banned from the 1994-95 FA Cup and docked six League points. These were later overturned by the English courts.

Wycombe Wanderers took Maidstone United's place in the Football League. They finished fourth in their first season in the Third Division and then won promotion through the play-offs, beating Preston North End in the Final at Wembley.

A week after England's failure to qualify for the 1994 World Cup Finals, their much-maligned manager Graham Taylor resigned and the FA announced that his successor would be Terry Venables. The former Tottenham chief executive would be known as coach rather than as manager.

Wales also failed to qualify for the World Cup Finals, and this meant the end for their manager, Terry Yorath. His replacement, John Toshack, was taken on part-time so that he could continue in charge of the Spanish club Real Sociedad. This was such an unpopular move that Toshack resigned after only 47 days in charge of the national side.

The Nineties

In Scotland, Rangers won the Premier Division for the sixth time in a row and also took the League Cup, beating Hibernian 2-1 in the Final.

Leading scorer in Scotland was Rangers' England international Mark Hateley, with 24 goals.

Dundee United won the FA Cup for the first time in their history, beating Rangers 1-0 in the Final. The Terrors had been losing finalists six times since 1974.

Italians AC Milan won the European Cup, beating Barcelona 4-0 in the Final in Athens.

Arsenal won the Cup Winners' Cup, beating Parma 1-0 in the Final in Copenhagen. The winning goal was scored by Alan Smith.

Inter Milan won the 1994 UEFA Cup, beating Salzburg 2-0 on aggregate in the Final.

The 1994 World Cup Finals were held in the USA. The 24 qualifying nations were Argentina, Belgium, Bolivia, Brazil, Bulgaria, Cameroon, Colombia, Germany, Greece, Holland, Italy, Mexico, Morocco, Nigeria, Norway, Republic of Ireland, Romania, Russia, Saudi Arabia, South Korea, Spain, Sweden, Switzerland and the USA.

Andres Escobar, the Colombian defender who scored an own goal in his country's 2-1 defeat by the hosts, was shot dead on his return home.

Diego Maradona failed a random drugs test after Argentina's second match against Nigeria and was sent home in disgrace.

 **Facts**

The Nineties

The top two countries in each group went through to the second, knockout phase. These were Brazil, Bulgaria, Germany, Holland, Mexico, Nigeria, Republic of Ireland, Romania, Saudi Arabia, Spain, Sweden and Switzerland.

They were joined in the knockout stage by the four best third-placed teams – Argentina, Belgium, Italy and the USA.

The Republic of Ireland went through to the second phase after winning one, drawing one and losing one of their three group matches. Their 1-0 victory over Italy came after a shot by Ray Houghton deceived the Italian keeper in the air.

Holland beat the Republic of Ireland 2-0 in the last 16 match at Orlando, Florida.

Germany beat Belgium 3-2 but the result might have been different if the Belgians had not had a penalty turned down by Swiss referee Kurt Rothlisberger. The official admitted his mistake after seeing the video replay and was not used again in the tournament.

Nigeria led for much of their game against Italy, who had Gianfranco Zola sent off. But then in the 88th minute Roberto Baggio equalised and then scored the winner in extra time from the penalty spot.

In the other second phase matches, Spain beat Switzerland 3-0, Sweden beat Saudi Arabia 3-1, Romania beat Argentina 3-2, Brazil beat the USA 1-0 and Bulgaria beat Mexico 5-4 on penalties after the two countries had finished 1-1 after extra time.

The Nineties

In the quarter-finals, Brazil beat Holland 3-2 after throwing away a two-goal lead; Romania went out on penalties for the second World Cup in succession, losing 5-4 to Sweden after a 2-2 draw, and Italy beat Spain 2-1. But the performance of the round was Bulgaria's 2-1 defeat of Germany, who were widely regarded as the holders even though they had won the World Cup in 1990 as West Germany.

Roberto Baggio scored both Italy's goals as they eliminated Bulgaria in one semi-final; in the other, Brazil beat Sweden 1-0 thanks to an 81st minute goal from Romario.

The 1994 World Cup Final was held on July 17 at the Pasadena Rose Bowl, Los Angeles, California, in front of 94,194 spectators.

BRAZIL: Taffarel, Jorginho (sub: Cafu), Aldair, Marcio Santos, Branco, Mauro Silva, Dunga, Mazinho, Zinho (sub: Viola), Babeto, Romario

ITALY: Pagliuca, Mussi (sub: Apolloni), Baresi, Maldini, Benarrivo, Berti, Albertini, D. Baggio (sub: Evani), Donadoni, R. Baggio, Massaro

The Final finished 0-0 after extra time and so for the first time the World Cup was decided on penalties.

Baresi missed the first kick; Pagliuca saved from Marcio Santos; Albertini scored; Romario scored; Evani scored; Branco scored; Taffarel saved the fourth Italian penalty from Massaro; Dunga scored; Roberto Baggio fired over the bar.

Brazil won the 1994 World Cup 3-2 on penalties.

The joint leading scorers in the 1994 World Cup were Salenko of Russia and Stoichkov of Bulgaria, each with six goals.

The tournament was the best-attended of all 15 World Cups, with an average gate of 68,592.

Facts

The Nineties

At the start of the 1994-95 season, Tottenham Hotspur swooped on three World Cup stars – Jurgen Klinsmann of Germany and Ilie Dumitrescu and Gica Popescu of Romania. Then, in October, they sacked manager Ossie Ardiles and replaced him with Gerry Francis.

In the close season, Liverpool paid Nottingham Forest £8.5 million for Stan Collymore and Arsenal bought Dennis Bergkamp from Inter Milan for the same amount and then David Platt from Sampdoria for £4.75 million. Manchester United sold Paul Ince to Inter Milan for £7.5 million.

Newcastle United bought Les Ferdinand from Queen's Park Rangers for £6 million, Warren Barton for £4 million from Wimbledon and David Ginola for £2.5 million from Paris St Germain.

Aston Villa bought Gareth Southgate from relegated Crystal Palace for £2.5 million, Savo Milosevic from Partizan Belgrade for £3.5 million, and Mark Draper from Leicester City for the same amount.

Blackburn Rovers won the 1994-95 FA Premier League Championship, finishing a point ahead of Manchester United in second place. This was the third League title in their history, but their first since 1914.

Kenny Dalglish thus joined Herbert Chapman, Brian Clough and Alex Ferguson in the select band of managers who had won a League championship with two clubs.

Everton won the FA Cup for the fifth time, beating Manchester United 1-0 in the 1995 Final through a goal by Paul Rideout.

Liverpool won the Coca-Cola Cup, beating Bolton Wanderers 2-1 in the Final. Steve McManaman scored both Liverpool's goals.

The Nineties

Facts

Crystal Palace reached the semi-finals of both the FA and the League (Coca-Cola) Cups and were then relegated from the Premier Division.

Eric Cantona was sent off while playing for Manchester United at Crystal Palace. On his way to the dressing room, the Frenchman attacked a spectator who had been hurling abuse at him.

Cantona was subsequently banned by the FA until the following season and a magistrate sentenced him to two weeks' imprisonment (although the judgment was overturned on appeal, and Cantona had to do 120 hours' community service.

Bruce Grobbelaar (Southampton), John Fashanu (Aston Villa) and Hans Segers (Wimbledon) were charged by the police with match-fixing.

George Graham, manager of Arsenal since 1986, was sacked by the club when a Premier League inquiry revealed that he had received a total of £425,000 in 'bungs' for himself when he signed John Jensen and Pal Lydersen in 1991 and 1992.

Scotland went over for the first time to the three-points-for-a-win system. The Scottish League was also restructured and increased in size from 38 to 40 clubs. From now on, there were to be four divisions, rather than three. The two new clubs were Caledonian Thistle and Ross County.

In 1995, Rangers won their seventh League Championship in a row, the 45th in their history.

After six years without a trophy, Celtic ended the drought when they beat Airdrieonians 1-0 in the Final of the FA Cup. The winning goal was scored by Dutchman Pierre Van Hooijdonk.

 **Facts**

The Nineties

The Scottish League Cup was won by Raith Rovers, who beat Celtic 6-5 on penalties after the match had finished 2-2 after extra time. This was the first major trophy in the history of the Kirkcaldy club.

Ajax Amsterdam won the European Cup, beating AC Milan 1-0 in the Final in Vienna.

Zaragoza won the Cup Winners' Cup, beating Arsenal 2-1 after extra time in the Final in Paris. The winning goal came less than a minute before the final whistle would have signalled a penalty shoot-out. Nayim – an ex-Spur whose real name is Mohamed Ali Amar – lifted the ball over Arsenal keeper David Seaman from the halfway line.

In an all-Italian Final, Parma won the UEFA Cup, beating Juventus 2-1 on aggregate.

In December 1995, the European Court of Justice made a historic ruling which had seismic repercussions throughout British and continental football.

The judgment concerned a Belgian player named Jean-Marc Bosman who had signed for RFC Liège in 1988. Two years later, when his contract expired, he was offered a new deal with the club but at less than half his previous wage. He said he would prefer a transfer to Dunkerque, who had expressed an interest in him, but Liège blocked this by putting him on the market at more than twice what Dunkerque were prepared to pay.

Bosman claimed that this was in restraint of trade and the European Court of Justice supported him. In their view, existing football transfer rules were in breach of EEC laws governing free movement of labour within all member states. They also ruled that restrictions on the number of foreign players in a team were likewise unlawful.

The Nineties

 **Facts**

As a result of the Bosman Ruling, any player who is out of contract is a free agent, and his present club can no longer expect anything from another club who buys his services. Today, more players than ever before are transferred when they are in the middle of a contract, so that the selling club can make money on the deal.

Manchester United won both the League and the FA Cup for the second time in three years and thus became the first English team ever to do a double double. They won the Premier League with 82 points, four points ahead of second-placed Newcastle United, and beat Liverpool 1-0 in the FA Cup Final with a goal by Eric Cantona.

Premiership leading scorer Alan Shearer of Blackburn Rovers became the first player ever to score more than 30 goals in three consecutive seasons.

Aston Villa won the League (Coca-Cola) Cup, beating Leeds United 3-0 in the Final with goals by Savo Milosevic, Ian Taylor and Dwight Yorke.

Terry Venables announced that he would not continue as England coach after the end of the 1996 European Championships (Euro '96). The FA appointed as his successor Glenn Hoddle, the former Tottenham Hotspur and England player who was currently manager of Chelsea.

First Division Leicester City lost their second manager in less than a year. Aston Villa had taken Brian Little from them in 1994, and in December, 1995, his replacement, Mark McGhee, was poached by Wolverhampton Wanderers. The parting was extremely acrimonious, but the club soon replaced him with Martin O'Neill, who led them to promotion through the play-offs at the end of the 1995-96 season.

 **Facts**   **The Nineties**

Chelsea appointed former Dutch international Ruud Gullit as player-manager in succession to Hoddle.

Bob Paisley died on February 14, 1996 at the age of 77. He was manager of Liverpool from 1974-83, during which time the club won the European Cup three times, the UEFA Cup once, the League Championship six times and the League Cup three times.

In Scotland, Rangers did the double, winning their eighth League Championship in a row and the FA Cup, beating Heart of Midlothian 5-1 in the Final with two goals from Brian Laudrup and three from Gordon Durie.

The Nineties

Facts

Aberdeen won the the League Cup, beating Dundee 2-0 in the 1996 Final.

Juventus won the European Cup, beating Ajax 4-2 on penalties after the Final in Rome had been drawn 1-1.

Paris St Germain became the first French club to win the Cup Winners' Cup, beating Rapid Vienna 1-0 in the Final in Brussels.

Bayern Munich won the UEFA Cup, beating Bordeaux 5-1 on aggregate in the 1996 Final.

Euro '96 – the 1996 European Championships – were held in England. There were 16 qualifying nations, twice as many as in Sweden in 1992. They were Bulgaria, the Czech Republic, Croatia, Denmark, England, France, Germany, Holland, Italy, Portugal, Russia, Scotland, Spain, Switzerland and Turkey.

England topped their group, drawing 1-1 with Switzerland and beating Scotland 2-0 and Holland 4-1.

The seven other countries that joined England in the quarter-finals were the Czech Republic, Croatia, France, Germany, Holland, Portugal and Spain.

England were lucky to draw 0-0 with Spain, who had a goal wrongly disallowed for offside. Then keeper David Seaman excelled himself in the penalty shoot-out, which England won 4-2.

In the other three matches, Germany beat Croatia 2-1, France beat Holland 5-4 on penalties after a 0-0 draw, and the Czech Republic beat Portugal 1-0.

Both semi-finals were decided on penalties. England took the lead against Germany after three minutes through Alan Shearer, but Stefan Kuntz equalised after 16. Both sides scored with their first five penalties, and then Gareth Southgate had England's sixth saved. Andreas Moller made no mistake with Germany's reply, to take them through 6-5.

The Czech Republic and France drew 0-0 after extra time, then won the penalty shoot-out 6-5.

The Euro '96 Final was played at Wembley in front of 73,611 spectators. The Czech Republic took the lead after 59 minutes when Karel Poborsky was fouled in the area and Patrik Berger scored from the penalty.

German manager Berti Vogts then brought on Oliver Bierhoff, who brought the scores level after 73 minutes.

Bierhoff scored again after five minutes of extra time – that was the end of the match, because Euro '96 was the first tournament in which the first team to score in extra time won the match – the so-called 'golden goal'.

Manchester United won the FA Carling Premiership in 1996-97 for the fourth time in five years. Their leading scorer, with 19 goals, was the Norwegian Ole Gunnar Solskjaer.

For the second year running, the leading scorer in the Premiership was Alan Shearer, with 25 goals for his new club, Newcastle United.

Chelsea won the FA Cup for the second time in their history. They beat Middlesbrough 2-0 in the Final with goals from Roberto Di Matteo and Eddie Newton.

Di Matteo's goal was the fastest in Cup Final history – he scored after only 43 seconds, thus beating the previous record set by Jackie Milburn, who scored after 45 seconds of the 1955 Cup Final for Newcastle United against Manchester City.

Leicester City won the League (Coca-Cola Cup), beating Middlesbrough 1-0 in the Final replay at Hillsborough with a goal by Steve Claridge.

The Nineties

Giantkillers of the year were Second Division Chesterfield, who reached the semi-final of the FA Cup.

The Wembley Coca-Cola Cup Final had ended 1-1 after extra time. Emile Heskey scored for Leicester and Fabrizio Ravanelli for Middlesbrough.

Middlesbrough achieved a unique and unwanted treble – they were beaten finalists in both Cups and were relegated from the Premiership. They would have avoided the drop had they not had three points deducted for cancelling a Premiership fixture against Blackburn Rovers without sufficient notice.

Kevin Keegan left his job as manager of Newcastle United in mid-season when his team were second in the Premiership. The club announced plans to become a public company and then, on January 14, 1997, appointed Kenny Dalglish as manager.

After eight years in charge, Howard Wilkinson was sacked as manager of Leeds United. He was later appointed Technical Director of the FA.

Former Arsenal manager George Graham replaced Howard Wilkinson at Elland Road after 18 months out of the game.

Macclesfield Town won the GM Vauxhall Conference and gained entry to the Football league for the first time. Their manager was former Manchester United and Northern Ireland international Sammy McIlroy.

Queen's Park Rangers were bought by music entrepreneur Chris Wright for £10 million.

Former England coach Terry Venables became Director of Football at First Division Portsmouth. He later also took on a part-time job as manager of Australia.

 **Facts**   **The Nineties**

Bruce Rioch was sacked as Arsenal manager after 61 weeks in the job. His replacement was Arsène Wenger, a Frenchman who had previously been coach at Grampus Eight in Japan.

In August 1996, Alan Ball resigned as manager of Manchester City. Six weeks later, the Maine Road board announced his replacement – Steve Coppell, formerly manager of Crystal Palace. Coppell lasted 33 days before resigning 'for health reasons'. He was replaced in December by Frank Clark, who had been manager of Nottingham Forest since 1993.

In Guatemala, 80 people were killed at a football match due to overcrowding in a stadium.

Chelsea director Matthew Harding was killed in a helicopter crash on his way back from watching his team's Coca-Cola Cup match at Bolton Wanderers.

Ray Harford resigned as manager of Blackburn Rovers. The club then announced that his replacement next season would be Sven Goran Eriksson, but he never came and they hired Roy Hodgson instead.

On December 22, 1996, Peter Shilton made his 1000th League appearance for Third Division Leyton Orient.

In Scotland, Rangers won the Premier League for the ninth year in succession, thus equalling Celtic's record of 1966-1974. They also won the League Cup, beating Heart of Midlothian 4-3 in the Final.

Kilmarnock won the 1997 Scottish FA Cup for the third time in their history, beating Falkirk 1-0 in the Final.

Alex Miller resigned as manager of Hibernian after 10 years in charge.

Borussia Dortmund won the European Cup, beating Juventus 3-1 in the Final in Munich.

The Nineties

Barcelona won the Cup Winners' Cup, beating Paris St Germain 1-0 in the Final in Rotterdam.

Schalke won the UEFA Cup, beating Inter Milan 4-1 on penalties after the Final had finished 1-1 on aggregate.

Arsenal won the FA Carling Premiership in 1997-98 – this was the 11th title in their history.

Frenchman Arsène Wenger thus became the first non-British manager to win the English League.

Arsenal completed the Double by winning the FA Cup, beating Newcastle United 2-0 in the Final at Wembley.

Arsenal's goals in the Final were scored by Marc Overmars and Nicolas Anelka.

The Premiership's leading scorer was Andy Cole, with 25 goals in all competitions.

Aston Villa sold controversial and disaffected Yugoslav striker Savo Milosevic to Real Zaragoza for a reported £3.5 million.

Chelsea won the League (Coca-Cola Cup), beating First Division Middlesbrough 2-0 in the Final with goals by Frank Sinclair and Roberto di Matteo.

All three of the clubs promoted to the Premiership at the end of the 1997 season were relegated from it again at the end of 1998 – Bolton Wanderers, Barnsley and Crystal Palace.

Crystal Palace let themselves down badly at home, where they won only one game. This was against Sheffield Wednesday, the only team from whom they took six points in the season.

 **Facts**   **The Nineties**

Everton flirted dangerously with relegation and only ensured safety through a 1-1 draw with Coventry City on the last day of the season.

Promoted automatically from the Nationwide Division One were Nottingham Forest (Champions) and Middlesbrough.

They were joined in the Premiership by Charlton who beat Sunderland 7-6 on penalties after the play-off Final at Wembley had ended 4-4 after extra time. Clive Mendonca scored a hat trick for Charlton in this match.

Kevin Phillips scored one of Sunderland's Wembley goals. It was his 35th of the season, making him the club's all-time leading marksman.

The crucial penalty was taken by Sunderland's Michael Gray and saved by Charlton keeper Sasa Ilic.

Celtic won the Scottish Premier League – their first championship since 1988. Their manager, Wim Jansen, then resigned, it is thought because of disagreements with club chairman Fergus McCann.

Tom Boyd became the first Celtic captain to lift the Premier League trophy for 10 years.

Heart of Midlothian won the Scottish FA Cup, beating Rangers 2-1 in the Final with goals by Colin Cameron (penalty) and Stephane Adam. Ally McCoist scored for Rangers.

Celtic won the Scottish League Cup, beating Dundee United 3-0 in the Final. Their goals were scored by Marc Rieper, Henrik Larsson and Craig Burley.

This was the first season since 1986 that Rangers had failed to win any of the major domestic trophies.

THE
PLAYERS

DISCIPLINE

Discipline

Facts

Only three teams in the Carling Premiership and three Nationwide League went through the 1995-96 season without a player being sent-off – Tottenham (Carling Premiership), Watford (Division One) and Swindon (Division Two).

November 20, 1982 became the worst day for dismissals in football history with 15 players sent-off. Twelve of those came in the third round of the FA Cup.

The most players ordered off on a League day was 13. That record number has been reached three times – December 14, 1985, August 19, 1995 and September 9, 1995.

The 376 sending-offs in the Carling Premiership and Nationwide League's in the 1994-95 season set a new record for England.

Alan Mullery became the first player to be sent-off for England when he was dismissed against Yugoslavia in an European Championship match in Florence, Italy on June 5, 1968.

Up to July 1997, only four players have been sent-off for England. Those players were: Alan Mullery v Yugoslavia (European Championship, June 5, 1968), Alan Ball v Poland (World Cup qualifyer, June 6, 1973), Trevor Cherry v Argentina (friendly, June 15, 1977) and Ray Wilkins v Morocco (World Cup Finals, June 6, 1986).

 **Facts**   **Discipline**

Stranraer set a Scottish record when four of their players were sent-off against Airdrie in a Scottish Division One match on December 3, 1994.

Five players from Brazilian club America Tres Rios were sent-off in the first 10 minutes of a Brazilian Cup match after a disputed goal awarded by opponents Itaperuna. As a result the game was abandoned and Itaperuna were awarded the match.

When Gremio of Brazil met Uruguay's Penarol in the South American Super Cup quarter-final in October 1993, eight players were sent-off, four from either clubs.

Up to July 1997, England have not had a player sent-off at Wembley.

Bologna's Giuseppe Lorenzo set a new world record when he was sent-off for striking an opponent after only 10 seconds of a League match against Parma on December 9, 1990.

Jose Batista of Uruguay set a World Cup Finals record when he was sent-off after only 55 seconds against Scotland in 1986.

Willie Johnston has the most sending-offs in a career. The breakdown of his 21 dismissals are: Rangers 7, West Bromwich Albion 6, Vancouver Whitecaps 4, Hearts 3 and Scotland 1.

Yugoslavia's Boris Stankovic became the first player to be sent-off at Wembley when he was dismissed in an Olympic Games match against Sweden in August 1948.

Manchester United's Kevin Moran is the only player to be sent-off in a FA Cup Final. He got his marching orders in the 1985 final against Everton in 1985.

Leeds' Billy Bremner and Kevin Keegan of Liverpool became the first players to be sent-off in the same match at Wembley. The two were dismissed for fighting in the 1974 Charity Shield.

Stockport had two players sent-off in the 1994 Second Division Play-Off final against Burnley at Wembley. Mike Wallace and Chris Beaumont the culprits.

Vinnie Jones has collected two of the fastest bookings in English football. He was shown the yellow card after three seconds for Chelsea against Sheffield United on February 15, 1992 and after five seconds for Sheffield United at Manchester City on January 19, 1991.

Discipline

Facts

Charlton's Derek Hales and Mike Flanagan were sent-off for fighting with each other against Southern League side Maidstone in an FA Cup third round tie on January 9, 1979.

Another warring pair were Hearts' Graeme Hogg and Craig Levein. The Scottish FA banned the two for ten matches in September 1994 when they fought in a pre-season friendly against Raith Rovers.

Eric Cantona of Manchester United suffered the longest suspension in modern times after his attack on a spectator during a Premiership match at Crystal Palace on January 25, 1995. He was banned from football by the FA for eight months.

Newcastle United's Faustino Asprilla was fined £10,000 and banned for the first match of the 1996-97 season by the FA after being found guilty of elbowing/head-butting Keith Curle of Manchester City in February 1996.

David Batty and Graeme Le Saux were both suspended for two European games by Uefa after the two Blackburn players started brawling with each other in a European Champions League match against Spartak Moscow in November 1995.

GOALSCORING

Goalscoring

The highest number of goals scored by a British club is 36, scored by Arbroath against Bon Accord in the Scottish Cup of 1885.

On the same day as Arbroath's record-breaking haul Dundee Harp beat Aberdeen Rovers 35-0.

The highest score recorded by a club in the Carling Premiership is nine, scored by Manchester United against Ipswich in March 1995.

Dixie Dean holds the record for English League goals in a season, scoring 60 in 1927-28 for Everton.

Luton's Joe Payne holds the record for goals in a League game, netting ten against Bristol Rovers in 1936 on his debut as a centre-forward.

The British record for League goalscoring in one season is held by Jimmy Smith of Ayr, who scored 66 goals in 38 appearances in the 1927-28 season.

Arthur Rowley has scored the greatest number of goals in League history with 434 strikes for WBA, Fulham, Leicester and Shrewsbury.

The record for League goals in the top flight is held by Jimmy Greaves, who scored 357 times for Chelsea, Tottenham and West Ham before becoming a television commentator.

Dixie Dean scored 349 goals for Everton between 1925 and 1937, a British goalscoring record for a player at one club.

Pele is reputedly the world's all-time biggest scorer with 1,282 goals from 1,365 matches, although some were in friendlies for his club, Santos.

Pele's 1000th goal was scored against Vasco de Gama in the Maracana Stadium in November 1969.

The first player to score more than 30 top-flight goals in three successive seasons was Alan Shearer between 1993 and 1996.

Iain Dunn was the first player in British football to settle a match with a golden goal when he scored in the 107th minute to seal Huddersfield's win over Lincoln in an Auto Windscreens Shield tie.

 **Facts**   Goalscoring

The first Wembley match to be decided by a golden goal was the Auto Windscreens final of 1995, Paul Tait giving Birmingham the win over Carlisle 13 minutes into overtime.

The first penalty to be scored in a first-class match was converted by John Heath for Wolves against Accrington Stanley in September 1891.

The first major international tournament to be decided by a golden goal was the 1996 European Championships – Oliver Bierhoff scoring the winner for Germany in the 95th minute.

Paul Mariner scored in six consecutive England appearances between November 1991 and June 1992.

Swindon conceded 100 goals in the 1993-94 season, a Carling Premiership record.

In 1993-94 Arsenal conceded only 28 goals in 42 Carling Premiership games, but in 1978-79 Liverpool claimed the post-war record with only 16 goals in 42 games.

In Tottenham's Championship year of 1960-61 they scored 115 goals. Two years later they scored 111 goals but finished the season as runners-up to Everton.

In 1930-31 the top three in the championship all scored a century of goals (Arsenal – 127, Aston Villa – 128, Sheffield Wednesday – 102)

The most goals to be scored in the Football League on one day was 209 in the 44 matches on February 1, 1936.

When Oxford United beat Shrewsbury 6-0 in April 1996 all six of the goals came from headers.

Alan Cork scored in all four divisions of the Football League and the FA Carling Premiership in an 18-year career with Wimbledon, Sheffield United and Fulham.

Billy Foulkes scored his first international goal for Wales against England in 1951, scoring with his first kick in his first game for his country.

Preston scored six goals in seven minutes in their 26-0 victory over Hyde in the FA Cup of 1887.

Goalscoring

The fastest Carling Premiership hat-trick was scored in August 1994 by Robbie Fowler. He netted three goals in 4 and a half minutes against Arsenal.

The fastest recorded hat-trick in history was scored by Maglioni for Independiente against Gimnasia de la Plata in March 1973. He completed his three goals in one minute 50 seconds.

In 1923-24 Chesterfield's goalkeeper, Arthur Birch, scored five goals in their Third Division campaign. All came from the penalty spot.

In August 1962 Reading's goalkeeper Arthur Wilkie injured a hand during the match against Halifax. He came out of goal to play as a striker and scored twice in a 4-2 win.

 **Facts**   Goalscoring

When Liverpool beat Crystal Palace 9-0 in December 1992 there were eight of their players on the scoresheet, with defender Steve Nicol the only man to score twice.

The English record for consecutive goalscoring is held by Bill Prendergast, who scored in 13 successive games for Chester in 1938.

Steve Bull was England's highest scorer for two consecutive seasons in 1987-88 (52) and 1988-89 (50).

Jimmy Greaves was First Division top scorer six times in 11 seasons between 1968 and 1969.

When West Ham beat Newcastle 8-1 in April 1986 Alvin Martin scored a hat-trick against three different keepers – goalkeeper Martin Thomas being replaced first by Chris Hedworth and then Peter Beardsley.

Manchester City are the only club to concede and score 100 goals in one season, scoring 104 and letting in 100 when they finished fifth in 1957-58.

Jim Dyet of Scottish club King's Park enjoyed a dream debut when he played against Forfar Athletic in 1930. He scored eight goals and surprisingly kept his place for their next fixture.

Alan Shearer scored a hat-trick on his full First Division debut at the age of 17. He scored his three goals for Southampton in their 4-2 win over Arsenal.

Jim Stannard of Gillingham set a new goalkeeper's record in 1995-96 when he kept 29 clean sheets in 46 matches, beating Ray Clemence's Liverpool record of 1978-79.

Chris Woods holds the British record for the longest shut-out by a goalkeeper. He did not concede a goal for 1,196 minutes when playing for Rangers in 1986-87, until he was finally beaten by a goal from Hamilton's Adrian Sprott.

Nottingham Forest hold the record for the longest unbeaten run in the Football League, playing 42 matches in 1977-78 and 1978-79 without being beaten. Defeat finally came at Liverpool with a 2-0 defeat.

Goalscoring

Facts

In 1960 Peterborough joined the Football league and won the Fourth Division at their first attempt, setting a scoring record of 134 goals in the process.

The Leeds side of 1973-74 were unbeaten in their first 29 League matches of the season. Their record was equalled by Liverpool in 1987-88.

In 1983-84 Cambridge United set a new Football League record when they played 31 consecutive matches without winning a game. They were later relegated from the Second Division.

The worst start to a Premier League season came at Swindon in 1993-94, the County Ground side waiting 15 matches before recording a win.

Only two clubs have completed a Football League season without being beaten – Preston North End in the League's inaugural season in 1888-89 and Liverpool in 1893-94.

On Boxing Day, 1994 the Carling Premiership was an away-day celebration as none of the 11 matches ended in a home win.

In 1957-58 Queens Park Rangers played out six consecutive 1-1 draws to set a record for the longest sequence of draws by the same score.

In 1993-94 there were 1195 goals scored in the Carling Premiership. The following year exactly the same number were scored once again.

In the nine seasons between 1961 and 1969 Northampton travelled from the Fourth Division to the First, and all the way back down from the top flight to the bottom again.

Halifax goalkeeper Steve Milton had a nightmare League debut when his side met Stockport in January 1934. They lost 13-0.

Manchester City were the highest-scoring team in the First Division in 1937-38 with 80 goals. But they ended the season in 21st and were relegated, despite scoring three more goals than champions Arsenal.

Robert Bell scored nine goals for Tranmere against Oldham in a Division Three (North) match on Boxing Day in 1935.

Preston North End's James Ross set a League record in it's first season when he scored seven goals against Stoke City in October, 1888.

 **Facts**   Goalscoring

Three other players have scored seven League goals in one match. They are: Ted Drake for Arsenal v Aston Villa, Division One, December 14, 1935. Tommy Briggs for Blackburn v Bristol Rovers, Division Two, February 5, 1955. Neville ('Tim') Coleman for Stoke City v Lincoln, Division Two, February 23, 1957.

On September 12, 1885, John Petrie set the all-time British individual record when he scored 13 goals in Arbroath's 36-0 win over Bon Accord in the Scottish Cup first round.

Denis Law scored seven goals in an FA Cup tie against Luton, but still finished a loser. Playing for Manchester City in 1961, Law scored all six goals in the fourth round tie but the game was abandoned with City leading 6-2. The re-arranged match was won by Luton 3-1, with Law scoring the consolation.

Vivian Woodward set a British record when he scored seven goals for England against France in an Amateur International in Paris on November 1, 1906. England won the game 15-0.

Woodward also scored six goals for England against Holland at Chelsea on December 11, 1909.

Ireland's Joe Bambrick set the British professional record when he scored six goals against Wales in Belfast on February 1, 1930.

Willie Hall set the record for fastest international hat-trick when he scored three goals in three minutes for England against Ireland at Old Trafford on November 16, 1938. Hall went on to score another two goals as England ran out 7-0 winners.

Up to the end of the 1996-97 season the top British international goalscorers are: England – Bobby Charlton (49 in 106 games), Scotland – Denis Law (30 in 55) and Kenny Dalglish (30 in 102), Northern Ireland – Colin Clarke (13 in 38), Wales – Ian Rush (28 in 73) and Republic of Ireland – Frank Stapleton (20 in 71).

Tinsley Lindley scored in nine consecutive games for England spanning three seasons. He scored in three games against each of Scotland, Wales and Ireland.

Paul Mariner has come the closest to beating Lindley's record. The England striker scored in six consecutive matches between November 1981 and June 1982.

Goalscoring

Peterborough United's Terry Bly set a new League record when he scored 52 Division Four goals in the 1960-61 season.

Albert Mundy set the quickest goal record by scoring after just six seconds for Aldershot against Hartlepool on October 25, 1958.

Two men have repeated Mundy's feat. Barrie Jones of Newport County v Torquay United, March 31, 1962; and Crystal Palace's Keith Smith v Derby County, December 12, 1964.

Huddersfield's Phil Starbuck scored after only three seconds of coming on as a substitute against Wigan in a Division Two match on April 12, 1993.

Malcolm Macdonald was officially timed with scoring a goal after just five seconds of Newcastle's 7-3 friendly win at St Johnstone on July 29, 1972.

Jimmy Scarth scored three goals in two minutes for Gillingham against Leyton Orient in a Division Three (South) match on November 1, 1952.

Arsenal scored six goals in 18 minutes in a 7-1 win over Sheffield Wednesday on February 15, 1992. The goals came between the 71st and 89th minute.

Notts County scored six goals in twelve second-half minutes when they beat Exeter 9-0 in Division Three (South) on October 16, 1948. Tommy Lawton and Jackie Sewell both scored hat-tricks.

The fastest international goal was set by San Marino's Davide Gualtieri against England in a World Cup qualifier on November 17, 1993. The official timing of the goal was 8.3 seconds.

The fastest First Division hat-trick since the war was set by Fulham's Graham Leggat. He scored three goals in three minutes when Fulham beat Ipswich 10-1 on Boxing Day, 1963.

Robbie Fowler set the fastest Carling Premiership hat-trick when he scored three goals in four-and-a-half minutes in Liverpool's 3-0 victory over Arsenal on August 28, 1994.

Blackburn's Chris Sutton and Dwight Yorke of Aston Villa share the record of fastest goal in the Carling Premiership. Both scored after 13 seconds, Sutton against Everton on April 1, 1995 and Yorke against Coventry on September 30, 1995.

 **Facts** Goalscoring

Jamie Cureton scored the fastest Carling Premiership goal from a substitute when he netted after only 13 seconds of coming on for Norwich against Chelsea on December 10, 1994.

The fastest Scottish hat-trick was timed at two-and-a-half minutes by Motherwell's Ian St. John. He managed the feat away at Hibernian in the Scottish League Cup on August 15, 1959.

The fastest all-time hat-trick was reported at one minute 50 seconds by Independiente's Maglioni against Gimnasia de la Plata in Argentina on March 18, 1973.

The fastest First Division own-goal was set by Arsenal's Steve Bould. He 'scored' after just 16 seconds at Sheffield Wednesday on February 17, 1990.

The fastest goal in World Cup Finals history was scored by Vaclav Masek of Czechoslovakia against Mexico in 1962. The goal was timed at 15 seconds.

Up to the start of the 1997-98 season, no Carling Premiership goals have been scored by a goalkeeper.

Peter Schmiechel scored for Manchester United against Rotor Volgograd in the Uefa Cup first round, second leg on September 26, 1995.

Jan Molby's first hat-trick in English football all came from the penalty spot in Liverpool's 3-1 win over Coventry in November 1986.

Arthur Birch scored five goals for Chesterfield in the 1923-24 season – as a goalkeeper. All came from the penalty spot.

Goalscoring

Maik Taylor was beaten by his opposite goalkeeper – on his League debut. Barnet's Taylor was beaten by Chris Mackenzie of Hereford in a Division Three match on August 12, 1995.

Liverpool set a Football League record when eight players scored in the same match. Steve Nicol (twice), Steve McMahon, Ian Rush, Gary Gillespie, Peter Beardsley, John Aldridge, John Barnes and Glenn Hysen all scored in the 9-0 win over Crystal Palace on September 12, 1989.

Nine different players scored for Striling Albion in their 20-0 win against Selkirk in the Scottish Cup first round on December 8, 1984.

Liverpool also hold the record for different scorers in a European match. Nine players scored in their 11-0 record home win over Stromsgodset of Norway in the European Cup-Winners' Cup first round, first leg on September 17, 1974.

Nearly matching Liverpool were Swansea City. They had eight different goalscorers when they beat Sliema of Malta 12-0 in the Cup-Winners' Cup first round, first leg on September 15, 1982.

Bill Prendergast set an English record when he scored in 13 consecutive matches for Chester City between September and December 1938.

Prendergast feat eclipsed the previous record set by Everton's Dixie Dean. Dean had scored on 12 consecutive appearances.

The Carling Premiership record for goals scored in consecutive games was set by Mark Stein. The Chelsea striker scored in seven consecutive matches between December 28, 1993 and February 5, 1994.

Brian Clough was the Second Division top goalscorer for three successive seasons while at Middlesbrough. He scored 40 goals in 1957-58, 42 in 1958-59 and 39 in 1959-60.

Middlesbrough's George Camsell scored a record nine hat-tricks in the 1926-27 season.

Dixie Dean holds the record for most League hat-tricks in a career. He scored 37 for Tranmere and Everton between 1924 and 1938.

The most Carling Premiership hat-tricks in a season was set by Alan Shearer. He scored five for Blackburn in the 1995-96 season.

 **Facts**   **Goalscoring**

Three players have scored three consecutive First Division hat-tricks: Frank Osborne (Tottenham) scored against Liverpool, Leicester and West Ham in 1925; Tom Jennings (Leeds), against Arsenal, Liverpool (four) and Blackburn (four) in 1926 and Jack Balmer (Liverpool) against Portsmouth, Derby County (four) and Arsenal in 1946.

Gilbert Alsop also scored three consecutive League hat-tricks for Walsall in Division Three (South). He scored against Swindon, Bristol City and Swindon (four) in 1939.

Up to the start of the 1997-98 season, there have been three hat-tricks scored from players on the same team in a League match: Nottingham Forest (Enoch West, Billy Hooper and Arthur Spouncer) against Leicester Fosse on April 21, 1909 in Division One; Wrexham (Ron Barnes, Wyn Davies and Roy Ambler) against Hartlepool on March 3, 1962 in Division Four; Manchester City (Tony Adcock, Paul Stewart and David White) against Huddersfield on November 7, 1987 in Division Two.

The record for most Football League goals scored on one day was set on February 1, 1936. In the 44 games played 209 goals were scored.

A Carling Premiership record was set on September 23, 1995 when three players scored hat-tricks on the same day. Robbie Fowler (Liverpool) scored four goals against Bolton, Tony Yeboah (Leeds) scored a hat-trick at Wimbledon and Alan Shearer (Blackburn) netted three against Coventry.

Hereford's Chris Pike scored a hat-trick against different goalkeepers on October 16, 1993. Hereford's opponents, Colchester, had two goalkeepers sent-off. The result of the game was 5-0.

Jim Dyet scored eight goals on his debut for King's Park against Forfar Athletic on January 2, 1930.

Len Shackleton holds the English record for scoring six goals on his debut for Newcastle in a 13-0 Division Two win against Newport County on October 5, 1946.

Alan Shearer became the youngest player to score a Division One hat-trick on his full debut when he scored for Southampton against Arsenal on April 9, 1988 at the age of 17.

Goalscoring

Stoke City equalled a Football League record in the 1984-85 season by scoring the fewest goals in a season. Both Stoke and Watford (1971-72) scored 24 goals.

Leeds set a new Carling Premiership record by scoring the fewest goals in 1996-97. They managed only 28 goals but still finished in 11th place.

The fewest goals scored by a relegated Carling Premiership side was Manchester City's 33 in 1995-96.

Crystal Palace set a Carling Premiership record when they went nine consecutive matches without scoring in the 1994-95 season.

The longest Football League sequence of a club not scoring a goal was 11 matches. Coventry (Division Two 1919-20) and Hartlepool (Division Two 1992-93) both hold the record.

 **Facts**   Goalscoring

Hartlepool actually went 13 games without scoring. Spanning over two months, and 1,227 minutes, they failed to score in 11 League games, one FA Cup match and an Autoglass Shield Trophy tie.

The British non-scoring record was set by Striling Albion in 1981. From January 31 to August 8 they went 14 matchs without netting. That run consisted of 13 Scottish League matches and one Scottish Cup game. It took them 1,292 minutes to score their next goal.

Arsenal's Ian Wright became the first player to score in each leg of each round for a club that reached a European Final. He achieved the feat in the 1994-95 European Cup-Winner's Cup, but failed to score in the Final, which Arsenal lost to Real Zaragova.

The most goals scored by one player in a first-class match was set by Polish striker Stephan Stanis. He scored 16 goals for Lens against Aubry-Austuries in a wartime French Cup match on December 13, 1942.

The record number of goals scored by one player in an international match is 10 goals, shared by two men, and both were in Olympic tournaments: Denmark's Sofus Nielsen against France in the 1908 Olympics and Gottfried Fuchs for Germany in the 1912 competition against Russia.

England's top 10 goalscorers:
Bobby Charlton (49 goals in 106 games)
Gary Lineker (48 in 80)
Jimmy Greaves (44 in 57)
Tom Finney (30 in 76)
Nat Lofthouse (30 in 33)
Vivian Woodward (29 in 23)
Steve Bloomer (28 in 23)
David Platt (27 in 62)
Bryan Robson (26 in 90)
Geoff Hurst (24 in 49)
Goals by Goalkeepers
Chris MacKenzie

Hereford United's Chris Mackenzie beat his opposite number, Barnet's Mark Taylor, in last season's Third Division encounter at Edgar Street.

Goalscoring

Facts

Iain Hesford
Iain Hesford scored Maidstone's winner against Hereford in a Fourth
Division match in November 1991. His clearance beat visiting keeper Tony
Elliot with one bounce.

Ray Charles
**East Fife's Ray Charles joined the exclusive list in February 1990.
His long ball deceived his opposite number, Stranraer's Bernard
Duffy, in the Scottish Second Division match.**

Alan Paterson
The 1989 Roadferry Cup Final in Belfast was brightened up when Glentoran
keeper Alan Paterson embarrassed Linfield's George Dunlop with a
towering clearance.

Andy McLean
**On his Irish league debut in August 1988, keeper Andy Mclean
scored for Cliftonville. The hapless goalkeeper at the other end
was once again Linfield's George Dunlop.**

Andy Goram
Scotland's international stopper Andy Goram scored once for his old club
Hibernian. It was in the Premier Division in May 1988, the unlucky
opposition keeper was Morton's David Wylie.

Steve Ogrizovic
**Coventry stalwart Ogrizovic grabbed his only goal for the Sky
Blues against Sheffield Wednesday in October 1986, his big-boot
beating Martin Hodge in the home goal.**

Steve Sherwood
Watford's Steve Sherwood got his name on the score sheet in a First
Division game in 1984. He beat Coventry's Raddy Avramovic in the match at
Highfield Road.

Ray Cashley
**The Division Two match between Bristol City and Hull City in
September 1993 produced another moment of goalkeeping
folklore when Bristol's Ray Cashley scored against Jeff Wealands.**

Peter Shilton
In over 900 league games England's Peter Shilton scored once. It was in
1967 playing for Leicester City, his obliging opposite number was
Southampton's Campbell Forsyth.

PLAYER AWARD WINNERS

PLayer Award Winners — Facts

THE FOOTBALL WRITERS ASSOCIATION
      PLAYER OF THE YEAR
1948 Stanley Matthews (Blackpool)
1949 Johnny Carey (Manchester United)
1950 Joe Mercer (Arsenal)
1951 Harry Johnston (Blackpool)
1952 Billy Wright (Wolverhampton Wanderers)
1953 Nat Lofthouse (Bolton)
1954 Tom Finney (Preston North End)
1955 Don Revie (Manchester City)
1956 Bert Trautmann (Manchester City)
1957 Tom Finney (Preston North End)
1958 Danny Blanchflower (Tottenham Hotspur)
1959 Syd Owen (Luton Town)
1960 Bill Slater (Wolverhampton Wanderers)
1961 Danny Blanchflower (Tottenham Hotspur)
1962 Jimmy Adamson (Burnley)
1963 Stanley Matthews (Blackpool)
1964 Bobby Moore (West Ham United)
1965 Bobby Collins (Leeds United)
1966 Bobby Charlton (Manchester United)
1967 Jack Charlton (Leeds United)
1968 George Best (Manchester United)
1969 Tony Book (Manchester City) and Dave Mackay (Derby County)
1970 Billy Bremner (Leeds United)
1971 Frank McLintock (Arsenal)
1972 Gordon Banks (Stoke City)
1973 Pat Jennings (Tottenham Hotspur)
1974 Ian Callaghan (Liverpool)
1975 Alan Mullery (Fulham)
1976 Kevin Keegan (Liverpool)
1977 Emlyn Hughes (Liverpool)
1978 Kenny Burns (Nottingham Forest)
1979 Kenny Dalglish (Liverpool)
1980 Terry McDermott (Liverpool)
1981 Frans Thijssen (Ipswich Town)
1982 Steve Perryman (Tottenham Hotspur)
1983 Kenny Dalglish (Liverpool)
1984 Ian Rush (Liverpool)
1985 Neville Southall (Everton)
1986 Gary Lineker (Everton)
1987 Clive Allen (Tottenham Hotspur)
1988 John Barnes (Liverpool)
1989 Steve Nicol (Liverpool); Special award to Liverpool players for their
      compassion to Hillsborough families

 **Facts**   **PLayer Award Winners**

990 John Barnes (Liverpool)
1991 Gordon Strachan (Leeds United)
1992 Gary Lineker (Tottenham Hotspur)
1993 Chris Waddle (Sheffield Wednesday)
1994 Alan Shearer (Blackburn Rovers)
1995 Jurgen Klinsmann (Tottenham Hotspur)
1996 Eric Cantona (Manchester United)
1997 Gianfranco Zola (Chelsea)

P.F.A. PLAYER OF THE YEAR
1974 Norman Hunter (Leeds United)
1975 Colin Todd (Derby County)
1976 Pat Jennings (Tottenham Hotspur)
1977 Andy Gray (Aston Villa)
1978 Peter Shilton (Nottingham Forest)
1979 Liam Brady (Arsenal)
1980 Terry McDermott (Liverpool)
1981 John Wark (Ipswich Town)
1982 Kevin Keegan (Southampton)
1983 Kenny Dalglish (Liverpool)
1984 Ian Rush (Liverpool)
1985 Peter Reid (Everton)
1986 Gary Lineker (Everton)
1987 Clive Allen (Tottenham Hotspur)
1988 John Barnes (Liverpool)
1989 Mark Hughes (Manchester United)
1990 David Platt (Aston Villa)
1991 Mark Hughes (Manchester United)
1992 Gary Pallister (Manchester United)
1993 Paul McGrath (Aston Villa)
1994 Eric Cantona (Manchester United)
1995 Alan Shearer (Blackburn Rovers)
1996 Les Ferdinand (Newcastle United)
1997 Alan Shearer (Newcastle United)

P.F.A. YOUNG PLAYER OF THE YEAR
1974 Kevin Beattie (Ipswich Town)
1975 Mervyn Day (West Ham United)
1976 Peter Barnes (Manchester City)
1977 Andy Gray (Aston Villa)
1978 Tony Woodcock (Nottingham Forest)
1979 Cyrille Regis (West Bromwich Albion)
1980 Glenn Hoddle (Tottenham Hotspur)
1981 Gary Shaw (Aston Villa)
1982 Steve Moran (Southampton)
1983 Ian Rush (Liverpool)

PLayer Award Winners

1984 Paul Walsh (Luton Town)
1985 Mark Hughes (Manchester United)
1986 Tony Cottee (West Ham United)
1987 Tony Adams (Arsenal)
1988 Paul Gascoigne (Newcastle United)
1989 Paul Merson (Arsenal)
1990 Matthew Le Tissier (Southampton)
1991 Lee Sharpe (Manchester United)
1992 Ryan Giggs (Manchester United)
1993 Ryan Giggs (Manchester United)
1994 Andy Cole (Newcastle United)
1995 Robbie Fowler (Liverpool)
1996 Robbie Fowler (Liverpool)
1997 David Beckham (Manchester United)

**SCOTTISH FOOTBALL WRITERS ASSOCIATION
PLAYER OF THE YEAR**
1965 Billy McNeill (Celtic)
1966 John Greig (Rangers)
1967 Ronnie Simpson (Celtic)
1968 Gordon Wallace (Raith Rovers)
1969 Bobby Murdoch (Celtic)
1970 Pat Stanton (Hibernian)
1971 Martin Buchan (Aberdeen)
1972 David Smith (Rangers)
1973 George Connelly (Celtic)
1974 Scotland's World Cup squad
1975 Dandy Jardine (Rangers)
1976 John Greig (Rangers)
1977 Danny McGrain (Celtic)
1978 Derek Johnstone (Rangers)
1979 Andy Ritchie (Morton)
1980 Gordon Strachan (Aberdeen)
1981 Alan Rough (Partick Thistle)
1982 Paul Sturrock (Dundee United)
1983 Charlie Nicholas (Celtic)
1984 Willie Miller (Aberdeen)
1985 Hamish McAlpine (Dundee United)
1986 Sandy Jardine (Heart of Midlothian)
1987 Brian McClair (Celtic)
1988 Paul McStay (Celtic)
1989 Richard Gough (Rangers)
1990 Alex McLeish (Aberdeen)
1991 Maurice Malpas (Dundee United)
1992 Ally McCoist (Rangers)
1993 Andy Goram (Rangers)

 **Facts**   PLayer Award Winners

1994 Mark Hateley (Rangers)
1995 Brian Laudrup (Rangers)
1996 Paul Gascoigne (Rangers)
1997 Brian Laudrup (Rangers)

SCOTTISH P.F.A. PLAYER OF THE YEAR
1978 Derek Johnstone (Rangers)
1979 Paul Hegarty (Dundee United)
1980 Davie Provan (Celtic)
1981 Mark McGee (Aberdeen)
1982 Sandy Clarke (Aidrieonians)
1983 Charlie Nicholas (Celtic)
1984 Willie Miller (Aberdeen)
1985 Jim Duffy (Morton)
1986 Richard Gough (Dundee United)
1987 Brian McClair (Celtic)
1988 Paul McStay (Celtic)
1989 Theo Snelders (Aberdeen)
1990 Jim Bett (Aberdeen)
1991 Paul Elliott (Celtic)
1992 Ally McCoist (Rangers)
1993 Andy Goram (Rangers)
1994 Mark Hateley (Rangers)
1995 Brian Laudrup (Rangers)
1996 Paul Gascoigne (Rangers)
1997 Paolo di Canio (Celtic)

SCOTTISH P.F.A. YOUNG PLAYER OF THE YEAR
1978 Graeme Payne (Dundee United)
1979 Ray Stewart (Dundee United)
1980 John McDonald (Rangers)
1981 Charlie Nicholas (Celtic)
1982 Frank McAvennie (St. Mirren)
1983 Paul McStay (Cektic)
1984 John Robertson (Heart of Midlothian)
1985 Craig Levein (Heart of Midlothian)
1986 Craig Levein (Heart of Midlothian)
1987 Robert Fleck (Rangers)
1988 John Collins (Hibernian)
1989 Billy McKinlay (Dundee United)
1990 Scott Crabbe (Heart of Midlothian)
1991 Eoin Jess (Aberdeen)
1992 Phil O'Donnell (Motherwell)
1993 Eoin Jess (Aberdeen)
1994 Phil O'Donnell (Motherwell)
1995 Charlie Miller (Rangers)

PLayer Award Winners

Facts

1996 Jack McNamara (Celtic)
1997 Robbie Winters (Dundee United)

EUROPEAN FOOTBALLER OF THE YEAR
1956 Stanley Matthews (Blackpool)
1957 Alfredo di Stefano (Real Madrid)
1958 Raymond Kopa (Real Madrid)
1959 Alfredo di Stefano (Real Madrid)
1960 Luis Suarez (Barcelona)
1961 Omar Sivori (Juventus)
1962 Josef Masopust (Dukla Prague)
1963 Lev Yashin (Moscow Dynamo)
1964 Denis Law (Manchester United)
1965 Eusebio (Benfica)
1966 Bobby Charlton (Manchester United)
1967 Florian Albert (Ferencvaros)
1968 George Best (Manchester United)
1969 Gianni Rivera (AC Milan)
1970 Gerd Muller (Bayern Munich)
1971 Johan Cruyff (Ajax)
1972 Franz Beckenbauer (Bayern Munich)
1973 Johan Cruyff (Barcelona)
1974 Johan Cruyff (Barcelona)
1975 Oleg Blokhin (Dynamo Kiev)
1976 Franz Beckenbauer (Bayern Munich)
1977 Allan Simonsen (Borussia Moenchengladbach)
1978 Kevin Keegan (SV Hamburg)
1979 Kevin Keegan (SV Hamburg)
1980 Karl-Heinz Rummenigge (Bayern Munich)
1981 Karl-Heinz Rummenigge (Bayern Munich)
1982 Paolo Rossi (Juventus)
1983 Michel Platini (Juventus)
1984 Michel Platini (Juventus)
1985 Michel Platini (Juventus)
1986 Igor Belanov (Dynamo Kiev)
1987 Ruud Gullit (AC Milan)
1988 Marco Van Basten (AC Milan)
1989 Marco Van Basten (AC Milan)
1990 Lothar Matthaus (Inter Milan)
1991 Jean-Pierre Papin (Marseille)
1992 Marco Van Basten (AC Milan)
1993 Roberto Baggio (Juventus)
1994 Hristo Stoichkov (Barcelona)
1995 George Weah (AC Milan)
1996 Matthias Sammer (Borussia Dortmund)

TRANSFERS

CARLING 10,000 FOOTBALL FACTS & QUESTIONS

British Transfers

The first £1m British player was Trevor Francis. He moved from Birmingham to Nottingham Forest for £1.18m in February 1979.

Alan Shearer became the most expensive player in the world when he moved from Blackburn to Newcastle for £15m in July 1996.

Duncan Ferguson cost £8m in two transfers in the space of 17 months. He moved from Dundee United to Rangers for £4m in July 1993, and then joined Everton for the same price in December 1994. The Dundee United-Rangers deal set a record transfer involving two Scottish clubs.

Alf Common became the first £1,000 player when he moved from Sunderland to Middlesbrough in February 1905.

Rushden & Diamonds set a new non-league transfer record when they bought Carl Alford from GM Vauxhall Conference side Kettering for £85,000 in March 1996.

The first £100,000 British player was Denis Law, when he moved to Italian club Torino from Manchester City in June 1961. Law became the most expensive British player for the second time when he returned to Manchester, but this time to United, for £115,000 in July 1962.

The first £200,000 British player was Tottenham's Martin Peters. The World Cup winning forward moved from London rivals West Ham in March 1970.

Kevin Keegan became the first £500,000 British player when he left Liverpool to join German club Hamburg in June 1977.

Paul Ince became the most expensive British player to sign for a foreign club when he moved from Manchester United to Italian club Inter Milan for £6m in June 1995.

Lee Bowyer became the most expensive teenager in British football when he left Charlton in July 1996 to join Leeds for £2.6m.

 **Facts**   British Transfers

Stan Collymore cost £17.7m in just three transfer deals in four years. He moved to Nottingham Forest for £2.2m from Southend in June 1993, then went to Liverpool in June 1995 for £8.5m and then arrived at Aston Villa for £7m in May 1997.

David Platt became Britian's most expensive player in history when Arsenal signed him from Sampdoria in July 1995. Platt cost just under £22m in total transfer deals in just four years. He moved from Aston Villa to Italian club Bari for £5.5m in July 1991, Bari to Juventus for £6.5m a year later, Juventus to Sampdoria for £5.2m in July 1993 and then to Arsenal for £4.75m in July 1995.

British Transfers

Dutch striker Dennis Bergkamp became the most expensive foreign import when he joined Arsenal in June 1995 for £7.5m.

Stan Collymore set three British records when he signed for Liverpool for £8.5m in June 1995. He became the record English club signing, the most expensive British striker and set a record all-British deal.

The record fee paid to a Scottish club was the £5m paid to Rangers from French club Marseille for Trevor Steven in August 1991.

Croatian Slaven Bilic became the most expensive footballer in Britain when he joined Everton from West Ham in May 1997 for £4.5m.

Bruce Dyer became the first £1m teenager when he joined Crystal Palace from Watford in March 1994 for £1.1m.

Alan Shearer has cost £18.3m in just two transfer deals. He moved to Blackburn from Southampton for £3.3m in July 1992 and then to Newcastle in July 1996 for £15m. Both transfer deals set British records.

YOUNGEST
AND OLDEST

Youngest and Oldest

Facts

The youngest player to be capped by England was James Prinsep, who played v Scotland in April 1879 at the age of 17 years 252 days.

The youngest player to score a goal in the top-flight was Ipswich schoolboy Jason Dozzell. He scored against Coventry in February 1984 at the age of 16 years, 57 days.

The youngest player to take part in a Carling Premiership match was West Ham's Neil Finn, who played in goals against Coventry in January 1996 when he was only 17 years and three days.

Neil McBain, manager of New Brighton, became the oldest player to figure in a League match when he came on as a goalkeeper in their game with Hartlepool in 1947 at the age of 51 years, 120 days.

Stanley Matthews holds the record as the oldest player to be capped by England, playing his final international against Denmark in May 1957 at the age of 42 years and 104 days.

British youngest capped players are:

Scotland – Denis Law, 18 years, 235 days (v Wales, October 18, 1958)

Northern Ireland – Norman Whiteside, 17 years, 42 days (v Yugoslavia, June 17, 1982)

Wales – Ryan Giggs, 17 years, 332 days (v Germany, October 16, 1991)

Republic of Ireland – Jimmy Holmes, 17 years, 200 days (v Austria, May 30, 1971)

Manchester United's Duncan Edwards became England's youngest capped player this century when he played against Scotland on April 2, 1955. He was 18 years, 183 days.

England's youngest goalscorer record was set by Tommy Lawton who was 19 years, 6 days when he scored a penalty against Wales in Cardiff on October 22, 1938.

Sunderland's goalkeeper Derek Foster became the youngest First Division player when he played against Leicester City on August 22, 1964. He was 15 years, 185 days.

 **Facts**   **Youngest and Oldest**

Andrew Cunningham became the oldest player to make his Football League debut. He was 38 years, 2 days when he turned out for Newcastle United against Leicester City in a First Division match on February 2, 1929.

Walter (Billy) Hampson became the oldest player to play in the FA Cup Final when he appeared for Newcastle United against Aston Villa in 1924. He was 41 years, 8 months.

The record for oldest Carling Premiership player was set by goalkeeper John Burridge on April 29, 1995. Aged 43 years, 4 months, 26 days, he appeared as a half-time substitute for Manchester City against Newcastle United. At the time he was goalkeeper coach for Newcastle.

The record for the youngest England captain was set by Bobby Moore. He captained his country away to Czechoslovakia on May 29, 1963 aged 22 years, 1 month, 17 days.

Tottenham's Andy Turner became the youngest Carling Premiership goalscorer when he scored against Everton on September 5, 1992. He was 17 years, 166 days.

Alan Shearer holds the record for the youngest First Division hat-trick scorer. He was 17 years, 240 days when he scored three for Southampton against Arsenal on April 9, 1988. It was Shearer's full debut.

Chelsea's Jimmy Greaves became the youngest player to score 100 Football League goals when he reached his ton against Manchester City on November 19, 1960 aged 20 years, 261 days.

Arsenal's average age of their 1950 FA Cup winning team was 31 years, 2 months, a record in the competition.

Stanley Matthews became England's oldest goalscorer when, aged 41 years, 248 days, he scored against Northern Ireland in Belfast on October 6, 1956.

The youngest FA Cup player record was set by Andy Awford. He played for Worcester City in a third round qualifying match against Borehamwood on October 10, 1987.

Youngest and Oldest

The youngest player to play in the FA Cup proper was Kettering Town's goalkeeper Scott Endersby. He was 15 years, 279 days when he played against Tilbury in the first round match on November 26, 1977.

The record for youngest goalscorer in an international match was set on April 22, 1995 by Mohamed Kallon of Sierra Leone. He was 15 years, 6 months, 16 days when he netted against Congo in an African Nations Cup match.

The oldest player to make his England debut was Leslie Compton. He was 38 years, 2 months when he played against Wales in Sunderland on November 15, 1950.

The oldest British international player was Wales' Billy Meredith on March 15, 1920. He was 45 years, 8 months when he played against England at Highbury.

The youngest player to score in the Football League was Bristol Rovers' Ronnie Dix. He was 15 years, 180 days when he scored against Norwich City in a Division Three (South) match on March 3, 1928.

David Nish still remains the youngest FA Cup Final captain. Aged 21 years, 7 months, Nish led out Leicester City against Manchester City in 1969.

Two men share the record for youngest Football League players. They are: Albert Geldard (Bradford v Millwall, Division Two, September 16, 1929) and Ken Roberts (Wrexham v Bradford, Division Three (North), September 1, 1951). Both were aged 15 years, 158 days.

Sunderland's Barry Venison became the youngest Wembley Cup Final captain when, at the age of 20 years, 7 months, 8 days, he led the club to the 1985 League Cup Final.

The record for youngest FA Cup-winning captain was set by Bobby Moore in 1964. He was 23 years, 20 days when he led West Ham to victory over Preston North End.

Chesterfield's Kevin Davies became the youngest League Cup player on September 22, 1993. He was 16 years, 180 days when he appeared as a substitute against West Ham in the second round, second leg tie.

 **Facts**   **Youngest and Oldest**

Aside from becoming the youngest England player, James Prinsep became the youngest FA Cup Final player when he appeared for Clapham Rovers against Old Etonians in 1879 aged 17 years, 245 days.

West Ham's Paul Allen has so far come closest to beating Prinsep's record. He was 11 days older than Prinsep when he played against Arsenal in 1980, and became the youngest FA Cup finalist this century.

The youngest FA Cup Final goalscorer was Manchester United's Norman Whiteside. He was 18 years, 19 days when he scored against Brighton and Hove Albion in the 1983 replay.

Whiteside is also the youngest goalscorer in a Wembley Cup Final. Aged 17 years, 324 days, he scored for Manchester United against Liverpool in the 1983 League Cup Final.

Chris Woods became the youngest Wembley Cup Final goalkeeper when he appeared for Nottingham Forest aged 18 years, 125 days against Liverpool in the 1978 League Cup Final.

THE RECORDS

CARLING 10,000 FOOTBALL FACTS & QUESTIONS

APPEARANCES

Appearances

Facts

Peter Shilton played his 1000th League game for Leyton Orient in December 1996, playing against Brighton and keeping a clean sheet. He became the first man to reach the thousand-mark in English football.

Tranmere Rovers' centre-half Harold Bell holds the record for consecutive appearances, playing in 459 games between 1946 and 1955 when he was ever-present for the first nine post-war seasons.

A broken finger prevented Dave Beasant extending his run of consecutive League games past 394, his nine-year run beginning in August 1981 and ending with his accident in October 1990.

Phil Neal made 366 consecutive First Division appearances for Liverpool between December 1974 and September 1983, a record for an outfield player in the top flight.

In 1952-53 the entire Huddersfield Town defence played in all 42 Second Division matches – the goalkeeper, two full-backs and three half-backs being ever-present for the whole season.

Eric Cantona played in Championship-winning teams for four consecutive seasons, first for Marseille (1990-91) and then in England for first Leeds then Manchester United.

The first substitute to be used in a League game was Keith Peacock, who came on for Charlton in a game at Bolton on August 21, 1965.

In 1992-93 Leeds United became the first club to fail to win a League match away from home in the season after claiming the Championship.

In 1986-87 goalkeeper Eric Nixon became the first player to play in all four divisions of the Football League in one season when he played for Manchester City, Southampton, Bradford City, Carlisle and Wolves.

When Preston played Bury in January 1990 the opposing keepers were brothers with Alan Kelly (Preston) lining up against Gary Kelly (Bury). Their father was a Republic of Ireland international goalkeeper.

In April 1915 a game between Middlesbrough and Oldham was abandoned after 55 minutes when Oldham defender Billy Cook refused to leave the field after his dismissal.

 **Facts**

Appearances

A game between Sheffield Wednesday and Aston Villa was abandoned through bad light after 79 and a half minutes in November 1898. The two teams reconvened four months later to play the last ten and a half minutes, Wednesday adding a fourth goal to make the final score 4-1.

Sweden's Tomas Ravelli overtook Peter Shilton's international goalkeeping record when he won his 126th cap for his country on June 8, 1995 in the Umbro Cup against, ironically, England.

After Peter Shilton, here are the players with most English League appearances:

Terry Paine – 824 (713 Southampton, 111 Hereford United)

Tommy Hutchinson – 797 (165 Blackpool, 314 Coventry City, 46 Manchester City, 92 Burnley, 180 Swansea City)

Robbie James – 782 (484 Swansea City, 48 Stoke City, 87 QPR, 23 Leicester City, 89 Bradford City, 51 Cardiff City)

Alan Oakes – 777 (565 Manchester City, 211 Chester City, 1 Port Vale)

EXTRA EXTRA TIME!

Appearances

John Trollope – 770 (all for Swindon Town – a record total for one club)

Jimmy Dickinson – 764 (all for Portsmouth)

Roy Sproson – 762 (all for Port Vale)

Billy Bonds – 758 (95 Charlton, 663 West Ham United)

Ray Clemence – 758 (48 Scunthorpe United, 470 Liverpool, 240 Tottenham)

Pat Jennings – 757 (48 Watford, 472 Tottenham, 237 Arsenal)

Frank Worthington – 757 (171 Huddersfield Town, 210 Leicester City, 84 Bolton Wanderers, 75 Birmingham City, 32 Leeds United, 19 Sunderland, 34 Southampton, 31 Brighton and Hove Albion, 59 Tranmere Rovers, 23 Preston North End, 19 Stockport County)

Trevor Steven has appeared in Championship-winning teams from three different countries. Steven played for Everton in England (1985, 1987), Scotland's Rangers (1990, 1991, 1993, 1994, 1995) and Marseille in France (1992).

ATTENDANCES

Attendances

Facts

The biggest World Cup attendance came in the final match of the 1950 tournament in Brazil. 199,850 saw Uruguay defeat Brazil to win the trophy.

The total attendance for the three World Club Cup matches between Santos and AC Milan in 1963 exceeded 375,000.

The first all-ticket match in Scotland was the 1937 international between Scotland and England at Hampden Park. 149,547 watched the game on April 17.

The biggest attendance for a British club match, apart from a Cup Final, was 143,470 for the Rangers v Hibernian at Hampden Park on March 27, 1948.

The FA Cup Final's highest attendance came in 1923 for the Bolton Wanderers-West Ham game. 126,047 were at Wembley although 150,000 were estimated to be in the ground.

120,000 watched Cameroon v Morocco in a World Cup qualifying tie in Yaounde in November 1981 – a record for a qualifying match.

The biggest British attendance for a World Cup qualifying match was 107,580 watching the Scotland and Poland at Hampden Park on October 13, 1965.

A record 127,621 saw the 1960 European Cup Final between Real Madrid and Eintracht Frankfurt at Hampden Park.

The highest attendance at an European Cup match is the 135,826 that watched the Celtic v Leeds semi-final at Hampden Park on April 15, 1970.

West Ham's victory over TSV Munich at Wembley in the 1965 European Cup-Winners' Cup Final produced a record crowd for the competition – 100,000.

Rangers and Celtic's match on January 2, 1939 provided a record attendance for a Scottish League match of 118,567.

The Scottish League Cup Final between Celtic and Rangers at Hampden Park on October 23, 1965 drew a record crowd of 107,609.

The English First Division's record attendance was set at the Manchester United v Arsenal match on January 17, 1948. 83,260 watched the match that was played at Maine Road.

 **Facts**

Attendances

The Second Division record crowd was at Villa Park on October 30, 1937 when 68,029 watched Aston Villa v Coventry City.

A record 49,309 for the Third Division watched the Sheffield Wednesday-Sheffield United match on Boxing Day in 1979.

The record attendance for a Football League season is 41,271,414 between the 88 clubs in the 1948-49 season.

The record single day attendance for Football League matches was the 1,269,934 on December 27, 1949.

Manchester United averaged a record 57,758 for matches in the 1967-68 season.

100,000 watched the 1953 FA Amateur Cup Final between Pegasus and Harwich & Parkeston at Wembley – a record for the competition.

The record British Cup tie aggregate is 265,199 for the two matches between Rangers and Morton in the Scottish Cup Final of 1948.

Attendances

Facts

Colchester United's record crowd of 19,072 turned up to watch the **FA Cup first round tie against Reading on November 27, 1948 only for the game was abandoned after 35 minutes because of fog.**

The lowest post-war League attendance was 450 for the Division Three game between Rochdale and Cambridge United on February 2, 1974.

The lowest First Division attendance since the war is the 3,121 that turned up to watch Wimbledon v Sheffield Wednesday on October 2, 1991.

The lowest Carling Premiership crowd is 3,039 at Selhurst Park on Boxing Day, 1993 for Wimbledon v Everton.

The smallest Wembley crowd for an England match is 15,628 for the match against Chile on May 23, 1989. The gate was affected by a tube strike.

Chile also featured in Northern Ireland's smallest gate when only 2,500 saw the match at Belfast on May 26, 1989.

The record FA Cup final attendance before Wembley was the 120,028 that saw the 1913 final between Aston Villa and Sunderland at Crystal Palace.

ENGLISH CLUB FEATS

English Club Feats

Liverpool went 85 competitive matches unbeaten from January 21, 1978 to January 31, 1981. That run covered 63 League games, nine League Cup, seven in Europe and six in the FA Cup.

Millwall were unbeaten at home in the League for 59 consecutive matches from 1964-67.

The first club to rise from the Fourth Division to the First were Northampton Town when they won promotion to Division One in 1965.

Wimbledon went from non-league football (Southern League) to Division One in just nine seasons. They reached the top-flight in 1986.

Manchester United completed the League and Cup 'double' twice in three seasons. They won both competitions in 1993-94 and 1995-96. They became the first club to win the 'double' twice.

Arsenal were the first club to win both FA and League Cup's in the same season – 1992-93.

Four clubs this century have won the League and Cup 'double'. They are Tottenham (1960-61), Arsenal (1970-71), Liverpool (1985-86) and Manchester United (1993-94 and 1995-96).

On their way to completing the first League and Cup 'double' in 1888-89, Preston North End did not lose a League match and didn't concede a goal in the FA Cup.

Liverpool's most successful League run was between 1976 and 1983 when they won the Championship six times in eight seasons.

Up to the start of the 1997-98 season, Liverpool are the only team to have won three major competitions in one season. They won the League Championship, League Cup and European Cup in the 1983-84 season.

Arsenal had seven players in the England side against Italy on November 14, 1935 – still a record.

Coventry City are the only club to have played in the Premier League, all four previous divisions of the Football League and both sections of the old Third Division (North and South).

 **Facts**

English Club Feats

Wolves, one of the founder members of the Football League, went from First Division to Fourth in successive seasons – 1984-5-6.

Lincoln City became the first club to be demoted from the Football League when they finished bottom of the Fourth Division in 1986-87. Scarborough, champions of the GM Vauxhall Conference, replaced them.

Aston Villa had seven ever-present players when they won the League Championship in 1980-81.

Birmingham City set a new record in the 1995-96 season by using 46 players during the League season.

Arsenal were defeated only once when they won the League Championship in 1990-91 – a record this century.

Up to the start of the 1997-98 season, only three teams have won the League Championship three times in succession. Huddersfield Town in 1923-24, 1924-25, 1925-26, Arsenal in 1932-33, 1933-34, 1934-35 and Liverpool in 1981-82, 1982-83, 1983-84.

Oxford United became the first club to win Division Three and Division Two titles in successive seasons – 1983-84, 1984-85.

The last team to win Second Division and First Division titles in successive years were Ipswich Town in 1960-61 and 1961-62.

The original 12 members of the Football League were Accrington, Aston Villa, Blackburn Rovers, Bolton Wanderers, Burnley, Derby County, Everton, Notts County, Preston North End, Stoke, West Bromwich Albion and Wolverhampton Wanderers.

English Club Feats

Up to the start of the 1997-98 season, Liverpool is the only city to have staged top-flight football in every season since the Football League began in 1888.

League Champions in successive seasons

Preston North End (1888-89, 1889-90)
Sunderland (1891-92, 1892-93)
Aston Villa (1895-96, 1896-97, 1898-99, 1899-1900)
Sheffield Wednesday (1902-03, 1903-04, 1928-29, 1929-30)
Liverpool (1921-22, 1922-23, 1975-76, 1976-77, 1978-79, 1979-80, 1981-82, 1982-83, 1983-84)
Portsmouth (1948-49, 1949-50)
Manchester United (1955-56, 1956-57)
Wolves (1957-58, 1958-59)

The highest goal-scoring team in the Premiership have been Newcastle United. They scored 82 goals in 42 games in the 1993-94 season.

Swindon Town hold the record for most goals conceded in a Premiership season when they let in 100 goals, also in the 1993-94 season.

FOOTBALL LEAGUE MILESTONES

Football League Milestones

Facts

The first code of football rules were compiled at Cambridge University in 1848.

The oldest Football League club, Notts County, were formed in 1862.

The Football Association was founded in 1863. The FA Cup was introduced eight years later.

The first football international match took place in 1872. Scotland and England drew 0-0.

Shinguards were introduced into football in 1874. A year later the crossbar replaced tape as part of the goal frame.

The Footbal League was founded by Wm. McGregor in 1888 with the first match taking place on September 8.

Goal-nets were introduced in 1891, as well as the penalty-kick.

The Football League opened a Second Division in 1892. Promotion and relegation was introduced six years later.

FIFA was founded by the seven member countries in 1904.

Transfer deadline day was introduced in 1911.

The Football League was extended to 44 clubs in 1919.

The Third Division (South) was formed in 1920. The North version came a year later.

England and Scotland met in the first Wembley International in 1924. The game ended 1-1.

Also in 1924, the Rules were changed to allow goals to be scored direct from corner-kicks.

The new offside law came into effect from 1925.

The first Football League match to be broadcast on radio was on January 22, 1927, for the match between Arsenal and Sheffield United. Other firsts in 1927: The FA Cup Final was broadcast on radio and Charles Clegg, president of the FA became the first knight of foootball.

 **Facts**   Football League Milestones

Britain's representatives withdrew from FIFA in 1928. They rejoined in 1946.

The Football League celebrate their 50th Jubilee. An arc on the edge of the penalty-area was introduced. FA secretary, Stanley Rous, re-drafts the Laws of the Game.

The numbering of players' shirts in Football League matches became compulsory in 1939.

Stanley Rous is knighted in 1949.

The Football League was extended from 88 clubs to 92 in 1950.

The last occasion of Football League matches played on Christmas Day was in 1957.

The Football League was re-structured into four divisions in 1958.

The Football League Cup was introduced in 1960.

The first Match of the Day was televised on August 22, 1964. The first match to be covered was the League match between Liverpool and Arsenal. Liverpool won 3-2.

Substitutes were allowed in Football League matches in 1965.

The Football League introduced the loan system in 1967 Originally two loan transfers a season were allowed to clubs.

League football was played for the first time on a Sunday on January 20, 1974.

Transfer Tribunal was formed by the Football League in 1978.

The Football League increase the points for a win to three instead of two in 1981. Queens Park Rangers become the first Football League club to install an artifical pitch in the same year. Also in the same year, referee's yellow and red cards are scrapped by the Football League. They were re-introduced in 1987.

The Football League Cup becomes a sponsored event when it is re-named the Milk Cup in 1982.

The Football League gains sponsorship and becomes the Canon Football League at the start of the 1983-84 season.

Football League Milestones

Facts

Charlton and Crystal Palace become the first clubs to share a ground (Palace's Selhurst Park) in the Football League's history in 1985.

Football League clubs are banned from European competition in 1985 after the Heysel disaster before the Liverpool-Juventus European Cup Final.

The Football League announced a new sponsor in 1986 when the Today newspaper put it's name to the competition.

The Football League introduce play-off matches to decide the final promotion/relegation places in 1987.

The Football League acquired their third sponsor, Barclays Bank, in 1987.

Football League clubs are allowed back into European competition after a five-year exile in 1990.

The Football League is reduced to three divisions, and 71 clubs, after the introduction of the FA Carling Premiership in the 1992-93 season.

Barclays Bank ended their sponsorship with the Football League in 1993. Endsleigh Insurance replace them.

For the start of the 1996-97 season, Nationwide Building Society were the new sponsors of the Football League.

In 1961 Fulham's Johnny Haynes became the first player to earn £100 a week wages.

MANAGERS

Managers

Facts

Fred Everiss holds the record as the longest-serving manager of one club – holding the reins at West Bromwich Albion for 46 years between 1902 and 1948.

Bill Lambton became the shortest-serving manager in British history when he served only three days at Scunthorpe United in April 1959.

Herbert Chapman became the first manager to win the League Championship with two different clubs when he led Arsenal to the title in 1930-31 after two earlier triumphs with Huddersfield Town.

The only manager to win the FA Cup with two different clubs is Billy Walker, who led Sheffield Wednesday to victory in 1935 and Nottingham Forest in 1959.

Les Allen was the first man to become player/manager of a top-flight team when he was appointed to the post at QPR in 1968.

Bob Paisley is the most successful manager in English club history, leading Liverpool to 20 trophies, including six League Championships, between 1974 and 1983.

Glenn Hoddle became the ninth England manager when he took over from Terry Venables in June 1996. Joe Mercer was caretaker-manager in 1974 before Don Revie took over.

Billy Bingham has managed Northern Ireland on two occasions. First from 1967 to 1971 and then from 1980 to 1993. He also coached Greece for two years from 1971.

Dave Bassett looked to have become manager of Crystal Palace in May 1984. But four days later he changed his mind, without signing the contract, and stayed at Wimbledon.

Up to the end of the 1996-97 season, West Ham have only had eight managers in their history. The list is: Syd King, Charlie Paynter, Ted Fenton, Ron Greenwood, John Lyall, Lou Macari, Billy Bonds and Harry Redknapp.

Tom Whittaker got a dream start with his new team at Arsenal in 1947-48. They were unbeaten for the first 17 League matches on their way to winning the First Division.

 **Facts** **Managers**

Only two managers have won the League Championship with different clubs – Herbert Chapman, Huddersfield Town (1923-24, 1924-25) and Arsenal (1930-31, 1932-33); Brian Clough, Derby County (1971-72) and Nottingham Forest (1977-78);

Kenny Dalglish became the first manager to win the League and Carling Premiership trophy. He led Liverpool to three League Championship titles in 1985-86, 1987-88, 1989-90 and then Blackburn to the Carling Premiership trophy in 1994-95.

Dalglish also became the first manager to win the 'double' as player-manager, when he led Liverpool in 1985-86.

The last man to win the First Division title as a player and as a manager with the same club was George Graham. He won the League with Arsenal as a player in 1970-71, and as a manager in 1988-89 and 1989-90.

Ruud Gullit became the first foreign manager to win the FA Cup when he led Chelsea to victory in 1997.

Managers

Facts

Billy McNeill and Dave Bassett both managed two clubs that were relegated in the same season. McNeill was in charge of Manchester City and Aston Villa who were relegated to Division Two in 1986-87. Bassett managed Watford (relegated to Division Two) and Sheffield United (down to the Third Division) in 1987-88.

Bob Paisley remains the most successful manager in English club football. Paisley won six League Championships, three European Cups, three League Cups, one Uefa Cup, one European Super Cup and six Charity Shields (one shared) as Liverpool manager between 1974 and 1983.

Up to the start of the 1997-98 season, Kenny Dalglish is the only man to have won the League Championship as player-manager. He led Liverpool to the title in 1985-86 and 1987-88 in dual roles.

The first winner of the Manager of the Year award was Celtic's Jock Stein.

By 1997, ten of the last 12 Manager of the Year were Scottish. Howard Kendall (Everton 1987) and Howard Wilkinson (Leeds (1992) are the only two English winners. The Scottish contingent are: Kenny Dalglish (Liverpool 1986, 1988, 1990 and Blackburn 1995), George Graham (Arsenal 1989, 1991) and Alex Ferguson (Manchester United 1993, 1994, 1996, 1997) are the other winners.

Jack Charlton was named Manager of the Year in 1974 when he was manager of Middlesbrough.

The League Managers' Association created their own Manager of the Year award in 1993. Given to "the manager who has made best use of the resources available to him", the winners have been: 1993 – Dave Bassett (Sheffield United), 1994 – Joe Kinnear (Wimbledon), 1995 – Frank Clark (Nottingham Forest), 1996 – Peter Reid (Sunderland), 1997 – Danny Wilson (Barnsley).

 **Facts**   **Managers**

Manager of the Year Awards

1966 Jock Stein (Celtic)
1967 Jock Stein (Celtic)
1968 Matt Busby (Manchester United)
1969 Don Revie (Leeds United)
1970 Don Revie (Leeds United)
1971 Bertie Mee (Arsenal)
1972 Don Revie (Leeds United)
1973 Bill Shankly (Liverpool)
1974 Jack Charlton (Middlesbrough)
1975 Ron Saunders (Aston Villa)
1976 Bob Paisley (Liverpool)
1977 Bob Paisley (Liverpool)
1978 Brian Clough (Nottingham Forest)
1979 Bob Paisley (Liverpool)

WHY CATS DON'T PLAY FOOTBALL!

Managers

Facts

1980 Bob Paisley (Liverpool)
1981 Ron Saunders (Aston Villa)
1982 Bob Paisley (Liverpool)
1983 Bob Paisley (Liverpool)
1984 Joe Fagan (Liverpool)
1985 Howard Kendall (Everton)
1986 Kenny Dalglish (Liverpool)
1987 Howard Kendall (Everton)
1988 Kenny Dalglish (Liverpool)
1989 George Graham (Arsenal)
1990 Kenny Dalglish (Liverpool)
1991 George Graham (Arsenal)
1992 Howard Wilkinson (Leeds United)
1993 Alex Ferguson (Manchester United)
1994 Alex Ferguson (Manchester United)
1995 Kenny Dalglish (Blackburn Rovers)
1996 Alex Ferguson (Manchester United)
1997 Alex Ferguson (Manchester United)

WEMBLEY

Wembley

Facts

Originally named the Empire Stadium, the famous home of English football was opened in 1923.

The original contract between the FA and the British Empire Exhibition was for the FA Cup final to be played there for 21 years.

Wembley was officially named England's national stadium in December 1996. It will cost an estimated £180m for re-development.

Wembley's first FA Cup Final was in 1923 when West Ham met Bolton Wanderers. The official attendance of 126,047 is still a record for the stadium.

The present contract, signed in 1983, by the FA ensured that Wembley will host England's home matches, the FA Cup Final and Charity Shield until 2002.

There have been only two England home games played away from Wembley since January 5, 1966. The two games were at Leeds' Elland Road against Sweden in the Umbro Cup on June 8, 1995 and the friendly against South Africa at Manchester United's Old Trafford on May 24, 1997.

The last 100,000 attendance at Wembley was for the 1985 FA Cup Final between Manchester United and Everton.

The first international played under floodlights at Wembley was on November 20, 1963 for the game between England and Northern Ireland. England won 8-3.

The first Wembley final to be decided on a 'Golden Goal' was the 1995 Auto Windscreens Shield. Paul Tait's goal in the 103rd minute ensured Birmingham beat Carlisle 1-0.

Nottingham Forest became the first club to reach two Wembley Finals in the same season when they reached the League Cup and Simod Cup Finals in 1989.

Three teams have reached both League and FA Cup Finals at Wembley in the same season. Arsenal and Sheffield Wednesday made both Finals in 1993, the first time the same two teams contested both Finals, and Middlesbrough in 1997. Sheffield Wednesday and Middlesbrough lost both games.

 **Facts** Wembley

Three players have scored hat-tricks in major Wembley Finals. They are Stan Mortensen (Blackpool v Bolton, FA Cup Final, 1953), Geoff Hurst (England v West Germany, World Cup Final, 1966) and David Speedie (Chelsea v Manchester City, Full Members Cup Final, 1985).

England's heaviest Wembley defeat to date was also their first in the stadium. They were beaten 3-6 by Hungary in November 1953.

The fastest goal in a Wembley match was scored after 20 seconds by Maurice Cox for Cambridge University against Oxford on December 5, 1979.

The fastest FA Cup Final goal at Wembley was scored by Chelsea's Roberto di Matteo after 42 seconds of the 1997 Final.

Up to June 1997, Wembley has hosted five European Cup Finals (1963, 1968, 1971, 1978, 1992). Two English clubs have won in the Wembley Finals. Manchester United in 1968 and Liverpool in 1978. The stadium has also hosted two European Cup-Winners' Cup Finals. Both finals have seen clubs win their first European trophy – West Ham in 1965 and Italian club Parma in 1993.

Only 12 players have been sent-off in major matches at Wembley. They are:

Boris Stankovic (Yugoslavia v Sweden, Olympic Games, August 1948)

Antonio Rattin (Argentina v England, World Cup, July 1966)

Billy Bremner (Leeds United v Liverpool, Charity Shield, August 1974)

Kevin Keegan (Liverpool v Leeds United, Charity Shield, August 1974)

Gilbert Dresch (Luxembourg v England, World Cup qual., March 1977)

Kevin Moran (Manchester United v Everton, FA Cup Final, May 1985)

Lee Dixon (Arsenal v Tottenham, FA Cup semi-final, April 1993)

Peter Swan (Port Vale v West Bromwich Albion, Play-off Final, May 1993).

IT'S A FUNNY OLD GAME

FAMOUS QUOTES

Famous Quotes

Facts

"A lot of hard work went into this defeat."
Malcolm Allison

"I went down to pass on some technical information to the team – like the fact the game had started."
Aston Villa manager Ron Atkinson, explaining why he had taken his seat in the dugout early in a match against Sheffield United.

Gordon Lee: "Well, what business has anyone got naming him Eamon O'Keefe if he isn't Irish?

Billy Bingham: "Probably the same business they have naming you Lee when you're not Chinese."

"Matt (Busby) always believed Manchester United would be one of the greatest clubs in the world. He was the eternal optimist. In 1968 he still hoped Glenn Miller was just missing."
Pat Crerand

"The game in Romania was a game we should have won. We lost it because we thought we were going to win it. But then again, I thought there was no way we were going to get a result there."
Republic of Ireland manager Jack Charlton in 1987

"The first thing that went wrong was half-time. We could have done without that."
England manager Graham Taylor in 1988.

"In terms of the Richter scale, this defeat was a force 8 gale."
John Lyall

"He's my man mountain – he would head aeroplanes away if it helped Birmingham City."
Barry Fry on Liam Daish

"Very few players have the courage of my convictions."
Brian Clough

"The last player to score a hat-trick in an FA Cup Final was Stan Mortensen. He even had a Final named after him – the Matthews Final."
Lawrie McMenemy

"I do want to play the long ball, and I do want to play the short ball. I think long and short balls is what football is all about."
Bobby Robson

"Certain players are for me, certain players are pro me."
Terry Venables

"Before the match I told my players they will be playing against 11 guys ready to fight for each other for 90 minutes...... but I didn't expect it to be with each other."
Spartak Moscow coach Oleg Romantsev after the infamous brawl between Blackburn's Graeme le Saux and David Batty.

"I don't drop players – I make changes."
Bill Shankly

Facts

Famous Quotes

"Women run everything. The only thing that I have done within my house in the last 20 years is to recognise Angola as an independent state."
Brian Clough

"Of course I didn't take my wife to see Rochdale as an anniversary present. It was her birthday, Would I have got married during the football season? And, anyway, it wasn't Rochdale, it was Rochdale reserves."
Bill Shankly

"A fan is a person who, when you have made an idiot of yourself on the pitch, doesn't think you've done a permanent job."
Francis Lee

"Remember, postcards only, please. The winner will be the first one opened."
Brian Moore

"A lot of people in football don't have much time for the press; they say they're amateurs. But I say to those people, 'Noah was an amateur, but the Titanic was built by professionals."
Malcolm Allison

"They must go for it now as they have nothing to lose but the match."
Ron Atkinson

"Kenny Dalglish has about as much personality as a tennis racket."
Mick Channon

"Don't tell those coming the final result of the fantastic match, but let's just have another look at Italy's winning goal."
David Coleman

"If in winning the game we only finish with a draw, we would be fine."
Jack Charlton

"Nottingham Forest are having a bad run....... they've lost six matches now without winning."
David Coleman

"Trevor Brooking floats like a butterfly, and stings like one too."
Brian Clough

"You know, the Brazilians aren't as good as they used to be, or as they are now."
Kenny Dalglish

"Lukic saved with his foot which is all part of the goalkeeper's arm."
Barry Davies

"He hit the post, and after the game people will say, well, he hit the post."
Jimmy Greaves

"If a week's a long time in politics, it is an equinox in football."
Stuart Hall

"The USA are a goal down, and if they don't get a goal, they'll lose."
John Helm

Famous Quotes

Facts

Interviewer: "You've devoted a whole chapter of your book to Jimmy Greaves.

Pat Jennings: "That's right. Well, what can you say about Jimmy Greaves?"

"Sporting Lisbon in their green and white hoops, looking like a team of zebras."
Peter Jones

"Bobby Robson must be thinking of throwing some fresh legs on."
Kevin Keegan

Dickie Davies: "What's he going to be telling his team at half-time, Denis?

Denis Law: "He'll be telling them that there are forty-five minutes left to play."

"Both of the Villa scorers – Withe and Mortimer – were born in Liverpool, as was the Villa manager – Ron Saunders – who was born in Birkenhead."
David Coleman

"Chesterfield 1, Chester 1. Another score draw there in that local derby."
Desmond Lynam

"If history is going to repeat itself, I should think we can expect the same thing again."
Terry Venables

"I hear Glenn Hoddle has found God. That must have been one hell of a pass."
Jasper Carrott

"He's (a fellow coach) not so much a coach as a hearse."
Tommy Docherty

"Last time we got a penalty away from home, Christ was still a carpenter."
Lenny Lawrence

"We've got grounds which are a state of the art and administration which is state of the Ark."
PFA chairman Gordon Taylor

"I'm not superstitious or anything like that, but I'll just hope that we'll play our best and put it in the lap of the Gods."
Terry Neill

"My only problem (after his transfer to Italy) seems to be with Italian breakfasts. No matter how much money you've got, you can't get any Rice Krispies."
Luther Blissett

 **Facts**

Famous Quotes

"We fought two wars with the Germans. We probably got on better with the smaller nations like the Dutch, the Belgians, the Norwegians and the Swedes, some of whom are not even in Europe."
Jack Charlton

"There's a hell of a lot of politics in football. I don't think Henry Kissinger would have lasted 48 hours at Old Trafford."
Tommy Docherty

Manchester United are buzzing around the goalmouth like a lot of red bottles."

David Coleman

"The news from Guadalajara, where the temperature is 96 degrees, is that Falcao is warming up."
Brian Moore

"The doctor at Lazio told me I should try drinking wine, because it would be good for me. When I did, he had one look at me and said: 'You'd better go back on the beer.'"
Paul Gascoigne

Famous Quotes

Facts

"Well, stone me. We've had cocaine, bribery and Arsenal scoring two goals at home. But just when you thought there truly were no surprises left in football, Vinnie Jones turns out to be an international player."
Jimmy Greaves

"I'm not giving away any secrets like that to Milan. If I had my way, I wouldn't even tell them the time of the kick-off."
Bill Shankly, on delaying his team line-up

"The World Cup – truly an international event."
John Motson

"I have Gary Lineker's shirt up in my hotel room, and it's only stopped moving now."
Mick McCarthy

"With Maradona, even Arsenal would have won it (the 1986 World Cup)."
Bobby Robson

STRANGE GOALS

Strange Goals

DENNIS EVANS (ARSENAL) v BLACKPOOL 12.56 – Hearing what he thought was the final whistle, Evans turned to celebrate Arsenal's 4-0 victory by whacking the ball into his own net. Unfortunately, the whistle had come from the crowd.

CHRIS MACKENZIE (HEREFORD) v BARNET 08.95 – Hereford keeper Mackenzie beat his opposite number, Barnet's Maik Taylor, who was making his League debut, when his wind-assisted kick sailed over Taylor's head.

GEOFF HURST (ENGLAND) v WEST GERMANY 06.66 – The most famous World Cup final goal ever. The scores stood 2-2 in extra-time when Hurst turned and thudded a shot against the German bar. The ball rebounded down onto the line and the referee awarded a goal, although television evidence suggests it did not cross the line.

GARY CROSBY (NOTTINGHAM FOREST) v MANCHESTER CITY 03.90 – City keeper Andy Dibble was balancing the ball on his palm when Crosby nipped in from behind him, headed the ball off Dibble's hand and turned it into the net.

PETER HUNT (CHARLTON) v OLDHAM 10.72 – Hunt was credited with his first goal for Charlton although his shot clearly hit the side netting before the ball rebounded into the advertising hoardings.

SAM CHEDGZOY (EVERTON) v SPURS 04.24 – A loophole in the law allowed Chedgzoy to take a corner to himself and dribble past the Tottenham defence before scoring. The law was subsequently changed.

MARCUS BROWNING (BRISTOL ROVERS) v BRENTFORD 10.96 – Brentford keeper Kevin Dearden, hearing a whistle in the crowd, placed the ball for a free-kick and then watched Browning knock the ball into the empty net.

JOHAN CRUYFF (AJAX) v HELMOND SPORTS 1982-83 – Awarded a penalty, Cruyff decided not to take a direct shot at goal, instead playing a one-two with Jesper Olsen before scoring.

DIEGO MARADONA (ARGENTINA) v ENGLAND 06.86 – Maradona used the 'Hand of God' to steer the ball past England keeper Peter Shilton in the 1986 World Cup quarter-final in Mexico City.

 **Facts**   **Strange Goals**

JIM FRYATT (BRADFORD PA) v TRANMERE 04.64 – Fryatt scored the quickest goal in British football history when he put Bradford Park Avenue ahead after only four seconds.

GARY SPRAKE (LEEDS) v LIVERPOOL 12.67 – Leeds goalkeeper Sprake decided at the last minute not to throw the ball out to a colleague. However, the momentum took the ball out of his hand and it ended up in his own net.

GARY SPRAKE (LEEDS) v CHELSEA, 05.70 – Another howler from the Welsh international, who allowed Peter Houseman's speculative long-range effort to creep beneath his diving body on a boggy Wembley pitch for the equaliser. Chelsea won the replay.

ANDY GORAM (HIBERNIAN) v MORTON 05.88 – One keeper who scored at the right end was Scotland international Goram whose Premier Division effort beat Morton's David Wylie.

TOMMY HUTCHISON (MANCHESTER CITY) v TOTTENHAM 05.81 – With eight minutes left of the FA Cup final, Hutchison, having earlier put City in front, deflected Glenn Hoddle's free-kick into his own net for the equaliser.

PETER SCHMEICHEL (MANCHESTER UNITED) v ROTOR VOLGOGRAD 09.95 – With his side trailing 2-1 in the final minute, United keeper Schmeichel went up for a corner and hammered his side level.

LARS RICKEN (BORUSSIA DORTMUND) v JUVENTUS 05.97 – The Dortmund substitute made his entrance into the 1997 European Cup final with Dortmund holding on to a 2-1 lead and within seconds chipped Juventus keeper Angelo Peruzzi with his first touch.

PAT JENNINGS (TOTTENHAM) v MANCHESTER UNITED 08.67 – The Spurs keeper launched a huge kick out of his hands in the 1967 Charity Shield. The ball bounced once over the head of his opposite number Alex Stepney and ended up in the net.

DAVID BECKHAM v WIMBLEDON 08.96 – Spotting Neil Sullivan off his line, Beckham hammered the ball over the Dons' keeper from inside his own half on the opening day of the 1996-97 season.

DAVID BATTY v WIMBLEDON 08.96 – Four days later, Sullivan was beaten with another long-distance effort as Batty chipped him from 35 yards.

Strange Goals

Facts

NAYIM (REAL ZARAGOZA) v ARSENAL 05.95 – Instead of playing out time at the end of 90 minutes in the European Cup Winners' Cup final, Nayim beat Arsenal keeper David Seaman with a looping shot from 40 yards to win the cup for Zaragoza.

SHAUN SMITH (CREWE) v BRENTFORD 04.97 – With a howling gale at his back, Smith caught Bees' keeper Kevin Dearden unaware by striking a free-kick from inside his own half straight into the net.

SCOTT MINTO (CHARLTON) v DERBY 10.92 – Charlton defenders Darren Pitcher and Scott Minto contrived to turn possession on the half-way line into a spectacular own goal. Pitcher sliced the ball 30 yards back to Minto, who headed past his own keeper.

ROD WALLACE (LEEDS) v ARSENAL 01.97 – Wallace lobbed keeper David Seaman, sending the ball towards the Arsenal goal. Martin Keown came across to clear but, expecting it to roll out for a goal-kick, left it. Instead, the ball struck the post and rebounded for Wallace to smash it home, while Keown also ended up in the net.

RONNIE BOYCE (WEST HAM) v MANCHESTER CITY – City keeper Joe Corrigan drop-kicked the ball out of his hands, but watched in horror as Boyce promptly volleyed it back past him.

RONNIE BOYCE (WEST HAM) v PRESTON 04.64 – Boyce deserves a second mention for his 30-yard chip in the 1964 FA Cup final, which struck the crossbar, came out and struck the diving body of Preston keeper Alan before rebounding into the net.

RAY CASHLEY (BRISTOL CITY) v HULL CITY 09.93 – The Division Two match produced another moment of goalkeeping folklore when City's Cashley scored against Jeff Wealands.

STAN COLLYMORE (LIVERPOOL) v BLACKBURN 02.95 – Collymore struck a shot from outside the area but was so convinced that Tim Flowers had it covered, he missed seeing the ball strike a divot and bounce over the stranded Rovers keeper.

ROBERTO RIVELINO (CORINTHIANS) v RIO PRETO – Goalkeeper Isadore Irandir was still on his knees saying his pre-match prayers when Rivelino hammered the ball home from the half-way line after only three seconds.

 **Facts**

Strange Goals

ROBERTO RIVELINO (BRAZIL) v EAST GERMANY 06.74 – More Brazilian magic when Rivelino scored one of the greatest free-kicks of all time. The Brazilians placed a man in the East German wall, who ducked his head at the last moment to allow Rivelino's shot to pass untouched into the net.

PAUL PARKER (ENGLAND) v WEST GERMANY 07.90 – England's World Cup hopes appeared to be in tatters when Andreas Brehme's free-kick cannoned off Parker's shoulder and looped over stranded keeper Peter Shilton.

DES WALKER (NOTTINGHAM FOREST) v LUTON 01.91 – Walker's only goal in a Football League career which stretches to 416 games came in the dying seconds against Luton. Walker strode forward to hammer the ball into the roof of the net but his manager Brian Clough didn't see it, having already left for the dressing room.

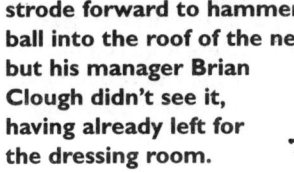

Strange Goals

Facts

DES WALKER (NOTTINGHAM FOREST) v TOTTENHAM 05.91 By contrast, Walker earned notoriety for the wrong reason in the 1991 FA Cup final with a spectacular diving header which handed Spurs a 2-1 victory.

HAROLD PHIPPS (CHARLTON) v ARSENAL 11.48 – Phipps beat keeper Ted Platt, playing his first game for two years, with a 45-yard free-kick in Charlton's 4-3 win.

BRYAN ROBSON (ENGLAND) v NORWAY 09.81 – Robson admitted his first international goal involved the use of a hand on the blind side of the referee before he belted the ball into the Norwegian net.

ESKANDARIAN (IRAN) v SCOTLAND 06.78 – Scotland needed a freak own goal to avoid an embarrassing World Cup defeat by Iran. Eskandarian's back-pass ended up in his own net after his keeper and a fellow defender collided with each other.

DENIS LAW (MANCHESTER CITY) v MANCHESTER UNITED 04.74 – In front of 56,996 United fans who used to adore him, Law produced an instinctive backheel to give City a 1-0 derby win over his former club. The goal sent United down to Division Two and Law, realising what he had done, left the field in tears.

IAIN HESFORD (MAIDSTONE) v HEREFORD 11.91 – Hesford scored Maidstone's winner against Hereford in a Fourth Division match. His clearance beat visiting keeper Tony Elliot with one bounce.

STAN MILBURN and JACK FROGGATT (LEICESTER) v CHELSEA 1954 – The only recorded instance of a shared own goal. Milburn and Froggatt owned up to getting simultaneous touches to the ball on its way past their own keeper.

TOMMY WRIGHT (EVERTON) v LIVERPOOL 03.72 – The England full-back scored one of the fastest League own goals in history after 33 seconds of the Merseyside derby.

TOMMY WRIGHT (EVERTON) v MANCHESTER CITY 03.72 – A week later he went one second better when he put through his own net after just 32 seconds.

RAY CHARLES (EAST FIFE) v STRANRAER 02.90 – Charles joined the exclusive list of goalkeepers who have scored when his long ball deceived Stranraer's Bernard Duffy in a Scottish Second Division match.

 **Facts**   **Strange Goals**

BENNY SMITH (NORWICH) v METROGAS 12.21 – The Norwich full-back struck such a fierce penalty that Metrogas keeper Leach was instantly knocked out, allowing Smith to hit the rebound into the unguarded net. The hapless Leach was carried off.

PETER ALDIS (ASTON VILLA) v SUNDERLAND 09.52 – Aldis scored what was thought to be the longest headed goal ever in the Football League from 35 yards.

GARRY JONES (BOLTON) v ROTHERHAM 11.72 – Rotherham keeper Jim McDonagh placed the ball for a goal-kick not realising the ball was still in play. Jones nipped in to score.

SANDY BROWN (EVERTON) v LIVERPOOL 02.70 – The Merseyside derby is the last match in which to score an own goal but Brown's searing header from a Liverpool corner would have been acknowledged as brilliant even if it had gone in at the right end.

WILLIE DONACHIE (SCOTLAND) v WALES 05.78 – A week before Scotland's departure for the 1978 World Cup Finals, defender Donachie hit a low backpass, without looking, towards his keeper Jim Blyth, who was on the other side of his area and could only watch the ball roll into the net.

PAT KRUSE (TORQUAY) v CAMBRIDGE 1977 – Kruse holds the unenviable record of scoring the quickest own goal in Football League history with a header in just six seconds.

DAN LEWIS (ARSENAL) v CARDIFF 04.27 – Probably the worst FA Cup Final blunder ever. Arsenal keeper Lewis allowed a weak 25-yarder from Hugh Ferguson to slip from his grasp and under his left arm. In an effort to retrieve the ball, he knocked it gently over the goalline with an elbow.

JOHNNY SUMMERS (CHARLTON) v MIDDLESBROUGH 10.60 – With Charlton trailing 5-6 in the 89th minute, striker Stuart Leary stood on goalkeeper Peter Taylor's foot so that Summers could score direct from the corner to make the score 6-6.

GEOFF NULTY (BURNLEY) v IPSWICH 03.71 – Nulty is credited with the latest Football League goal ever. He equalised for Burnley with a goal officially timed at one second from the end.

Strange Goals

SAM LAWRIE (CHARLTON) v LIVERPOOL 11.60 – A month later, The Valley witnessed another bizarre goal when winger Lawrie's back-pass from the half-way line caught his keeper Frank Reed looking the other way.

NAT LOFTHOUSE (BOLTON) v MANCHESTER UNITED 05.58 – Wanderers centre forward Lofthouse set up his side's FA Cup final victory when he charged United keeper Harry Gregg and the ball into the Wembley net.

ANDY GRAY (EVERTON) v WATFORD 05.84 – Twenty six years later, Watford keeper Steve Sherwood felt sympathy with Gregg when he caught a cross only for Gray to head the ball through his hands into the net.

 **Facts**   **Strange Goals**

ANDY GRAY (EVERTON) v NOTTS COUNTY 03.85 – Always
renowned for his heading ability, Gray stooped to conquer with a
diving header only inches off the ground when it would have been
easier to reach it with his foot.

BRIAN GAYLE (SHEFFIELD UNITED) v LEEDS 04.92 – Gayle's cock-up gave
Leeds their first championship in 25 years. With the score tied at 2-2, Gayle
reached a through ball ahead of his outrushing keeper and promptly headed
it into his own net.

STEVE OGRIZOVIC (COVENTRY) v SHEFFIELD WEDNESDAY
10.86 – Coventry stalwart keeper Ogrizovic grabbed his only goal
for the Sky Blues when his big-boot beat Martin Hodge in the
home goal.

STEVE SHERWOOD (WATFORD) v COVENTRY 01.84 – It was a
Coventry keeper's turn to be on the wrong end of a goal from his opposite
number when Raddy Avramovic was beaten by Sherwood.

JACK ALLEN (NEWCASTLE) v ARSENAL 04.32 – Newcastle
inside-forward Jimmy Richardson chased a long ball which crossed
the by-line before he centred it. Eddie Hapgood and his fellow
Arsenal defenders didn't bother to intercept it, allowing Allen to
turn it home.

ANDY HINCHCLIFFE (EVERTON) v LEICESTER 11.96 – With the Leicester
players still protesting about the referee's decision to award a free-kick against
them, Everton's Nick Barmby snatched the ball out of Kasey Keller's hands
and quickly placed it for Hinchcliffe to strike the ball into the empty net.

BARRY DAINES (TOTTENHAM) v BRISTOL ROVERS 03.78 – In
a goalmouth melee following a Rovers corner, Daines tripped over
when attempting to clear the ball only to volley it into the roof of
his own net.

DAVE SYRETT (MANSFIELD) v TOTTENHAM 03.78 – The same month,
Daines experienced another calamitous moment when he raced out of his
area to clear the ball. It took a strange bounce on the muddy pitch and the
keeper connected only with fresh air, leaving Syrett an easy tap-in.

EDDIE KELLY (ARSENAL) v LIVERPOOL 05.71 – With Arsenal
trailing 1-0 in the FA Cup final, Kelly slipped the ball forward to
George Graham, who appeared to flick it past keeper Ray
Clemence. Graham wheeled away in triumph to claim the goal
only for television replays to give it back to Kelly.

Strange Goals

KENNY DALGLISH (SCOTLAND) v ENGLAND 05.76 – England keeper
Ray Clemence produced a Hampden Park howler when he allowed
Dalglish's tame shot to trickle through his legs and gift Scotland a 2-1 win.

**OLMO (BARCELONA) v TOTTENHAM 04.82 – Clemence
assured himself another piece of unwanted fame when he allowed
Olmo's long-range shot to swerve past him despite having a clear
view of it for over 30 yards.**

JIMMY GREENHOFF (MANCHESTER UNITED) v LIVERPOOL 05.77 – A
crazy FA Cup final winner when Jimmy Greenhoff inadvertently deflected
Lou Macari's mishit shot past the stranded Ray Clemence. Greenhoff was
actually trying to get out of the way.

**BILLY BONDS (CHARLTON) v PORTSMOUTH 12.65 – Bonds
always claimed the fastest goal he ever scored was the one he
headed past his own 18-year-old debutant keeper Les Surman,
who was stranded on an icy Fratton Park pitch after just 18
seconds.**

PETER SHILTON (LEICESTER) v SOUTHAMPTON 1967 – In over 1000
league games, England's Peter Shilton scored only once. It was in 1967
playing for Leicester City, when his obliging opposite number was
Southampton's Campbell Forsyth.

**ROBERTO BAGGIO (ITALY) v ENGLAND 07.90 – Shilton figures
again, this time for the wrong reason. In his 125th and final game
for England, he was trying to dribble the ball to the edge of the
area when Baggio dispossessed him and slid the ball home.**

RONNIE WHELAN (LIVERPOOL) v MANCHESTER UNITED 03.90 –
Whelan sent a superb 30-yard chip, which dipped just under the crossbar.
The trouble was it was past his own keeper Bruce Grobbelaar.

**STEVE McMANAMAN (LIVERPOOL) v TOTTENHAM 12.97 – A
weak shot from McManaman appeared to be rolling straight to Ian
Walker but, as the Spurs keeper got down to the ball, a sudden
bobble took it over his hands and into the back of the net.**

ALAN MULLERY (FULHAM) v SHEFFIELD WEDNESDAY 01.61 –
Wednesday scored the easiest goal in their history when Mullery contrived
to score an own goal past his own keeper without a Sheffield player
touching the ball.

 **Facts** **Strange Goals**

JOHN BARNES (LIVERPOOL) v SOUTHAMPTON 12.96 –
Southampton keeper Dave Beasant attempted to clear his area
but succeeded only in finding Barnes whose shot just beat Beasant
into the corner of the net.

ERNIE HUNT (COVENTRY) v EVERTON 10.70 – Awarded a free-kick on
the edge of the box, Coventry's Willie Carr held the ball between his heels
and flicked the ball up for Hunt to blast the ball home. The move was later
outlawed.

**CHARLIE DYKE (CHELSEA) v CHARLTON 11.50 – Dyke scored
direct from a corner when legendary Charlton keeper Sam
Bartram caught the ball but staggered over the goal-line.**

ALAN PATERSON (GLENTORAN) v LINFIELD 04.89 – The 1989
Roadferry Cup Final in Belfast was brightened up when Glentoran keeper
Paterson embarrassed Linfield's George Dunlop with a towering clearance.

**ANDY McLEAN (CLIFTONVILLE) v LINFIELD 08.88 –
Unfortunately for the hapless Dunlop, Paterson's goal was not a
new experience for him. Eight months earlier he had been beaten
in similar fashion by McLean, who was making his Irish League
debut.**

PAUL INCE (MANCHESTER UNITED) v IPSWICH 03.95 · Shellshocked
Ipswich keeper Craig Forrest was on the edge of his area protesting to the
referee about the award of a United free kick when the quick-thinking Ince
stepped up to chip into an empty goal. It stood to give United a Carling
Premiership record 9-0 win.

**ROGER MILLA (CAMEROON) v COLOMBIA 06.90 – With
Colombia 1-0 down to Cameroon in the 1990 World Cup, keeper
Rene Higuita decided to help out by dribbling the ball out of his
area. Unfortunately he was tackled by Milla, who stroked it into an
empty net.**

RENE HIGUITA (ATLETICO NACIONAL) v RIVER PLATE 09.95 – The
legendary Colombian keeper scored at the right end in a Copa Libertadores
match. When his side were awarded a free-kick, Higuita raced from his goal
to smack home the only goal of the game.

**LEE DIXON (ARSENAL) v IPSWICH 03.94 – Dixon, possibly
feeling sorry for Ipswich, sent an unstoppable header whistling into
the roof of his own net, but Arsenal won 5-1.**

Strange Goals

Facts

LEE DIXON (ARSENAL) v COVENTRY 09.91 – The feeling was nothing new for the England full-back, who has made a habit of scoring spectacular own goals. Against Coventry, he lobbed his own keeper from outside the area after just 54 seconds.

IAIN DOWIE (WEST HAM) v STOCKPORT 12.96 – Dowie's classic downward header into the bottom corner was far too good for his own keeper Ludek Miklosko. It helped Stockport to a Coca-Cola Cup shock and to make matters worse for Dowie, he limped off soon afterwards with a broken bone in his leg.

CHRIS NICHOLL (ASTON VILLA) v LEICESTER 03.76 – To score one own goal in a match is unlucky. To do it twice smacks of carelessness, but that was Nicholl's fate in a League match. However, he made up for his errors by scoring both of Villa's goals as well in a 2-2 draw.

BARROW v PLYMOUTH 1968 – A Barrow shot was sailing harmlessly wide when it struck referee Ivan Robinson and was deflected into the net for the only goal of the game.

MIKE MILLIGAN (NORWICH) v ASTON VILLA 10.94 – The greatest goalmouth scramble ever? Darren Eadie headed against the post, Mike Sheron's follow-up hit the bar, Eadie's second effort was then cleared off the line before Milligan finally headed home.

ROBERTO DI MATTEO (CHELSEA) v MIDDLESBROUGH 05.97 – Chelsea's Italian star scored the quickest FA Cup final goal ever when his long-range effort sailed over Ben Roberts' hand after only 42 seconds.

 **Facts**   **Strange Goals**

BRUCE GROBBELAAR (LIVERPOOL) v WIMBLEDON 08.88 – In a mad goalmouth scramble, Liverpool keeper Grobbelaar lay on the ground when the ball was kicked off the line behind him, struck his head and ricocheted into the net.

JOHN LUKIC (LEEDS) v GLASGOW RANGERS 10.92 – English champions Leeds were leading their Scottish counterparts in a European Cup tie at Ibrox when their keeper Lukic punched a harmless-looking corner into his own net.

GARY MABBUTT (TOTTENHAM) v COVENTRY 05.87 – Dave Bennett's extra-time cross deflected off the left knee of Spurs skipper Mabbutt and looped over Ray Clemence to win the 1987 FA Cup final for the Sky Blues.

DENNIS TUEART (MANCHESTER CITY) v NEWCASTLE 03.76 Tueart had kids up and down the country practising overhead kicks after his spectacular bicycle effort won the League Cup final for City.

TREVOR SINCLAIR (QPR) v BARNSLEY 01.97 – Sinclair brought off the bicycle kick to end them all when he volleyed home a cross which was drifting behind him into the top corner.

ALEX STEPNEY (MANCHESTER UNITED) v LEICESTER 09.94 – United's keeper charged upfield when his side were awarded a penalty, grabbed the ball and fired home the spot-kick. To prove it was no fluke, he did it again five weeks later.

MADJER (FC PORTO) v BAYERN MUNICH 05.87 – With his back to goal in the area, the Algerian international produced a moment of European Cup magic when he cleverly backheeled the ball into the Bayern net.

ERIC VISCAAL (AA GENT) v LOKEREN 1994 – Outfield player Viscaal was forced to take over in goal when Gent's keeper was sent off in the last five minutes. His first act was to save a penalty and then, in the dying seconds when Gent were awarded a spot-kick, he went up the other end and scored.

ANDRE BAL (SOVIET UNION) v BRAZIL 06.82 – Brazilian keeper Valdir Peres still has nightmares about the World Cup match in which he caught Bal's shot and then dropped it over his line.

Strange Goals

NICK CUSACK (FULHAM) v SCARBOROUGH 01.96 – Borough keeper Ian Ironside dropped a horrendous clanger by trying to keep a back-pass in play. Knocking the ball high in the air he failed to grab it three times when it dropped, allowing Cusack to side-foot it home.

JOHN PEMBERTON (SHEFFIELD UNITED) v MANCHESTER CITY 04.93 – Desperately stretching to intercept David White's cross, Pemberton succeeded only in volleying the ball low into his own net.

MARK CROSSLEY (NOTTINGHAM FOREST) v BLACKBURN 09.92 – Blackburn defender Colin Hendry powered in a header from a corner. Crossley initially caught the ball only to throw it over his own line as he fell to the ground.

NACIONAL v PENAROL 1932 – A Nacional player's shot missed the post but struck a cameraman's briefcase, which had been left close to the by-line. The ball rebounded to another Nacional player, who turned it home.

ANDRES ESCOBAR (COLOMBIA) v USA 06.94 – The most tragic own goal of all time. Escobar's outstretched leg deflected the ball past his own keeper and ended Colombia's hopes in the 1994 World Cup. Just 72 hours after returning to Colombia, Escobar was gunned down outside a restaurant in his home town of Medelin, the assasin allegedly shouting: "That's for the own goal."

STRANGE BUT TRUE

Strange but True

With an injury crisis at the club, non-league Tring Town were forced to name their 37-year-old chairman, David Lane, as one of the substitutes for the game against Berkhamsted in the 1990-91 season. Lane was put on, but was sent-off before kicking the ball.

With his Brazilian side San Lorenzo 2-1 up over Estudiantes in the final minutes, defender Siminiota picked up the ball thinking it had already gone out of play. To his amazement the referee, Humberto Dellacasa, awarded a penalty. The spot-kick was converted and two players were sent-off for manhandling the referee who had to be escorted from the pitch by riot police.

One of the easiest spot-the-ball competition's came in Welsh newspaper The Western Mail in January 1993. Instead of publishing that week's competition the newspaper showed the previous week's answer. One thousand copies of the paper were run off before the mistake was realised.

When they entered their first Scottish Cup in 1873 Kilmarnock were more accustomed to playing rugby than football. As they tried to brush up on their football knowledge, opponents Renton were constantly awarded free-kicks after the Kilmarnock players had used their hands rather than their feet. To no-one's surprise Renton won the match 3-0.

Despite losing 10-0 to Liverpool in the 1986 League Cup first round, first leg, Fulham still printed details of what would happen if the tie should finish as a draw. Unfortunately they managed only two goal, with Liverpool scoring three.

Brazilian Roberto Rivelino scored some fantastic goals for club and country, but surely the one he scored against Rio Preto will remain one of the strangest. Rio Preto goalkeeper Isadore Irandir always prayed in his goalmouth before every game. When Corinthians kicked off, Irandir took up his praying position only to look up and see Rivelino's half-way line shot sail past him en route to the net.

Nat Lofthouse became one of England's best strikers, but it was not always like that. As a schoolboy in Bolton, Lofthouse played his first football match in goal. His team lost 7-1.

 Facts   **Strange but True**

It's not only players that can score world-class goals, one referee also got in on the act. In a Sunday League fixture in Southampton, the referee told the two teams that he would abandon the match if the persistent fouling continued in the second period. With the message not seeming to get through to the players the ref had had enough. With the ball in play on the edge of the penalty area, he produced an unstoppable shot that flew into the net. "That is how you are supposed to play the game," he said as he handed his whistle to his linesman and walked off the pitch.

Strange but True

Facts

Leicester Fosse were already relegated from the First Division in 1909 before playing Nottingham Forest in a match that Forest needed to win to stay up. The day before the game one of the Leicester players was getting married so his team-mates decided to celebrate in style. They lost the game 12-0 and a Football League inquiry was launched to find out the secret for the then-Football League record victory. They found that the large defeat was due to the fact that the Leicester players were stil hung over from their wedding celebrations.

Despite losing all their 26 matches in the 1992-93 Darlington and District League, Barton Athletic still managed to pick up a trophy – the League's fair-play award. A club official said: "We've always been a very popular club – particularly with our opponents."

Raith Rovers' first overseas tour was not a happy one. Travelling to the Canary Islands in 1930, the Scottish club found themselves shipwrecked after their boat had capsized. Fortunately all players and officials were rescued, but a decision to play friendlies closer to home was quickly announced.

Bognor's Paul Pullen became involved in a difference of opinion with the referee during a Diadora League match. The referee, however, called twin brother Mick over to him and sent him off. Despite protesting his innocence Mick, Bognor's player-manager at the time, was ordered off, with his brother laughing loudly in the background.

In a desperate bid to stave off relegation a French team laced the opposing team's drink with knock-out drops. The scenes were hilarious as players started to collapse during the match. The authorities became aware, and when they unearthed the reason for the bizarre behaviour they condemned the offending club to relegation.

When two teams of referees met for a friendly game in Spain it should have boasted 22 of the best-behaved players. But when the match official sent off one of the players he was approached and hit by the player's father, who also happened to be a referee.

Former England goalkeeper Dave Beasant presented one of the more bizarre injury excuses when he missed out on the start of the 1993-94 season with a foot injury. The cause of the injury? He dropped a jar of salad cream and tried to stop it smashing on the floor with his foot, severing a tendon.

 **Facts**   **Strange but True**

Cardiff City received a bumper pay-out when they entertained Queens Park Rangers in a third round FA Cup tie in 1990. Record receipts of £50,000 were taken, but soon discovered that thieves had stolen the money.

When Milwall opened their new stadium, The Den, in 1910 Lord Kinnaird, President of the FA, was asked to to conduct the ceremony. Unfortunately, Lord Kinnaird went to the opposing end of the ground and while club officials were waiting he was being pushed over the wall. He then ran across the pitch to perform the dignitaries.

Kidderminster were ecstatic when their protest of their 3-1 FA Cup defeat to Darwen was approved and the match was to be replayed. Joy quickly turned to tragedy when Darwen beat them 13-0 to record the highest score in the competition.

Goalkeeper Jonathan Gould suffered ill-effects on hearing his fate was to play for the Coventry City first team against Southampton in 1993. Within two hours of the news, his car was pranged twice.

It was the proudest moment in West Ham's Jimmy Barrett's career when he was picked to make his England debut against Northern Ireland on October 19, 1929. But after only eight minutes he was injured and carried off. He never played for England again and holds the record for shortest England career.

After watching their side lose 2-0 in a Uefa Cup tie in September 1992, two Celtic fans were drowning their sorrows in a bar in Cologne. When they hailed a taxi to take them to their hotel they could not remember the name of the digs, or even what town it was located. After consulting each other they decided on Dortmund which was 90 miles away. After the £70 fare they remembered it was Dusseldorf, which was another 70 miles away.

Queens Park Rangers chairman was so anxious to find out the latest news on his club that he rang the Clubcall line on his carphone. Unfortunately he did not replace the handset correctly and only discovered his mistake the next morning when he was hit with a £335 phone bill.

Strange but True

Facts

Billy Abercrombie created history in 1986 by being sent-off three times in the same match. The St. Mirren captain was shown the red card from referee Louis Thow for an offence, then another for talking back and then a third one for dissent. He was banned for 12 matches by the Scottish League.

Stockport United FC of the Stockport Football League created the unenviable record of losing 39 consecutive League and Cup matches from September 1976 to February 1978.

Peruvian broadcaster Mario Sanchez received a terrible shock when he asked the striker Corina why he had missed three easy heading chances and how could that part of his game be improved. Corina answer was a swift head-butt to Sanchez, who was knocked unconscious by the blow. Corina was later arrested by the police.

Reaching your local Cup Final is a dream for thousands of footballers across the country, but for one team their success back-fired. After winning their semi-final Lags XI, a prison team from Stockton, Cleveland, were thrown out of the competition because they could only play home matches.

 **Facts**   **Strange but True**

A Danish league match in April 1960 produced a remarkable and controversial finish. With Norager leading 4-3 in the final minute against Ebeltoft, referee Henning Erikstrup was on the verge of blowing the final whistle when his dentures fell out. While he was looking for them, Ebeltoft equalised. To protestations from the Ebeltoft team, Mr Erikstrup disallowed the goal and blew for full-time with the result standing at 4-3.

When Exeter City were beaten 5-1 at Millwall in 1982 manager Brian Godfrey decided to keep the team in London and play Millwall reserves the next day. It didn't get any better for Godfrey, Millwall reserves won 1-0.

Hearts director Douglas Park was so infuriated by the refereeing of David Symes after the game with Rangers in 1988 he locked the Symes in the dressing room for 18 minutes after the game and left with the key. Park was fined £1,000 by the Scottish League for his actions.

Stephen Gould thought he could play in goal for his struggling works side, Little Aston in Staffordshire. As he began his warm-up on his debut he jumped up to touch the crossbar, only for the bar to fall on his head. He was carried back to the dressing room before the start of the match.

Nottingham Forest secured promotion to the First Division in 1977 thanks to an own goal from Millwall's Jon Moore. Later that evening Forest supporters voted Moore their Player of the Year.

Bernie Marsh of Mid Sussex League side Balcombe Reserves suffered the uneviable honour of being tackled by a Ford Sierra. With the ball on the half-way line a spectator decided to reverse his car onto the pitch so he could turn round to leave the playing fields. But then came a long shot toward Marsh's goal. Without looking behind him Marsh began moving towards his goal to stop the shot. He tipped the ball over the crossbar but his momentum sent him crashing into the car and knocking him straight out.

Because of bad weather Inverness Thistle's Scottish Cup tie against Falkirk in 1979 was postponed a record 29 times. The game was not exactly worth the wait – Thistle lost the match 4-0.

When Scottish club Greenock Morton won their first game with their new mascot, Toby the sheep, the celebrations were cut short when Toby was left in the changing room and drowned in the players' bath.

Strange but True

In 1924 Cardiff City had the opportunity to become the first, and only, Welsh club to win the Football League Championship. Needing a victory to take the title, City were awarded a penalty in the final game of the season against Birmingham. But Len Davies missed the kick and Huddersfield won the title on goal avaerage.

 **Facts**   Strange but True

There was no place to hide for Chelsea defender John Sillett when, hearing a whistle, caught the ball in his penalty area thinking the referee had blown up. Unfortunately the whistle came from a spectator and Chelsea's opponents, Sheffield Wednesday, were awarded one of the bizaare penalties in history.

Derby County's Andy Comyn made an immediate impact when he came on as a substitute against Bristol City in September 1992. The defender arrived onto the field to face a City free-kick. He rose to head the ball away but only succeeded in putting the ball past stand-in goalkeeper Paul Williams to give Bristol City a goal within 10 seconds of coming on.

Denis Law could even injure himself watching a match on the substitutes bench. In Manchester United's 1968 European Cup semi-final against Real Madrid, Law got so carried away when Bill Foulkes scored that he went to punch the air but smashed his fist through the roof of the dug-out and suffered a broken bone in his hand.

Quiz Score Sheets

 Quiz Score Sheets

Quiz Score Sheets

Quiz Score Sheets

Quiz Score Sheets

 # Quiz Score Sheets

Quiz Score Sheets